IDENTIFYING BIBLICAL PERSONS IN NORTHWEST
SEMITIC INSCRIPTIONS OF 1200–539 B.C.E.

Society of Biblical Literature

Academia Biblica

Saul M. Olyan,
Old Testament Editor

Mark Allan Powell,
New Testament Editor

Number 12

IDENTIFYING BIBLICAL PERSONS IN NORTHWEST
SEMITIC INSCRIPTIONS OF 1200–539 B.C.E.

# Identifying Biblical Persons in Northwest Semitic Inscriptions of 1200–539 B.C.E.

Lawrence J. Mykytiuk

Society of Biblical Literature
Atlanta

# Identifying Biblical Persons in Northwest Semitic Inscriptions of 1200–539 B.C.E.

Copyright © 2004 by the Society of Biblical Literature

All rights reserved. No part of this work may be reproduced or transmitted in any form or by any means, electronic or mechanical, including photocopying and recording, or by means of any information storage or retrieval system, except as may be expressly permitted by the 1976 Copyright Act or in writing from the publisher. Requests for permission should be addressed in writing to the Rights and Permissions Office, Society of Biblical Literature, 825 Houston Mill Road, Atlanta, GA 30329, USA.

**Library of Congress Cataloging-in-Publication Data**

Mykytiuk, Lawrence J.
  Identifying Biblical persons in Northwest Semitic inscriptions of 1200-539 B.C.E. / by Lawrence J. Mykytiuk.
      p. cm. — (Society of Biblical Literature Academia Biblica ; no. 12)
  Includes bibliographical references and index.
  ISBN 1-58983-062-8 (paper binding : alk. paper)
  1. Names in the Bible. 2. Inscriptions, Semitic. 3. Inscriptions, Hebrew. 4. Paleography, Semitic. 5. Bible. O.T.—Antiquities. I. Title. II. Academia Biblica (Series) (Society of Biblical Literature) ; no. 12.
  BS435.M95 2004
  221.9'22—dc22
                                    2004010934

08 07 06 05 04      5 4 3 2 1

Printed in the United States of America
on acid-free paper

# Identifying Biblical Persons in Northwest Semitic Inscriptions of 1200–539 B.C.E.

Lawrence J. Mykytiuk

Society of Biblical Literature
Atlanta

# Identifying Biblical Persons in Northwest Semitic Inscriptions of 1200–539 B.C.E.

Copyright © 2004 by the Society of Biblical Literature

All rights reserved. No part of this work may be reproduced or transmitted in any form or by any means, electronic or mechanical, including photocopying and recording, or by means of any information storage or retrieval system, except as may be expressly permitted by the 1976 Copyright Act or in writing from the publisher. Requests for permission should be addressed in writing to the Rights and Permissions Office, Society of Biblical Literature, 825 Houston Mill Road, Atlanta, GA 30329, USA.

**Library of Congress Cataloging-in-Publication Data**

Mykytiuk, Lawrence J.
  Identifying Biblical persons in Northwest Semitic inscriptions of 1200-539 B.C.E. / by Lawrence J. Mykytiuk.
     p. cm. — (Society of Biblical Literature Academia Biblica ; no. 12)
  Includes bibliographical references and index.
  ISBN 1-58983-062-8 (paper binding : alk. paper)
  1. Names in the Bible. 2. Inscriptions, Semitic. 3. Inscriptions, Hebrew. 4. Paleography, Semitic. 5. Bible. O.T.—Antiquities. I. Title. II. Academia Biblica (Series) (Society of Biblical Literature) ; no. 12.
BS435.M95 2004
221.9'22—dc22
                                        2004010934

08 07 06 05 04       5 4 3 2 1

Printed in the United States of America
on acid-free paper

To my wife,
Joy A. Mykytiuk,

to my father,
Nicholas S. Mykytiuk,

and to the memory of my mother,
Ruth E. Mykytiuk,

and of my stepmother,
Mary F. Scheckel Mykytiuk

# Contents

Preface     xi
Acknowledgments     xiii
Abbreviations     xv
Symbols and Chronological Conventions     xvii
Figures     xix

Introduction: Background and Statement of Thesis     1

### Part 1: An Identification System

Chapter 1: Identification Criteria     9
1.1    Three approaches which call for an identification system     9
1.2    Development of basic criteria for making identifications     10
1.3    Definitions     10
1.4    Underlying factors in the process of identification     11
1.5    Ancient Near Eastern ways of identifying an individual     12
1.6    Prosopography     13
1.7    Survey of the literature, first of two parts     15
1.8    Methodology for choosing criteria     18
1.9    Instructive misidentification number one: the seal of "Jotham"     19
1.10    Instructive misidentification number two: the seal impressions of Eliakim, steward of "Jehoiachin"     23
1.11    The criteria not met by these two misidentifications     26
1.12    Avigad's criteria     27
1.13    Survey of the literature, second of two parts     29
1.14    Foundational data for making identifications     31
1.15    Non-foundational facts relevant to identifications     34
1.16    Rationale for a way of evaluating identifications that is more refined and more complete than Avigad's     34
1.17    Principles for measuring the strength of identifications     37
1.18    The three main diagnostic questions about potential identifications     38
1.19    A three-question system for evaluating potential identifications     40
1.20    Question one: how reliable are the inscriptional data?     40
1.21    Criterion 1, means of acquisition or access     40
1.22    Criterion 2, provenance of the inscription     40
1.23    Criterion 3, how the matter of the inscription's authenticity has been or should be regarded     41

viii                                    Contents

1.24    Question two: does the general setting of the inscription *permit* a
        match between the inscriptional person and the biblical person?    43
1.25    Criterion 4, the date of the person                                 43
1.26    Criterion 5, the identity of the language of the inscription        45
1.27    Criterion 6, the socio-political classification of the inscription  47
1.28    Question three: how strongly do specific identifying data in the
        the inscription count for or against an identification?             49
1.29    Criterion 7, the name of person in the inscription                  49
1.30    Criterion 8, family and other interpersonal relations               50
1.31    Criterion 9, title information                                      52
1.32    Criterion 10, other identifying information (marks of the individual) 53
1.33    Criterion 11, identification on grounds of singularity              54
1.34    Summary and Limitation                                              56

Chapter 2: Taxonomy of Identifications and Two System Refinements          57
2.1     Taxonomy: grades of identifications and of non-identifications      57
2.2     Grade S identifications, including SI and SB: certain               57
2.3     Grade 3 identifications: virtually certain to reliable              67
2.4     Grade 2 identifications: reasonable but uncertain                   73
2.5     Grade 1 identifications: doubtful                                   77
2.6     Grade 0 (zero) non-identifications: without any clear basis         79
2.7     Grade D non-identifications: disqualified                           82
2.8     The place of explanatory hypotheses in evaluation                   84
2.9     Historical frameworks to minimize the danger of circularity         85
2.10    Potential circularity in the interpretation of inscriptional data   85
2.11    The purpose and composition of historical frameworks                86
2.12    The procedure of evaluation                                         86
2.13    An example of the anti-circular identification system: Is the
        biblical Hoshea, king of Israel, named in the seal of Abdi?         87


                    Part 2: Application of the Identification System
            to Hebrew Inscriptions and Two Stelae from before the Persian Era
                              Published before October 1997

Chapter 3: Identifications in Provenanced Inscriptions                     93
3.1     The scope and possible evidential value of potential identifications
        evaluated in Chapters 3 and 4                                       93
3.2     The order of research and presentation                              95
3.3     Is the biblical Mesha, king of Moab, named in the Mesha
        Inscription?                                                        95
3.4     Is the biblical Omri, king of Israel, named in the Mesha
        Inscription?                                                       108

| | | |
|---|---|---|
| 3.5 | Is the biblical King David named in the Tel Dan stele? | 110 |
| 3.6 | Is the biblical Jeroboam II, king of Israel, named in the Megiddo seal of Shema, the minister of Jeroboam? | 133 |
| 3.7 | Is the biblical Shaphan the scribe, father of Gemariah, named in the city of David bulla of Gemaryahu? | 139 |
| 3.8 | Is the biblical Gemariah, son of Shaphan the scribe, named in the city of David bulla of Gemaryahu? | 147 |
| 3.9 | Is the biblical Hilkiah the high priest, father of Azariah, named in the city of David bulla of Azaryahu? | 148 |
| 3.10 | Is the biblical Azariah, son of Hilkiah the high priest, named in the city of David bulla of Azaryahu? | 151 |
| | | |
| Chapter 4: Identifications in Unprovenanced Inscriptions | | 153 |
| 4.1 | The scope of potential identifications evaluated in this chapter | 153 |
| 4.2 | Is the biblical Uzziah, king of Judah, named in the seal of Abiyaw? | 153 |
| 4.3 | Is the biblical Uzziah, king of Judah, named in the seal of Shubnayaw? | 159 |
| 4.4 | Is the biblical Ahaz, king of Judah, named in the seal of Ushna? | 163 |
| 4.5 | Is the biblical Hoshea, king of Israel, named in the seal of Abdi? | 169 |
| 4.6 | Is the biblical Hezekiah, king of Judah, named in the bulla of Yehozaraḥ? | 169 |
| 4.7 | Is the biblical Hilkiah, the high priest, named in the seal ring of Ḥanan? | 177 |
| 4.8 | Is the biblical Baruch the scribe named in the bullae of Berekyahu? | 188 |
| 4.9 | Is the biblical Neriah, father of Baruch, named in the bullae of Berekyahu? | 189 |
| 4.10 | Is the biblical Jerahmeel, the king's son, named in the bulla of Yeraḥmeʾel? | 191 |
| | | |
| Chapter 5: Conclusions | | 197 |
| 5.1 | Tabulation of identifications of individuals | 197 |
| 5.2 | Conclusion in relation to the thesis | 200 |
| 5.3 | Conclusions as they would be developed if unprovenanced inscriptions were demonstrated to be authentic | 200 |
| 5.4 | Nine biblical episodes which include more than one individual identified or conditionally identifiable in an inscription | 201 |
| 5.5 | Promising directions for further investigation | 205 |

Appendix A: The Significance of the Title ʿ*Ebed* in Northwest Semitic Seals and Seal Impressions — 207

Appendix B: Evaluations of Potential Identifications in Socio-Political, then Chronological Order, Updated through July 2002 — 211

Appendix C: The Corpus and the Remainder: Evaluations of Potential Identifications in Descending Order of Strength, Updated through July 2002 — 244

Appendix D: Index of Biblical Persons in Appendixes B and C — 262

Appendix E: Is the Biblical King David Named in the Mesha Inscription? — 265

Appendix F: Numerical Tabulation of Identifications in Appendixes B and C by Grade — 278

Bibliography, Updated through July 2002 — 287

Index of Modern Authors and Editors — 319

# Preface

*The original scope and later development of this study*

This book is the published version of my 1998 dissertation at the University of Wisconsin-Madison, titled "Identifying Biblical Persons in Hebrew Inscriptions and Two Stelae from before the Persian Era," in which the two stelae are the Aramaic stele from Tel Dan and the Mesha stele. The text of the Introduction and of Chapters 1–5 has been only slightly revised. The footnotes, appendixes, and bibliography are more freely revised and are updated. Chapters 1–5 are intended to include all published Hebrew inscriptions in which biblical persons can be systematically identified, except as limited in the following list (for details, see section 3.1 below). Chapters 1–5 of the original study—hence of this book, in order to observe the rules of this monograph series—do *not* treat:

1. inscriptions that were initially published and actually became available in the United States after the beginning of October 1997,

2. unreliable identifications, including those in grade 2, because they are unresolved (an example appears in section 2.4; there see the first paragraph),

3. non-Hebrew texts besides the two stelae mentioned above, and

4. inscriptions from after 539 B.C.E.

Readers may wonder why some inscriptions are treated in detail, whereas others are not. The above limits help explain the differences historically, in terms of the development of the detailed, less broadly defined original study into a book with expansive, updated appendixes.

In revising the dissertation for publication, despite minor changes and updates, I have tried to avoid any changes of substance in the text of the Introduction and Chapters 1–5. (The dissertation was written without any access to *WSS*. Fortunately, access to *WSS* months later did not necessitate adding any inscription to be treated in Chapters 1–5.) With editorial permission, I have modified some footnotes and all appendixes, especially by updating Appendixes B and C, changing some evaluations in them, and adding Appendixes E and F.

*The two main contributions of this work: system and corpus*

Readers who are interested only in the results, i.e., the corpus of inscriptions that name biblical persons, should turn to Chapter 5 and to Appendix C, sections C.1 through C.4. Appendixes B and C broaden the corpus far beyond the inscriptions treated in the main body of the work in an attempt to include all relevant, published *Northwest Semitic* inscriptions from before the Persian era (cf. note 54 near the end of Appendix C). They also update coverage of publications through July 2002. To my knowledge, *nowhere else are such inscriptions specifically indexed as a distinct group, nor does any previous published corpus of such inscriptions approach completeness.*

Surprisingly, the search for ways of evaluating potential identifications located only two earlier methods, both of which are meant to apply only in limited circumstances. The first appeared in a 1985 article by Pierre Bordreuil (see section 1.7 below). Although its premises and claims are possible and very plausible, they remain unproven, so it has not withstood adverse criticism. The other method was initially set forth in a 1987 article by Nahman Avigad (see section 1.12 below). Fortunately, its two paragraphs on methodology contain perhaps the wisest advice possible. Advancing beyond the limited applicability of these two earlier methods, Chapters 1 and 2 develop *the first comprehensive system* for evaluating potential identifications in Northwest Semitic inscriptions. This system and the extended corpus that results from applying it are, I hope, useful advances following after their precursors, which I gratefully acknowledge. The fortunes of these precursors lend guidance and confidence to this work.

*The technical and repetitive nature of this book*

This volume is essentially a technical piece. By making the evaluation of potential identifications more explicit than it is in earlier works, it makes the process easier to examine and improve. Like many a lab report, this study is also by nature repetitious, because it applies the same steps of analysis repeatedly and because many of the inscriptions are similar, yielding similar observations. The payoff is in the Conclusions and the Appendixes.

# Acknowledgments

It is a pleasant duty to acknowledge my indebtedness to others in producing this book and the dissertation that preceded it, including my prayerful family. I am especially grateful to my wife, Joy, and to John M. Turner, our friend and brother-in-law and a scholar in his own right. John provided crucial computer software, technical support, and encouragement.

I am sincerely grateful to these members of academe for their substantial help: the late Professor Nahman Avigad of the Hebrew University of Jerusalem, for his publication of Northwest Semitic epigraphic sources and his all-important analysis of some identifications they offer; Professor Avraham Biran, Director of the Nelson Glueck School of Biblical Archeology, Hebrew Union College-Jewish Institute of Religion, for his decades of work at Tel Dan and his encouragement; Madame Josette Elayi, Chargée de Recherche, CNRS, for her articles of critical importance and her correspondence; Professor Michael V. Fox, Department of Hebrew and Semitic Studies, University of Wisconsin-Madison, my academic advisor and second reader; Professor Nili S. Fox, Hebrew Union College-Jewish Institute of Religion, for kindly providing a copy of her dissertation long before it was published; Dr. and Mrs. Alon Kantor, while at Purdue University, for key translation help; Professor André Lemaire, École Pratique des Hautes Études (Paris-Sorbonne), for his writings, his correspondence, and key bibliographic information; Professor Cynthia L. Miller, Department of Hebrew and Semitic Studies, University of Wisconsin-Madison, who joined the faculty when this study was nearly complete, for her well-placed challenges, diligence in indicating needed corrections, and perceptive advice; James Ernest Miller, a gifted Bible scholar and my former fellow student in Madison, Wisconsin, for extending my awareness of issues and sources; my patient series editor, Professor Saul M. Olyan of Brown University, along with my two anonymous reviewers in the SBL, for their careful reading, corrections, and sound advice; Professor Benjamin Sass, Tel Aviv University, for revising and completing Avigad's corpus for publication (as *WSS*); Dr. Keith N. Schoville, Professor Emeritus, Department of Hebrew and Semitic Studies, University of

Wisconsin-Madison, director of my dissertation research, for accepting me as his last graduate student and for his advice and energizing encouragement; Professor Andrew G. Vaughn, Gustavus Adolphus College, for his epigraphic labors with Professor Gabriel Barkay of Bar Ilan University and The Hebrew University of Jerusalem, for invaluable information on the paleography of chronologically diagnostic letters, and for his encouragement; Dr. D. J. Wiseman, Emeritus Professor of Assyriology, University of London, for his writings and ready encouragement; Professor Gordon D. Young, Department of History, Purdue University, for his advice, for his personal encouragement, and for serving on my Ph.D. Committee at the University of Wisconsin-Madison; Dr. Ronald F. Youngblood, Bethel Theological Seminary—West Campus, for his interest and correspondence.

The following persons in the academic and publishing worlds helped in a variety of other ways: Ms. Leigh Andersen, Managing Editor, SBL; Professor Jeffrey A. Blakely, University of Wisconsin-Madison; Professor J. Andrew Dearman, Austin Presbyterian Theological Seminary; Professor Gary N. Knoppers, Pennsylvania State University; Dr. Rex D. Matthews, then Dr. Frank Ritchel Ames, successive Editorial Directors, SBL; Ms. Lilia P. Mavrikova, Digital Resources Specialist, Purdue University Libraries; Professor Nicholas K. Rauh, Department of History, Purdue University; Professor Christopher A. Rollston, Emmaus School of Religion, when he was a doctoral student at Johns Hopkins University; Rev. Amy Vaughn, Parish Associate, Union Presbyterian Church, St. Peter, Minnesota; Ms. Suzanne M. Ward, Head of Access Services, including Interlibrary Loan, with Ms. Mary C. Aagard, Ms. Marjorie M. Boeckman, Ms. Kathryn L. Garner, Ms. Deborah J. Heemstra, Ms. Helen J. Hill, Ms. Amy J. Winks, and others on Purdue's heroic Interlibrary Loan staff.

The dissertation was written between mid-1993 and August 1998, while I served in a full-time, twelve-month-per-year capacity as History Bibliographer and Reference Librarian in the Humanities, Social Science & Education Library, Purdue University, West Lafayette, Indiana. I am deeply grateful to my former supervisor, Professor J. Mark Tucker, Ph.D., for his support, which proved to be decisive, and to my colleague Dr. Jean-Pierre V. M. Hérubel for his encouragement. Professor Emily R. Mobley, Dean of Libraries, Purdue University, deserves special thanks for authorizing financial support for me to attend two Annual Meetings of the SBL and for granting me two months' personal leave.

To me alone falls the dubious distinction of accepting full responsibility for all flaws and shortcomings of this study. Yet for whatever benefit it may bring to others, I add with deepest gratitude of all, *soli deo gloria*.

L. J. M.
West Lafayette, Indiana
September 25, 2003
Nahman Avigad's birth anniversary

# Abbreviations

The Bibliography spells out the names of bibliographic items, e.g., journal and series titles, that are abbreviated in the notes. Abbreviations are those of Patrick H. Alexander et al., eds., *The SBL Handbook of Style: for Ancient Near Eastern, Biblical, and Early Christian Studies* (Peabody, Mass.: Hendrickson, 1999), except *CAH* (italicized below, referring to the latest edition only), *DDD* (latest edition below), and *KAI* (3d edition below). Additional abbreviations are:

| | |
|---|---|
| *AHI* | Graham I. Davies, *Ancient Hebrew Inscriptions* (New York: Cambridge University Press, 1991). |
| A.0. | A = Assyrian Periods; 0 = Dynasty Inapplicable (RIMA 3:xiii). |
| BM | British Museum |
| *BullBib* | *Bulletin of Bibliography* |
| *CAH* | John Boardman et al., eds., *The Cambridge Ancient History*, (2d ed.; New York: Cambridge University Press, 1970). |
| CNRS | Centre national de la recherche scientifique (France) |
| *CSOSI* | Pierre Bordreuil, *Catalogue des sceaux ouest-sémitiques inscrits* (Paris: Bibliothèque Nationale, 1986). |
| D | a grade of non-ID which is disqualified because it is known to be impossible or virtually so (see key to Appendix B) |
| *DDD* | *Dictionary of Deities and Demons in the Bible DDD* (ed. Karel van der Toorn, Bob Becking, and Pieter W. van der Horst; 2d extensively rev. ed.; Boston: Brill, 1999). |
| Diringer | David Diringer, *Le iscrizioni antico-ebraiche Palestinesi* (Florence: Felice Le Monnier, 1934). |
| DN | deity's name |
| Fowler | Jeaneane D. Fowler, *Theophoric Personal Names in Ancient Hebrew: A Comparative Study* (JSOTSup 49; Sheffield, England: JSOT Press, 1988). |
| Gibson 1 | John C. L. Gibson, *Textbook of Syrian Semitic Inscriptions*, vol. 1: *Hebrew and Moabite Inscriptions* (New York: Oxford University Press, 1971, corrected 1973). |
| GN | geographical name |
| *HAE* | Johannes Renz and Wolfgang Röllig, *Handbuch der althebräischen Epigraphik* (3 vols. in 4; Darmstadt: Wissenschaftliche Buchgesellschaft, 1995– ). |
| ID | identification (only abbreviated when it means a result, not when referring to a process or when used as an adjective or in headings) |

| | |
|---|---|
| IM | Iraq Museum |
| Jackson | Kent P. Jackson, *The Ammonite Language of the Iron Age* (HSM 27; Chico, Calif.: Scholars Press, 1983) |
| *KAI* | Herbert Donner and Wolfgang Röllig, *Kanaanäische und aramäische Inschriften* (3 vols.; 3d ed.; Wiesbaden: Otto Harrassowitz, 1971–1973). |
| Maraqten | Mohammed Maraqten, *Die semitischen Personennamen in den alt- und reichsaramäischen Inschriften aus Vorderasien* (Texte und Studien zur Orientalistik 5; New York: Georg OlmsVerlag, 1988. |
| *MNDPV* | *Mittheilungen und Nachrichten des Deutschen Palästina-Vereins.* |
| *NEA* | *Near Eastern Archaeology* (titled *Biblical Archaeologist* before 1998) |
| Nr. | number (in *KAI*) |
| RawlCu 1 | British Museum, Department of Egyptian and Assyrian Antiquities, *A Selection from the Miscellaneous Inscriptions of Chaldaea, Assyria, and Babylonia* (ed. Henry C. Rawlinson and Edwin Norris; vol. 1 of RawlCu (London: R. E. Bowler, 1861). |
| RawlCu 3 | British Museum, Department of Egyptian and Assyrian Antiquities, *A Selection from the Miscellaneous Inscriptions of Assyria* (ed. Henry C. Rawlinson and George Smith), vol. 3 of RawlCu (London: R. E. Bowler, 1870). |
| RN | royal name |
| S, SI, SB, & SI + SB | grades of ID which are certain because of singular circumstances, based on inscriptional and/or biblical data (see key at the beginning of Appendix B) |
| *SANSS* | Larry G. Herr, *The Scripts of Ancient Northwest Semitic Seals* (HSM 18; Missoula, Mont.: Scholars Press, 1978). |
| *WSS* | Nahman Avigad and Benjamin Sass, *Corpus of West Semitic Stamp Seals* (Jerusalem: The Israel Academy of Sciences and Humanities, Israel Exploration Society, and The Hebrew University of Jerusalem, The Institute of Archaeology, 1997). |

# Symbols and Chronological Conventions

√           A check beside an identifying criterion means it has been met.

(number)    Parentheses ( ) enclose the number of each *person* potentially to be identified. Numbers of persons are assigned by the order in which they appear in Appendix B.

[number]    Brackets [ ] enclose the number of each *inscription*. Numbers of inscriptions are assigned by their order in Appendix B.

[author's name]    Brackets [ ] around an author's name mark the attribution of authorship of an unsigned article to the editor of the publication in which it appeared.

/letter(s)/    Phonemes appear between virgules (slash marks) / /.

[page no.]n    In the Index below, a letter *n* suffixed to a page number indicates the notes on that page.

All years referring to modern persons and events, such as publications and excavations, are C.E. All other years are B.C.E. unless specified otherwise. For persons mentioned in the Bible, this study uses Galil's dates for the monarchs of Israel and Judah, Kitchen's for the rulers of Egypt, Grayson's for Neo-Assyrian kings, and Wiseman's for Neo-Babylonian kings (see Chapter 1, note 109, below).

# Figures

In Chapter 2, Unprovenanced:
Fig. 1: The Seal "of Abdi, the Minister of Hoshea" 59
Fig. 2: The First-known Bulla "of Berekyahu, Son of Neriyahu, the Scribe" 70
Fig. 3: A Modern Impression of the Seal "of Asayahu, the King's Minister" 75
Provenanced:
Fig. 4: The Tel Dan Jar-handle Seal Impression, "Zekaryaw" 78
Fig. 5: Portions of the ʿIzbet Ṣarṭah Ostracon 81
Fig. 6: A Modern Impression of the Tel El-Kheleifeh Seal Ring "of Yatom" 83

In Chapter 3, Provenanced:
Fig. 7: Portions of the Mesha Inscription from Dibon Bearing the Names of Mesha, King of Moab, and Omri, King of Israel 98
Fig. 8: A Portion of the Tel Dan Stele Bearing the Name of "the House of David" 114
Fig. 9: A Bronze Cast from the Megiddo seal "of Shema, the Minister of Jeroboam" 135
Fig. 10: The City of David bulla "of Gemaryahu, Son of Shaphan" 141
Fig. 11: The City of David bulla "of Azaryahu, Son of Ḥilqiyahu" 149

In Chapter 4, Unprovenanced:
Fig. 12: The Seal "of Abiyaw, the Minister of Uzziyaw" 155
Fig. 13: The Seal "of Shubnayaw, the Minister of Uzziyaw" 161
Fig. 14: The Seal "of Ushna, the Minister of Aḥaz" 165
Fig. 15: The Bulla "of Yehozaraḥ, Son of Ḥilqiyahu, the Minister of Ḥizqiyahu" 170
Fig. 16: The Seal ring "of Ḥanan, Son of Ḥilqiyahu, the Priest" 178
Fig. 17: The Bulla "of Yeraḥmeʾel, the King's Minister" 192

In Appendix E, Provenanced:
Fig. 18: Portions of the Mesha Inscription Bearing the Name of King David 269

The author has made all drawings except: 1) two in Fig. 5, used by permission of *AUSS*: line 4a of the Izbet Sartah Ostracon, excerpted from William H. Shea, "The ʿIzbet Ṣarṭah Ostracon," *AUSS* 28 (1990): 63, Fig. 1, and a portion of line 4a of the same inscription, in idem, "Hophni in the Izbet Sartah Ostracon," *AUSS* 36 (1998): 278, Fig. 1; and 2) in Figs. 7 and 18, portions of the Mesha Inscription, which are from a drawing by Mark Lidzbarski that is in the public domain.

Researchers are well advised to see the photograph(s) of inscriptions before making final judgments on paleography or iconography. Citations in each section of Chapters 3 and 4 and in Appendixes B, C, and E below generally refer to sources containing photographs. In such visual matters, it is hazardous to rely on drawings alone.

# Introduction:

# Background and Statement of Thesis

## 0.1 Background

*A Growing Wealth of Hebrew Inscriptions*

For a century and a half, a great mass of "new" data from the discovery of Hebrew inscriptions has been quietly accumulating. Ancient Hebrew seals and bullae,[1] for example, were published irregularly since 1828, if not earlier. Between 1858 and 1950, they were usually published at least three of every five

---

[1] In this study, for the sake of clarity, the noun "seal" is reserved for the hard object which makes the impression in the softer material, such as clay or wax. Seals were made of semiprecious stone, metal, bone, or common stone. If they were inscribed with letters intended to be legible in the impression, the letters needed to appear on the seal in retrograde (i.e., mirror-image) script. The terms for impressions made by seals are: "seal impression," "sealing," and, if the seal impression is made in material that is used to seal a document (usually written on papyrus), "bulla."

In both biblical and ancient inscriptional Hebrew, the common word for "seal," *ḥôtām*, may refer to a seal as defined above or to the impression made by a seal. The Hebrew word is probably borrowed from the Egyptian noun *ḥtm*, "seal." The Hebrew word *ṭabbaʿat*, probably borrowed from the Egyptian *ḏbʿ.t*, "seal [ring]," yet related to the Hebrew word *ṭabaʿ*, "sink down," means a signet-ring, signet, or simply a ring (Thomas O. Lambdin, "Egyptian Loan Words in the Old Testament," *JAOS* 73 [1953]: 145–55; Benedikt Otzen, "חתם, *ḥātām*, חותם, *ḥôtām*," in *TDOT* 5:264). For background on seals

1

years.² Since the mid-twentieth century, the discovery of Hebrew inscriptions has continued unabated.³ We now know the names of more than 1,200 preexilic Israelites from inscriptional sources alone, primarily Hebrew seals, bullae, and ostraca.⁴ The names of exilic and postexilic Israelites from inscriptions of those periods can be added to these, as can the names of many Gentiles in Northwest Semitic inscriptions of other peoples of Syria-Palestine.⁵

---

and their uses in the ancient Near East, see Larry G. Herr, "Seal," *ISBE* 4:369–75; Elizabeth E. Platt, "Jewelry, Ancient Israelite," *ABD* 3:823–34.

²From 1858 through 1950, Hebrew seals and bullae were published during at least 55 of 93 years. Diringer mentions no Hebrew seal or bulla published before 1828. After that, he lists only five published during 1828–1849, then publications of seals and bullae during 1858–1932 with only one gap (1872–1879) of more than three years (Diringer, 158–261). Continuing from Diringer's registry to cover through 1950, Moscati reveals that "new" seals and bullae were published in all but three of the following 16 years (*EEA*, 47–65).

³Since 1950, the rate of publication of "new" Hebrew seals and bullae has continued at a rate which is at least comparable, as is evident in Francesco Vattioni, "I sigilli ebraici [I]," *Bib* 50 (1969): 370–85; idem, "I sigilli ebraici II," *Aug* 11 (1971): 447–54; idem, "I sigilli ebraici III," *AION* 41 (1981): 177–93. More than twenty anthologies and other broad-based studies of Hebrew inscriptions have appeared since 1970, several of which also cover other Northwest Semitic inscriptions. For these, see the bibliog. below under Aharoni, Aḥituv, Avigad, Avigad and Sass, Bordreuil, G. I. Davies, Deutsch, Deutsch and Heltzer, J. C. L. Gibson, Herr, Hestrin and Dayagi-Mendels, F. Israel, Israel Museum, Lemaire, Lindenberger, Pardee, Renz and Röllig, Stern, Suder, Tigay, and Zadok. Among these, *WSS* is especially important, because of its scope, photographs, and scholarly discussion. Also among these, a nearly complete corpus of extant Hebrew inscriptions from before 200 B.C.E. known as of 1991 is *AHI*. Its content is incorporated into a tool which is unique for its coverage of both biblical and inscriptional Hebrew: David J. A. Clines, ed., *The Dictionary of Classical Hebrew*, 10 vols. projected (Sheffield, England: Sheffield Academic Press, 1993– ), of which vols. 1–5, covering *aleph* through *nun*, appeared by 2001.

⁴Jeffrey H. Tigay, *You Shall Have No Other Gods: Israelite Religion in the Light of Hebrew Inscriptions* (HSS 31; Atlanta: Scholars Press, 1986), 9.

⁵For an extensive bibliography which traces the publication of Northwest Semitic inscriptions from 1616 to 1896, see Lidzbarski's indispensable *NE* 1:5–83. Lidzbarski carried his work forward to cover from 1900 to 1915 in idem, *Ephemeris für semitische Epigraphik* (3 vols.; Giessen: J. Ricker, Alfred Töpelmann, 1902–1915). More recent bibliography through 1969, coverage of inscriptions discovered up to some point in 1966, and discussion of Northwest Semitic inscriptions (except those then considered Ammonite and Edomite) is available in *KAI*. The chronological sequence continues with Javier Teixidor, *Bulletin d'épigraphie sémitique (1964–1980)* (Bibliothèque archéolo-gique et historique 127; Paris: Librarie orientaliste Paul Guenther, 1986). See also Joseph Naveh, *Early History of the Alphabet: An Introduction to West Semitic Epigraphy and Palaeography* (2d rev. ed.; Jerusalem: Magnes Press, 1987). The most current work strictly on

That this inscriptional material has significant implications for the study of the Bible and the ancient Near East is evident in countless publications. As ever increasing numbers of Northwest Semitic inscriptions are unearthed, including more that seem to mention persons named in the Bible, these will call for ever greater attention, including attention to the potential identifications they offer.

*Little-Researched Aspects of the Inscriptional Corpus*

Until now, the significance of Northwest Semitic inscriptions has been observed on the level of individual inscriptions and small groupings of them. Despite piecemeal attention in the treatment of historical details, their potential significance as a corpus has thus far attracted relatively little research.[6] To be sure, the Hebrew material is but a small piece of a larger whole, as is all material in Northwest Semitic languages. Other inscriptions of the era to which the Hebrew Bible refers, whether they be Hamito-Semitic (Egyptian), East Semitic (Akkadian), or Indo-European (Hittite, Greek, etc.), are abundant. Yet the fact that Egyptian, Assyrian, and Babylonian inscriptions, especially, are much more abundant and contain much useful information does not mean that Hebrew inscriptions as a corpus or other Northwest Semitic inscriptions ought to be ignored. A lack is evident in the facts that 1) previous studies have only rarely fo-

---

Hebrew inscriptions is *HAE*. The new standard dictionary for Northwest Semitic inscriptions is *DNWSI*, which, though published in 1995, understandably includes no material published after 1991.

For potential identification of biblical persons among Northwest Semitic inscriptions, after those that are Hebrew, the next most relevant group is Aramaic, followed by Ammonite and Moabite. See the bibliography below: for all three kinds, Aḥituv, Avigad and Sass, Bordreuil, Fowler, Herr, Hestrin and Dayagi-Mendels, Israel Museum, and Suder; on Aramaic inscriptions, see Fitzmyer and Kaufman, J. C. L. Gibson, Hackett, Hoftijzer and van der Kooij, Lemaire, Lindenberger, Lipiński, Maraqten, Naveh, Porten and Yardeni, and Rosenthal; on Ammonite inscriptions, Aufrecht (mainly) and Jackson; on Moabite inscriptions, Dearman, J. C. L. Gibson, Lemaire, and Rainey. A bibliographic essay that notes limitations of current works and describes some that are forthcoming is Lawrence J. Mykytiuk, "Accessing Voices of the Biblical World, Part 2: Tools and Corpora of Northwest Semitic Inscriptions of 1190–333 B.C.," *BullBib* 59 (2002): 151–66.

[6]For example, among treatments of Hebrew inscriptions, works which focus on Hebrew onomastics and the significance of the religious concepts in the Hebrew onomasticon are a precious few, e.g., *IPN*; George Buchanan Gray, *Studies in Hebrew Proper Names* (London: Adam & Charles Black, 1896); Fowler. Works, however, which focus on the *historical* significance of a large corpus of Hebrew inscriptions in comparison with the picture of history presented in the Hebrew Bible, e.g., Tigay, *You Shall Have No Other Gods*, are even fewer.

cused on more than a handful of the Hebrew inscriptions that offer potential identifications of persons named in the Hebrew Bible, and 2) only a few potential identifications have been evaluated in a way that can be called at all systematic (because that presupposes an existing method or system), therefore, the accuracy and reliability of a number of identifications has not been made clear.

*The Scope of This Study*

Most of the Hebrew inscriptions unearthed during the past century and a half originated during the course of the first millennium B.C.E. This study is about those that precede the Persian period, i.e., before 539, because of their variety and because of historical interest in the First Temple and exilic periods.

The corpus of inscriptions investigated in the main body of this study consists of eleven Hebrew inscriptions, the Mesha Inscription, and the Tel Dan stele. These thirteen artifacts were chosen both because they exemplify the kinds of conditions (e.g., annalistic content, fragmentation, etc.) that permit a demonstration of the capabilities and limits of the identification system and because they offer identifications whose historical significance makes them too important to ignore. Appendixes B and C enlarge the scope of the coverage by briefly evaluating potential identifications of more than 75 persons in over ninety Northwest Semitic inscriptions. The positive identifications they list without discussion add considerably to those established in the main body of the work.

Although Aramaic inscriptions of the preexilic period offer more than fifteen strong identifications of Gentile rulers who are mentioned in the Bible, lack of space prohibits treatment of them in the main body of this study. (Appendixes B and C list them.) Instead, this book is concerned with Hebrew inscriptions, partly because they offer potential identifications not only of rulers, but also of lesser government officials and of priests, providing glimpses of governmental and religious organizational structures.

**0.2 Statement of Thesis and proposed application of results**

This study attempts to establish and to gauge the strength of identifications or non-identifications between persons named in the above-mentioned corpus and persons named in the Hebrew Bible. The thesis of this work is that a relatively small, slowly growing number of identifications of biblical persons in Hebrew inscriptions and the two stelae (using provenanced materials) and conditional identifications (using unprovenanced Hebrew inscriptions) can indeed be systematically established. The study has two main thrusts. The first is to develop a sound methodology for making identifications of biblical persons in Hebrew inscriptions and the two stelae from before the Persian era. The second is to define a corpus of inscriptions that refer to biblical persons.

## 0.3 Method

The first two chapters develop a system for evaluating identifications. Chapter 1 selects appropriate criteria, and Chapter 2 subjects several potential identifications to these criteria. The resulting examples of six categories of identifications or non-identifications illustrate a taxonomy. Chapter 2 also builds refinements into the system to avoid accepting explanatory hypotheses as facts and to avoid circular thinking.

Chapter 3 uses the system set forth in Chapters 1 and 2 to evaluate potential identifications of persons named in the Hebrew Bible in inscriptions that are provenanced. Chapter 4 conducts the same process in unprovenanced inscriptions from the antiquities market.

The fifth and final chapter draws the conclusion indicated by the provenanced inscriptions in Chapter 3. It also specifies conditional findings which depend on verdicts regarding authenticity of unprovenanced inscriptions in Chapter 4. This final chapter also indicates promising areas for further research.

The most important appendixes are B, C, and F. Appendix B takes preliminary steps in further research, covering not only Hebrew but all (or almost all) Northwest Semitic inscriptions from before the Persian era. Appendix C rearranges Appendix B's identifications in descending order of strength. Appendix F presents numerical summaries of the results of all chapters and appendixes. In general, the chapters give intense scrutiny to Hebrew inscriptions and the two stelae, whereas the appendixes deal more broadly, but more briefly, with Northwest Semitic inscriptions.

# PART 1

## AN IDENTIFICATION SYSTEM

# Chapter 1

# Identification Criteria

**1.1 Three approaches which call for an identification system**

Rather frequently, treatments of potential identifications between persons named in the Bible and persons named in inscriptions exhibit the following ways of responding to the inscriptional and biblical data:

1. Some identifications are made with minimal evidence. The writer seizes on one or more bits of evidence or speculation and concludes that this or that biblical person is named in an inscription.

2. Other identifications, for which abundant evidence is available, are made too reluctantly or not at all.

3. Still other identifications are not made, because no analysis is conducted. The writer cites the possibilities, but does not reach a conclusion.

In all three kinds of response, it is readily observable that some reasonable system or set of criteria for making identifications could be very helpful.[1] Even

---

[1] E.g., the fact that no applicable identification system existed at the time may have helped lead Hackett to *assume* (this term is hers, emphasis mine) that the Balaam, son of Beor, a "seer of the gods" in the Deir ʿAllā inscription on plaster, was to be identified with the biblical Balaam (Jo Ann Hackett, *The Balaam Text from Deir ʿAllā* [HSM 31;

a very basic system could help to curb conclusions made for flimsy reasons, might provide assurance that an identification is justifiable, and could encourage writers to attempt an analysis.

This chapter and the next attempt to fill a long-standing need by developing a full-fledged[2] system for measuring the strength of potential identifications or non-identifications between persons named in the Hebrew Bible and persons named in ancient Northwest Semitic inscriptions. The principles used in this study may be extended to identifications of persons named in any literary sources received from tradition with persons named in excavated inscriptions.

From this point onward in this study, the noun *identification* will be spelled out if it signifies a process, but it will be abbreviated ID if it signifies the result of the process. For example: "The identification of the steward was difficult," but "An ID based on such clear evidence could hardly be more secure." The abbreviation will not be used as an adjective or in headings.

## 1.2 Development of basic criteria for making identifications

Although this chapter considers several approaches to making IDs, it develops identification criteria in three main ways. First, it takes into account ancient Near Eastern ways of identifying individuals, as known through inscriptions and the Bible. Second, it analyzes two well-known, modern misidentifications. Finally, it compares the results from the first two steps with the criteria adopted by a senior epigrapher after decades of trial and error.

## 1.3 Definitions

The following are working definitions for identifying individuals:

An *identity* is a unique self which belongs to a particular individual. This study assumes that an identity is outwardly recognizable by explicit phenomena, including such things as name, patronymic, and position in society.

To *identify* has two definitions: 1) to recognize a specific person by factual data; 2) to decide that those who might be perceived as two persons are really one and the same person. Below, the person(s) is or are usually named in two or more sources, therefore, the second definition will usually apply.

An *ID* (identification) is the recognition of a specific individual by evaluating outwardly discernible traits (see Appendix F, first paragraph).

---

Chico, Calif.: Scholars Press, 1984], 33–34, 36; idem, "Some Observations on the Balaam Tradition at Deir ʿAllā," *BA* 49 [1986]: 216).

[2] A *full-fledged* system is not necessarily fully developed or complete, but rather, one that takes into account all categories of factors. A fully fledged bird may not be full-grown, but it has every kind of feather that full-grown birds use in flight. A *method* that has very limited applicability can hardly be called a *system*.

An *identifying mark* is a specific bit of information about a person that an observer can use to distinguish him or her from others in the same group, such as parentage or occupation. Below, it can simply be called a "mark."

## 1.4 Underlying factors in the process of identification

The following factors underlie the practical (as opposed to fanciful) process of identification. As each of these factors increases, it tends to increase the number of identifying marks needed to identify a person with reasonable confidence. As these factors decrease, they may decrease the number of marks needed to make such an ID. The factors are:

1. Group size, i.e., the size of the group to which the person belongs *which forms the frame of reference*. Today, in a nation of millions, a full name and a multi-digit number may be necessary to identify someone, but if that individual works in an office in which only five persons work, there only a first name may suffice. In the agricultural societies of the ancient Near East, settled patterns of habitation in small villages and towns where families were linked to their ancestral land made for a lack of mobility. This in turn tended to make few marks suffice for an ID, e.g., name and patronymic. War or social dislocation could break up the reference group or put the person into a new reference group, necessitating new or additional identifying marks.[3]

2. Commonness of marks. A relatively high number of other persons within the group forming the frame of reference who have the same name or other identifying mark tends to reduce the likelihood of a correct ID on the basis of that mark alone. In this way, large groups tend to make more marks necessary in order to identify someone.

3. Vagueness of "location." Uncertainties regarding the social position(s), temporal span, or geographical location(s) of a person can necessitate more identifying marks, because they tend to increase the size of the potential reference group. After many generations, loss of knowledge of what these marks used to be and how common they were also makes identification difficult.

---

[3] In the rare situation of the return of Jewish exiles, multiple patronymics, as found, e.g., in Neh 11: 4–24, may have been added to show qualification for leadership (cf. Ezra 7:1–5) or as evidence of lineage, hence of the right to hold a particular office and the more basic right to membership in the Jewish community of Second Temple era Judah.

## 1.5 Ancient Near Eastern ways of identifying an individual

Generally in the ancient Near East, and specifically in ancient Syria-Palestine, the following were conventional ways of identifying persons:

1. The individual's given name.

2. A patronymic. It was occasionally used as a substitute for the individual's given name.[4] Sometimes several patronymics were used after a given name, asserting continuity of lineage despite change and social upheaval:

> ... Ezra, the son of Seraiah, the son of Azariah, the son of Hilkiah, the son of Shallum, the son of Zadok, the son of Ahitub, the son of Amariah, the son of Azariah, the son of Meraioth, the son of Zerahiah, the son of Uzzi, the son of Bukki, the son of Abishua, the son of Phineas, the son of Eleazar, the son of Aaron the chief priest—this Ezra went up from Babylon.... (Ezra 7:1b–6a)

3. The person's official post, e.g., "the governor of the city," or position in relation to a superior, e.g., "Malkiyahu, the steward [*na ʿar*] of Shaphat".

4. A pictured symbol, such as a depiction of an animal, plant, inanimate object, or geometric symbol which perhaps indicates a religious loyalty, clan membership, or cultural orientation.[5] A few seals have a tiny portrait, possibly of the seal owner, wearing foreign-style clothing, sometimes with a symbol of office.[6] Although there have been advances in our understanding of Syro-Palestinian iconography, it is still not thoroughly understood.[7]

---

[4] See Albrecht Alt, "Menschen ohne Namen," *ArOr* 18 (1950): 9–24; repr. in *Kleine Schriften zur Geschichte des Volkes Israel* (Munich: C. H. Beck, 1959), 3:198–213; ET, *Essays on Old Testament History and Religion* (trans. R. A. Wilson; Garden City, N.Y.: Doubleday, 1967); David J. A. Clines, "X, X ben Y, ben Y: Personal Names in Hebrew Narrative Style," *VT* 22 (1972): 282–87; Joseph Naveh, "Nameless People," *IEJ* 40 (1990): 108–23.

[5] Gibson 1:25–26, no. 9; cf. W. Robertson Smith, *Kinship and Marriage in Early Arabia* (London: Adam & Charles Black, 1903; repr., Boston: Beacon Press, n.d.), 217–51.

[6] E.g., the seal of Shubnayaw, the minister of Uzziyaw (see section 4.3 below). Other examples are listed in Gibson 1:60–62.

[7] Among noteworthy studies of iconography are Kurt Galling, "Beschriftete Bildsiegel des ersten Jahrtausends v. Chr. vornehmlich aus Syrien und Palästina: Ein Beitrag zur Geschichte der phönikischen Kunst," *ZDPV* 64 (1941): 121–202; Ruth Hestrin, "Understanding Asherah: Exploring Semitic Iconography," *BAR* 17, no. 5 (September/October 1991): 50–59; Othmar Keel, *Die Welt der altorientalischen Bildsymbolik und das Alte Testament: Am Beispiel der Psalmen* (5th ed.; Göttingen: Vandenhoeck & Ruprecht,

## 1.6 Prosopography

The categories of information which are useful in making IDs, such as an individual's name(s) and family, social, and career relationships in a given time and place, are also used in prosopographical studies. Prosopography[8] has to do with situating individuals and groups in their societal context in order to study various things, such as typical career paths, the social fabric of political power structures, traditional alliances and rivalries, or the living conditions of groups at various levels in society. "There is no agreed or official definition of prosopography," and it even "goes under different names in different disciplines."[9]

In such a fluid situation, one is free to view the study of identifying individuals as a subset of prosopography.[10] Of course, the identification of individuals can be an important factor in prosopographical study. As prosopography has developed, however, at least in the field of history, it exhibits a characteristic tendency to focus on groups or aggregates within their social contexts, whereas identification study has no intrinsic impulse to go beyond individual IDs.

Prosopography with an orientation toward history commonly appears in classical and medieval studies, although it is found elsewhere, including ancient

---

1996); idem, *Corpus der Stempelsiegel-Amulette aus Palästina/ Israel: Von den Anfängen bis zur Perserzeit Einleitung* (OBO Series Archaeologica 10; Göttingen: Vandenhoeck & Ruprecht, 1995). See note 28 below.

[8] Perhaps the best essay for gaining a grasp of the value and limitations of prosopography is T. Robert S. Broughton, "Senate and Senators of the Roman Republic: the Prosopographical Approach," in *Von den Anfängen Roms bis zum Ausgang der Republik* (ed. Hildegard Temporini; Part 1 of *ANRW*), 1:250–65. A much-cited classical essay on the topic is Lawrence Stone, "Prosopography," *Daedalus* 100 (1971): 46–79, repr. in *Historical Studies Today* (ed. Felix Gilbert and Stephen R. Graubard; New York: Norton, 1972), 107–40. See also Thomas F. Carney's essay in conversational style, "Prosopography: Payoffs and Pitfalls," *Phoenix* 27 (1973): 156–79 (this *Phoenix* is the one published by the University of Toronto); George Beech, "Prosopography," in *Medieval Studies: An Introduction* (ed. James M. Powell; 2d ed.; Syracuse, N.Y.: Syracuse University Press, 1992), 185–226. Beech credits the German classicist, Otto Seeck (1850–1921), with conceiving and carrying out the first prosopographical study (ibid., 188). One issue of *Annales: Économies, Sociétés, Civilisations* contains three articles which are also important: André Chastagnol, "La prosopographie, méthode de recherche sur l'histoire du Bas-Empire," *Annales* 25 (Septembre-Octobre 1970): 1229–35; Claude Nicolet, "Prosopographie et histoire sociale: Rome et l'Italie à l'epoque républicaine," *Annales* 25 (Septembre-Octobre 1970): 1209–28; Jacqueline Sublet, "La prosopographie arabe," *Annales* 25 (Septembre-Octobre 1970): 1236–39.

[9] Simon Hornblower and Anthony J. S. Spawforth, "Prosopography," *OCD*, 1262.

[10] E.g., Nili S. Fox, *In the Service of the King: Officialdom in Ancient Israel and Judah* (Cincinnati: Hebrew Union College Press, 2000), 36–42. This book is the published revision of idem, "Royal Functionaries and State-Administration in Israel and Judah During the First Temple Period" (Ph.D. diss., University of Pennsylvania, 1997).

Near Eastern studies.[11] The study of identification as presented here is rooted in extant data of the first half of the first millennium B.C.E. from peoples whose languages were Northwest Semitic. Perhaps identification study has sprung up in the context of this field of study because there is great interest in potential IDs of people known from the Bible and, at the same time, little available data about particular individuals, especially non-royal persons. There is less, for example, than in classical Roman history.[12] Generally, the problem is to find enough data of the kind necessary to make a secure ID.

---

[11] E.g., James R. Jordan, "Studies in Sumerian Prosopography: Sheshkalla" (Ph.D. diss., University of Minnesota, 1971); Lucio Milano, "L'étude prosopographique des textes cunéiformes d'Ebla (IIIe millénaire avant J.-C.): Quelques réflexions à propos du projet et de ses finalités," in *Informatique et Prosopographie: Actés de la Table Ronde du CNRS, Paris, 25–26 octobre 1984* (ed. Hélène Millet; Paris: Éditions du Centre National de la Recherche Scientifique, 1985), 91–114; Simo Parpola, ed., *The Prosopography of the Neo-Assyrian Empire* (2 vols. to date; Helsinki: The Neo-Assyrian Text Corpus Project, 1998– ); Ran Zadok, *The Pre-Hellenistic Israelite Anthroponomy and Prosopography* (OLA 28; Leuven: Uitgeverij Peeters, 1988).

[12] In general, the usual ways of making IDs within the field of classical Roman history are of little help in ancient Near Eastern IDs, because of differences in the nature and quantity of the available data. E.g., distinguished Romans usually had a *praenomen* (i.e., individual name), followed by the *nomen* (the name of the *gens*, or clan), and a cognomen (surname or family name), such as Marcus Tullius Cicero. Such a combination furnishes its own classification system, locating the individual within specific intermediate and large kinship groups. The simpler system of name and patronymic found among Semitic peoples and the ancient Greeks usually provides a two-generation genealogy (not found in Roman names), but does not reveal clan or tribal membership. Further, the quantity of literary and inscriptional material available to researchers in classics far exceeds that available in Northwest Semitic studies from before the Persian era.

In the field of classical history, there is an observable tendency to present IDs as results, without the rationale. In that field, I have not been able to find any system for making IDs of individuals (taken one by one) with certainty. It is difficult to imagine that no classicist ever formulated one, but such a formulation, if it exists, seems to be buried in the scholarly literature.

Further, prosopographers in the field of classics, despite the rigor of their research and the large amount of information available, tend to express IDs in terms of possibility and likelihood, rather than certainty. When firm IDs are necessary, confidence tends to arise from the overall quantity of data surveyed, rather than any ironclad certainty in particular cases. E.g., Rauh, in attempting to trace the business activities of Roman and other Italian aristocrats, matches many names found in literary and epigraphic sources. He finds that eighty-five families represented in the pre-Sullan Roman Senate left contemporary epigraphic evidence of business transactions in commercial centers. After presenting many of the matches somewhat tentatively, Rauh concludes that these eighty-five matches are more than can be attributed to coincidence (Nicholas K. Rauh, "Senators and

## 1.7 Survey of the literature, first of two parts

Although there are important works on Israelite personal *names*[13] and what they reveal about religious loyalties and concepts of the day,[14] little has been written on the process of *identification*. To be sure, studies on names can be of great help in making IDs, as can various writings on paleography, etc. Nevertheless, there is a dearth of material on general criteria for making IDs in Northwest Semitic inscriptions. The probable reason is that during most of the last century, only a few Northwest Semitic inscriptions that seem to name persons named in the Bible were discovered and published.[15] Moreover, almost all treatments concern specific matches, rather than the identification process in general. Many of these leave the reasons for the IDs implicit, with little or no reference to general identification criteria. Very few works discuss general criteria, and although gatherings of a few citations can be found in a few places in the literature, it appears that there is only one bibliography specifically on this subject.[16]

Because the beginnings of sound, comprehensive criteria for making IDs have developed through a long process of educated guess, discovery of error, and correction, each study which has contributed to any of these stages in the formulation of these criteria can be considered important. There are two historical sequences in the development of identification methodology. The longer of these two sequences has to do with the use of epigraphy, as over against iconography, in making IDs. It originates with a 1932 article by William F. Albright,[17] leads to a landmark article by Nahman Avigad in 1987,[18] and continues to the present. The shorter historical sequence has to do with the use of iconography in the making of IDs. It begins with a 1985 article by Pierre Bordreuil,[19] which

---

Business in the Roman Republic, 264–44 B.C." [Ph.D. diss., University of North Carolina at Chapel Hill, 1986], 78–86).

[13] E.g., *IPN*; Gray, *Studies in Hebrew Proper Names*.

[14] E.g., Tigay, *You Shall Have No Other Gods*; Fowler.

[15] As late as 1978, Nahman Avigad lamented that up to that time, no Hebrew seal or seal impression had yet been found whose owner could "be identified with absolute certainty with a person mentioned in the Bible" (Nahman Avigad, "Baruch the Scribe and Jerahme'el the King's Son," *IEJ* 28 [1978] 52).

[16] Lawrence J. Mykytiuk, "Did Bible Characters Really Exist? Part 1: An Annotated Bibliography on Methods of Evaluating Evidence in Hebrew Inscriptions," *BullBib* 55 (1998): 243–49.

[17] William F. Albright, "The Seal of Eliakim and the Latest Pre-Exilic History of Judah, with Some Observations on Ezekiel," *JBL* 51 (1932): 77–106.

[18] Nahman Avigad, "On the Identification of Persons Mentioned in Hebrew Epigraphic Sources," *ErIsr* 19 (Michael Avi-Yonah Volume, 1987): 235–37 (Hebrew), English summary 79*.

[19] Pierre Bordreuil, "Inscriptions sigillaires ouest-sémitiques, III: sceaux de dignitaires et de rois syro-palestiniens du VIIIe et du VIIe siècle avant J.-C.," *Syria* 62 (1985):

along with later articles occasions Josette Elayi's criticisms of Bordreuil's criteria in 1995.[20] It will probably continue also. Perhaps one day it may even merge with the longer sequence on identification using epigraphic data.

Bordreuil's main criterion involves West Semitic inscribed seals depicting a standing or striding human figure in profile with one hand held up, palm forward, and the other hand holding a scepter or staff. If the figure is crowned, it represents a monarch who is the seal owner; such a figure with a scepter or staff but without a crown represents a dignitary, not a monarch, who is the seal owner.[21] It is understood that a dignitary could have become a monarch sometime after the seal was made. Having determined the apparent rank of the seal owner by the iconographic representation, the researcher then searches for the name of the seal owner (inscribed on the seal) in inscriptions which are contemporary with or refer back to the time of the seal. If the iconography depicts a king, and if a king with the same name and (apparently) the same realm at the same time is named in another inscription, the ID may be made.

The assumption underlying this criterion is that the human figures on the seals depict the seal owners, never anyone else. Elayi observes that this assumption is groundless; therefore all six IDs of allegedly "royal" seal owners which have been made on the basis of iconographic criteria, though possible, cannot be established on those grounds.[22] Similarly, Benjamin Sass finds that "'royal' or 'official' iconography of a seal could imply royal or official ownership, but this cannot be proved . . . ."[23] Elayi also notes iconography that does not fit Bordreuil's main criterion very tidily: "Sass has distinguished three different principles in the representation of so-called 'kings' and 'dignitaries': the figure holding in one hand a scepter and the other hand hanging down—or the other hand raised—or without a scepter and both hands raised."[24]

---

21–29. Ten subsequent articles by Bordreuil which use his identification criteria are listed in Josette Elayi, "Les sceaux ouest-sémitiques 'royaux': mythe ou réalité?" *Quaderni ticinesi di numismatica e antichità classiche* 24 (1995): 39–40, n. 4.

[20] Ibid., 39–71.

[21] Bordreuil, "Inscriptions sigillaires ouest-sémitiques, III," 29.

[22] ʾAbibaʿal, king of Šamsimuruna; Muṣuri, king of Moab; Ḥanunu, king of Gaza; Peqaḥ, king of Israel; Menaḥem, king of Šamsimuruna; and Milki-Asapa, king of Byblos (Elayi, "Les sceaux ouest-sémitiques 'royaux,' 39–71).

[23] Benjamin Sass, "The Pre-Exilic Hebrew Seals: Iconism vs. Aniconism," in *Studies in the Iconography of Northwest Semitic Inscribed Seals: Proceedings of a Symposium Held in Fribourg on April 17–20, 1991* (ed. Benjamin Sass and Christoph Uehlinger; OBO 125; Göttingen: Vandenhoeck & Ruprecht, 1993), 230.

[24] Elayi, "Les sceaux ouest-sémitiques 'royaux,'" 49 (translation mine), citing Sass, "Pre-Exilic Hebrew Seals," 229–31.

Eric Gubel has followed Bordreuil in the use of these criteria since 1990, and in 1994, Christoph Uehlinger also used them.²⁵ Elayi's critique and adverse conclusions appeared the following year.²⁶ Although iconography seems to offer hope of becoming useful in making IDs,²⁷ it has thus far proven difficult to perceive under what circumstances or in what ways it may be used reliably.²⁸

For a bibliographic discussion of the longer historical sequence of publications, i.e., those which base IDs on epigraphy, see section 1.13 below. It accompanies an examination of the content of the main articles in the sequence.

Turning from the matter of identification criteria to the inscriptions in which the IDs might appear, it is noteworthy that the specific inscriptions in which biblical persons might reasonably be identified have never been completely listed *as such* in any published source. Publications specifically about inscriptions that may name persons in the Bible uniformly take a piecemeal approach; none of these publications covers more than a few of these inscriptions, and most cover only one. Many of these treatments are now out of date, and some of their IDs of persons known from the Bible have later been shown to be erroneous (see, e.g., sections 1.9 and 1.10 below). Relevant information is very thinly sprinkled, for the most part, through a wide variety of reference works,

---

²⁵ Eric Gubel, "Le sceau de Menahem et l'iconographie royale sigillaire," *Sem* 38 (1990): 167–71; idem, "Notes sur l'iconographie royale sigillaire," in Congresso Internationale di Studi Fenici e Punici 1987, *Atti del IIo Congresso Internationale di Studi Fenici e Punici* (ed. Enrico Acquaro et al.; Collezione di Studi Fenici 30; Rome: Consiglio nazionale delle recherche, 1991), 2:913–22; Christoph Uehlinger, "Ahabs königliches Siegel: Ein antiker Bronzering zwischen Historismus und Reliquienkult, *Memoria* und Geschichte," in *Peregrina curiositas: Ein Reise durch den Orbis antiquus: zu Ehren von Dirk van Damme* (ed. Andreas Kessler, Thomas Ricklin, and Gregor Wurst; NTOA 27; Göttingen: Vandenhoeck & Ruprecht, 1994), 86–89.

²⁶ Elayi, "Les sceaux ouest-sémitiques 'royaux,'" 39–71.

²⁷ Ibid.

²⁸ Two sources which seem likely to be useful in constructive discussion on using both epigraphy and iconography in making IDs are Irene J. Winter, "Legitimation of Authority through Image and Legend: Seals Belonging to Officials in the Administrative Bureaucracy of the Ur III State," in *The Organization of Power: Aspects of Bureaucracy in the Ancient Near East* (ed. McGuire Gibson and Robert D. Biggs; SAOC 46; Chicago, Illinois: The Oriental Institute of the University of Chicago, 1987), 69–106, Pl. 1–10; and Sass and Uehlinger, *Studies in the Iconography*. Although Winter's article treats Sumerian materials of 2112–2004, rather than Hebrew inscriptions of 1000–586, some of the same conventions of seal composition using text and image may apply. Winter finds that *the iconography reflects the level of the office of the seal owner* (italics mine) (Winter, "Legitimation," 90–91). Sass' and Uehlinger's collection of essays will undoubtedly provide some of the bases for future perspectives on the potential use of the iconography in identification study. See note 7 above.

archaeological reports, other monographs, scholarly journals, Bible commentaries,[29] popular-level magazines, and dissertations.

Because no previously published study or bibliography covers this topic as a whole or for any particular time period (though one might wish otherwise), the survey of the literature (in this section and section 1.13 below) is fairly short. Broader bibliographic coverage extending beyond the focus of this study is contained in the anthologies, published corpora, and bibliographies of inscriptions listed in section 0.1, notes 2 through 6, above.

**1.8 Methodology for choosing criteria**

Past attempts at finding matches between persons named in literary and epigraphic sources have produced some IDs of uncertain validity and others which are now known to be failures. An effective way to discover how to make valid IDs and avoid mistaken ones would be to shun the uncertain matches and instead, as ironic as it may sound, proceed on the firmer ground of known failures. By examining how mistakes have been made in the past, it is reasonable to expect that sound criteria might emerge as unreliable criteria fall away or as the need for other criteria becomes evident.

Many factors in archaeological, epigraphic, and identification processes were unknown or little understood by the pioneer archaeologists of the nineteenth and twentieth century. Therefore, despite their mastery of existing knowledge in several relevant fields of study (not least, ancient Near Eastern languages), they had to resort to trial and error. The field of archaeology advanced not only because they were willing to risk the possibility of later being shown to be wrong, but also because their educated guesses were often right. This chapter examines some of their mistakes in an attempt to discern both reliable and unreliable criteria for making IDs.

It is generally acknowledged that a contributing factor in the decline of the biblical archaeology movement[30] has been a tendency to interpret discoveries by

---

[29] The information in Bible commentaries, unfortunately, is less common, less current, and less useful. A new species of commentary, known as the archaeological Bible commentary or archaeological companion to a book or books of the Bible, has only begun to remedy this problem. The best example is Philip J. King, *Jeremiah: An Archaeological Companion* (Louisville, Ky.: Westminster/John Knox Press, 1993), esp. 85–101.

[30] Biblical archaeology may be defined as field archaeological work, such as survey and excavation, along with the analysis and interpretation of discoveries, undertaken in order to elucidate the Bible. Although its beginnings can be traced to the nineteenth century with the work of such men as Edward Robinson, Sir William M. Flinders Petrie, Henry Creswicke Rawlinson, Austen Henry Layard, and Charles Simon Clermont-Ganneau, biblical archaeology did not begin to assume the proportions of a movement until the 1920s. The biblical archaeology *movement* flourished from that time through the 1960s under the leadership of William Foxwell Albright (1891–1971), followed by his

relating them as closely as possible to biblical locations, persons, objects, and events, sometimes without a sound factual basis. Speaking more generally, J. Maxwell Miller has observed that archaeologists tend to be overly optimistic regarding their finds (these include inscriptions and the potential IDs they offer), whereas historians tend to be too skeptical regarding ancient texts (which include inscriptions).[31] Prudence, therefore, would suggest a more stringent approach to the identification process than that usually taken by archaeologists.

The overall pattern of reasoning that lies behind the method used below is called abductive, i.e., reasoning back and forth between the specific and the general. To develop criteria, reasoning will go back and forth between specific examples of error or correctness and general criteria or principles of identification.

**1.9 Instructive misidentification number one: the seal of "Jotham"**

The seal of "Jotham"[32] is the simpler of the two misidentifications to be considered. It was discovered in 1940 at "the last minute of the last day of the

---

student, George Ernest Wright (1909–1974). Other leaders in the field, such as Father Roland G. de Vaux, Dame Kathleen M. Kenyon, Yigael Yadin, Benjamin Mazar, Ruth Amiran, Nelson Glueck, and D. J. Wiseman, to name but a few, have considered themselves biblical archaeologists. Albright gave the chronological dimensions of biblical archaeology as 9,000 B.C.E. to 700 C.E. and the geographical dimensions as Spain and Northwest Africa to the Indus Valley (William F. Albright, "The Impact of Archaeology on Biblical Research—1966," in *New Directions in Biblical Archaeology* [ed. David Noel Freedman and Jonas C. Greenfield; Garden City, N.Y.: Doubleday, 1969], 1–2).

P. Roger S. Moorey, *A Century of Biblical Archaeology* (Louisville, Ky.: Westminster/John Knox Press, 1991) presents the history of biblical archaeology from 1800 to the late twentieth century in a generally positive light. Thomas W. Davis, "A History of Biblical Archaeology" (Ph.D. diss., University of Arizona, 1987), written under the direction of Professor William G. Dever, analyzes the movement under Albright's and Wright's leadership and arrives at predominantly negative conclusions. Amihai Mazar, *Archaeology of the Land of the Bible, 10,000–586 B.C.E.* (New York: Doubleday, 1990), 31–33, points out a few of the errors of the older biblical archaeology movement and presents the favorable attitude of a contemporary Israeli archaeologist toward the increasingly secular, professional, and multidisciplinary transformation of biblical archaeology.

[31] J. Maxwell Miller, "Approaches to the Bible through History and Archaeology: Biblical History as a Discipline," *BA* 45 (1982): 211–16.

[32] See Chapter 2, Fig. 6, below. Discoverer Nelson Glueck always vocalized *ytm* with o in the first syllable followed by ā in the second, from his first mention of this seal in "The Third Season of Excavation at Tell el-Kheleifeh," *BASOR* 79 (October 1940): 2–18. Currently, however, many scholars are inclined to reverse the vowels to ā followed by o, yielding the name Yatom, "orphan." Among the latter group is, e.g., Gibson 1:61, no. 4, and 63, n. 4.

last of three seasons of ... excavations"[33] at Tell el-Kheleifeh, at the northern tip of the Gulf of Aqaba. Pioneer archaeologist Nelson Glueck believed it to be the site of the biblical cities Ezion-Geber and, later, Elath. Abbas, the Arab foreman of Glueck, found a seal ring under a mud brick wall. Believing that this beautifully executed seal ring most likely belonged to Jotham, son of Uzziah, king of Judah, Glueck wrote,

> In a room belonging to Period III [which he assigned "to the eighth century B.C."[34]], was found a beautiful signet ring (Figs. 8–9). The seal itself, enclosed in a copper casing, had incised on it in retrograde, in the clearest possible ancient Hebrew characters, the following inscription: LYTM, "belonging to Jotham." Below the inscription is a beautifully carved, horned ram, which seems to be Syrian in style. In front of the ram seems to be the figure of a man. It cannot definitely be proven that the YTM of the seal is the very king of Judah, whose dominion included also Elath, but the likelihood is a strong one[9] [i.e., Glueck's footnote 9]. Even if this JOTHAM was merely the governor of Elath, he was apparently a Judaean. In all events, it is quite appropriate that during the period of Judaean control over Elath extending throughout the reigns of Uzziah, Jotham, and the beginning of the reign of Ahaz, the Hebrew name of JOTHAM should be found ....[35]

In the first half of the accompanying note 9, Albright stated:

> It appears that the identification is almost certain. The absence of the usual patroymic suggests that the owner of the seal was a very important person, and this impression is amply confirmed by the beautiful execution of the seal itself. A date between cir. 750 and 650 is fixed both stratigraphically and epigraphically. High officials seem always to have given their titles or the general title "servant of the king." If the seal belonged to Jotham as crown prince, we might expect the usual addition, often found in Jewish seals, "son of the king." If it belonged to him as regent or as king no addition would have been needed. We know from ample material that Near Eastern rulers often had their seals made in numerous examples, to facilitate the execution of royal business, so the copper or bronze (instead of silver or gold) mounting need occasion no difficulty ... [Albright then discusses the vocalization of the name].[36]

In an "imaginative study"[37] published in 1961, Nahman Avigad supported this ID with his interpretation of the significance of the ram and the unidentified

---

[33] Nelson Glueck, *Rivers in the Desert: A History of the Negev* (New York: Farrar, Strauss and Cudahy, 1959; repr. as vol. 5 of Evergreen Encyclopedia; New York: Grove Press, Evergreen Books, 1960), 166.
[34] Idem, "Third Season," 12.
[35] Ibid., 13, 15. Quotation courtesy of ASOR.
[36] Ibid., 15, n. 9. Quotation courtesy of ASOR.
[37] Gibson 1:63, n. 4.

shape in front of the ram.[38] Yet even in that article, Avigad observed, "This identification, however, remained open to question as long as no supporting internal evidence was available to prove that the said YTM was indeed an official authority of any kind."[39]

Avigad's article attempted to buttress the ID partly by interpreting the unidentified shape as a bellows, symbolizing the local copper smelting industry, and the ram (*'ayil* in Hebrew) as a symbol of the imputed provenance, Elath. Nevertheless, it failed to establish that the seal owner had any official authority, let alone royal blood. Because they were pioneers, these men did not have access to the great mass of information available today, much of which is based on their work. To their credit, both Glueck and Avigad stopped short of claiming certainty for this ID. In 1978, by examining the seal's paleographic traits, Larry G. Herr identified it as Edomite, from the first half of the seventh century, rather than mid-eighth century and Hebrew.[40] This correction has withstood scholarly scrutiny. As early as 1971, Glueck tacitly abandoned the ID he had originated for this seal's owner.[41]

Why did this ID fail? An examination of Albright's argument,[42] quoted above, reveals that the stratigraphy (at least at this site), paleography, and knowledge of linguistic development were not yet accurate enough to prevent this misidentification.[43] For example, Albright dated the seal between 750 and 650, whereas later on, Herr was able to set the date more accurately at 700 to 650. Jotham ruled Judah from 758/7 to 742/1.[44] The ability to distinguish Edomite from Hebrew script reliably was also a development that came long after Albright's comments appeared in Glueck's 1940 article.

But two factors of which Glueck, Albright, and Avigad were aware could have kept them from this error if they had given them more weight. The first, "the absence of the usual patronymic," which Albright listed first in his observations,[45] should have served as a reason for caution. Albright, however, chose to regard it as a suggestion "that the owner of the seal was a very important per-

---

[38] Nahman Avigad, "The Jotham Seal from Elath," *BASOR* 163 (October 1961): 18–22.

[39] Ibid., 19.

[40] *SANSS*, 163, no. 2.

[41] Nelson Glueck, "Tell el-Kheleifeh Inscriptions," in *Near Eastern Studies in Honor of William Foxwell Albright* (ed. Hans Goedicke; Baltimore: Johns Hopkins Press, 1971), 225, 226, Pl. 1.

[42] In Glueck, "Third Season," 15, n. 9.

[43] E.g., on the linguistic development of the first vowel, cf. Gibson 1:63, n. 4.

[44] Gershon Galil, *The Chronology of the Kings of Israel and Judah* (Studies in the History and Culture of the Ancient Near East 9; New York: Brill, 1996), 147.

[45] Glueck, "Third Season," 15, n. 9.

son,"[46] and would therefore be recognized without any further identifying information. As for the absence of a title, which could also have served as a warning, Albright added, "If it belonged to him as regent or as king no addition [*sc.*, of a title] would have been needed."[47] This comment appears to be based on the same reasoning: that very important people need no further identifying information. This reasoning, however, fails on five points (cf. section 2.7 below):

1. Regarding the lack of a patronymic for a person who was so well known that he or she needed no further identifying information, Albright overlooked the possibility that precisely the same result could also have resulted from illegitimacy of birth. How were the two to be distinguished from each other?

2. It does not explain the practical matter of how a seal that belonged to an untitled person was to be distinguished from that of a titled person having the same name.

3. Surviving material evidences of the culture of the Israelites of the divided kingdoms reveal no hesitancy to include titles relating to royalty. Such phrases as "the king's son," "the king's daughter," and "the minister of the king" are in standard usage among the phrases included in Hebrew seals and bullae. In Hebrew epigraphic sources, as Albright himself notes,

> High officials seem always to have given their titles or the general title, "servant of the king." If the seal belonged to Jotham as crown prince, we might expect the usual addition, often found in Jewish seals, "the son of the king."[48]

4. A further point applies to seals, which were in many instances used not merely to signal the owner's identity by name and patronymic, but to express the owner's full authority and accountability in relation to the sealed item by a title.[49] To omit an official title or a patronymic perhaps relevant to an inherited office would have been contradictory to the official function of a seal. Albright and Glueck did not give due weight to the lack of patronymic and title in the seal whose owner they identified as Jotham, king of Judah. It was primarily the failure to emphasize patronymic and title as essential elements that led to the misidentification.

---

[46] Ibid.
[47] Ibid.
[48] Ibid.
[49] See the parallels to offices of preexilic Hebrew kingdoms and the description of seal functions in *Seals and Sealing in the Ancient Near East* (ed. McGuire Gibson and Robert D. Biggs; Bibliotheca Mesopotamica 6; Malibu, Calif.: Undena Publications, 1977), 142–44, 148; cf. 75–76, 79–80, 98, 111.

5. In a matter of underlying principle, the ID leaned too heavily on the reasoning of twentieth-century scholars about the recognition of very important persons, rather than on ancient practice in the making and use of seals. The cessation of the original social context and the relative scarcity of data about it in modern times have forced modern scholars to identify persons by using the same categories of data by which their ancient society identified them. The surviving material remains reveal the means by which the ancient societies identified persons, and we have little choice but to use those same means.

Albright and Glueck cannot be held responsible for not dating the seal accurately and for not discerning its "nationality," since they did not have the information at their disposal that we do. Nevertheless, the specific categories of information which contributed to this misidentification point to the importance of patronymic and title as well as date and socio-political classification[50] of inscriptions in the identification process.

## 1.10 Instructive misidentification number two: the seal impressions of Eliakim, steward of "Jehoiachin"

While excavating Tell Beit Mirsim in 1928 and 1930, Albright found two stamped jar handles that read, in paleo-Hebrew, לאליקם / נער יוכן, "belonging to Eliakim, the steward of Yokan." In 1930, before Albright's second such inscription was found, Elihu Grant, digging at Beth Shemesh, unearthed a jar handle with this same inscription. All three of these impressions were made with the same seal. Near the two stamped jar handles at Tell Beit Mirsim, Albright also found two jar handles bearing the royal seal impression, "*lmlk*." Along with many seal impressions of private individuals, all of these were stamped on double-ridged jar handles made of the same dark, reddish-brown clay. Combining the three factors, that Eliakim was the servant, that Yokan was the master, and that the royal stamp seemed to be used on the same jars, Albright concluded that the name Yokan must somehow be related to that of Jehoiachin, king of Judah. Albright's colleague, Father Louis Hugues Vincent, explained the form *ywkn* to him as "Jochin," a hypocoristicon of *ywykyn*[51] (in the Hebrew Bible, the consonants *ywykyn* form King Jehoiachin's name only in Ezek 1:2).

---

[50] Reasons for the selection of this term, rather than "nationality," etc., appear under Criterion 6 in section 1.27 below.

[51] This summary is from Albright, "Seal of Eliakim," 77–78, 81; and Yosef Garfinkel, "The Eliakim *Naʿar* Yokan Seal Impressions: Sixty years of Confusion in Biblical Archaeological Research," *BA* 53 (1990): 74–75. See also Anson F. Rainey, "A Rejoinder to the Eliakim *Naʿar* Yokan Seal Impressions," *BA* 54 (1991): 61.

The dating of these finds was a corollary of the dating of the *lmlk* jars, about which a major debate was settled much later. This argument about their stratigraphic dating spanned half a century,[52] and it was not settled until David Ussishkin's excavation of Lachish Level III. This stratum at Lachish corresponds approximately to the levels at Tell Beit Mirsim and Beth Shemesh in which the Eliakim-steward-of-Yokan jar handles were found. In 1977, Ussishkin showed that this level was destroyed by the Assyrian invasion of 701, not the Babylonian invasions of 597 or 587/586, as Albright and other leaders had contended.[53]

Albright had used the Eliakim-steward-of-Yokan jar handles as part of the basis of his date for this stratum, which was incorporated into an overall scheme of stratigraphic dating for all of Palestine that dominated the field for about half a century of modern scholarly work. As a result,

> A mysterious gap between the tenth and seventh centuries seemed to appear at most of the excavated sites in Judah. In this way a distorted picture emerged, not only of the archaeology of the kingdom of Judah but also of other related disciplines such as ancient Hebrew epigraphy, the historical geography of the Bible, and biblical studies.[54]

It should now be clear that 1) some IDs can be crucial to several fields of study, a fact that underscores the importance of correctness in making IDs, and 2) the stratigraphy of the period of the divided kingdoms became well established in the late 1970s, and it was not at all accurate when the Eliakim-steward-of-Yokan jar handles were discovered. How, then, might Albright have avoided this crucial misidentification?

Unlike the previous example of a misidentification, the trouble was caused not primarily by the lack of a patronymic or title (of the seal owner's master). To be sure, such information would have precluded the possibility of this error, and in retrospect one might wish that Albright had suspended judgment because this sort of information was absent for Yokan. The pivotal problem, however, originated from a misunderstanding of the ancient Hebrew usage of the title, *na'ar*, translated "steward" or "servant." It was Nahman Avigad who in 1976 first called for an end to the identification of Eliakim's master with King Jehoiachin. He was able to do so because, on the basis of the study of other seals (many of which were not available to Albright in 1932), it had by then become clear that the title *na'ar* was not a guarantee that the title holder was an official in the royal household. Rather, it was a title bestowed on a certain class of ser-

---

[52] Garfinkel, "Eliakim *Na'ar* Yokan," 74–79; esp. the bibliog.. on 79.
[53] Ibid., 77.
[54] Ibid., 76.

vants, apparently private stewards, who served individuals who were not necessarily connected to the palace at all.[55]

Albright was aware that in seals and bullae of the Hebrew monarchic period, the Hebrew formula "[PN] 'ebed [PN]" implied that the second person named was a king (see Appendix A). The title na 'ar seemed so close semantically to 'ebed that Albright considered them virtually synonymous, hence the name following na 'ar also seemed to belong to a king.[56] It should be pointed out that the biblical examples of the use of na 'ar that Albright adduced did not require that the master be a king at all. Nevertheless, the failure to apprehend the distinction in usage between these two titles is not surprising, because the precise meaning of such titles was not as clear in the 1930s as it is today.

The second-most-serious difficulty Albright faced had to do with the orthography of the name of the seal owner's master. The spelling remained ambiguous, no matter what attractive possibilities Father Vincent mentioned to Albright.[57] On this point, in view of the available evidence as he understood it, he had at least a very good chance of being correct. His error came in treating it as more than a very good chance. He had at first vocalized the name as Yokan, but in light of the additional evidence of the royal stamps and of Grant's discovery of the same seal impression, Albright opted for the king's name and found his original vocalization much less likely.[58]

To summarize, even in 1932, the ID could have been questioned. The biblical evidence did not support the conclusion that the title na 'ar always implied the master was a king. Also, the precise vocalization of the master's name was open to question. Nevertheless, partly because of Albright's great prestige and partly because of his persuasiveness in arguing his case, this misidentification prevailed for about fifty years in the archaeology of Palestine and related fields. It made the dates assigned to the many archaeological discoveries dated with

---

[55] Nahman Avigad, "New Light on the Na 'ar Seals," in *Magnalia Dei, the Mighty Acts of God: Essays in the Bible and Archaeology in Memory of G. Ernest Wright* (ed. Frank M. Cross, Werner E. Lemke, and Patrick D. Miller; New York: Doubleday, 1976), 294–300; idem, "Titles and Symbols on Hebrew Seals" (in Hebrew), *ErIsr* 15 (1981): 303–5, Pl. 57). On the possibility that the na 'ar of a private individual might simultaneously be the 'ebed of the king, see Andrew G. Vaughn, *Theology, History and Archaeology in the Chronicler's Account of Hezekiah* (Archaeology and Biblical Studies 4; Atlanta: Scholars Press, 1999), 130–35. Nevertheless, this possibility does not make the two titles synonymous or their usage *in seals and bullae* interchangeable.

[56] Albright, "Seal of Eliakim," 79–80, 82–84.

[57] Ibid., 81. Diringer, 197, no. 38, read Albright's "excellent parallel" (i.e., *ywqm* as a parallel to *ywkn* [Albright, "Seal of Eliakim," 81]) as Joqim, just as Albright did. But Noth (*IPN*, 176, no. 638) read Joqam, a parallel which does not support Albright's ID.

[58] Albright, "Seal of Eliakim," 82.

reference to this seal impression about a century too late.⁵⁹ Finally, accurate dating, if it had been possible, would have enabled archaeologists to avoid this misidentification altogether, along with the distortion it caused in several fields. This fact underscores the importance of establishing an accurate date for an inscription *before* identifying someone named in it. This misidentification, then, indicates that name vocalization, title usage, and dating can be crucial criteria.

### 1.11 The criteria not met by these two misidentifications

The above two cases of mistaken identity reveal the following things about the criteria needed to make accurate IDs:

1. The vocalization of PNs in inscriptions must be treated as accurately and objectively as possible. A range of possible vocalizations should not be narrowed to only one option without well established reason(s) for doing so. Both examples above illustrate the need for caution in vocalization.

2. A name without an additional identifying mark or marks, such as patronymic or title, cannot furnish an accurate ID at all. More data are needed. In other words, a patronymic and/or a title must accompany the given name. Both of the examples above failed to meet this criterion.

3. Regarding such additional marks, if a title is used, its significance for the ID must be demonstrated by biblical and/or epigraphic examples of the *usage* of that particular title, no matter how close it may seem to a parallel title. The second example above failed to meet this criterion.

4. Dating of an inscription within fifty years before or after the biblical depiction of the person must permit the ID. In the second example above, the jar-handle seal impression of Eliakim *na'ar* Yokan, which was in reality a century earlier than King Jehoiachin, was ultimately shown to fail to meet this criterion. The earlier example of the seal ring of Yathom as originally dated had, at best, only a borderline chance of meeting it.

5. The implied or stated socio-political classification of the person named in the inscription must agree with that of the person named in the Bible; e.g., Yatom, implicitly an Edomite according to the paleography, could not have been Jotham, the Judahite⁶⁰ king in the Bible.

---

⁵⁹ Garfinkel, "Eliakim *Na'ar* Yokan," 75, 77.
⁶⁰ In this study, the term *Judahite*, parallel to *Israelite*, means of or pertaining to the *kingdom* of Judah (i.e., until 586). *Judean* has no necessary reference to that kingdom.

It is evident, therefore, that in order to be reliable, modern identification criteria need to follow the ancient method, i.e., explicit presentation of the given name, patronymic, title, and/or epithet. Date and socio-political classification are usually not explicitly indicated, but are also crucial to consider.

## 1.12 Avigad's criteria

Nahman Avigad's three-page article, "On the Identification of Persons Mentioned in Hebrew Epigraphic Sources,"[61] made him one of only two authors who have published major articles dedicated to laying down and applying general principles on making IDs (the other author is Bordreuil; see section 1.7 above). Other articles and passages in books are intent on making or suggesting IDs based on principles which they only occasionally make explicit. For the principles themselves, other writings offer only a slight rationale at most, and many of the rationales are what Avigad would call speculation.

When he set out on his career as an epigrapher, Avigad did not posit stringent rules for making IDs. As noted above, in his article on the seal of "Jotham," he was willing to make an ID with little more than the three consonants of the given name and a plausible geographical site to support it.[62] At an international congress of scholars in 1961, with this scant evidence, a fifty-five-year-old Avigad spoke in favor of the identification of the seal owner with King Jotham.[63] As years went by and other IDs failed, however, he became not only more astute but also more cautious in making IDs. Writing in 1976 about a postexilic Judean inscription, "*yhwd ʾwryw*," meaning, "Yehud [i.e., the Persian province that Judah eventually became], Uriyaw," Avigad commented,

> I have sought elsewhere [[64]] to identify this Uriaw with Uriah son of Hakkoz, father of Meremoth who was the Temple treasurer in the days of Ezra (Ezra 8:33). From the chronological aspect, this identification would hold even if the impression were pushed back to ca. 500 B.C.E. *But now* [emphasis mine] we would avoid making any such identifications, nor have we any proof for our earlier assumption that this Uriaw was an overseer of tax collection for the Temple rather than for the secular authorities.[65]

---

[61] Avigad, "On the Identification," 235–37 (Hebrew), English summary 79*.

[62] Idem, "Jotham Seal," 18–22.

[63] Ibid. is an "abridged version of a paper read at the Third World Congress of Jewish Studies which took place in Jerusalem, 25th July–1st August 1961" (ibid., 18, note under asterisk).

[64] Idem, "A New Class of Yehud Stamps," *IEJ* 7 (1957): 146–53.

[65] Idem, *Bullae and Seals from a Post-Exilic Judean Archive* (trans. Rafi Grafman; Qedem 4; Jerusalem: The Hebrew University of Jerusalem, The Institute of Archaeology, 1976), 22, no. 6.

In two places in his article on identifying persons mentioned in Hebrew epigraphic finds, Avigad summarizes the requirements for making an ID. He introduces his treatment of individual seals and bullae by remarking that the name and patronym of the seal owner must match those of the biblical person, that a distinctive title makes a better case, and that there must be a chronological match.[66] But this is not a complete list. He closes his article with a second list of more refined, more rigorous requirements for making an ID:

> Finally, the question may be asked: To what extent is it possible to rely on identifications like these which we have treated above? Inasmuch as correlations between the names of both of the sources (the biblical and the epigraphic) are multiplying, we are then obliged to treat with extra caution the fixing of the identity. On principle, identicalness of the names does not always mean also identicalness of the people. Many people were named with identical names, and also linkings of similar names of a father and his son were undoubtedly common enough. Therefore, the identification will always remain within the limit of an assumption, even if the assumption is reasonable—unless it is supported by additional evidence, such as: a title, an epithet, or [אוֹ] a genealogical sequence of three generations (in an instance like this, coincidence is unlikely). An additional criterion which is to be brought into the reckoning is a chronological consideration—whether there exists a common chronological basis belonging to the identified persons.[67]

Avigad regards these requirements as the foundations of a reliable ID. Of course, there are other, non-foundational considerations, and he mentions some of these in the article. These can count for or against a particular ID, but the requirements of the kind mentioned a few pages above in section 1.11, must be satisfied first. Examples of the use of similarly reasonable but non-foundational factors are not lacking.[68]

---

[66] Idem, "On the Identification," 235 (translation mine).

[67] Ibid., 237 (translation mine).

[68] A recent example is the discussion about the seal that bears the text, "belonging to Shelomith, the maidservant of Elnathan the Gover[nor]" in relation to 1 Chr 3:19b, which mentions Shelomith, the daughter of Zerubbabel, the grandson of King Jehoiachin and governor of the Persian province of Yehud. The seal is published in idem, *Bullae and Seals from a Post-Exilic Judean Archive*, 11–13, no. 14, 31–32, Pl. 15. A brief description and bibliog. of the discussion appears in André Lemaire, "Populations et territoires de la Palestine a l'epoque perse," *Transeuphratene* 3 (1990): 34–35, no. 5; 34, n. 20.

## 1.13 Survey of the literature, second of two parts

This part of the survey of the literature treats IDs based on epigraphy, including the articles whose content has been examined above in sections 1.9, 1.10, and 1.12 and in related studies. The main items containing the errors and corrections treated above, plus other publications, may be outlined as follows. Albright's misidentification of "Jehoiachin" in 1932,[69] was corrected by Ussishkin in 1976[70] and 1977,[71] Avigad in 1976[72] and 1981,[73] and Cross by 1983.[74] In 1990, Garfinkel surveyed that discussion,[75] and Rainey offered his corrections to Garfinkel's article that same year.[76] Glueck's misidentification of "Jotham" in 1940[77] and 1965,[78] seconded by Avigad in 1961,[79] was implicitly abandoned by Glueck in 1971.[80] Avigad had abandoned it by 1979.[81] Explicit corrections of the "Jotham" misidentification were published by Gibson in 1973,[82] Herr in 1978,[83] Naveh in 1987,[84] and DiVito in 1993.[85] In 1980, Zevit[86] classified it as

---

[69] Albright, "Seal of Eliakim," 77–84, 102.

[70] Ussishkin, "Royal Judean Storage Jars and Private Seal Impressions," *BASOR* 223 (1976): 1–13. His dating of Lachish Stratum III agrees with that previously assigned by Olga Tufnell, *Lachish III* (New York: Oxford University Press, 1953), 72–73, 344.

[71] Ussishkin, "The Destruction of Lachish by Sennacherib and the Dating of the Royal Storage Jars," *TA* 4 (1977): 28–60.

[72] Avigad, "New Light on the Naʿar Seals," 294–300.

[73] Idem, "Titles and Symbols on Hebrew Seals" (in Hebrew), 303–5, Pl. 57.

[74] Frank M. Cross, "The Seal of Miqneyaw, Servant of Yahweh," in *Ancient Seals and the Bible* (ed. Leonard Gorelick and Elizabeth Williams-Forte; International Institute for Mesopotamian Area Studies Monographic Journals of the Near East, Occasional Papers on the Near East 2/1; Malibu, Calif.: Undena Publications, 1983), 57–58.

[75] Garfinkel, "Eliakim Naʿar Yokan," 74–79.

[76] Rainey, "Rejoinder," 61.

[77] Glueck, "The Third Season of Excavation at Tell el-Kheleifeh." *BASOR* 79 (October 1940): 13–15.

[78] Glueck, "Ezion-geber." *BA* 28 (1965): 86.

[79] Avigad, "Jotham Seal," 18–22.

[80] Nelson Glueck, "Tell el-Kheleifeh Inscriptions," 225–26, Pl. 1.

[81] Nahman Avigad, "Hebrew Epigraphic Sources," in *The Age of the Monarchies: Political History* (ed. Abraham Malamat; vol. 4, no. 1 of *The World History of the Jewish People*; ed. Benzion Netanyahu et al.; New Brunswick, N.J.: Rutgers University Press, 1979), 43.

[82] Gibson 1:61, no. 4, 63, n. 4.

[83] *SANSS*, 163, no. 2, Fig. 78.

[84] Joseph Naveh, *Early History of the Alphabet: An Introduction to West Semitic Epigraphy and Palaeography* (2d ed.; Jerusalem: The Hebrew University, Magnes Press, 1987), 102.

an eighth-century Hebrew seal, but made no biblical ID. A third ID, later seen to be unfounded, is that of one Uriyaw (without patronym or title) of the Persian period as Uriah, son of Hakkoz, the temple treasurer of Ezra 8:33. It was both made by Avigad in 1957[87] and corrected by him in 1976.[88] These errors and corrections seem to have contributed to Avigad's 1987 formulation of criteria for identifying biblical persons in Hebrew inscriptions.[89] These criteria must now be taken into account in any further developments in methodology. Since 1990, Avigad's criteria have been cited with approval by Lemaire[90] and Sass.[91] Fox apparently agrees with them in principle.[92] Elayi[93] and Schneider[94] have used these criteria in making IDs, and Barkay has used them in modified form.[95]

---

[85] Robert A. DiVito, "The Tell el-Kheleifeh Inscriptions," in Gary D. Pratico, *Nelson Glueck's 1938–1940 Excavations at Tell el-Kheleifeh: A Reappraisal* (ASOR Archaeological Reports 3; Atlanta: Scholars Press, 1993), 52, 53, 218, Pl. 79.

[86] Ziony Zevit, *Matres Lectionis in Ancient Hebrew Epigraphs* (ASOR Monograph Series 2; Cambridge, Mass.: ASOR, 1980), 14, no. 17, 15.

[87] Avigad, "New Class of Yehud Stamps," 146–53, Pl. 33, no. 4.

[88] Idem, *Bullae and Seals from a Post-Exilic Judean Archive*, 22, no. 6.

[89] Avigad, "On the Identification," 235–37.

[90] André Lemaire, "Les critères non-iconographiques de la classification des sceaux nord-ouest sémitiques inscrits," in Sass and Uehlinger, *Studies in the Iconography*, 1–26.

[91] Sass, "Pre-Exilic Hebrew Seals," 194–256.

[92] Nili S. Fox, *In the Service of the King*, 36–37. Fox raises no specific objections to Avigad's criteria in themselves, mentioning only "the pitfalls of Avigad's criteria" (ibid., 37), which I understand to exist in their omissions. The omissions are not due to negligence, but are brought about by the fact that Avigad's article deals with a particular set of inscriptions. E.g., all of them are Hebrew, therefore he saw no need to specify a common socio-political classification. Fox states that if they are applied to the corpus of extant inscriptions, i.e., those that were known at the time when she was writing, only the two bullae impressed with the seal of Berekyahu, son of Neriyahu, the scribe, meet Avigad's criteria. These, however, are problematic, because they "were acquired on the antiquities market and their authenticity has been called into question" (ibid., 37; see *WSS*, 12, no. 417).

Most of Fox's book is a model of thorough, judicious scholarship. Unfortunately, a tiny flaw, rendering אן as "and" instead of "or," led to a misstatement of Avigad's criteria, making them far more stringent than they really are: ". . . Avigad advanced three criteria by which to establish a sound identification. In addition to a corresponding PN, there should be (1) a matching title or epithet *and* (2) a genealogy of three generations and (3) chronological synchronism" (Fox, *In the Service of the King*, 36–37, emphasis mine). The crucial phrase should read "or [אן] (2) a genealogical sequence . . . ." Following this misstatement of Avigad's requirements, Fox's examples seem to show awareness that they are not as rigorous as she stated (cf. section 1.12).

[93] Josette Elayi, "New Light on the Identification of the Seal of Priest Ḥanan, son of Ḥilqiyahu," *BO* 49 (1992): cols. 681–83.

Fox finds that analysis of certain materials according to Avigad's criteria does not produce any reliable IDs, but only because of the limitations of the available materials. After examining the bases for several methods, she selects one which, though practical, produces only tentative results.[96]

Fox considers Rivkah Harris' analysis of materials from Old Babylonian Sippar in which, among hundreds of names, no two men of the same generation had the same combination of name and patronym.[97] Harris found it likely that a registry of names was kept in a central office; duplication of name-and-patronym combinations might have been avoided by consulting such a registry when babies were named. It is not known, however, whether such a practice was observed in the Hebrew kingdoms. The examples of seals unearthed at Arad show that one individual could own several different seals bearing the same name and patronym.[98] Therefore, examples of the same combination of name and patronym in different seals and the impressions made by different seals, for example, among the personal seal impressions appearing on *lammelek* storage jar handles, are ambiguous evidence.[99] That is, it is not known whether only one person owned all the seals bearing a particular combination of name and patronym. That means that in a given generation, there could have more than one person in the Hebrew kingdoms who had the same combination of name and patronym. For Fox, this ambiguity means that rather than clear IDs, only "tentative associations" can be established in the materials she studied.[100]

## 1.14 Foundational data for making identifications

In this attempt to avoid erroneous IDs by learning from past mistakes, the two examples of error treated above lead to agreement with Avigad's criteria. Another criterion must be added, since his article treated only Hebrew sources:

---

[94] Tsvi Schneider, "Azariahu Son of Hilkiahu (High Priest?) on a City of David Bulla," *IEJ* 38 (1988): 139–41; idem, "Six Biblical Signatures: Seals and Seal Impressions of Six Biblical Personages Recovered," *BAR* 17, no. 4 (July/August 1991): 26–33.

[95] Gabriel Barkay, "A Bulla of Ishmael, the King's Son," *BASOR* 290–291 (1993): 110.

[96] Fox, *In the Service of the King*, 36–42.

[97] Rivkah Harris, "Notes on the Nomenclature of Old Babylonian Sippar," *JCS* 24 (1972): 102–4.

[98] Yohanan Aharoni, *Arad Inscriptions*, ed. and rev. by Anson F. Rainey, trans. Judith Ben-Or (Jerusalem: Israel Exploration Society, 1981), 119–20.

[99] Among the personal seal impressions on *lammelek* storage jars, twelve different name-plus-patronym combinations are each found in impressions made from two or more different seals (Vaughn, *Theology, History and Archaeology*, 121).

[100] Fox, *In the Service of the King*, 42. Some of these tentative associations seem to correspond approximately to grade 2 IDs as described in section 2.4 below.

the socio-political classification of an inscription, sometimes termed "nationality." This aspect may be explicit, as in the title, "King of [name of sociopolitical entity]" or implicit, as in some theophoric names or in the paleography.

A reliable ID of a person named in an inscription(s) as a person named in the Bible, then, is based on matches of the following foundational data:

1. The name of the person. Given the variety of ancient ways of expressing a particular name, it is necessary to consider various forms of a name, including alternative spellings, hypocoristica, etc., without confusing different names.

2. Two or more of the following: patronymic(s), epithet, title, or other identifying data of a comparable degree of particularity.

3. Time period within fifty years. The inscriptional person, who is usually dated through the inscription, should be no more than fifty years earlier or later than the biblical person. Ideally, the range really should be narrower, but inscriptions dated solely by paleography, of which there are many, usually cannot be dated more narrowly. If possible and reasonable, other data from sources independent of the Bible should be used to narrow the range of dates.

4. Socio-political classification.

Five different lines of evidence support the validity of these foundational identification criteria. It is evident both from first-millennium Northwest Semitic inscriptions and from biblical practice that in the original social context, name and patronym (and/or title) were a requisite minimum. The two instructive misidentifications discussed above show the necessity of all four foundational criteria. Finally, since Avigad learned from these same two misidentifications, as well as others, no doubt, his criteria tend toward similar requirements. Because his article is about *Hebrew* inscriptions, it implicitly assumes the same socio-political classification. He also set the requirement of a third identifying mark besides name and patronym (i.e., title, epithet, or second patronym) to insure the validity of IDs made in modern times.

The following chart summarizes these five lines of evidence for various aspects of foundational data. The pattern of arrangement of information in the chart below is above the dotted line:

*Identification Criteria* 33

## Foundational element useful in establishing IDs

| Custom in NW Semitic inscriptions | Custom in Hebrew Bible | Analysis of wrong ID of "Jotham" | Analysis of wrong ID of "Jehoiachin" | Avigad's 1987 criteria |
|---|---|---|---|---|
| **Identifying mark: name** | | | | |
| √Present | √Present | √Present | √Present | √Required |
| **Name correctly vocalized** | | | | |
| Occasional *matres lectionis* | Vocalized in textual traditions | √Needed | √Needed | Not mentioned |
| **Second identifying mark, usually patronym (or husband's name)** | | | | |
| √Present | √Present | √Needed | √Needed | √Need for reasonable hypothesis |
| **Third identifying mark, e.g., title, epithet, or second patronym** | | | | |
| Infrequently present | Sometimes present | √Needed | √Needed | √Need for reliable ID |
| **Title's usage correctly understood** | | | | |
| No explanations given | Explanations rare (1 Sam 9:9) | Not applicable; no title present | √Needed | Not mentioned (but see n. 55 above) |
| **Element of setting: date** | | | | |
| Rare in seals & bullae | Infrequent except for rulers | √Needed | √Needed | √Required |
| **Element of setting: socio-political classification** | | | | |
| Usually implicit | Usually indirect | √Needed | Not mentioned | √Implied by article title |

## 1.15 Non-foundational facts relevant to identifications

As observed above in section 1.12, non-foundational facts alone are not conclusive. Nevertheless, they are relevant to making IDs and cannot be ignored. They can appear in almost any category of information. An example of a non-foundational fact is the presence of the bulla "of Yeraḥmeʾel, the king's son," in the same hoard of bullae with the first known bulla "of Berekyahu, son of Neriyahu, the scribe." This phenomenon documents them as officials in the same royal administration. Avigad noted that these two men appeared together in Jer 36 and that their bullae appeared in the same lot. The latter fact provided an identifying mark. When Avigad considered this along with the match of Jerahmeel's name and title in the Bible and in the bulla, he became assured of the ID.[101] (In the system presented in sections 1.18 through 2.13 below, such items go under Criterion 10, other identifying information; see section 1.32).

## 1.16 Rationale for a way of evaluating identifications that is more refined and more complete than Avigad's

From the two examples above in sections 1.9 and 1.10, in concurrence with Avigad's 1987 article setting forth identification criteria, this chapter has inferred that in order to make a reliable ID, the foundational data in section 1.14 should agree in both sources. Yet there are more aspects involved:

1. There is a whole category of ID which is implicitly recognized by many epigraphers but which Avigad did not mention in his article on identifying persons in epigraphic materials. Here it is called an *ID on grounds of singularity*. This sort of ID is based on there being only one person to whom extant inscriptional sources, biblical sources, or both, can refer (see section 1.33, Criterion 11, below). In contrast, Avigad's criteria are designed to lead to correct IDs by reducing the odds of a misidentification to an acceptable minimum.

2. Avigad's system has no discussion of the socio-political classification of an inscription, because the article treats only Hebrew inscriptions. This classification can be difficult to determine (see section 1.27, Criterion 6, below).

3. There are differences in *reliability* of data, most obviously between inscriptions that have been excavated under controlled conditions and those that appear on the antiquities market, which could well be forgeries.

4. In several of the criteria mentioned above, there can be *relative degrees of strength*. For example, a match between a biblical name that appears in full

---

[101] Avigad, "On the Identification," 235–36.

and an inscriptional name in which one of the triliteral root letters has been broken off is not as strong as a match between a complete name in both sources. Also, a missing letter in the theophoric element usually creates less doubt about a name than a missing letter in a triliteral root does.

5. There can also be *varying degrees of precision*. For example, the date of a destruction layer established by a comparison of stratigraphy with literary sources that agree can be more precise than the date of a different destruction layer as established only by paleographic analysis of that layer's inscriptions.

6. Some data are *vague, rather than specific*. For example, the iconography of an inscribed seal may indicate that the seal owner was an official in the royal court, without spelling out his title. It would be hazardous to match such a vague datum with a specific title given in the Bible.

7. Some biblical and inscriptional data are *ambiguous*. For example, in the pattern of PN followed by patronymic phrase followed by title, the syntax permits application of the title to either the first PN or to the patronymic (see section 1.31, Criterion 9, below).[102]

---

[102] In the Hebrew syntactical pattern of PN plus patronymic phrase plus title, the title can refer to the patronym as easily as to the first name that appears. For example, in the phrase X *bat* Y followed by a title, the title can belong to Y. This fact is doubly clear in the phrase "Athaliah, the daughter of Omri, king of Israel" (2 Kgs 8:26), in which the king is not Athaliah but Omri. Athaliah was queen of Judah, not king of Israel. Similarly, in "Jezebel, the daughter of Ethbaal king of the Sidonians" (1 Kgs 16:31) and "Maacah, the daughter of Talmai king of Geshur" (1 Chr 3:2), the title applies to the patronym only.

The same general pattern is found in X *ben* Y followed by a title, in which the title can belong to the father, not the son. The following two examples are cited in Avigad, "On the Identification," 236 (see note 121 in this chapter). First is "Jonathan, the son of Abiathar the priest" in 1 Kgs 1:42. There the title "the priest" refers to the high priest (in section 4.7 below, see under "Title[s]"). Jonathan never became high priest; his prospect of succeeding his father, Abiathar, as high priest ended when Solomon removed Abiathar from the high priesthood (1 Kgs 2:26–27) and made Zadok high priest instead (1 Kgs 4:4). Thereafter, not Abiathar's but Zadok's descendants became high priests (e.g., 2 Chr 5:34–36; 31:10).

Avigad's second example is "Zechariah, the son of Jehoiada the priest" in 2 Chr 24:20. That Jehoiada was high priest is evident in 2 Kgs 11–12 and 2 Chr 22–24. His son Zechariah is never listed among the high priests, apparently because he was stoned by royal command before he could succeed his father in that office (2 Chr 24:17–22).

Similarly, in the phrase "Gemariah, the son of Shaphan the scribe" in Jer 36:10, the title does not apply to Gemariah. In 2 Kgs 22:8, 9, 10, and 12, it is clear that Shaphan

Because the seven factors listed immediately above present themselves in the available data, it is appropriate to measure the relative strength of IDs by using a more complete and more refined system than that of Avigad. This study demonstrates that it is also possible. Although Avigad's general criteria can be found underlying part of the system set forth below, it should be remembered that his system results only in confirmation or disqualification of *a particular kind* of potential ID. It indicates only two gradations of strength in its IDs; it does not take into account several classes of factors which affect IDs; and it lacks the important category of IDs on grounds of singularity.

---

was a scribe, but in the list in Jer 36:12, which includes "Gemariah the son of Shaphan," only "Elishama the scribe" is accorded the title "scribe." Gemariah is listed only as one of the śarim (Avigad, "On the Identification," 236–37). Cf. the example of Gehazi and Elisha two paragraphs below.

All of the above are instances of a more general syntactical pattern: PN + appositive phrase 1 + appositive phrase 2, in which appositive phrase 2 refers not to the initial PN, but to a patronymic PN within appositive phrase 1. E.g., in "Rachel, the daughter of Laban, his [i.e., Jacob's] mother's brother" (Gen 29:10), there is no question that appositive phrase 2 must refer to the patronymic PN Laban within appositive phrase 1. The same is true in "Milcah, the daughter of Haran, the father of Milcah, and the father of Iscah" (Gen 11:29), in which a third appositive phrase also refers to the patronymic PN within appositive phrase 1. The difference in gender between the initial PN and the patronymic PNs contained within the appositive phrases permits the clearest observations, but there is no reason that the same syntax cannot apply when the initial PN and the patronymic PNs and other nouns within the appositive phrases all have the same gender.

A likely example of such a same-gender pattern, in which the second appositive phrase refers to the PN in the first appositive phrase is "Gehazi, the servant (naʿar) of Elisha the man of God" (2 Kgs 5:20). Here the phrase "the man of God" refers to Elisha, not Gehazi. Elisha is called "the man of God" in 2 Kgs 5:8, but Gehazi, a relatively minor character in the narrative, is never called that, but only "the servant (naʿar) of the man of God" (2 Kgs 8:4; in accord with 2 Kgs 4:12, 25).

But because the syntax is ambiguous, in the Hebrew syntactical pattern of PN plus patronymic phrase plus title, the title can *also* refer to the *first* name that appears, as easily as to the patronym or other noun in the first appositive phrase. E.g., in the phrase, "Elihoreph and Ahijah, the sons of Shisha, scribes" (1 Kgs 4:3), the plural "scribes" refers to the two sons, not to Shisha. Another example is found in the parallels to the recurrent phrase, "Isaiah the son of Amoz, the prophet" (2 Kgs 20:1; Isa 37:2; 38:1; 2 Chr 26:22; 32:20, 32). It is sometimes varied as "Isaiah the prophet, the son of Amoz" (2 Kgs 19:2) and "Isaiah the prophet" (2 Kgs 20:11, 14; Isa 39:3). The office of prophet was not hereditary, and it is reasonable to infer that the text is pointing to the fact that *Isaiah* was a prophet. Also, cf. Jer 28:1 with vv. 5, 10, 12, 15, and 17.

Cf. Chapter 3, note 28, below, on similar ambiguity of appositives in Moabite syntax.

## 1.17 Principles for measuring the strength of identifications

The system set forth below for making IDs and measuring their strength is based on the following general principles:

1. Modern rationales are not as reliable as explicit data in ancient sources (e.g., Albright's critique in section 1.9 above). Of course, the explicit statements of ancient sources must be evaluated critically, since they might be misleading. Nevertheless, modern thinking is separated from the original context of a primary historical source by millennia. A high degree of cultural isolation and a relative lack of assurance of historical genuineness underlie all such modern reasoning. As a general rule, therefore, it must be considered secondary at best.

2. A datum which is established by *more* means that are independent of each other is usually more reliable than a datum established by *fewer* means. For example, a date established by ceramics, epigraphy, and the historical content of the inscription is more reliable than a date indicated by epigraphy alone.

3. Data which are more reliable, clearer, more explicit, less ambiguous, and more precise tend to produce stronger IDs than data which are less so. If these qualities are set in order of priority, reliability is paramount, followed by clarity, with its subsets of explicitness and unambiguousness, and then by precision. The rationale for this order of priority is:

a. Putting reliability first helps to protect the findings from pollution by false data gathered from forgeries. All systems that attempt to arrive at truth operate between two opposing emphases. One emphasis is to include as much truth as possible while accepting that there may be a certain admixture of error in it. The opposite emphasis is to eliminate as much error as possible while accepting that some truth may be excluded along with the error. These two emphases may be called, respectively, inclusivist (alias liberal) versus purist (alias conservative). After the initial period of inscriptional discoveries and speculative biblical IDs, in which nineteenth- and twentieth-century scholars tended to try to include all that were true or that seemed potentially to be true, a conservative shift became more and more needed. Such a shift was marked by Avigad's decision by 1976[103] (possibly earlier) to adopt more stringent criteria for making IDs. This conservative shift, a comparative luxury made possible by the growing number of inscriptions, was in the direction of the exclusion of error. By that time, a purist approach was becoming more and more practical, both because more and more inscriptions were being excavated under controlled conditions and because

---

[103] See section 1.12 above.

an increasing number of inscriptions of dubious origin were appearing on the antiquities market. In the system proposed below, the priority on reliability of data extends Avigad's conservative approach by placing the highest value on purity of data rather than inclusiveness of data. The emphasis is on distinguishing more firmly established IDs from weaker ones. The conservative emphasis is needed in view of the wishful, ultimately weak IDs that continue to be made or suggested and in view of the increasing number of available inscriptions.

b. It would seem obvious that clarity should precede precision, since a precise datum that is ambiguous tends to lose its value. This priority of clarity over precision is a rational protection against precision's rhetorical value. From time immemorial, storytellers have known that an insignificant but precise detail can give the entire narration a ring of truth in the mind of the audience.[104] Further, in our technological age, precision connotes scientific verisimilitude. The rhetorical and connotative appeal of precision can lure researchers away from the criteria established above. One must resist the temptation to abandon the criteria.

### 1.18 The three main diagnostic questions about potential identifications

In gathering information relevant to a potential ID, researchers have three main questions: 1) Are the inscriptional data *reliable*? 2) Do the *settings* of the inscriptional person and the biblical person match? (Recall "Jotham's" seal.) And 3) does the combination of *specific identifying marks* of the individual eliminate, or at least render negligible, the chance of confusing two different persons? (Recall "Jotham's" seal and "Jehoiachin" in the seal impression.) *All three of these questions must be answered satisfactorily before an ID can be considered valid.* Rather than permitting only a yes-or-no answer, the criteria described below attempt to gauge the relative degree of strength in these areas.

The following outline is expanded in sections 1.19 to 1.34 below:

Question 1. How reliable are the inscriptional data? The first three criteria ask this question in different ways:

Criterion 1, means of acquisition or access: was it excavated under controlled conditions, was it observable above ground, or did it appear on the antiquities market?

Criterion 2, provenance of the inscription: how precisely can we say from where it was recovered? Do we know the exact findspot, a site or tell, or only a vague region?

---

[104] Note, e.g., the rhetorical effect of 1 Sam 17:4, "His height was six cubits and a span." Because the last word indicates a rather precise measurement, it connotes veracity. This rhetorical effect, however, is no indication of the truth or falsehood of the statement.

Criterion 3, authenticity: how has it been regarded? Or how should it be? The advanced technologies listed below in section 1.25, Criterion 4, Date, under "Other," if applied to inscriptions, can be of help in discovering whether an artifact is authentic or not. But antiquity is still not a complete guarantee of genuineness; even ancient items can be altered to become fakes.

Question 2. Does the general setting of the inscription permit a match between the inscriptional person and the biblical person? Criteria 4 through 6 cannot determine an ID; they can only prohibit or permit (i.e., not prohibit) it.

Criterion 4, the date of the person: how well can it be established? By what means?

Criterion 5, the language of the inscription: how specifically can it be determined? By what indicators? In the specific instance, is the language relevant to the potential ID?

Criterion 6, the socio-political classification of the person and/or the inscription: how strongly can it be established? By what means? Since the general setting of any inscription may be revealed in data gathered from other inscriptions, it is appropriate here to ask how a particular inscription may fit in with its historical framework and what contribution the inscription might make to that framework.

Question 3. How strongly do specific data in the inscription count for or against an ID? In contrast with the general setting listed immediately above, Criteria 7 through 11 *can* determine an ID or a disqualification.

Criterion 7, the name of person in the inscription: how does it compare with the biblical name? If there are differences, are they minor, reconcilable, or irreconcilable?

Criterion 8, interpersonal relations: how do available data on family and associates compare with the biblical data? Are there matches in the names of persons around the candidate which increase the likelihood of an ID?

Criterion 9, title information: if the person had a title, how does it compare with the biblical title, if any? Is it possible, perhaps even likely, that they might be consecutive titles, or perhaps multiple titles, in one person's career?

Criterion 10, other identifying information: are there any other data that can help determine whether an ID should be made or not made?

Criterion 11, ID on grounds of singularity (see section 1.33 below): among the known data, do any point to only one person, thereby requiring that this ID be made? If so, are they found in the inscription, in the Bible, or in both?

## 1.19 A three-question system for evaluating potential identifications

The system described here and in Chapter 2 attempts to take into account all classes of factors which may affect an ID. It was created and repeatedly revised as a summary of ways of dealing with various features presented by real inscriptions. If other kinds of features appear in "new" inscriptions, future revisions may be necessary. Its structured approach implies a firm rejection of the facile, unsystematic process of making IDs without explicit criteria that has appeared in popular and even in scholarly literature. This system deals mainly with *inscriptional* phenomena; on the *biblical* side, it is unnecessary to describe the usual processes, such as text criticism, which are involved in thorough and careful handling of a text, since there is extensive literature on these.

Readers may prefer to skim or skip over the rest of this chapter and resume reading in Chapter 2. The way this system works becomes easier to understand with the six examples in sections 2.2 through 2.7 below. Like the circuitry of a television, it is easier to *use* it than to describe it in schematic form, as below.

## 1.20 Question one: how reliable are the inscriptional data?

### 1.21 Criterion 1, means of acquisition or access

1) Excavated under controlled conditions. The distinctive trait of this form of access is that researchers have accurate, recorded information about the excavation, so that the authenticity of the discovered object(s) is established.

2) Observed without excavation, apparently at or near the original location. The Mesha Inscription, which was only partly covered with earth when discovered, is a good example of this classification. Cliff inscriptions also qualify.

3) Marketed for sale by an antiquities dealer(s), including items that are intentionally dug up for profit from sale and chance finds sold to dealers.

### 1.22 Criterion 2, provenance of the inscription

Unverified claims to a particular provenance for items which have appeared on the antiquities market, being notoriously untrustworthy, are excluded from consideration in all categories. Only provenances from excavations under controlled conditions count. In descending order of strength, subcategories are:

1) Within the site of the find, the exact findspot is known.

2) Provenance, i..e., the site, is known.

*Identification Criteria* 41

3) Provenance, i.e., the region, is known.

4) Provenance is unknown.

## 1.23 Criterion 3, how the matter of the inscription's authenticity has been or should be regarded

With the intent to be evenhanded, this study assumes neither that artifacts not proven fraudulent are genuine nor that those without established authenticity are fraudulent.[105] Various kinds of technical analysis (see "Other" in Criterion 4 below) may help answer the question of authenticity.

1) Regarded as authentic because recovered in a controlled excavation or else observed at or near the location where an exposed inscription, e.g., on a monument, was placed in ancient times.

2) Presumable, even though purchased on the antiquities market. During almost all of the nineteenth century, knowledge of epigraphy was not sufficient to forge letters that would fit in with the typology of letter shapes that developed with later discoveries. Paleographic details that were consistent both with each other and with the date of the biblical person to be identified were then unknown. Therefore, a mid- or even late nineteenth-century date of purchase tends to uphold the authenticity of the inscription. Also, if a seal and bulla match, or if two bullae were made by the same seal, and one is provenanced and one not, then, unless disqualified, the unprovenanced exemplar is presumably authentic.

3) Technical analysis yields clear, unbiased results confirming authenticity.

4) Expert opinion favors authenticity by consensus or substantial support.

---

[105] According to Sass,
One school of thought maintains, "If the material, shape, technique, iconography, epigraphy, and names pass our test, the seal must be genuine." André Lemaire put it differently in our conference: "You may be able to prove a seal to be a fake; you cannot prove its genuineness", or if I am permitted a paraphrase, "Any seal is presumed genuine until proven false." (Sass, "Pre-Exilic Hebrew Seals," 245)
If classical gems with their hard stones and intricate subject-matter could be so artfully reproduced, then West Semitic seals, mostly in soft stone and with simpler iconography must be, if I may be allowed an exaggeration, a *Kinderspiel* for a talented forger. Who can tell which of the unprovenanced seals, "tasteful" or otherwise, are fakes and which are not? On the other hand, it is well known that controlled excavations yield from time to time unusual finds that, if acquired on the antiquities market, would raise suspicion. (Ibid., 246)

5) Unknown, because purchased on the antiquities market, and neither technical analysis nor expert opinion provide a clear verdict

6) Shows possible signs of a forgery or fake, or 3) and 4) above conflict.

7) To be regarded as a forgery or a fake because of clear indications in the inscription or for other reasons.[106]

The seven classifications above show considerable nuance, but respected scholars take both nuanced and simpler positions.[107] Unprovenanced materials raise serious concerns: ethics, discerning between authentic items and frauds,

---

[106] See, e.g., Charles S. Clermont-Ganneau, *Les fraudes archéologiques en Palestine* (Paris: Ernest Leroux, 1885); *NE* 1:129–32; Diringer, 319–25; Joseph Naveh and Hayim Tadmor, "Some Doubtful Aramaic Seals," *AION* (68): 448–52, Pl. I–III; Joseph Naveh, "Aramaica Dubiosa," *JNES* 27 (1968): 317–25; idem, "Some Recently Forged Inscriptions," *BASOR* 247 (Summer 1982): 53–58; idem, "Clumsy Forger Fools the Scholars—But Only for a Time," *BAR* 10, no. 3 (1984): 66–72; Ulrich Hübner, "Fälschungen ammonitischer Siegel," *UF* 21 (1989): 217–26; Dominique Collon, *Near Eastern Seals* (Interpreting the Past 2; Berkeley, Calif.: University of California Press, 1991), 56–57; Pierre Bordreuil, "Sceaux inscrits des pays du Levant," in *Dictionnaire de la Bible, Supplément* (ed. Louis Pirot et al.; Paris: Letouzey & Ané, 1996), 12:137–38; Sass and Uehlinger, *Studies in the Iconography*, 245–46, 270–71.

Warnings against using unprovenanced materials seem to be growing ever sharper (cf. section 1.17, paragraph a, on conservatism). In *WSS*, of 711 inscriptions identified as Hebrew, only 132, or 19%, are provenanced (*WSS*, 549, Table 1); on this phenomenon, see Sass, "Pre-Exilic Hebrew Seals," 245–46. Fox presents strong reasons to exercise great caution with data from unprovenanced materials and altogether avoids using even unprovenanced artifacts generally accepted as genuine to arrive at interpretations and conclusions (Fox, *In the Service of the King*, 23–32). See also the thorough treatments in Christopher A. Rollston, "Non-Provenanced Epigraphs I: Pillaged Antiquities, Northwest Semitic Forgeries, and Protocols for Laboratory Tests," *Maarav* 10 (2003): 135–93.

On detecting the likely presence of forgeries in *groups* of inscriptions, see Andrew G. Vaughn and Carolyn Pillers Dobler, "A Provenance Study of Hebrew Seals and Seal Impressions—A Statistical Analysis," in *I Will Tell Secret Things from Long Ago (Abiah Chidot Menei-Kedem)—Ps. 78:2b): Archaeological and Historical Studies in Honor of Amihai Mazar on the Occasion of his Sixtieth Birthday* (ed. Aren M. Maeir and Pierre R. de Miroschedji; Winona Lake, Ind.: Eisenbrauns, in press). Certain features invite suspicion but do not establish clear fraudulence. Inscriptions which are members of suspect *groups* may perhaps be assigned to a new class *between* two categories in the system as it now stands, i.e., between "5 Unknown, because purchased on the antiquities market and without a clear verdict from technical analysis or expert opinion," and what is now "6 Shows possible signs of being a forgery or a fake."

[107] Herr, for example, in his published diss., written under the direction of Frank M. Cross, treats seals and bullae which are suspected of being forgeries (*SANSS*, 51, no. 109; 74–75, nos. 45, 46; 148–49, nos. 161, 162; 159, no. 9; 186–88, nos. 3, 5, 7).

and loss of sometimes crucial archaeological contexts.[108] This study separates and labels as conditional the potential findings which are based on them. On the other hand, because unprovenanced inscriptions may be authentic, it observes conditional findings without building on them.

**1.24 Question two: does the general setting of the inscription** *permit* **a match between the inscriptional person and the biblical person?**

**1.25 Criterion 4, the date of the person**

For assigning dates to various persons, this study uses Galil's dates for the monarchs of Israel and Judah, Kitchen's for the rulers of Egypt, Grayson's for Neo-Assyrian kings, and Wiseman's for Neo-Babylonian kings.[109]

1) Between the date of the person as calculated using the date of the inscription and the date of the person in the biblical account, agreement can be established by all possible factors (six appear in the list below). Agreement means that these two dates fall usually within fifty years of each other. Note: during the eighth through sixth centuries, there were very few changes in the script that are helpful in dating seals and bullae more precisely. The date of the inscription can be assigned by using applicable means from among the following: a) partly by

---

[108] Fox, *In the Service of the King*, 33.

[109] Galil, *Chronology*; Kenneth A. Kitchen, "The Basics of Egyptian Chronology in Relation to the Bronze Age," in *High, Middle, or Low: Acts of an International Colloquium on Absolute Chronology Held at the University of Gothenburg 20$^{th}$–22$^{nd}$ August 1987, Part 1* (ed. Paul Åström; Gothenburg, Sweden: Paul Åström Förlag, 1987), 37–55. In Part 3 of the same publication (Gothenburg, 1989), Kitchen raises the New Kingdom dates by a single year in his "Supplementary Notes on 'The Basics of an Egyptian Chronology,'" 152–59. To continue: idem, *The Third Intermediate Period in Egypt (1100–650 B.C.)* (2d ed. with supplement; Warminster, England: Aris & Phillips, 1986), 466–68; A. Kirk Grayson, *Assyrian Rulers of the Early First Millennium BC, II (858–745 BC)* (RIMA 3; Buffalo, N.Y.: University of Toronto Press, 1996); idem, "Assyria: Ashur-dan II to Ashur-nirari V (934–745 B.C.)," in *CAH*, vol. III, part I, 238–81; idem, "Assyria: Tiglath-pileser III to Sargon II (744–705 B.C.)," in *CAH*, vol. III, part II, 71–102; idem, "Assyria: Sennacherib and Esarhaddon (704–669 B.C.)," in *CAH*, vol. III, part II, 103–41; idem, "Assyria 668–635 B.C.: The Reign of Ashurbanipal," in *CAH*, vol. III, part II, 142–61; Donald J. Wiseman, "Babylonia 605–539 B.C." in *CAH*, vol. III, part II, 229–51.

As more and more archaeological data have become available during the past two centuries, ancient Near Eastern and biblical chronologies have become stable enough to avoid major changes in the years assigned to various rulers, but they are not fixed with utter precision. Since much of the dating of inscriptions in this study is done by approximate means, esp. paleography, variations of a few years in dating the inscriptional and biblical persons usually make no difference for IDs.

stratigraphy (of course, marketed inscriptions, already removed from their archaeological context or else forged, cannot be dated stratigraphically); b) partly by ceramics, using typology of pottery; c) partly by epigraphy, especially using paleographic typology; d) partly by historical linguistics, i.e., datable linguistic changes which can be detected in the inscription or in later inscriptions, e.g., the contraction of a diphthong; e) partly by historical content in the inscription; and f) partly by other means of dating, especially highly technical methods which make use of modern scientific discoveries. These may be applicable to the inscribed object or to its archaeological context. They include archaeomagnetism, carbon 14, collagen content, dendrochronology, electronic spin resonance, fluorine absorption, neutron activation analysis of clay, nitrogen analysis, obsidian dating, pollen analysis, potassium 40-argon, examination of bore marks in seals with a scanning electron microscope (SEM), thermoluminescence (TL), uranium series, varve dating, etc.[110]

At least one priority applies. Except where the strata are disturbed, dating by stratigraphy generally takes precedence over dating by epigraphy. Epigraphic typology is not usually as clear cut; rather, it represents an attempt to trace the trends in the development of letter shapes made by any number of scribes over long periods of time. Within reasonable parameters, epigraphers generally attempt to adjust the dating of inscriptions to fit their stratigraphic location.[111]

---

[110] For lists and brief descriptions of dating methods, see Martin J. Aitken, "Dating Techniques," *OEANE* 2:113–17; Keith N. Schoville, *Biblical Archaeology in Focus* (Grand Rapids, Mich.: Baker, 1978), 115, 117, 118; Fox, *In the Service of the King*, 32–36. For longer surveys of such methods, see Stuart J. Fleming, *Dating in Archaeology: A Guide to Scientific Techniques* (London: J. M. Dent, 1976); Penelope A. Parkes, *Current Scientific Techniques in Archaeology* (New York: St. Martin's Press, 1986); Colin Renfrew and Paul Bahn, *Archaeology: Theories, Methods and Practice* (London: Thames and Hudson, 1991), 101–48.

Two particularly useful techniques are SEM for perforations in stone seals and thermoluminescence for bullae fired in ancient times. On SEM, see Leonard Gorelick and A. John Gwinnett, "Ancient Seals and Modern Science: Using the Scanning Electron Microscope as an Aid in The Study of Ancient Seals," *Expedition* 20 (1978): 38–47; A. John Gwinnett and Leonard Gorelick, "Seal Manufacture in the Lands of the Bible: Recent Findings," in *Ancient Seals and the Bible* (ed. Gorelick and Williams-Forte), 44–49, Pl. III–VIII.

On thermoluminescence, see Stuart J. Fleming, *Authenticity In Art: The Scientific Detection of Forgery* (New York: Crane, Russack, 1976), 73–97; idem, *Thermoluminescence Techniques in Archaeology* (New York: Oxford University Press, 1979); Martin J. Aitken, *Thermoluminescence Dating* (Studies in Archaeological Science; Orlando, Fla.: Academic Press, 1985); and the journal, *Thermoluminescence*.

[111] Recognition of such precedence is clear in statements occasionally made by excavators and epigraphers. E.g., Ussishkin has remarked, "Other chronological considerations, such as paleography or stylistic criteria, are beyond the scope of this study, and

2) As immediately above, except that the agreement in dating is determined by one less means, i.e., only five of the means listed above.

And so on: 3) would indicate that agreement is established by a combination of one less means, i.e., four; a 4) indicates by three means; a 5) by two means, and a 6) by only one.

7) There is no known disagreement in date. The dating of the inscription or the dating of the biblical person (or both) *cannot be narrowed down* to a time span of a century, therefore *neither agreement nor disagreement is clear*. The ID may stand or fall on the basis of other factors.

8) There is disagreement between the date of the person as calculated by the dating of the inscription and the date of the person according to the biblical account. The factors listed above may be mentioned to clarify the dating method.

**1.26 Criterion 5, the identity of the language of the inscription**

Because in most instances the identity of the language can be compared directly with a language expectation created by the biblical text, language stands as a separate criterion. This criterion is established on strictly linguistic grounds. Other factors, such as onomastics, paleography, etc., should properly be considered under Criterion 6, the socio-political classification of the inscription. For example, Aramaic is used in Assyrian, Babylonian, and Persian inscriptions, as well as in West Semitic inscriptions. But the onomastic and paleographic characteristics, etc., of eastern and western Aramaic inscriptions are not identical. Criterion 6 distinguishes between particular socio-political entities, each having its own traditional onomastic array, paleographic traits, etc.

---

are, at any rate, secondary to stratigraphy" (David Ussishkin, "Gate 1567 at Megiddo and the Seal of Shema, Servant of Jeroboam," in *Scripture and Other Artifacts: Essays on the Bible and Archaeology in Honor of Philip J. King* [ed. Michael D. Coogan, J. Cheryl Exum, and Lawrence E. Stager; Louisville, Ky.: Westminster John Knox Press, 1994], 423).

Cross also implicitly acknowledges the same precedence (in instances where there is no insurmountable contradiction) in the following:

> The paleographical data assembled above establishes a date for the Idalion inscription between 350 and 300 B.C.E. Were it not for the archaeological context of the sherd, I should be inclined to date it to the mid-fourth century. However, the paleographical evidence fits easily into the assignment of the inscription to the fiftieth year of Pumayyaton, 312 B.C.E. (Frank M. Cross, "A Phoenician Inscription from Idalion: Some Old and New Texts Relating to Child Sacrifice," in ibid., 96)

On the other hand, the finding on Criterion 5 is considered under Criterion 6. Because the inscriptions of particular socio-political entities exhibit specific language choices, the identity of the language can be useful in determining the socio-political classification or at least narrowing down the number of possibilities. This criterion takes into account not only the language, but also the dialect. In this study, it is sometimes useful to distinguish between the dialect of the northern kingdom of Israel and that of the southern kingdom of Judah.

1) The language in which the inscription is written, as *specifically determined* by the vocabulary, morphology, and syntax of the inscription, agrees with the language expectation raised by the biblical account. For example, a biblical narrative that presents a Hebrew king ruling a Hebrew kingdom raises the expectation that his inscriptions would be written in Hebrew, and the vocabulary, morphology, and/or syntax specifically indicate Hebrew.

2) The language of the inscription, unknown or unrecognized until this inscription was discovered, was deduced from the self-identification of the author in the inscription as being of the nation whose people spoke this language. It agrees with the language expectation raised by the biblical account. For example, a biblical narrative that presents Mesha, a Moabite king ruling a Moabite kingdom raises the expectation that his inscription(s) would, of course, be written in Moabite.

3) The language of the inscription, *although not specifically determined* by the vocabulary, morphology, and syntax of the inscription, presents no known disagreement with the language expectation raised by the biblical account. Since it offers neither specific support nor any disagreement with that expectation, it cannot count for or against an ID.

4) The language of the inscription has been specifically determined by its vocabulary, morphology, and syntax. This classification is used when the context in which an inscription is viewed does not include the Hebrew Bible (see section 2.11 and point 2 in section 2.12 below).

5) The language of the inscription cannot be determined from its vocabulary, morphology, or syntax. This classification, too, is used when the context in which an inscription is viewed does not include the Hebrew Bible (again, see section 2.11 and point 2 in section 2.12 below).

6) The inscription is unintelligible at our current level of understanding, either because it is not a text, i.e., words in syntactical relationships with each other, or because the language is not known well enough to translate it.

7) There is disagreement between the language of the inscription and the language expectation raised by the biblical account.

## 1.27 Criterion 6, the socio-political classification of the inscription

Every inscription has a socio-political classification.[112] The term *nationality* cannot properly apply to such entities as Phoenicia or Aram, both of which had a fairly homogenous language and culture, but in which were found several independent city-states, not a single, united nation. At the other extreme, it would not be suitable to say that someone from ancient Tyre had a Tyrian nationality, since Tyre in that era is best described as a city-state. Nor could the term *ethnicity* be used with any certainty or precision in such instances. Ethnicity is not a suitable category, e.g., for Judahite,[113] which was, properly speaking, a nationality within the Hebrew people, and besides, the Hebrews were ethnically mixed. Since statehood is an attribute of political collectivities, not of individuals, perhaps a useful term relative to a government may be that person's *state identity*. Yet the person also belonged to a society. All three of these terms are examples of socio-political classification. This study is free to select the most appropriate term to indicate a socio-political classification, even if the alternatives, being ethnicities, nationalities, and states, are not exactly parallel to each other.

An important point here is that biblical persons could be named in inscriptions of states and societies other than their own, as would make sense, for example, in a victory stele written by their enemies. Therefore, the socio-political classification of an *inscription* which potentially names the biblical person to be identified cannot be expected always to match that of the biblical person. Further, it is not unheard of that the socio-political classification of an inscription may be uncertain or, as in a few instances, that scholars may change their minds about a previously assigned classification.

In considering agreement on the basis of eight factors, seven factors, etc., as represented by numbers immediately below, it should be kept in mind that in determining the socio-political classification, a single factor, such as an explicit reference, can be weightier than several other factors combined. The system keeps track of the number of factors, but good judgment is still indispensable in discerning the strength of the evidence.

1) The socio-political classification of the inscription is in agreement with the biblical account, as determined (or permitted) by all possible factors, eight

---

[112] The best discussion in print regarding socio-political classification ("ethnie") is André Lemaire, "Les critères non-iconographiques," 1–26.

[113] In this study, the term "Judahite" makes a good parallel to the terms "Israelite," "Ammonite," "Hittite," etc. See note 60 above.

being listed here: a) explicit references or statements in the inscription which reveal its socio-political classification, b) theophoric elements or theological references in the inscription (usually including one or more DNs), c) onomastic features *except* theophoric elements, d) paleographic analysis of the script, with its auxiliary elements, such as word dividers, e) the identity of the language of the inscription (see Criterion 5 above), f) the spatial arrangement of the text on the writing surface, including possible placement in relation to iconography and dividing lines, which may create multiple registers,[114] g) the provenance of the inscription, and h) the material characteristics of the inscribed object, such as shape (e.g., scarab, scaraboid, stamp, ring, conoid, button, or cylinder, some possibly perforated) and the composition of the material on which the inscription is written (specific kinds of semiprecious stone, metal, bone, common stone, clay, etc.). The technical means of analysis listed above under Criterion 4, "Other," can reveal such things as the composition of clay, which may indicate the geographical location of a likely source.

2) As immediately above, except that the agreement in dating is determined by one less means, i.e., only seven of the means listed above.

And so on: 3) would indicate that agreement is established by a combination of one less means, i.e., six; a 4) indicates by five means; a 5) indicates by four means; a 6) three means; a 7) two means, and an 8) only one means.

9) The socio-political classification of the inscription is clearly determined, but because the biblical account is not specific about it, the most that can be said is that there is no known disagreement between the socio-political classification of the inscription and the biblical account.

10) The socio-political classification of the inscription is narrowed to a few alternatives.

11) The socio-political classification of the inscription is undetermined.

---

[114] See Lemaire's three observations on the placement of the writing in Ammonite, Moabite, and Edomite seals (Lemaire, "Les critères non-iconographiques," 7–8). These observations appear in a larger discussion about ways to determine the ethnic group to which a given seal should be assigned. By including it there, Lemaire implies that the conventions regarding how the writing is positioned may well be a clue to the identity of the socio-political entity in which the seal inscription was produced. The quantity of recovered inscriptions has now become sufficient to permit the study of this aspect of sigillography as a possible indicator of socio-political classification.

*Identification Criteria* 49

12) The socio-political classification of the inscription disagrees with the biblical account.

**1.28 Question three: how strongly do specific identifying data in the inscription count for or against an identification?**

**1.29 Criterion 7, the name of person in the inscription**

1) Completely present, clearly legible, and in exact agreement with the consonants of at least one biblical spelling of the personal name of the biblical candidate for an ID. Other spellings of the person's name should usually be noted.

2) A difference in the presence, absence, form, placement, or degree of preservation of the theophoric element, including the changes made in a hypocoristicon, must be reconciled before an ID can be made. Frequently, the difference is an inconsequential discrepancy between the ending -*yah* in one source and the ending -*yahu* in the other source. The placement of the theophoric element at the beginning or at the end of the name is occasionally in question. A biblical example of such variations is Jehoiachin (2 Kgs 24:6ff; Jer 52:31; 2 Chr 36:8, 9), alias Jeconiah (Jer 24:1ff; 1 Chr 3:16), alias Coniah (Jer 22:24, 28; 37:1). An inscriptional example is Ahaziah in one source and Jehoahaz in the other source (see section 4.4 below). If part of a theophoric element is difficult to read or is broken off, it is usually much easier to restore than a missing root letter.

3) The name in one source is other than the name in the other source, but the complete difference between the names is reconcilable by a demonstration that the same person bore both names. In such instances, a discrepancy in the name used to identify a person should not be regarded as a real disagreement in identity. It may be that a throne name accounts for the difference, e.g., Azariah, king of Judah, is also called Uzziah (2 Kgs 15:1–34; 2 Chr 26:1–27:2; Isa 1:1; 7:1). Jehoahaz in 2 Kgs 23:30–34 and Shallum in Jer 22:11, 12 and 1 Chr 3:15 are widely recognized to be the same person, even though these two names are entirely different.[115] Cf. Abram/Abraham (Gen 17:5), Jacob/Israel (Gen 35:10),

---

[115] This ID is based on the following identifying marks, ascribed to the bearer of each name:

1) Jehoahaz and Shallum are each said to have been the son of Josiah, king of Judah, i.e., the immediate son, with no intervening generation(s) (2 Kgs 23:30; Jer 22:11). Note: 1 Chr 3:15 lists three other immediate sons of Josiah.

2) Jehoahaz and Shallum are each said to have been a captive (2 Kgs 23:33; Jer 22:12).

Jehoiakim/Eliakim (2 Kgs 23:34; 2 Chr 36:4), and Daniel/Belteshazzar with his three friends (Dan 1:7). Patronymics (and in Second Temple times, nicknames) may also have substituted for given names (see note 4 above in this chapter).

4) A difference which occurs specifically because of the presence or absence of one or more *matres lectionis*. Despite negligible instances, the difference may be the result of a dialectical difference, especially between the Israelite Hebrew of the northern kingdom and the Judahite Hebrew of the southern kingdom. Such differences as diphthongs being uncontracted or contracted and the use or non-use of *matres lectionis* can indicate a northern or southern dialect of Hebrew, which might have a direct bearing on the ID.

5) There is a problem with legibility due to poor preservation of one or more root letters (and/or letters from another non-theophoric part of the name): the letter(s) are indistinct, fragmentary, or broken off. In such instances, a sure restoration is usually impossible without a clear parallel in the same inscription or an ancient copy of that inscription.

6) It is uncertain whether the letters represent a personal name.

7) The person's name is or seems to be completely absent.

8) The name of the inscriptional person to be identified disagrees irreconcilably with the name of the person in the biblical account.

## 1.30 Criterion 8, family and other interpersonal relations

1) The inscriptional patronymic or inscriptional filionymic (m.) or filianymic (f.) matches the biblical one. A maritonymic (husband's name), uxoronymic (wife's name), dominonymic (master's name), or servonymic (name of servant or slave) may substitute for a patronymic.

---

3) Jehoahaz and Shallum are each said to have left Jerusalem (2 Kgs 23:33), which seems to be referred to as "this place" in Jer 22:11.
4) Jehoahaz and Shallum are each assigned the fate of being exiled out of the land of Judah, never to return, as an accomplished fact in 2 Kgs 23:34 and as a prophecy of Jeremiah in Jer 22:11–12.
5) The land outside of Judah to which Jehoahaz and Shallum were taken away in captivity is said to be the place of the death of each, as an accomplished fact in 2 Kgs 24:34 and as a prophecy of Jeremiah in Jer 22:12.
6) Both Jehoahaz and Shallum are referred to in language used for the immediate successor of Josiah to the throne of Judah (2 Kgs 23:30; Jer 22:11). Whereas the previous five points could conceivably apply to two different sons of Josiah, within the Hebrew Bible, this is a singular identifying mark, making for a strong ID on biblical grounds.

2) Family or other relational information is implicit. Usually these implied data are explicit in a literary source(s) or other inscription(s). They may relate to semantic usage, literary conventions, specific families, etc.[116]

3) A paternal title is substituted for a patronymic, e.g., "the king's son."

4) The generation to which the inscription's family information refers is uncertain due to the practice of papponymy in that era and region.

5) In the Bible, any name in the category of a patronymic, filionymic, *vel cetera* as in 1) above under this criterion—*whichever category of relationship is filled by any name in the inscription*—is absent; there is none to match or contradict the inscriptional counterpart (patronymic *vel cetera*). The Hebrew Bible may name persons in other relationships to the biblical candidate with whom the inscriptional person might potentially be identified, but it contains no reference to anyone in the particular relationship which is specified in the inscription.

Alternatively, in the *inscription*, any such name—*in whichever category is filled by any name in the Bible*—is absent; there is none to match or contradict the biblical counterpart. As above, the inscription contains no reference to the associated person in the particular relationship which is specified in the Bible.

6) Although some family or other relational information appears in the inscription or in the Bible or in both, it includes no names.

7) It is uncertain whether family or other relational information is present, whether such information in the inscription applies to the inscriptional person to be identified, or whether it can be relied on for a match. Fragmentation of the inscription may be the cause. Another difficulty is that, although societies or governments might have exercised controls in given regions to avoid letting more than one individual have the same combination of name and patronymic,[117] we do not know whether they did. As Fox states, "it cannot be as-

---

[116] It is legitimate to regard family or other relational information supplied by literary sources as a potentially valid supplement to inscriptions if the references to the persons concerned clearly specify them. Even though such data may not be as reliable as an explicit statement of family or other relations in an inscription, if a literary source is reliable, its relational information about the person might still provide valid help in making IDs. In this study, such literary sources would have to be not only extrabiblical, but independent of the Bible as a source of such information.

[117] Remarkably, among hundreds of examples documented at the Old Babylonian city of Sippar, within a given generation, no two persons bearing the same combination of name and patronymic are attested (Harris, "Notes on the Nomenclature," 104, cited in

sumed that such a system could encompass more than one city and its environs," therefore, "among royal functionaries, even those residing at court, probably there were natives of towns and cities outside the capital who could have borne identical names and patronyms."[118] Because this was possible, a name and patronymic alone cannot be considered sufficient for a reliable ID.

8) Family or other relational information is or seems to be completely absent, both from the inscription as it has survived and from the Bible.

9) Family or other relational information disagrees with that in the Bible.

## 1.31 Criterion 9, title information

1) The title[119] unambiguously belongs to the inscriptional person to be identified and matches that of the biblical person.

2) The title as implied clearly indicates the position of the inscriptional person to be identified, even though the expressed title may not be stated as belonging to that person (e.g., the title *'ebed* implies that the master of the *'ebed* was a *melek*),[120] or even though no title may be explicit, as in dynastic names (e.g., the phrase, "the house of Omri," when used as the name of a dynasty or of its territory, implies that Omri was a king).

3) Paternal title or filial title: the title in the inscription is complete and unambiguously applies, if paternal title, to the candidate's ancestor or father or, if filial title, to an offspring of the candidate.

---

Fox, *In the Service of the King*, 39). Harris reasons that a central registration process prevented such duplication.

[118] Ibid., 39.

[119] For lists of titles and descriptions of the offices they signified, first see Fox, *In the Service of the King*, 43–203; then *WSS*, 25–30; Bordreuil, "Sceaux inscrits," cols. 182–202; Ruth Hestrin and Michal Dayagi-Mendels, *Inscribed Seals: First Temple Period* (Jerusalem: Israel Museum, 1979), 11–15; Tryggve N. D. Mettinger, *Solomonic State Officials: A Study of the Civil Government Officials of the Israelite Monarchy* (ConBOT 5; Lund: CWK Gleerup, 1971); Roland de Vaux, *Les Institutions de l'Ancien Testament* (Paris: Editions du Cerf, 1961); ET, *Ancient Israel* (trans. John McHugh; London: Darton, Longman & Todd, Ltd., 1961); repr., *Ancient Israel* (New York: McGraw Hill Paperback Edition, 1985), 69–70, 119–20, 120–32, 155, 226, 346.

[120] See Appendix A.

4) Title of the candidate or paternal or filial title: the title in the inscription is ambiguous in its application. It could belong to the candidate or to a relative named in the inscription.[121]

5) The inscriptional title is other than the title in the Hebrew Bible. One must consider whether the biblical person might have held the inscriptional title earlier or later in his or her career. It is even possible that one person might have held two or more titles concurrently, as in Ur III, but no extant Hebrew inscriptions of the biblical era document concurrent titles.

6) It is uncertain whether a title is present or whether it applies to the inscriptional person in question, because the inscription is damaged or illegible.

7) An inscriptional title is or appears to be completely absent.

## 1.32 Criterion 10, other identifying information (marks of the individual)

1) Other information[122] about the inscriptional person to be identified is explicit and clear, and it agrees with the biblical account.

2) Other information about the inscriptional person to be identified is implicit, and it agrees with the biblical account. The implied data may be clear in a literary source(s) or other inscription(s).

3) Other identifying information is vague in its meaning. For example, the iconography of an inscribed seal may imply that the owner was an official in the king's court without indicating his precise title.[123]

---

[121] Avigad points out the ambiguity of the title when it is placed after both the name and the patronymic:
... The owner of the seal can indicate in his seal the title of his father. Even in an ordinary text, this formula can also be explained otherwise; compare similar formulas in the Tanach: Jonathan, the son of Abiathar, the priest (1 Kgs 1:42) in which it is known that Abiathar was the priest, and not Jonathan, and the same goes for Zechariah, the son of Jehoiada, "the priest" (2 Chr 24:20), in which also it is known that Jehoiada was the priest, and not Zechariah. (Avigad, "On the Identification," 236, translation mine)
See also the fuller evidence in note 102 above. Note: in this article, Avigad does not address the question of whether the title "the priest" means high priest. He simply uses the terminology found in the texts under consideration.

[122] Whereas most classification systems, such as filing systems, place the "miscellaneous" category last, here it is penultimate, in order that all relevant data might be made explicit before they are considered in relation to the final criterion, identification on grounds of singularity.

4) Other identifying information is uncertain in its application to the inscriptional person to be identified, usually because of the fragmentary state of an inscription.

5) Other identifying information appears to be completely absent.

6) Other identifying information disagrees with the biblical account.

**1.33 Criterion 11, identification on grounds of singularity**

Since all reasonable IDs include or aspire toward an element of singularity, this criterion needs to be described by the distinctive phrase "*grounds* of singularity." Although the word "uniqueness" is tempting, its clear meaning, "one of a kind," cannot apply when more than one inscription provides this kind of ID of a particular person. Speaking more analytically, an ID on grounds of singularity means that an ID is required by data which indicate at least two of the three things in the following list: a and/or b, plus c:

a) that there was only one individual who could be indicated by the *inscriptional* identifying marks, and/or

b) that there was only one individual who could be indicated by the *biblical* identifying marks; plus

c) that the match between the known inscriptional and biblical identifying marks *requires* the conclusion that the same individual is indicated by both. Of course, such an ID may not be made if there is an overriding consideration against it, such as a lack of provenance for an inscription, hence an objective reason to doubt its authenticity. In such a case, the ID would remain conditional upon demonstrated authenticity of the inscription.

Although the phrase, "grounds of singularity," means that there is no other tenable alternative supported by known, ancient evidence, *this criterion cannot be met by depending on absence of evidence*, since available evidence from both inscriptional and biblical sources is and will always be only part of all the data that once existed. Beyond absence of tenable alternatives for the ID, *there must be unequivocal linkage* between the inscriptional and the biblical persons. Such linkage may consist in matching historical circumstances of the two, as with

---

[123] Bordreuil, "Inscriptions sigillaires ouest-sémitiques III," 27–29. On the other hand, aniconism might also be significant. On aniconism in general, see Tryggve N. D. Mettinger, *No Graven Image? Israelite Aniconism in Its Ancient Near Eastern Context* (ConBOT 42; Stockholm: Almqvist & Wiksell International, 1995).

Mesha, king of Moab, in the Mesha Inscription (see section 3.3 below), or it may present itself in terms of a set of identifying marks that are sufficient to specify one and only one individual, eliminating any chance of duplication.

To illustrate a refinement of this category, an ID on grounds of singularity is one which meets one or both of the following conditions:

a) One or more *inscriptions* may provide enough information to situate clearly a person whom it names in a singular historical context. For example, the Mesha Inscription mentions the son(s) of Omri, king of Israel, as king(s) of Israel who were contemporary with Mesha. Elsewhere, the name Omri appears as the name of a king of Israel in Assyrian inscriptions, used in such a way as to refer to only one Hebrew monarch who bore that name, and he can be dated to the period just before that of Mesha. The Mesha Inscription also supplies other historical details that allow modern scholars to identify Omri, king of Israel, in the inscription, with the Omri, king of Israel, to whom 1 Kgs 16:16ff refers. This is an example of an ID on grounds of *inscriptional* singularity (on the ID of Omri, see section 3.4 below).

b) An inscription may clearly indicate a person concerning whom *literary* sources allow no ambiguity. For example, only one Hezekiah who was a king of Judah appears in biblical sources. The decisive data are 1) that the Bible presents its lists of kings of Israel and of Judah as a complete lists of consecutive rulers,[124] and 2) that according to the Bible, no other king of Judah (or Israel) bore that name. Suppose, for example, that a seal or bulla of known authenticity from late eighth-century Judah, for example, names an ʿebed Ḥizqiyahu. It is understood that on seals and bullae, ʿebed is always followed by a DN, the name of a king, or the word *hammelek* (on this phenomenon *in seals and bullae* in which the *title* ʿebed appears, see Appendix A below). Thus the biblical text and that seal or bulla each refer to a Hezekiah who was king of Judah in the late eighth century. Suppose also that there is no evidential reason to differentiate the Hezekiah of one source from the Hezekiah of the other source, for example, on the basis of different circumstances or different individual identifying marks. According to the Bible, there was only one such king. This, then, would be an example of an ID on grounds of *biblical* singularity. (On the process of identifying Hezekiah, see section 4.6 below, keeping in mind that the bulla treated there is unprovenanced, therefore, the ID is only conditional.)

---

[124] The complete, consecutive continuity of the Davidic royal line and the First Temple high-priestly line as presented in the Bible is challenged, however unconvincingly, in W. Boyd Barrick, "Genealogical Notes on the 'House of David' and the 'House of Zadok,'" *JSOT* 96 (2001): 29–58.

Since grounds of singularity might be present on the inscriptional side, the biblical side, or both, there are degrees of strength in these grounds:

1) Available data require an ID on double grounds of singularity, i.e., the ID is to be made on grounds of *both* singularity according to inscriptional data *and* singularity according to biblical data.

2) Available data require an ID on single grounds of singularity, i.e., *either* singularity in inscriptions *or* singularity in the Bible.

3) Available data do not require an ID on grounds of singularity.

**1.34 Summary and Limitation**

This part of the system for identifying biblical persons in Northwest Semitic inscriptions subsumes all criteria under three general questions regarding authenticity, setting, and specific identifying marks. Not just one or two, but *all three* of these general questions must be answered satisfactorily before an ID can be considered valid. This requirement amounts to a threefold assertion that to establish an ID, the inscription must be authentic, the setting of the biblical and inscriptional individuals must match, and that (by a combination of specific marks) the chance of confusing two different persons must be rendered negligible or eliminated altogether.

The eleven identification criteria are divided into three groups, each of which is designed to help answer one of these three questions accurately. Each criterion, in turn, must take into account various factors, many of which call for techniques capable of revealing evidence relevant to the criterion. In other words, this chapter's attempt to take into account all categories of factors under each criterion is an attempt to consider all relevant evidence. The abstract discussion in this chapter calls for concrete examples, which are given below.

The presentation thus far is limited in that *this chapter does not completely describe the identification system*. Chapter 2 completes the description.

## Chapter 2

# Taxonomy of Identifications and Two System Refinements

### 2.1 Taxonomy: grades of identifications and of non-identifications

Fortunately, the identification system is not nearly as complicated in practical use as the latter part of the previous chapter may suggest. Application of the criteria enables researchers to sort IDs or non-IDs into six grades of strength or weakness. In descending order, these range from grade S IDs, "on grounds of singularity," through grades 3, 2, 1, and 0 (zero), depending on the number of specific identifying criteria met, to grade D for disqualified. IDs in grade S are certain. Grade 3 IDs range from virtually certain to reliable, depending on the factors involved. Grade 2 IDs are unresolved and appear to be risky, but they are usually reasonable enough to invite assumption. Those in grades 1 and 0 are not reliable IDs at all. Some of the examples below are in unprovenanced inscriptions. Though the IDs they may offer are conditional on authenticity, this conditionality is not relevant to their use here as examples of the six grades.

### 2.2 Grade S identifications, including SI and SB: certain

Grade S identifications are made on grounds of singularity. As mentioned in section 1.18, *all three* of the questions in the three-question identification system must be answered satisfactorily in order for there to be an ID. The inscriptional data must be authentic, the general setting of the inscription must *permit* a match, and specific identifying marks in the inscription must be sufficient for a match. Grounds of singularity cannot satisfy the requirements of the first and second questions; *singularity counts only in relation to the third question.*

IDs made on grounds of singularity must be established by specific, unequivocal linkage, i.e., only one individual could be indicated on inscriptional grounds, on biblical grounds, or on grounds of both (as in section 1.33, Criterion 11). As a supporting fact, there must be no other tenable alternative IDs which are supported by ancient evidence. Grade S IDs differ not in degree, but in kind, from those in grade 3, which are based on reduced chances of misidentification.

An example of a grade S ID (conditional upon the authenticity of the seal) is Hoshea, son of Elah, the last king of the northern kingdom of Israel (2 Kgs 15:30ff) in the seal of Abdi. It was first published in 1995 by André Lemaire, who made the ID in that article.[1]

Description: The seal of Abdi is a scaraboid of translucent orange chalcedony (or possibly "brown" carnelian) one inch long, slightly over one-half inch wide, and one-third inch thick. It is perforated lengthwise. On its face strides a male courtier wearing an Egyptian wig and a long skirt. One of his hands grasps a papyrus scepter, and the other is raised above his shoulder in a palm-down gesture, apparently of blessing. In the register beneath his feet is a winged solar disk. A vertical inscription behind and before him reads, in retrograde script, לעבדי / עבד הושע, "belonging to Abdi, / the minister of Hoshea."

An ID on grounds of singularity is always a grade S ID, regardless of how many other specific identifying criteria are met under question 3. Nevertheless, all criteria that have been met are recorded below.

### (2.2) Question 1: How reliable are the inscriptional data?

**Acquisition**: 3) It was purchased on the antiquities market, at a Sotheby's auction in New York City on December 14, 1993. The purchaser was Mr. Shlomo Moussaieff, an Israeli collector of antiquities who lives in London.

**Provenance**: 4) The location of the inscription when found is unknown.

**Authenticity**: 4) Expert opinion substantially supports authenticity.

### (2.2) Question 2: Does the general setting of the inscription permit a match between the inscriptional person and the biblical person?

**Date**: 6) There is no known disagreement in dating, which is determined by epigraphy alone. This is surely an eighth-century inscription, yet in searching for a more precise date using the other epigraphic evidence, one finds that the

---

[1] André Lemaire, "Name of Israel's Last King Surfaces in a Private Collection," *BAR* 21, no. 6 (November/December 1995): 48–52.

## Fig. 1

### The Seal "of Abdi, the Minister of Hoshea"

(The inscription is in retrograde, i.e., mirror-image, script.
Drawing by the author)

basis exists partly in a relatively slender amount of evidence regarding *daleth*. Most of the letter forms are broadly eighth through seventh century, but the dates of two diagnostic letters are more precise. The *daleth* apparently comes from the late eighth century to the second half of the seventh.[2] The *waw* (shaped much like the English capital letter Y) is composed of three straight strokes; similar examples come from the eighth century but no later.[3] The chronological overlap in this seal between these forms of *daleth* and *waw* indicates the late eighth century. In view of the small number of inscriptions whose *daleth*s form part of the basis for dating, this date is tentative, but *it is the most accurate date currently possible.*[4] The biblical king Hoshea reigned ca. 732/1–722.

**Language**: 3) The twelve letters of the seal do not permit the language of the inscription to be specifically determined by the vocabulary, morphology, or syntax. Nevertheless, the script is Hebrew, and there is no known disagreement with the language expectation raised by the biblical account: Hebrew.

**Socio-political classification**: 4) The agreement is *determined* by:

1. The script, which is clearly and distinctively Hebrew. All of the letters find comparable exemplars in Hebrew seals of the mid- to late eighth century. In particular, the *he* with long, horizontal rungs, of which the bottom rung is the

---

[2] *SANSS*, Fig. 67.

[3] Ibid., 127, no. 102, Hebrew Seal Script Fig. 67, nos. 67, 4, 30, 123, and 102. In agreement with Herr, Vaughn finds that "the archaic form of the *waw* without the intersecting bar is early and not found in any of the late seventh century forms. Thus, this should be recognized as a distinctive trait dating the letter to the earlier period" (Vaughn, "Palaeographic Dating of Judaean Seals," 54.)

In his diss., completed in November 1995, Vaughn seems originally to have defined this "earlier period" for *waw* as early to mid-eighth century, i.e., previous to the conclusively dated late-eighth-century *lmlk* seal impressions found in Stratum III of Ussishkin's excavations at Lachish (idem, "The Chronicler's Account of Hezekiah: The Relationship of Historical Data to a Theological Interpretation of 2 Chronicles 29–32" [Ph.D. diss., Princeton Theological Seminary, 1996], 24–25, 113–46; idem, "Palaeographic Dating of Judaean Seals," 45). But after the diss. was completed, one instance became known which exhibited, on a late-eighth-century jar handle, "an archaic *waw* from the impression יהוקם / [. . .]ל . . . on which the intersecting bar is absent" (ibid., 53, referring to an unsigned article attributable to the editor: [Heidi L. Nordberg], "Photoessay: New Photographic Techniques for Documenting Inscribed Objects," *Religious Studies News* 11, no. 3 [September 1996]: 29, Fig. 8). That seal impression expanded the chronological range of this form of *waw* to the entire eighth century.

[4] Andrew G. Vaughn, "Methodological Issues in the Palaeographic Dating of Hebrew Seals," paper presented November 19, 1995, at the Annual Meeting of the ASOR, Philadelphia, Pa., 19 and appended chart, "Early Eighth to mid Eighth Century Letters," photocopied. Presumably because the number of exemplars of *daleth* is very small, this letter is not included among the diagnostic letters in idem, "Chronicler's Account," nor is it in idem, "Palaeographic Dating of Judaean Seals."

longest, the *beth* that leans slightly back, against the direction of reading, and the "double check" *shin* all appearing together distinguish the Hebrew seal script.

The agreement is *permitted* by:

2. The onomastic features. The PN עבדי is in one unprovenanced Hebrew seal and ten Hebrew seal impressions on excavated jar handles (*WSS*, 519). Although this exact name is unattested in any other socio-political classification, PNs formed from the root *'bd* (or equivalent) appear in the inscriptions of at least five other socio-political classifications (Fowler, 282). The PN הושע appears in three other unprovenanced Hebrew seals, seven or eight excavated Hebrew bullae, one wooden tag (?) in Aramaic from fifth-century Elephantine (*WSS*, 506), and one other Aramaic inscription (Maraqten, 155–56). With a suffix (usually theophoric), it is in twenty-three or twenty-four Hebrew inscriptions and one unprovenanced Ammonite seal (*WSS*, 506). Only Hebrew, Aramaic, and Ammonite inscriptions contain PNs based on the form הושע (cf. Fowler, 289).

3. The inscription's broad language parameters, which include Hebrew.

4. The vertical arrangement of the text on the writing surface, which has precedents among Hebrew seals. See sections 4.2 and 4.3 below; those Hebrew inscriptions may be regarded as authentic, as explained in section 5.1. Similar, vertical arrangements are found on unprovenanced seals which are Phoenician (*WSS*, no. 724), Aramaic (*WSS*, nos. 751, 775, etc.), and Ammonite (*WSS*, nos. 858, 885, etc.), but apparently not on Moabite or Edomite seals.

5. The material characteristics of the inscribed object. Several known Hebrew seals are scaraboids of semiprecious stone and perforated lengthwise.

## (2.2) Question 3: How strongly do specific data in the inscription count for or against an identification?

A check (√) means that a criterion has been met.

√ **Name**: 1) The name of Hoshea, person (16) in seal [15] (both as numbered in Appendix B) is completely present, clearly legible, and in exact agreement with the consonants of the uniform biblical spelling of the name of the biblical candidate for identification, Hoshea, in 2 Kgs 15:30ff.

The objection might be raised that if this seal were from the kingdom of Israel during the late eighth century, it would not include *waw* as the second letter in Hoshea's name, because in Israelite Hebrew and in Phoenician, the diphthongs /ay/ and /aw/ were contracted to the monophthongs /ê/ and /ô/, respectively. Although this view expresses Garr's general perception of the geographical spread of the contraction of diphthongs,[5] yet the linguistic picture as shown by the eighth century evidence regarding /aw/ and /ô/ in Israelite Hebrew reveals a state of transition. The diphthong /aw/ and its contraction, /ô/ were being used simultaneously. In eighth-century Israelite inscriptions, Ziony Zevit finds the contraction in unaccented syllables (e.g., the first syllable of *ḥōrōn* in Tell Qasile ostracon 2) but not in accented ones (e.g., several PNs ending in accented *-yaw* in the Samaria Ostraca).[6] The Hebrew name of the last king of Israel to be named in Assyrian inscriptions, Hoshea, who reigned in 731, is rendered ᵐ*a-ú-si-'i*[7] or ᵐ*a-ú-si-'a*.[8] These transcriptions, which represent what was heard by a

---

[5] W. Randall Garr, *Dialect Geography of Syria-Palestine, 1000–586 B.C.E.* (Philadelphia: University of Pennsylvania Press, 1985), 38–39, 206, no. 2:8, under Hebrew, N[orthern]. Observing that the contraction of these two diphthongs occurred earliest in those language groups which were closest to Phoenicia and progressively later among language groups which were progressively more distant from Phoenicia, Garr theorizes as follows:

> Two models can account for this distribution. Monophthongization may have originated in Phoenicia, and thence spread to northern Israel, later to Ammon, Moab, and finally reached Edom centuries later. Alternatively, monophthongization developed independently in several dialects as it did, for example, in Akkadian. As a result, it is unclear whether monophthongization is a shared innovation in N[orth] W[est]S[emitic]. The distribution of the phenomenon, however, suggests a Phoenician origin. (Ibid., 40)

[6] Ziony Zevit, *Matres Lectionis in Ancient Hebrew Epigraphs*, ASOR Monograph Series 2 (Cambridge, Mass.: ASOR, 1980), 11–12, no. 3, 12, no. 6, 12–13, no. 7, 15. Sass suggests the Tel Qasile ostraca may have been forged (*WSS*, 457–58).

Zevit's strongest evidence for the contraction of /aw/ to /ô/ is Tel Qasile ostracon 2 (Zevit, *Matres*, 11–12, no. 3; Gibson 1:15–17). In that ostracon, the first vowel of חרן in לביתחרן may safely be considered /ô/, contracted from /aw/. The main problem is that in לביתחרן, the diphthong /ay/, which contracted to /ê/ earlier than /aw/ to /ô/, is apparently uncontracted, reversing the accepted chronological order. Zevit's other evidence for contraction of /aw/ to /ô/ in unaccented syllables, however, is not nearly as strong. The PN *ywyšb* in Samaria ostracon 36, line 3, derives support from Akkadian syllabic transcription of similar Hebrew names (Zevit, *Matres*, 12–13, no. 7, and 13, n. 16), but its transcription is somewhat uncertain, and it can be vocalized as *yawyašb* just as easily (so P. Kyle McCarter, "'Yaw, Son of Omri': A Philological Note on Israelite Chronology," *BASOR* 216 [1974]: 5). In that ostracon, either 1) לביתחרן means "to/for Beth-Horon," a GN of adjacent upper and lower towns in the territory of Ephraim in southern Israel, or 2) חרן in לביתחרן is a DN, and ביתחרן is a temple of that deity (on whom see *KAI*, Nr. 27, line 16). On these alternative interpretations, see *HAE* 1:230–31, n. 4. *HAE* 2/1:209 lists ביתחרן as a GN. The GN may, of course, contain a DN.

[7] Summary (alias Display; see *ITP*, 25) Inscription 4, discovered at Calah on a fragmentary slab and left *in situ*, lines 15–18 (*ITP*, 140–41, Pl. XLIX–LI; RawlCu 3, Pl. 10, no. 2); *ANET*, 284; Galil, *Chronology*, 153.

scribe(s) of the Assyrians, indicate that the Israelite speech of that time included the diphthong /aw/ in its uncontracted state.[9] It may have been retained in this instance because it formed part of a PN, and archaic linguistic features tend to linger on in PNs,[10] or possibly because of a dialectical difference in the background of the King Hoshea whose name the Assyrians transcribed.[11] Therefore, the *waw* in the royal name on the seal does not represent merely conservative spelling or an archaizing tendency in orthography.[12]

The preservation of the uncontracted diphthong in this name, however, reflects a phonological usage which is different from that of the contracted diphthong in the first syllable of *ḥôrōn* in Tell Qasile ostracon 2. Noting that "regarding -*aw*-, there was still some fluctuation: forms with the diphthong existed along with monophthongized ones," Zadok nevertheless emphasizes the fact that "the indigenous sources from the northern kingdom reflect a mo-

---

[8] Anson F. Rainey, "The Word *Ywm* in Ugaritic and in Hebrew," *Lešonenu* 36 (1972): 189.

[9] As Harris also observes, ". . . The Assyrian transcription *a-u-si-'* (III Rawlinson [i.e., RawlCu 3] 10.2.28) [háwši‛], later > [hôšê<sup>a</sup>‛], shows the form . . . before the reduction of the diphthong. (Zellig S. Harris, *Development of the Canaanite Dialects: An Investigation in Linguistic History*, AOS 16 [New Haven, Conn.: American Oriental Society, 1939], 31).

Cody also sees this transcription as representing an uncontracted diphthong:

It is true that a . . . cuneiform transcription of the name of Hoshea, ruler of the Northern Kingdom in the third quarter of the eighth century, shows (= \**Hawši‛*), with -*aw* uncontracted, and this, moreover, in a name which never had a still unsyncopated intervocalic -*h*- to postpone the contraction of the diphthong . . . . (Aelred Cody, "A New Inscription from Tell āl-Rimaḥ and King Jehoash of Israel," *CBQ* 32 [1970]: 338–39)

[10] Layton bases his recent study on this premise:

It is a generally accepted tenet of ancient Near Eastern studies that proper names tend to preserve archaic features of a language. As such, they constitute an important source for reconstructing the older stages of any language. This statement holds true for PNN as well as for GNN, though these two sources may not complement one another in some instances. (Scott C. Layton, *Archaic Features of Canaanite Personal Names in the Hebrew Bible*, HSM 47 [Atlanta: Scholars Press, 1990], 8)

[11] Cody suggests a dialectical reason:

. . . The uncontracted diphthong in Hoshea's name may be explained as reflecting the pronunciation of a dialect different from that of Samaria and close to that of Judah. The Hoshea concerning us here came to the throne in Samaria by usurpation (2 Kgs 15, 30). We do not have any information on his provenance, but his speech may not have been that characteristic of Samaria. (Cody, "New Inscription," 339)

[12] Harris, *Development of the Canaanite Dialects*, 25.

nophthongization of -*aw*-."[13] Whereas the PN *hwš*ʿ preserves the diphthong, "Beth-Horon" in Tell Qasile ostracon 2, apparently an Israelite GN, does not preserve it. This phenomenon contradicts the general characteristic of GNs that Layton observes, i.e., "that GNN are 'super-archaic' in comparison to PNN. They evidence an extreme resistance to change . . . ."[14] Still, the GNs of inhabited sites change with less difficulty than the names of permanent geographic features, "as a result of renaming after the conquest, abandonment, or destruction of a settlement."[15] It should also be noted that "there is no way of knowing whether . . . [Tell Qasile ostracon 2] represents the pronunciation at Tell Qasile on the coast or at Beth Horon in the hills of Ephraim . . . ."[16]

Two later Assyrian transcriptions of the PN *hwš*ʿ are ᵐ*ú-si-a*, from Aššur, and ᵐ*ú-si-'a*, from Gozan.[17] Presumably, these are names of exiled Israelites (cf.

---

[13] Zadok summarizes the relevant textual evidence as follows:

N[eo-]A[ssyrian] *A-ú-se-'* occurs only once ([Hayim] Tadmor [*ITP*] 1994, 140: 4,17), whereas all the other three NA occurrences of this name (all referring to individuals living in Assyria and other regions of the Jezireh, very probably deportees) start with *Ú-* (*Ú-se-'* / *Hwš*ʿ, [Theodore] Kwasman and [Simo] Parpola [eds., *Legal Transactions of the Royal Court of Nineveh, Part I: Tiglath-Pileser III through Esarhaddon* (State Archives of Assyria 6; ed. Simo Parpola; Helsinki: Helsinki University Press)] 1991, 111, 3; *Ú-se-'*, [Johannes] Friedrich et al., [eds., *Die Inschriften von Tell Halaf* (Archiv für Orientforschung Beiheft 6; Berlin: published by the editors)] 1940, 111, 4, 7; [B.] Parker ["Administrative Tablets from the North-west Palace, Nimrud," *Iraq* 23] 1961, 39 and pl. 20: ND 2629, 10). This name (of the causative verbal stem *hpʿl*) cannot refer to Phoenicians (the Phoenician causative is *ypʿl*), but only to Israelites or Transjordanians, more likely to the former group (Samarians and Judahites, see [Israel] Ephʿal ["On the Identification of the Israelite Exiles in the Assyrian Empire" (in Hebrew), in *Excavations and Studies: Essays in Honour of Professor Shemuel Yeivin* (ed. Y. Aharoni; Publications, Tel Aviv University, Institute of Archaeology 1; Tel Aviv: CARTA)] 1973) [201–3], seeing that there is hardly any evidence for Assyrian mass deportations of Transjordanians. It can be argued that -*ay*- was monophthongized in Samarian Hebrew, but regarding -*aw*-, there was still some fluctuation: forms with the diphthong existed along with monophthongized ones, e.g., NA *Ia-a-ú* along with *Ia-ú-a* (*Iu-ú-a* in view of NA *A-sa-a-ú* along with *Su-ú-a*, to be discussed in a forthcoming publication by N. Naʾaman and myself). However, the indigenous sources from the Northern Kingdom reflect a monophthongization of -*aw*- (See [W. Randall] Garr [*Dialect Geography of Syria-Palestine, 1000–586 B.C.*] . . . , 38f.). The same fluctuation (-*aw*- along with -*ō*-) existed among the Judeans in Babylonia during the last third of the 5th century BC . . . . (Ran Zadok, "Notes on Syro-Palestinian History, Toponomy, and Anthroponomy," *UF* 28 [1996]: 726–27)

[14] Layton, *Archaic Features of Canaanite Personal Names*, 4.

[15] Ibid., 4–5.

[16] Zevit, *Matres*, 12.

[17] See notes 8 and 13 above.

2 Kgs 17:6). The first syllable of these names attests the contraction of the diphthong /aw/. The documents containing these two examples are from about 611. Although these examples could have resulted from exposure to the Assyrian contracted diphthong, Zevit argues that it is more likely that because they come from two different Israelite communities in exile, preserving "a linguistic pattern which was completely developed before their exile, ca. 722."[18] That argument also would tend to place the diphthong /aw/ and its contraction, /ô/, in use at about the same time (731 and 722; cf., in the Samaria Ostraca, likely of the early eighth century, McCarter's vocalization of *ywyšb* as *yawyašib*).[19]

The point of the above discussion is that the presence of a diphthong in the royal name not only is no obstacle to this ID, but, moreover, it tends to strengthen the link, because the earlier Assyrian transcription of this name records this diphthong in its uncontracted state in the name of precisely the individual whom the seal seems to indicate. The above evidence for the original diphthong /aw/ in the late eighth-century pronunciation of this name also points to leveling of the original diphthong /aw/ to the later /ô/ in the Bible, as reflected in the vocalization of the MT הוֹשֵׁעַ and the LXX 'Ωσηε.[20]

**Relations**: 5) In the inscription, there is no patronymic to match or contradict the biblical phrase, "son of Elah." In the Bible, there is no servonymic to match or contradict the inscriptional "Abdi." (Note: if this ID were to be made on grounds of biblical singularity, the family information found in 2 Kgs 15:30; 17:1 could be applied to the inscriptional Hoshea, and the relationship to Abdi found in the inscription could be applied to the biblical Hoshea.)

√ **Title**: 2) The title clearly implies that of the inscriptional candidate for the ID, even though the title belongs to his servant. In a seal, the servant's title, ʿ*ebed*, unequivocally indicates that the master was a king (see Appendix A).

**Other**: 3) Other identifying information is vague in its significance. The Egyptianizing iconography of this inscribed seal depicts a courtier, which implies that the owner was probably an official in the king's court without indicating his precise title. This implication only supports what is already known from the title. Egyptianizing iconography commonly accompanies Hebrew and other Northwest Semitic inscriptions in inscribed seals. The fact that this seal is made of semiprecious stone signifies that its owner was a man of some means, as one would expect of a king's minister.

---

[18] Ibid., 25, n. 43.

[19] McCarter, "'*Yaw*, Son of Omri,'" 5. See also note 74 above in Chapter 1.

[20] Layton observes, "As a general rule, PNN lie outside the mainstream of language change and thus are immune to the editorial and linguistic revision to which the surrounding text is subject. There are, however, some exceptions to this general rule" (Layton, *Archaic Features of Canaanite Personal Names*, 19).

√ **Singularity**:  2) Available data indicate that identification on grounds of singularity in the Bible is required. The evidence in this instance is three-sided, coming from an Assyrian inscription, the biblical narrative, and this seal

On the Assyrian inscriptional side, a fragmentary, annalistic text of Tiglath-pileser III, king of Assyria (r. 744–727), names Hoshea ($^{m}A$-*ú-si-'i* or $^{m}A$-*ú-si-'a*) as the king of Israel who immediately succeeded Pekah during the reign of this Assyrian monarch.[21] The succession of two kings of Israel with these names during this eighteen-year period is a singular identifying mark common to the Assyrian inscription and the biblical account. According to the biblical data in 2 Kgs, there was only one Hebrew king named Hoshea, the immediate successor of Pekah, and they ruled Israel during the same narrow time period. The match between 2 Kgs and Tiglath-pileser III's inscription on this point unmistakably shows that the biblical and the Assyrian source refer to the same King Hoshea.

The short inscription on the seal in question, however, not being an annal, of course, makes no mention of Hoshea's predecessor, and so it makes no connection with the singular identifying mark shared by 2 Kgs and the Assyrian inscription. The question is whether the Hoshea of the seal in question can be linked to the Hoshea of the biblical and/or Assyrian sources in any other way(s). If the identifying links to the biblical Hoshea were established, then, because the biblical list of the kings of the northern and southern kingdoms presents itself as complete, it would be possible to make an ID which on the basis of the biblical data is singular.

The seal in question exhibits distinctive Hebrew script, gives no indication that it is in a language besides Hebrew, and implies in the servant's title that the master was a king. The royal name is spelled in a way that is compatible with the Assyrian transcription and matches the uniform sequence of consonants that appears in all biblical spellings of this name. Paleographic analysis of the seal's script, though tentative, places it in the second half of the eighth century, the same time period as that of the Israelite King Hoshea who is named in the biblical and Assyrian sources. Taken together, these factors point to this person alone. On the biblical side, there is no other king Hoshea in the Bible with whom the Hoshea of the seal may be identified. The Hebrew Bible presents the reigns of consecutive kings in a way which purports to include every monarch in the Hebrew kingdoms. Provided this inscription is authentic, then, this ID is made on grounds of biblical singularity.

The ID on grounds of biblical singularity, however, cannot be allowed to influence the decision regarding singularity in inscriptions, in order that it might remain precisely what it is called (see sections 2.10 through 2.13 below). Assyrian inscriptions differ from the Bible in that they are not at all complete in their

---

[21] Summary Inscriptions from Calah, Summary Inscription 4, lines 17'–18', *ITP*, 140–41; *ANET*, 284; Galil, *Chronology*, 153.

records of Hebrew monarchs. The Assyrian inscriptions unearthed thus far contain the names of only seven of the Bible's twenty kings of Israel. Regarding Hebrew monarchs, therefore, singularity in Assyrian inscriptions is usually more difficult to document than singularity in biblical materials. Before considering the potential ID on grounds of singularity in inscriptions, it should be recalled that, as described in section 1.33, criterion 11, above, singularity implies not merely that only one such person is *known* to have existed, but, more crucially, that there is unequivocal linkage between the inscriptional person and the biblical person. Therefore, the fact that only one Hoshea, king of Israel, appears in known extrabiblical data (i.e., the inscription of Tiglath-pileser III referred to above) does not establish this ID on grounds of inscriptional singularity. Three factors prevent unequivocal linkage between the Hoshea of this seal and the Hoshea of Tiglath-pileser III's inscription: 1) the approximate epigraphic time frame leaves enough room for another Hoshea, king of Israel, hypothetically to have reigned; 2) the incompleteness of the Assyrian records regarding Hebrew monarchs also permits another such Hoshea, and 3) the seal does not specify its Hoshea as the successor of Pekah, because seals do not name unrelated predecessors. No ID can be made on grounds of singularity in inscriptions. Because two specific identifying criteria have been met (name and title), the strongest connection that can be made using inscriptional data alone is Avigad's "reasonable assumption," a grade 2 ID. (On the analogy of SI, it could be called 2-I.)

**Remarks**: The second and third questions can be answered satisfactorily for this ID, and under the third question, it meets the criterion of singularity on biblical grounds (SB). Therefore, but for the first question, regarding reliability, it would be considered a grade S ID. Because forgery has not been proven, the first question has not been answered in the negative, and the ID has not been disqualified. A convenient way to state suspension of judgment on this ID is to say that it is conditional upon demonstration of the genuineness of the seal. Until a verdict is reached on authenticity, this is a *conditional* grade SB ID.

## 2.3 Grade 3 identifications: virtually certain to reliable

These IDs meet at least three identifying criteria but are not made on grounds of singularity. Some of them qualify as near-certain IDs, because the possibility of their being wrong is so unlikely as to be considered utterly negligible. Others in this grade are not as redundantly secure, but they are reliable. In his 1987 article, which presented foundational criteria for making IDs, Avigad had in mind what this study calls grade 3 IDs.[22]

An example of a grade 3 ID (again, depending on the authenticity of the bulla) is Baruch the scribe, son of Neriah, (Jer 32:12ff) in the bulla that was first

---

[22] Avigad, "On the Identification," 235–36, on Baruch and Jerahmeel.

published in 1978 by Avigad, who made the ID in that article.[23] Its number in the Israel Museum is 76.22.2299 (A9). A second marketed bulla, apparently made from the same seal, was first published in 1994.

Description: The first known bulla of Baruch is a 16 x 17 mm. lump of dark brown clay bearing the impression of an 11 x 13 mm. oval seal. It is aniconic. A single line surrounds the impression, and two double horizontal lines divide the face of the impression into three registers. The inscription, which occupies all three registers, reads, לברכיהו / בן נריהו / הספר, "belonging to Berekyahu, son of Neriyahu, the scribe." The reverse side bears the impression of papyrus fibers and a deep, curved impression, apparently made by the loop of a thick string used to bind the papyrus which this bulla sealed.

### (2.3) Question 1: reliability of the inscriptional data

**Acquisition**: 3) It was purchased on the antiquities market.
**Provenance**: 4) The location of the inscription when found is unknown.
**Authenticity**: 4) Expert consensus affirms its authenticity. See note 32.

### (2.3) Question 2: whether the setting of the inscription *permits* a match between the inscriptional person and the biblical person

**Date**: 5) Agreement in dating is determined by epigraphy alone to be late seventh to early sixth century, when Baruch, the scribe who is mentioned in the book of Jeremiah, flourished. The first and second letters *he* in the inscription are diagnostic. The top crossbar extends to the other side of the vertical shaft,

---

[23] Nahman Avigad, "Baruch the Scribe and Jerahmeel the King's Son," *IEJ* 28 (1978): 52–56. Other works on this bulla are: idem, "Jerahmeel & Baruch, King's Son and Scribe," *BA* 42 (1979): 114–18; idem, *Hebrew Bullae*, 28–29, no. 9; Larry G. Herr, "Paleography and the Identification of Seal Owners," *BASOR* 239 (Summer 1980): 67–70; Hershel Shanks, "Jeremiah's Scribe and Confidant Speaks from a Hoard of Clay Bullae," *BAR* 13, no. 5 (September/October 1987): 58–61, 63, 65; *WSS*, 175–76, no. 417; *AHI*, 186, no. 100.509.

Works on the second known bulla from the same seal are Robert Deutsch and Michael Heltzer, *Forty New Ancient West Semitic Inscriptions* (Tel Aviv: Archaeological Center Publication, 1994), 37–38, no. (11) 1; Hershel Shanks, "Fingerprint of Jeremiah's Scribe," *BAR* 22, no. 2 (March/April 1996): cover, large digital image in color, 37, large color photograph. That it was made by the same seal was not an automatic conclusion; from Aharoni's excavations at Arad, it is evident that several seals could belong to the same person, presumably for administrative use by subordinates (Yohanan Aharoni, *Arad Inscriptions* [Jerusalem: Israel Exploration Society, 1981], 119–20, nos. 105–107). This practice has Mesopotamian parallels: "Finally, we know that, at least in the Middle Assyrian period, a senior official could authorize the use of his seal by subordinates on official business" (Winter, "Legitimation of Authority," 82).

*Taxonomy of Identifications and Two System Refinements* 69

and the three crossbars are not parallel but tend to converge toward the open side of the letter. This form of the letter is found only during this time period.[24]

**Language**: 3) The language of the inscription, *although not specifically determined* by the vocabulary, morphology, or syntax of the inscription, presents no known disagreement with the expectation raised by the biblical account, i.e., Hebrew.

**Socio-political classification**: 3) The agreement is *determined* by:

1. Two theophoric elements -*yahu*, which indicate a Judahite origin (see Chapter 3, note 136, below).

2. Script that is clearly and distinctively Hebrew. See under "Date" above.

The agreement is *permitted* by:

3. The onomastic features. The PN ברכיהו appears in one provenanced Hebrew seal, two provenanced Hebrew bullae, and one other unprovenanced Hebrew bulla (*WSS*, 490). Although this name is not found in any non-Hebrew inscriptions, PNs formed from the root ברך are in the inscriptions of at least three other socio-political classifications (Fowler, 284). The PN נריהו appears in twenty-five other Hebrew inscriptions: one provenanced and thirteen unprovenanced seals, two provenanced and nine unprovenanced bullae (*WSS*, 516). Inscriptions of at least seven other socio-political classifications contain PNs derived from the root נור or נר (Fowler, 280; *WSS*, 516).

4. The broad language parameters of the inscription, that include Hebrew.

5. The arrangement of the text in three registers in aniconic seals of titled officials is found among unprovenanced Hebrew seals (*WSS*, no. 20, face B, nos. 22, 23, 24, 28, etc.). If there are three or more registers, it is more common to have iconography in one of the registers. Similar layouts are found on unprovenanced seals which are Phoenician (*WSS*, nos. 717, 718, etc.), Ammonite (*WSS*, nos. 876, 985), and Moabite (*WSS*, no. 1010) but apparently not Edomite.

6. The material characteristics of the inscribed object. The back of the bulla bears the impression of unusually coarse papyrus fibers which are not crisscrossed, but rather all point in the same direction. It also exhibits thick, curved

---

[24] Vaughn, "Palaeographic Dating of Judaean Seals," 47, 52–53.

## Fig. 2

**The First-known Bulla
"of Berekyahu, Son of Neriyahu, the Scribe"**

(Drawing by the author)

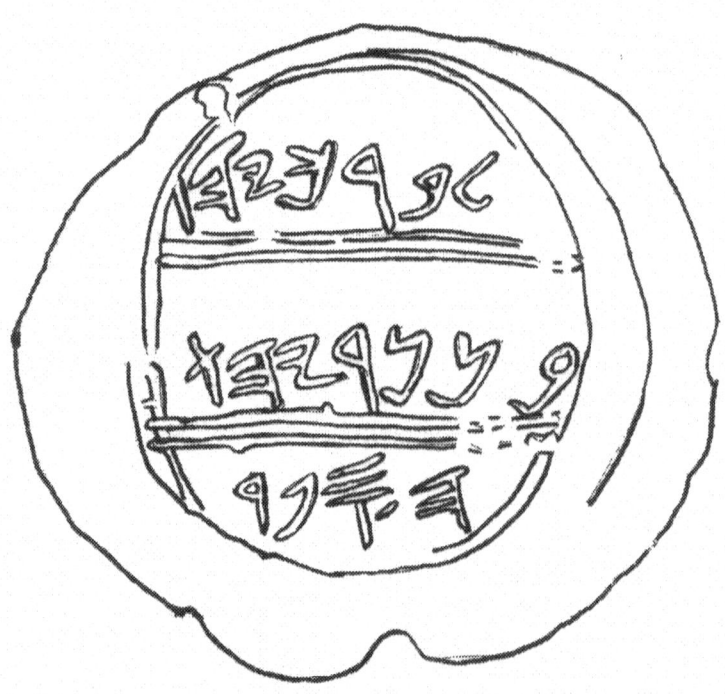

impressions, apparently from the string that tied the document, with some string fibers still present. These two features are also found in provenanced, preexilic bullae of Judah and in a postexilic, Judean archive.[25] Though these features do not prove authenticity or a Judahite origin, they are consistent with them.

## (2.3) Question 3: how strongly the specific data in the inscription count for or against an identification

A check (√) means that a criterion has been met.

√ **Name**: 3) Conversion of a hypocoristicon into the corresponding full form of the name found in the bulla is necessary to make the ID (see person (47) in [57 group] in Appendix B). All twenty-three references to Baruch by name in the Hebrew Bible use the hypocoristicon בָּרוּךְ (Jer 32:12ff).

√ **Relations**: 1) The inscriptional patronymic, i.e., Neriyahu, matches the biblical patronymic. Complete and clearly legible, its full form in the inscription is in exact agreement with the consonants of the less frequent form found in the Hebrew Bible, נריהו, e.g., in Jer 36:14, 32. The consonants of the more frequent biblical form (e.g., in Jer 36:4, referring to the same man) are נריה.

√ **Title**: 4) The title is complete and clearly legible. It is that of a senior government official. The office of scribe is attested in some other Northwest Semitic seals, where it is interpreted as a governmental position. Grammatically, it is ambiguous in its reference. It could be either the title of the seal owner or his father.[26] The context in a hoard of bullae, discussed immediately below, leads to a logical choice. It is important to note that the consonantal text of Jer 36:32 contains a very close parallel to the text of the bulla: "ברוך בן נריהו הספר." This phrase is represented in the Syriac version. That it is not represented in the LXX could be the result of abridgement on the part of the translator.[27] In much of the book of Jeremiah, Baruch seems to be the personal secretary of the prophet Jeremiah, but in Jer 36:10, it becomes clear that he had access to the temple chamber of Gemariah, the son of Shaphan, a top-level governmental official. Further, Baruch was invited into the scribe's chamber in the royal palace (Jer 36:11–14). The fact that he gained access there is perhaps explained best by the possibility that he had at one time been a scribe in the ser-

---

[25] This point is made in *WSS*, 175–76, no. 417. See Avigad, *Bullae and Seals*, Pl. 4b, 7d, 11f; idem, *Hebrew Bullae*, 19, 28, no. 9, photograph.

[26] Avigad, "On the Identification," 236.

[27] Contra William L. Holladay, *Jeremiah 2* (Hermeneia; Minneapolis: Fortress, 1989), 253, and J. Gerald Janzen, *Studies in the Text of Jeremiah* (HSM 6; Cambridge, Mass.: Harvard University Press, 1973), 72, 107, 114. Note Janzen's recognition of a scholarly consensus "that a number of G minuses represent . . . intentional deletion by the translator" (ibid., 87).

vice of the king. At some point, caught in the political tension between the Judahite monarchy and the prophet Jeremiah, who certainly seemed to be pro-Babylonian, Baruch may have been forced to choose between the two.[28]

When purchased, the first-known bulla of Berekyahu "was found among a hoard of bullae of royal officials."[29] Therefore, the title, which most likely designates a government post, should be ascribed to the seal owner, Berekyahu, rather than Neriyahu.[30]

√ **Other**: 1) Other identifying information explicitly agrees with the biblical account. The late seventh- to early sixth-century bulla "of Jerahmeel, the king's son" was discovered in the same hoard of bullae as this one. See Jer 36:26 and section 1.15 above.

Also, although it does not add to the identifying marks, it is consistent with the biblical narrative that this bulla has the marks of papyrus fibers on its reverse side and was somehow fired. These two circumstances fit both the custom of using papyrus for official documents in the late First Temple period and the fact that the Babylonian army burned Jerusalem in 586. The same fire that incinerated the papyrus would have fired the clay bulla, making it a durable ceramic piece. Precisely this process has been archaeologically attested in the finds in the "house of the bullae" in the city of David.[31]

**Singularity**: 3) Available data require no ID on grounds of singularity. The most that can be said is that the four identification criteria that have been met make it extremely unlikely that there was more than one person who fit this description during the time period indicated by the epigraphy.

**Remarks**: The second and third questions have been answered satisfactorily. Under the third question, it meets not three, but four specific identifying criteria. Therefore, it would be legitimate to create a grade 4 for IDs such as this, but, working within the grades as set forth above, this is a grade 3 ID which is virtually certain.

---

[28] Cf. the support for Jeremiah the prophet from the descendants of Shaphan the scribe, perhaps unknown to the monarchy. Shaphan's sons Elasa, Gemariah, and Ahikam, as well as his grandson Gedaliah, all acted on Jeremiah's behalf, perhaps because they also felt that it was best for Judah to submit to Babylon. This family loyalty and the tensions it involved are described and diagrammed in John Rogerson and Philip R. Davies, *The Old Testament World* (Englewood Cliffs, N.J.: Prentice-Hall, 1989), 50–51.

[29] Avigad, "Baruch the Scribe and Jerahmeel the King's Son," 55.

[30] Avigad suggests,
> The presence of Baruch's bulla in an archive amidst bullae of royal officers seems to indicate that at some time Baruch belonged to the category of royal scribes.... Later, however, Baruch apparently gave up his office to join Jeremiah in his religious and political struggle against the policy of the last kings of Judah, which was to result in the destruction of Jerusalem. (Ibid.)

[31] Yigal Shiloh, "A Group of Hebrew Bullae from the City of David," *IEJ* 36 (1986): 25.

It has been observed that it is more difficult for forgers to produce a bulla than a seal, and it is easier to detect a forged bulla than a forged seal.[32] The fact that only one other bulla[33] made from the same seal has surfaced on the antiquities market seems incompatible with the profit motive of forgers and would appear to make forgery unlikely.[34] These observations are in addition to the consensus of experts affirming authenticity.

## 2.4 Grade 2 identifications: reasonable but uncertain

These IDs meet only two specific identifying criteria under the third question, and they are not IDs on grounds of singularity. Although there is some chance of their being correct, from our perspective they cannot be considered reliable IDs, because there remains a reasonable doubt. For example, two individuals might have had the same name and patronym or the same name and title. Although grade 2 IDs are entirely possible and reasonable, they are unresolved.

A cursory inspection of the 1,215 seals and bullae in *WSS*, 49–460, or of the 370 seals and seal impressions in *AHI*, 118–246, reveals that most inscribed seals and bullae include no more than 1) the name of the seal owner and 2) a patronym. It seems obvious that in preexilic times, at least, only two identifying marks usually sufficed. This evidence, which is massive, shows that Avigad's requirement of a third mark in order to make a secure ID can be seen as a modern addition. The third specific identifying mark under question three is a concession to the fact that, more than 2,500 years later, we lack the information found in the original social context which evidently enabled the ancients to make secure IDs with only two specific identifying marks.

That an ancient government might have maintained a central office which kept a list of names and patronyms and that new or prospective parents might

---

[32] In reference to the hoard of Hebrew bullae which includes the bulla of Berekyahu, son of Neriyahu, the scribe (Avigad, *Hebrew Bullae*, 28–29, no. 9), Vaughn observes,

> The authentication of bullae is somewhat easier than with the actual seals. In order to fake a seal, the forger need only fashion and inscribe a semi-precious stone. However, the process required to create a fake bulla is more complicated and entails several steps, thus enabling experts to identify forgeries more readily. Since many experts have examined the bullae published by Avigad and confirmed that they are authentic both in terms of their fabric and in terms of the seal impressions found on them, it seems safe to use this hoard of bullae [to supplement those of known provenance]. (Vaughn, "Chronicler's Account," 24)

[33] The second bulla "of Berekyahu ben Neriyahu, the scribe" is now in the Shlomo Moussaieff collection, London. A computer-enhanced picture of it is on the front cover of *BAR* 22, no. 2 (March/April 1996). A photograph of it appears in ibid, p. 36.

[34] Deutsch and Heltzer, *Forty New*, 37–38, no. (11) 1.

have consulted it before naming babies[35] would seem to be more than a possibility. Rather, a central registry would have been a governmental tool of great practical value for levying taxes, conscripting royal work forces,[36] and raising armies, therefore, it seems likely that something of the sort existed. Nevertheless, the possibility exists that there was not a central registry for the whole of each Hebrew kingdom, but perhaps regional registries, which would have been more easily accessible to regional officials who would have used such lists, as well as to the populace.[37] Theoretically, duplicate combinations of name and patronym could have appeared in separate regional registries. The biblical way of referring to some individuals partly by a reference to their home city or region may suggest the possibility of regional registries of names. Jer 28:1, for example, refers to "Hananiah the son of Azzur, the prophet, who was of Gibeon," as if to distinguish him from other Hananiahs whose fathers were named Azzur, who were from other places. The available evidence, however, is inconclusive.[38]

Treatments of examples of IDs in grades 2, 1, 0, and D will be shorter than those above, because although they help illustrate the complete system, they do not contribute directly to the thesis of this study, as the previous examples did. An example of a grade 2 ID (depending on authenticity) is Asaiah, the king's minister, (2 Kgs 22:12, 14; 2 Chr 34:20) in the seal that was first published in 1994 by Deutsch and Heltzer, who made the ID in that work.[39]

---

[35] See the last paragraph of section 1.13 above.

[36] I.e., הַמַּס in 2 Sam 20:24; 1 Kgs 4:6; 5:28; 9:15; 12:18 (= 2 Chr 10:18). Cf. the seal obv. לפלאיה / ו מתתיהו, rev. אשר על / המס (WSS, 56–57, no. 20, unprovenanced). An alternative term is סֵבֶל in 1 Kgs 11:28. Conscripted labor is also referred to in 1 Kgs 15:22; Jer 22:13–19. Regardless of whether it was given continual, explicit references in scripture, it was a reality of the Hebrew monarchic era.

[37] Fox observes that

... it cannot be assumed that such a system could encompass more than one city and environs. Among royal functionaries, even those residing at court, probably there were natives of towns and cities outside the capital who could have borne identical names and patronyms. (Fox, *In the Service of the King*, 39.)

[38] The following are recorded similarly: "Shimei the son of Gera, the Benjamite, who was of Bahurim" (2 Sam 19:17); "Jeroboam the son of Nebat, an Ephraimite of Zeredah" (1 Kgs 11:26); Amon's "mother's name was Meshullameth, the daughter of Haruz of Jotbah" (2 Kgs 21:19); Josiah's "mother's name was Jedidah, the daughter of Adaiah of Bozkath" (2 Kgs 22:1); Jehoiakim's "mother's name was Zebudah, the daughter of Pedaiah of Rumah" (2 Kgs 23:36); and Jehoiachin's "mother's name was Nehushta, the daughter of Elnathan of Jerusalem" (2 Kgs 24:8). These examples do not prove that regional or urban registries existed; they only suggest the possibility.

[39] Deutsch and Heltzer, *Forty New*, 49–51. This seal is also treated in Hershel Shanks, "Fingerprint of Jeremiah's Scribe," *BAR* 22, no. 2 (March/April 1996): 37–38.

*Taxonomy of Identifications and Two System Refinements* 75

**Fig. 3**

**A Modern Impression of the Seal
"of Asayahu, the King's Minister"**

(Drawing by the author)

Description: This seal of Asaiah is a perforated, reddish limestone scaraboid measuring 16.5 x 13 x 8 mm. A single line surrounds the face of the seal, on which a riderless horse gallops. The inscription above and below the horse reads, לעשיהו / עבד המלך, "Belonging to Asaiah, the king's minister."

## (2.4) Questions 1 and 2: temporarily assumed reliability of inscriptional data and matching settings

Although this seal is unprovenanced, for the sake of an example, we will treat it as if it were provenanced, having reliable data. Although there is no clearly diagnostic letter to narrow the range of possible dates to a shorter span than the eighth to early sixth century,[40] we will assume also that its date matches that of the biblical Asaiah, the king's minister, ca. 622. The Judahite origin in the form of the theophoric ending (-*yahu* rather than -*yaw*) matches.

## (2.4) Question 3: how strongly the specific data in the inscription count for or against an identification

A check (√) means that a criterion has been met.

√ **Name**: 2) Spelling does not agree precisely with the consonants of any biblical spelling of the candidate's name, but the difference is negligible, i.e., the ending -*yah* in one source and the ending -*yahu* in the other source. Here the inscription has a final *waw*, but the biblical occurrences do not (2 Kgs 22:12, 14; 2 Chr 34:20). (In Appendix B, see person (40) in seal [53].)

**Relations**: 6) Although some relational information appears both in the inscription and in the Bible (see Title), it includes no names.

√ **Title**: 1) Title is complete, clearly belongs to the inscriptional candidate and matches that of the biblical person (2 Kgs 22:12; 2 Chr 34:20).

**Other**: 3) Other identifying information is vague in its significance. Red limestone was probably not especially valuable, and the depiction of a horse on a seal has no known relevance to a specific identifying mark.

**Singularity**: 3) Available data require no ID on grounds of singularity. It cannot be demonstrated that there was only one Asaiah who was the king's minister during the time period indicated by the epigraphy. Indeed, this name is one

---

[40] The *he* in the upper line cannot definitely be considered diagnostic because, although the two lower crossbars tend to converge toward the open side of the letter, available photographs leave some doubt as to whether the top crossbar clearly extends to the other side of the vertical shaft (cf. Vaughn, "Palaeographic Dating of Judaean Seals," 47, 52–53), notwithstanding the top crossbar going beyond the vertical shaft in Deutsch's drawing (Deutsch and Heltzer, *Forty New*, 50, Fig. 21).

of the most frequently attested in Hebrew epigraphy; yet on the other hand, the title עבד המלך is attested less than a dozen times in seals and bullae.[41]

**Remarks**: Although the inscription contains two marks of a particular individual, more than one Asaiah could have held this title at this same time. Therefore, this conditional grade 2 ID would not be secure even if proven genuine. The possibility only invites Avigad's "reasonable assumption."

## 2.5 Grade 1 identifications: doubtful

These IDs meet only one specific identifying criterion under question three and have no grounds of singularity. Their chance of being correct is remote.

An example of a grade 1 ID is Zechariah, king of Israel (r. 750/49; 2 Kgs 14:29; 15:8–11), in the Tel Dan jar-handle seal impression of Zecharyaw, unearthed in 1988 and published by Avraham Biran in 1992.[42]

Description: This jar-handle seal impression of Zekaryaw is an oval whose face measures 2 cm. x 1.5 cm. A double line marks the edge of the impression, on which five letters appear on an open field, the first three letters above the last two, with no line between them. The inscription consists of one PN, זכר / יו.

### (2.5) Questions 1 and 2: reliable data and matching settings

This excavated inscription provides reliable data. It is dated paleographically to the mid-eighth century, and several factors indicate that it is Israelite. It matches the setting of Zechariah, king of Israel.

---

[41] Deutsch and Heltzer, *Forty New*, 49. The infrequent attestation of this title suggests that many other seals and bullae bearing this title have not been recovered, because administration of a kingdom undoubtedly required many. Apart from this:
> ... The real reason few bullae have been found is that bullae are small, and sieving is not yet widely practiced. Also, to the uninitiated, an unbaked clay bulla looks like an ordinary lump of clay if it is not carefully examined. (King, *Jeremiah*, 93)

And with regard to ostraca,
> Aharoni . . . introduced the practice of soaking and dipping sherds in water and then inspecting them carefully for possible inscriptions before proceeding with the more vigorous washing process. The traditional procedure of scrubbing the pottery with a brush without dipping in advance may have obliterated countless inscriptions from ostraca (ibid., 100).

[42] Avraham Biran, *Biblical Dan* (Jerusalem: Israel Exploration Society and Hebrew Union College-Jewish Institute of Religion, 1994), 255, 258, Fig. 213; *WSS*, 246, no. 669; *AHI*, 243, no. 100.882. The Hebrew version of Biran, *Biblical Dan*, appeared in 1992. For a photograph of the jar handle and the drawing of the seal impression, see *BAR* 20, no. 2 (March/April 1994), 32.

**Fig. 4**

**The Tel Dan Jar handle Seal Impression, "Zekaryaw"**

(Drawing by the author)

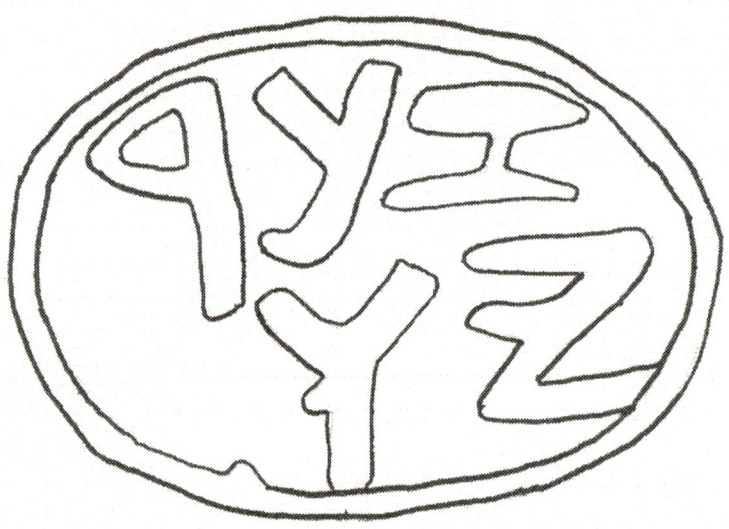

## (2.5) Question 3: identifying mark(s) in the inscription

A check (√) means that a criterion has been met.

√ **Name**: 2) The inscriptional spelling זכריו does not agree precisely with the consonants of either biblical spelling of the name, זכריהו or זכריה. The inscriptional spelling in fact includes the common way of spelling the Yahwistic theophoric ending in the northern kingdom of Israel.[43] The different biblical spelling can be attributed to leveling on the part of the scribes who transmitted the text using spellings common in Judah. (See person (13) in Appendix B.)

**Relations**: 5) In the inscription, a patronymic is absent; there is none to match or contradict the biblical patronymic, Jeroboam (2 Kgs 14:29; 15:8).

**Title**: 7) An inscriptional title is absent.

**Other**: 5) Other identifying information is absent.

**Singularity**: 3) Available data require no ID on grounds of singularity.

**Remarks**: Any attempted ID would rest on only one point: the seal owner's name. A large number of individuals in the kingdom of Israel bore this name. That this one should be the king or a then-future king is very unlikely. A high degree of unlikelihood characterizes all grade 1 IDs.

## 2.6 Grade 0 (zero) non-identifications: without any clear basis

Because grade 0 non-IDs lack clear data which might serve as a basis for meeting identification criteria, they cannot be considered IDs, but rather are non-IDs. Usually because of missing letters or difficulties with intelligibility, these non-IDs *might* meet but do not necessarily meet any identifying criteria and have no grounds of singularity. Their chance of being correct is infinitesimal.

An example of a grade 0 non-ID is Hophni, the son of Eli the priest, (1 Sam 1:3ff) in the ʿIzbet Ṣarṭah ostracon, which was first published by Moshe Kochavi in 1977.[44] William H. Shea made the ID in 1990.[45]

---

[43] See Chapter 3, note 136.

[44] Moshe Kochavi, "An Ostracon of the Period of the Judges from ʿIzbet Ṣarṭah," *TA* 4/1–2 (1977): 1–13.

[45] William H. Shea, "ʿIzbet Ṣarṭah Ostracon," *AUSS* 28 (1990): 59–86. For a treatment of Shea's attempt, see Lawrence J. Mykytiuk, "Is Hophni in the ʿIzbet Ṣarṭah Ostracon?" *AUSS* 36 (1998): 69–80. A response is found in William H. Shea, "Hophni in the ʿIzbet Ṣarṭah Ostracon: A Rejoinder," *AUSS* 36 (1998): 277–78, to which Mykytiuk did not reply. Works which treat this ostracon in general are Frank M. Cross, "Newly Found Inscriptions in Old Canaanite and Early Phoenician Scripts," *BASOR* 238 (Spring 1980): 1–20; Aaron Demsky, "The ʿIzbet Sartah Ostracon Ten Years Later," in Israel Finkelstein, *ʿIzbet Ṣarṭah: An Early Iron Age Site Near Rosh Haʿayin, Israel* (British Archaeological Reports International Series 299; Oxford, England: B.A.R., 1986), 186–97;

80    *Identifying Biblical Persons in Northwest Semitic Inscriptions*

Description: The ʿIzbet Ṣarṭah ostracon is an approximately trapezoidal sherd from a large storage jar, 9 cm. wide, 16 cm. long, and an average of 8 mm thick. Five bent lines of Proto-Canaanite letters are incised on its surface. The scratches that form the letters are never more than 0.1 mm. wide and deep. Line 5 is clearly an abecedary to be read from left to right. It is scratched more deeply than lines 1 through 4. The shallowness of the slight scratches that form the letters in the first four lines has produced much uncertainty regarding the presence of many letters. The number of letters scholars read in lines 1 through 4 varies from sixty-one to eighty-one! Also, the identity of many letters is uncertain.[46]

### (2.6) Questions 1 and 2: reliable data and matching settings

This inscription, recovered in Moshe Kochavi's 1976 excavation and now on display in the Israel Museum (identification number IDAM 801), is dated between the late thirteenth century and the end of the twelfth.[47] Still, a date in the first half of the eleventh century is not out of the question. That would place it at the time the Bible assigns to Hophni, son of Eli. Although it could be Canaanite or Philistine, its provenance makes the author most likely a Hebrew.

### (2.6) Question 3: how strongly the specific data in the inscription count for or against an identification

A check with a question mark (√?) means that it is uncertain whether a criterion has been met.

√? **Name**: 8) It is uncertain whether the letters represent a personal name. In the first part of line 4, Shea's perceived letter sequence *heth, pe, nun*, read from left to right (biblical חׇפְנִי defectively spelled?) is questionable as to its presence and order. Some scholars read *gimel* instead of *pe*.[48] In the literature, only one perceives a *nun* here.[49] It is further questionable whether these

---

Aron Dotan, "New Light on the ʿIzbet Ṣarṭah Ostracon," *TA* 8 (1981): 160–72; Benjamin Sass, *The Genesis of the Alphabet and Its Development in the Second Millenium* [sic] B.C. (Ägypten und altes Testament 13; Wiesbaden: Harrassowitz, 1988), 65–69, 106–34, 152–56, 185 Table 6, Pl. 175–77.

[46] Kochavi, "Ostracon of the Period," 4–5; Cross, "Newly Found Inscriptions," 9; Dotan, "New Light," 161, 167; Sass, *Genesis of the Alphabet*, 67; Shea, "ʿIzbet Ṣarṭah Ostracon," 62. See the summary tables in Mykytiuk, "Is Hophni," 74–77.

[47] The chronological chart in Sass, *Genesis of the Alphabet*, 155, dates the script paleographically between ca. 1230 and 1100. Most scholars adopt a twelfth-century date. Light," 161. Sass reads it as either *pe* or *gimel* (Sass, *Genesis of the Alphabet*, 67).

[49] Shea, "ʿIzbet Ṣarṭah Ostracon," 62, 77.

*Taxonomy of Identifications and Two System Refinements* 81

### Fig. 5

### Portions of the 'Izbet Sartah Ostracon

(Drawings courtesy of *Andrews University Seminary Studies*)

These drawings present one scholar's changing perceptions. The point is that with many faint scratches on the ostracon, one can overlook or perceive "letters" which might easily have been "written" by random scratches made with or without human agency, as earthquakes apparently jostled this potsherd upward, into the stratum above its original stratum.

Immediately below is an excerpt from William H. Shea's first published drawing of the ostracon (1990). It includes three letters which he perceives in the sequence *ḥeth, pe, nun* (double-underlining of these letters below is mine). He reads these as a proper noun, the PN Hophni, followed by an *aleph*, which he understands to be the first letter of a following word. (Because of the direction of writing from *aleph* to *tav* in the abecedary in line 5, it is generally agreed that the Proto-Canaanite letters in this ostracon are to be read from left to right.)

line 4a

Below is Shea's entire second published drawing (1998) of part of the very same ostracon. It consists of only part of line 4a, because it is part of a reply to adverse criticism of his identification of the biblical Hophni, son of Eli the priest, in this ostracon. This time, he perceives the letter sequence *ḥeth, pe, nun*, and *yodh*, followed by an *aleph*, and he interprets this different sequence also as the PN Hophni followed by an *aleph*. Note the difference in the size and shape of the newly perceived *nun* superscripted over the *pe*, the disappearance (without explanation) of the larger supposed *nun* seen above the *pe* in his previous drawing, and, above the *aleph*, a newly perceived letter, which he claims is a *yodh*

line 4a

perceived letters form a common noun with first person pronominal suffix or a proper noun. (See person (1) and inscription [1] in Appendix B.)

**Relations**: 7) It is uncertain whether family or other relational information is present in the inscription and, if present, whether it applies to the candidate for an ID. Only one scholar finds a reference to a relative, Hophni's brother Phinehas, but that reference as he perceives it does not name Phinehas.[50]

**Title**: 7) A title is absent in the inscription.

**Other**: 5) Other identifying information appears to be absent.

**Singularity**: 3) No ID is required on grounds of singularity.

**Remarks**: The inscription is unintelligible, either because it does not consist of words, let alone words in syntax, or because its language is not understood. The two attempts to treat it as readable have produced utterly different translations.[51] Most scholars view this inscription as a penmanship exercise that never was intelligible. The reading of the name Hophni is fraught with serious difficulties. No ID can be made, because identifying information is either unintelligible or, almost certainly, absent.

## 2.7 Grade D non-identifications: disqualified

It is known or virtually certain that these non-IDs fail to answer one or more of the three questions satisfactorily; thus they are disqualified.

An example of a grade D non-ID is "Jotham," son of Uzziah, king of Judah (2 Kgs 15:5ff), formerly thought to be mentioned in the seal ring of Yatom from Tell el-Kheleifeh. This seal ring was first published in a 1940 article by Nelson Glueck, in which also he was the first to make the ID.[52]

Description: This copper signet ring contains a stone seal 12 mm. wide and 15 mm. long. An approximately oval line surrounds the face of the seal. Inscribed on the face, above a side view of a striding, horned ram is ליתם, "belonging to *Yatom*." In front of the ram is an unknown object or letter shaped like the English capital letter H with an extremely thick crossbar.

## (2.7) Questions 1 and 2: reliable data, but very different settings

This seal ring is authentic. Its provenance could well have been within Uzziah's, Jotham's, and Ahaz's realm. At other times, the territory in which it was discovered was Edomite.

---

[50] Ibid., 62, 76–78.
[51] Dotan, "New Light," 160–71; Shea, "ʿIzbet Ṣarṭah Ostracon," 59–86.
[52] Glueck, "Third Season," 2–18, see especially 13, 14, Fig. 8 and 9, 15; *WSS*, 392, no. 1054, where it is classified as an Edomite seal.

*Taxonomy of Identifications and Two System Refinements* 83

**Fig. 6**

**A Modern Impression of the Seal Ring "of Yatom"**

(Drawing by the author)

Nevertheless, there is about a century of difference between the date of the seal ring, i.e., the first half or the middle of the seventh century, and the dates of the biblical King Jotham, who ruled ca. 758/7–742/1 (person (21) in Appendix B). Paleographic analysis indicates that the script is not Hebrew, but Edomite (or, less likely, Moabite).[53] The provenance, combined with the seventh-century date, strongly supports an Edomite socio-political classification.[54] Because these factors disagree with the expectation of an eighth-century Judahite classification raised by the biblical account of Jotham, king of Judah, the ID must be disqualified. Because the answer to the second question, regarding settings, is unsatisfactory, it would be pointless to consider question three (see section 1.9 above).

## 2.8 The place of explanatory hypotheses in evaluation

An explanatory hypothesis is not a fact but a thought brought in to explain certain phenomena or facts in a situation. Although these may suggest such a hypothesis, they do not demonstrate it. A good example is the potential ID of J(eh)oram, king of Israel, son of Ahab, in the Aramaic stele discovered at Tel Dan, which is listed and evaluated in Appendixes B and C. How strong is the case for such an ID? Let us assume here, for the sake of an example, that the date and socio-political identity of the stele are appropriate for such an ID, but that the only data in the inscription that specifically support *this* ID are the two consonants רם- followed by the word בר. We have what might potentially be the last two consonants of the name Joram or Jehoram. Since the stele elsewhere mentions "the king of Israel," it is entirely possible that the remaining letter sequence [יו]רם . בר . [אחאב] . / . מלך . ישראל, i.e., "[Jo]ram, the son of [Ahab,] / the king of Israel." Yet this "ID" is not an ID at all, but rather a hypothesis intended to explain the appear-

---

[53] This disagreement in dating is determined by epigraphy alone. The high upper horizontal stroke and slightly raised foot of the *yodh* strongly resemble *yodh* in the late eighth or early seventh century Moabite seal of כמש / יהי (*SANSS*, 158, no. 7, Fig. 75). The *taw*, like the English letter X except for a long, high upper left arm, is most like that in the seal of בעלנתן (ibid., 158, no. 8, Fig. 75), which is clearly seventh century (Herr feels it is probably from the second half) and is probably Moabite. This form of *taw* seems to be peculiar to Moabite and Edomite inscriptions. The form of the *mem* is apparently distinctively Edomite. The "double-L" head is common to Hebrew and Moabite *mem*, but a three-stroke version of it attached to a nearly straight vertical shaft appears only in Edomite inscriptions, such as the seal impression of קוסג . . . מלכא (ibid., 162, no. 1, Fig. 78) and the seal of שמעאל (ibid., 165, no. 5, Fig. 78), both from the first half of the seventh century.

[54] The Edomites occupied the territory at the northern tip of the Gulf of Aqaba from a time early in the reign of Ahaz (r. 742/1–726), Jotham's successor (2 Kgs 16:5, 6).

## Taxonomy of Identifications and Two System Refinements 85

pearance of the letters . בר . םר- in this fragment and possibly also the appearance of the phrase מלך . ישראל on a different fragment (see section 3.5 below). That "Joram" is a hypothesis becomes clear when one considers that for all we know, םר- could be part of the PNs אבירם, אחירם, אדנירם, vel cetera.

Explanatory hypotheses deserve to be considered, but they are too uncertain to be given weight in the identification process. They should not be allowed to change the grade of an ID, but they may be acknowledged as a "decimal" and be given one "tenth" for each of the extant letters of the potential name Joram (though it is really an integer to the right of a period). Here, then, we have a grade 0.2 ID.[55] Normally, explanatory hypotheses are noted in grade 2, 1, or 0 IDs. Grades S and 3 have no need to be buttressed by them.

It is important to distinguish between criterion 10, other identifying information, which includes merely factual data, and hypotheses, which are not facts. Identifying data in criterion 10 can, in some instances, provide one of three identifying marks needed for an assured ID, but explanatory hypotheses cannot.

### 2.9 Historical frameworks to minimize the danger of circularity

The remaining sections in this chapter deal with the question of the *interpretation* of inscriptions. The system must include well-defined steps to prevent the interpretive process from falling victim to circular reasoning.

### 2.10 Potential circularity in the interpretation of inscriptional data

If inscriptional data are interpreted according to biblical data and then compared with biblical data, there is a risk of circular reasoning which will bias the results in the direction of making biblical IDs in the inscriptions.[56] In order

---

[55] Because of the uncertain nature of hypotheses, even ten of them ought not to raise the grade of an ID to the next higher whole number. If, e.g., eleven hypotheses based on eleven observations about an inscription were formulated, they would add .11 to the grade, rather than 1.1. The .11 should be understood as an integer following a dividing period, not as tenths or hundredths.

[56] After this identification system was designed, its author learned that Smelik follows a similar methodological pattern of isolating biblical materials from extrabiblical materials, then comparing the results of an examination of each (Klaas A. D. Smelik, *Converting the Past: Studies in Ancient Israelite and Moabite Historiography*, [OtSt 28; New York: Brill, 1992], 22–25). "Only in the final stage is the evidence from the biblical and extrabiblical sources combined for historical reconstruction. We have postponed doing this up till now in order to avoid circular arguments" (ibid., 25).

Cf. some alleged "confirmations of the Bible" of which Miller speaks: "Obviously, when a written source has served as a determining factor in the interpretation of any

to avoid such circularity in interpretation, the independence of the inscriptional data must be preserved by avoiding the use of biblical material to interpret it. This study attempts to interpret inscriptions according to historical frameworks constructed from inscriptional data, rather than according to biblical material.

Avoiding the use of the Bible in interpreting inscriptions, however, is extremely difficult. Ever since the beginnings of scientific archaeology in the nineteenth century, when there was little else to use as a guide, archaeologists in the Middle East have understandably consulted the Bible. The result today is that the influence of the Bible is widespread in the fields of ancient Near Eastern archaeology, chronology, and history. One might easily use biblically based concepts, data, interpretations, or evaluations without even being aware of doing so. Nevertheless, this study tries to avoid biblical influence as much as possible within the constraints of research requirements. That is, it does not attempt to eliminate all biblical influence from the fields of archaeology and history; such a project could take lifetimes. Instead, it simply acknowledges the existing influence and attempts to limit as much as possible its effects on this study.

## 2.11 The purpose and composition of historical frameworks

The immediate purpose of the historical frameworks used in this study is to determine on a purely inscriptional basis whether specific social structures and individuals existed. They do not need to be anything more than elementary outlines, built on inscriptional data, registering the existence, approximate location, and occasionally some distinctive facts about the political entities and the persons whom the inscriptions mention. In order to construct such frameworks, it is not necessary to include all the various kinds of detailed information supplied by an exhaustive corpus, but rather only information which is *most closely related to the potential IDs evaluated in later chapters*. Avoiding many details, and with them many controversies, each section sets forth a relatively simple historical framework for the interpretation of the inscription under consideration. In Chapters 3 and 4, as each inscription is interpreted in light of its framework, it also adds to it.

## 2.12 The procedure of evaluation

In order to minimize circularity, Chapters 3 and 4 consider each inscription in a three-part discussion:

---

given archaeological data, it is misleading to cite the interpreted archaeological data in turn as 'proof' of the accuracy of the written source" (J. Maxwell Miller, *The Old Testament and the Historian* [GBS, Old Testament Series; Philadelphia: Fortress Press, 1976], 47).

1. The first part describes the inscription itself, presenting part or all of its text, with an English translation. Next, this part asks how reliable are the inscriptional data, considering Criteria 1 through 3. Then this part considers the general setting of the inscription by itself: date, language, and socio-political classification. These three attributes are the inscriptional side of Criteria 4 through 6, which are described in sections 1.25–1.27.

2. The second part presents matters related to the historical framework at the level of social hierarchies and, if appropriate, in the identity of individuals named in other inscriptions. First, it interprets the inscription according to the framework. Second, it observes the contributions of the inscription to the historical framework, which, for Hebrew inscriptions, grows through these chapters. Thus far, biblical data have not yet been considered.

3. After the two preparatory parts, which attempt to isolate inscriptional data from biblical data, the third part under each inscription evaluates the potential ID by comparing data from inscriptional sources and data from biblical sources in order to answer the second and third questions.

## 2.13 An example of the anti-circular identification system: Is the biblical Hoshea, king of Israel, named in the seal of Abdi?

On the inscription itself, how reliable its data may be, and the inscriptional side of Criteria 4 (date), 5 (language), and 6 (socio-political classification), see section 2.2 above.

### (2.13) Historical framework: Does the seal of Abdi, the minister of Hoshea, *correlate* with it? If so, how?

In light of Assyrian inscriptions, which name seven kings of the northern kingdom of Israel who are also named in the Hebrew Bible,[57] it is possible ten-

---

[57] 1. Omri: earliest attestations of the name of Omri as a ruler in Syria-Palestine are: a) in one of the epigraphs labeling the reliefs on the Black Obelisk of Shalmaneser III, b) in a long version of the annals of Shalmaneser III, and c) on the Kurbaʾil statue of Shalmaneser III, all of which mention Omri as an ancestor of Jehu:

a) The epigraph over relief B on the Black Obelisk discovered at Calah (BM 118885 = 48-11-4,1), line 1, names ᵐ*ia-ú-a* DUMU ᵐ*ḫu-um-ri-i*, "Jehu son of Omri," in connection with tribute received from him during the eighteenth year of Shalmaneser III, i.e., 841 (Grayson, *Assyrian Rulers (858–745 BC)*, 149, A.0.102.88 [for the narration on the Black Obelisk, see 3:63–71, A.O. 102.14]; Galil, *Chronology*, 153; *ANET*, 281).

b) The long version of the annals of Shalmaneser III, which closes with the date of the twentieth year of his reign (839), is on a large stone tablet discovered in the outer

tatively to interpret this seal as that of a minister of Hoshea, king of Israel, who, according to an inscription of Tiglath-pileser III, succeeded Pekah as king, and whose rule began during the reign of that same Tiglath-pileser (r. 744–727).

---

wall of Aššur (IM 55644). The reference to "Jehu son of Omri" is in col. 4, line 11: <sup>m</sup>ia-a-ú DUMU <sup>m</sup>ḫu-um-ri-i (Grayson, *Assyrian Rulers (858–745 BC)*, 54, col. 4, line 11 of A.0.102.10; Galil, *Chronology*, 153).

c) The inscription on the "Kurbaʾil statue" of Shalmaneser III dedicated to Adad (a DN) of Kurbaʾil (a GN), discovered at Calah and dated to 839 or 838 (ND 10000; IM 60497), lines 29–30, refers to "Jehu son of Omri," <sup>m</sup>ia-ú-a DUMU <sup>m</sup>ḫu-um-ri-i (Grayson, *Assyrian Rulers (858–745 BC)*, 60, lines 29–30 of A.0.102.12; Galil, *Chronology*, 153).

All three of the latter references document that during the reign of Shalmaneser III, Omri became so noteworthy that his name was incorporated into customary Assyrian terminology referring to the kingdom of Israel.

2. Ahab: a monolith inscription of Shalmaneser III (r. 858–824) assigns to the sixth year of his reign a reference to the military forces of "Ahab the Israelite" at the Battle of Qarqar in 853 (the Kurkh Monolith of Shalmaneser III [BM118884], col. 2, lines 91–92; Grayson, *Assyrian Rulers (858–745 BC)*, 23, col. 2, lines 91–92 of A.0.102.2; RawlCu 3, Pl. 7–8; *ANET*, 279; Galil, *Chronology*, 153).

3. "Jehu [<sup>m</sup>ia-ú-a or <sup>m</sup>ia-a-ú] son of Omri" is first mentioned in Assyrian inscriptions as a payer of tribute during the eighteenth year of Shalmaneser III (841), according to the latter's Black Obelisk. But the Bible clearly calls Jehu "the son of Jehoshaphat, the son of Nimshi" in 2 Kgs 9:2, 14. A genuine contradiction seems evident. On whether Jehu was really a descendant of Omri, see Galil, *Chronology*, 33, n. 2; *CAH*, vol. 3, no. 2, 490; Tammi J. Schneider, "Did King Jehu Kill His Own Family?" *BAR* 21, no. 1 (January/ February 1995): 26–33, 80, 82; idem, "Rethinking Jehu," *Biblica* 77 (1996): 100–107.

4. "Joash the Samarian" (<sup>m</sup>ia-ʾa-su KUR sa-me-ri-na-a-a) paid tribute to Adad-Nirari III (r. 810–783), according to the latter's Tell al-Rimah inscription (Stephanie Page, "A Stela of Adad-Nirari III," *Iraq* 30 [1968]:142–45, line 8, Pl. 38–41; read as <sup>m</sup>iu-ʾa-su in Grayson, *Assyrian Rulers (858–745 BC)*, 211, line 8 of A.0.104.7, now in the Iraq Museum; Galil, *Chronology*, 153).

5. Menahem: according to the annalistic records on slabs from Calah, Tiglath-pileser III (r. 744–727) in an unknown year "received tribute . . . from Menahem the Samarian" (<sup>m</sup>me-ni-ḫi-im-me URUsa-me-ri-na-a-a) (The Calah Annals of Tiglath-pileser III, Annal 13, line 10; *ITP*, 68–69, Pl. IX; *ANET*, 283; Galil, *Chronology*, 153).

6 and 7. As for Pekah and Hoshea, a fragmentary annalistic text, also from an unknown year of Tiglath-pileser III, records: "The land of Israel (KUR bît ḫu-um-ri-a), . . . [. . .] its] 'auxiliary army,' [. . .] all of its people, [. . .] I carried off to Assyria. Pekah (<sup>[m]</sup>pa-qa-ḫa) their king [I/they killed] and I installed Hoshea (<sup>m</sup>a-ú-si-ʾi) [as king] over them" (Summary [alias Display; see *ITP*, 25] Inscription 4, discovered at Calah on a fragmentary slab and left *in situ*, lines 15–18 (*ITP*, 140–41, Pl. XLIX–LI; RawlCu 3, Pl. 10, no. 2); *ANET*, 284; Galil, *Chronology*, 153).

**(2.13) Historical framework: If the authenticity of the seal of Abdi, the minister of Hoshea, were verified, how would this seal *contribute* to it?**

The seal of Abdi would provide Israelite inscriptional corroboration to the reference to Hoshea, king of Israel, in the fragmentary annalistic text of Tiglath-pileser III, who claimed in that text to have made Hoshea king.[58]

**(2.13) Question 2: Provided the seal of Abdi, the minister of Hoshea, were authentic, would its setting *permit* a match?**

Yes. See section 2.2 above for a comparison of the inscriptional and the biblical setting (Criteria 4, 5, and 6: date, language, socio-political classification) related to matching the inscriptional person and the biblical person.

**(2.13) Question 3: Provided it were authentic, how strongly would specific data in [15] the seal לעבדי / עבד הושע count for or against an identification with the biblical (16) Hoshea, son of Elah, king of Israel (2 Kgs 15:30ff; r. 732/1–722)?[59]**

The specific identifying criteria (Criteria 7 through 11: name, interpersonal relations, title, other identifying information, and identification on grounds of singularity) are exactly the same as those listed above in section 2.2, and there is no change in the discussion or the conclusions in that section. Provided the inscription is authentic, this ID is required on grounds of biblical singularity.

The above example illustrates the three-part discussion: the inscription itself, the inscription within a historical framework derived from inscriptional sources, and a comparison of data from the inscription and from the Bible in order to answers questions 2 and 3. Chapters 3 and 4 provide more examples.

---

[58] See the last paragraph of the preceding note.
[59] The number of each person is indicated in parentheses ( ) and the number of each inscription is indicated in brackets [ ]. The order in Appendix B determines the numbers.

# PART 2

## APPLICATION OF THE IDENTIFICATION SYSTEM TO HEBREW INSCRIPTIONS AND TWO STELAE FROM BEFORE THE PERSIAN ERA PUBLISHED BEFORE OCTOBER 1997

# Chapter 3

# Identifications in Provenanced Inscriptions

## 3.1 The scope and possible evidential value of potential identifications evaluated in Chapters 3 and 4

Chapters 3 and 4 comprise a corpus of all (or almost all) pre-Persian-era *Hebrew* inscriptions published before October 1997 that name biblical persons. In Appendix C, sections C1 through C4 expand this corpus, attempting to include all pre-Persian-era *Northwest Semitic* inscriptions naming biblical persons. Until now, no book or article in print has listed *as such* all known, extant Hebrew inscriptions or Northwest Semitic inscriptions of any period that name such persons. Chapters 3 and 4 include only inscriptions that fall within all of the following parameters:

1. They were actually available in published form in the United States before the beginning of October 1997.

2. They are all from periods before the Persian era, i.e., before 539 B.C.E.

3. They are Hebrew inscriptions, or they are stelae containing historical data directly related to the kingdoms of Israel or Judah. The term "Hebrew inscriptions" refers to the language in which they are written. Although very short inscriptions frequently do not contain enough linguistic data to make clear the identity of the language, still their script, provenance, and/or theophoric endings

can indicate that they are from a Hebrew-speaking kingdom, whether the united kingdom of Israel, the northern kingdom of Israel, or the kingdom of Judah.[1]

It is appropriate to include the Mesha Inscription and the Tel Dan stele, because their narrative form and fragmentary state serve to illustrate the capabilities and limitations of the identification system. They are also appropriate for inclusion in light of the historical interest which partly motivates this study, because their content is directly related to the history of the Hebrew kingdoms. Unfortunately, lack of space prohibits treatment of the Aramaic inscriptions which, according to preliminary evaluations, offer more than fifteen other, strong IDs of rulers (see section 0.1 above). Nor does this study propose to focus on the corpora of all Egyptian, Assyrian, Babylonian, and other inscriptions which relate to the history of Israel and Judah. Instead, it uses the most relevant of these others to provide historical frameworks for interpreting inscriptions.

4. They are relevant to the thesis of this study. Therefore, Chapters 3 and 4 cover only inscriptions which offer IDs in grades S (i.e., SI and/or SB) and 3 (see sections 2.2 and 2.3 above). Not included are grade 2 (reasonable assumptions that are ultimately unresolved) and grades 1, 0, and D, because they neither support nor contradict the thesis (stated in section 0.2 above). Rather, they simply indicate inscriptions which, after evaluation, offer no clear, reliable matches with biblical persons. To observe the overall scope of the preliminary investigations of materials that later proved to be relevant or irrelevant, see Appendix B or C. The mere fact that *then-potential* (but unproven) *candidates* for IDs appear in those appendixes *does not necessarily mean* that these biblical persons are to be identified in any inscription at all.

This study seeks to measure the strength of potential IDs only between individuals whose PNs appear in the sources. It does not attempt to make IDs by tracing connections between PNs and GNs or between PNs and clan or tribal names, e.g, Ḥeleq, Ḥoglah, or Levi, or between PNs and kingdom names, e.g., Israel, Judah, Ammon, Moab, or Edom.[2] Of these, the names mentioned in

---

[1] It is unnecessary to show that the people of these two kingdoms spoke Hebrew, as attested by the many hundreds of Hebrew inscriptions discovered in the territory held by these two kingdoms in ancient times.

[2] This study does not cover, e.g., the six GNs in the Samaria Ostraca which appear to be the same as the names of clans or of tribal subdivisions of Manasseh named after their progenitors in Num 26:29–33 and Josh 17:2–3: Abiezer, Ḥeleq, Shechem, Shemidaʿ, Noah, and Ḥoglah (*DOTT*, 205). Nor does this study cover such things as a fragment of a game board discovered at Beth-Shemesh and inscribed with the PN Ḥanan, which may or may not relate to the GN Elon Beth-Ḥanan in 1 Kgs 4:9 (Shlomo Bunimovitz and Zvi Lederman, "Beth-Shemesh: Culture Conflict on Judah's Frontier," *BAR* 23, no. 1 [January/February 1997]: 48). To undertake the identification of individuals

Egyptian and Assyrian sources appear not as PNs, but as GNs or the names of socio-political groups.

### 3.2 The order of research and presentation

The first step in the research for this book was to gather the publications, both of provenanced and of unprovenanced inscriptions. (The dissertation was written and defended without any access to *WSS*; see Preface.) Then it was necessary to evaluate all potential IDs treated in the original version of Appendix B and to classify them in grades S through D, as defined in sections 2.2 through 2.7 above. This study took those in grades S and 3 that fit the above parameters and treated them in Chapter 3 or 4. In order to begin with the most reliable data, this chapter treats the IDs furnished by provenanced inscriptions. Chapter 4 treats those in unprovenanced inscriptions. Chapter 5 tabulates the results of all previous chapters, and Appendixes B, C, and F gather and tabulate the results for the larger, Northwest Semitic corpus.

### 3.3 Is the biblical Mesha, king of Moab, named in the Mesha Inscription?

**Description, transcription, and translation**

The thirty-four extant lines of the Mesha Inscription[3] are engraved across the face of the Moabite Stone, a smoothed, aniconic block of basalt approximately 1 m. tall, 60 cm. wide, and 60 cm. thick (Clermont-Ganneau's measurements). Its most relevant lines, including Lemaire's improved readings,[4] appear below:

---

from GNs, clan names, or national names would be a more complicated and hazardous attempt to demonstrate more than this study attempts, with less evidence than this study uses. That evidence also seems less clear than that which is used here.

[3] The first publication about the Mesha Inscription is a letter from Charles Clermont-Ganneau to E. Melchior Comte de Vogüé which was published in Paris in 1870.

[4] In line 12 Lemaire reads היה instead of the problematic ריה, which appears in earlier treatments of the Mesha Inscription, and in line 31, he supplies the *daleth* in בת[ד]וד. These readings appear in André Lemaire, "'House of David' Restored in Moabite Inscription," *BAR* 20, no. 3 (May/June 1994): 33. His reading, "house of [Da]vid," in line 31 appears also in idem, "La dynastie Davidique (*byt dwd*) dans deux inscriptions ouest-sémitiques du IXe s. av. J.-C.," *SEL* 11 (1994): 17–19. For a systematic evaluation of the potential ID of King David in line 31, see Appendix E below. To understand why chapter 3 does not include the evaluation of the potential ID of King David in the Mesha Inscription, which is instead placed in Appendix E, there see note 3.

*Identifying Biblical Persons in Northwest Semitic Inscriptions*

| line | |
|---|---|
| 1 | אנך · משע · בן · כמש[ית] · מלך · מאב · הד |
| 2 | יבני | אבי · מלך · על · מאב · שלשן · שת · ואנך · מלב |
| 3 | תי · אחר · אבי | ואעש · הבמת · זאת · לכמש · בקרחה · במ[ת · י] |
| 4 | שע · כי · השעני · מכל · השלכן · וכי · הראני · בכל · שנאי | עמר |
| 5 | י · מלך · ישראל · ויענו · את · מאב · ימן · רבן · כי · יאנף · כמש · באר |
| 6 | צה | ויחלפה · בנה · ויאמר · גם · הא · אענו · את · מאב | בימי · אמר · כן | ו [ |
| 7 | וארא · בה · ובבתה | וישראל · אבד · אבד · עלם · וירש · עמרי · את · א[ר] |
| 8 | ץ · מהדבא | וישב · בה · ימה · וחצי · ימי · בנה · ארבען · שת · ויש |
| 9 | ב · כמש · בימי · ואבן · את · בעלמען · ואעש · בה · האשוח · ואב[ן · ] |
| 10 | את · קריתן | ואש · גד · ישב · בארץ · עטרת · מעלם · ויבן · לה · מלך · |
| 11 | שראל · את עטרת | ואלתחם · בקר · ואחזה | ואהרג · את · כל · העם [ · ו] |
| 12 | הקר · הית · לכמש · ולמאב | ואשב · משם · את · אראל · דודה · וא[ס] |
| 13 | חבה · לפני · כמש · בקרית | ואשב · בה · את · אש · שרן · ואת · א[ש ·] |
| 14 | מחרת | ויאמר · לי · כמש · לך · אחז · את · נבה · על · ישראל | וא |
| 15 | הלך · בללה · ואלתחם · בה · מבקע · השחרת · עד · הצהרם | ואח |
| 16 | זה · ואהרג · כל[ה] · שבעת · אלפן [·] ג[ב]רן · ו[גר]ן | וגברת · ו[גר] |
| 17 | ת · ורחמת | כי · לעשתר · כמש · החרמתה | ואקח · משם · א[ת · כ] |
| 18 | לי · יהוה · ואסחב · הם · לפני · כמש | ומלך · ישראל · בנה [·] את [·] |
| 19 | יחץ · וישב · בה · בהלתחמה · בי | ויגרשה · כמש · מפני | ו [ ] |
| . . . . | |
| 31 | [ צאן · הארץ | וחורנן · ישב · בה · בת[ד]וד[ ] אש] |
| 32 | וי[מ]ר · לי · כמש · רד · הלתחם · בחורנן | וארד · ו[ ] |
| 33 | [ בה · כמש · בימי · ועל] ·[ד]ה · משם · עש] |
| 34 | [שת · שדק | ואנ]ך [·] |

line
1  I am Mesha, the son of Kemosh[yat], the King of Moab, the Da / ibonite.
2  My father ruled over Moab thirty years, and I rul / ed
3  after my father. And I have made this high place for Kemosh in Qarhoh, a hig[h place of vic-] / tory,
4  because he delivered me from all attackers and because he let me prevail [lit., "see"] against all my enemies. Omr / i
5  was the king of Israel, and he had oppressed Moab many days, because Kemosh was angry with his la/ nd.
6  Then his son succeeded him, and he, too, said, "I will oppress Moab." In my days he said th[is],
7  but I prevailed [lit., "saw"] against him and against his house, and Israel

*Identifications in Provenanced Inscriptions* 97

    utterly perished forever. Now Omri had taken possession of the la[n] / d
8  of Mehadaba, and he lived in it during his days and half the days of his
    son(s), forty years. But
9  Kemosh lived in it during my days. And I built Baalmeon, and I made the reservoir in it, and I buil[t]
10  Qiryaten. Now the Gadites had lived in the land of ʿAtaroth perpetually, and the king of I / srael
11  had rebuilt ʿAtaroth for himself. But I fought against the city [or: Qir] and took it, and I killed all the people, [so]
12  the city [or: Qir] became the property of Kemosh and Moab. I captured from there its Davidic lion and [d] / ragged
13  it before Kemosh in Qiryath. I settled in it the men of Sharon and the men of
14  Maharith. Now Kemosh said to me, "Go seize Nebo from Israel." So I
15  went at night and fought against it from the break of dawn until noon. I sei / zed
16  it and killed all in it—seven thousand native m[e]n, foreign [m]en, native women, [for]eign
17  women, and concubines—for I had devoted it to ʿAshtar-Kemosh. I took from there th[e ves] / sels
18  of Yahweh and dragged them before Kemosh. Now the king of Israel had built
19  Yahaṣ, and he occupied it while he was fighting against me. But Kemosh drove him out from before me. [And]. . . .
31  ] sheep of the land. As for Ḥawronen, the house of [Da]vid had settled in it. [ ] ʿš[
32  But] Kemosh said to me, "Go down, fight against Ḥawronen." So I went down[
33  and] Kemosh [retur]ned it in my days. As for ʿl[ ]dh, from there ʿš [
34  ] št šdq. And I

### (3.3) Question 1: reliability of the inscriptional data

**Access**: 2) Observed at or near its original location. *Banî Ḥamîdi* bedouin observed this stele lying partly buried at the site of the modern ruin of Dhiban. They showed it to a European, F. A. Klein of the Church Missionary Society, in 1868. In late 1869, during the negotiations to purchase the stele, the bedouin broke it in pieces. Largely through the efforts of Charles Clermont-Ganneau, in

*Identifying Biblical Persons in Northwest Semitic Inscriptions*

### Fig. 7

### Portions of the Mesha Inscription from Dibon Bearing the Names of Mesha, King of Moab, and Omri, King of Israel

(Excerpted from a drawing by Mark Lidzbarski)

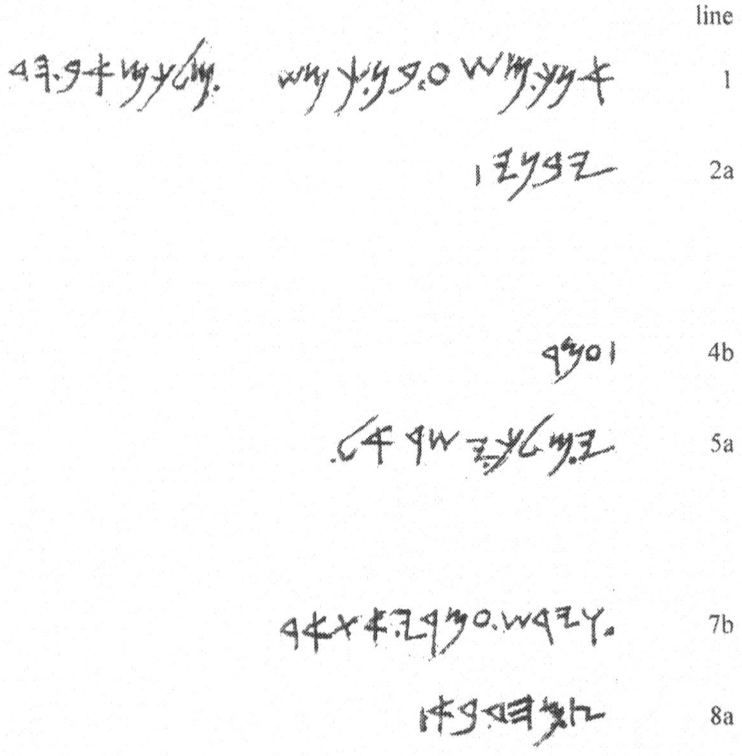

| | line |
|---|---|
| 𐤀𐤍𐤊.𐤌𐤔𐤏.𐤁𐤍.𐤊𐤌𐤔 𐤌𐤋𐤊.𐤌𐤀𐤁.𐤄𐤃 | 1 |
| 𐤁𐤍𐤉׀ | 2a |
| 𐤏𐤌𐤓𐤉 | 4b |
| 𐤉𐤌𐤋𐤊.𐤁𐤉𐤔𐤓𐤀𐤋. | 5a |
| .𐤉𐤒𐤃𐤔.𐤏𐤌𐤓𐤉׀𐤇𐤋𐤐 | 7b |
| 𐤇𐤑𐤉𐤉𐤌𐤉 | 8a |

1873 the recovered pieces were sent to the Louvre Museum in Paris. With the help of paper squeezes and sketches, most of the upper portion was restored.[5]

**Provenance**: 2) Site: the modern ruin of Dhiban.

**Authenticity**: 1) Regarded as authentic, because observed at or near its original location. The 1868 date of discovery also clearly upholds the authenticity of the stele, because, as Patrick D. Miller Jr. observed, "The form of the letters is consistent with other inscriptions of the 9$^{th}$ cent. B.C. and could not have been known when the stone was discovered."[6]

### (3.3) The setting of the Mesha Inscription, apart from biblical data

**Date**: 5) Dated by epigraphy: ninth century. Relatively little Moabite epigraphic material is available for comparison. Extant, discernibly Moabite seals number only about forty, and they are mostly dated to the eighth through sixth centuries.[7] This inscription dates to an earlier period, during which Hebrew/Moabite lapidary script shared a common development away from the Phoenician/Aramaic lapidary script.[8] In the Mesha Inscription, for example, the *tav* looks like an English letter X, with arms and legs of approximately equal length. In Phoenician/Aramaic lapidary scripts, however, *tav* has a lower left leg (reader's left) about three times as long as the shortest arm or leg, as if it were a tilted cross. This Phoenician/Aramaic "tilted cross" *tav* began to appear in the ninth century and was used consistently beginning in the eighth century. In Hebrew script, the pattern was inconsistent. *Tav* was sometimes an X and sometimes a "tilted cross." During the sixth century, it was usually the lower *right* leg that became longer. The *daleth*, which in both scripts developed a stubby right leg mainly in the eighth and following centuries, has no such leg in the Mesha Inscription. Whereas *beth* has a foot at approximately a right angle to the vertical shaft in Phoenician/Aramaic lapidary scripts of the eighth and seventh centu-

---

[5] Dearman, *Studies*, 73, n. 118.

[6] Patrick D. Miller Jr., "Moabite Stone," *ISBE* 3:396. This is one of the strongest arguments for the authenticity of the Mesha Inscription. On the history of the debate about its authenticity, see Dearman, *Studies*, 75–78, which summarizes both Löwy's arguments against authenticity and Clermont-Ganneau's arguments in its defense (Albert or Abraham Löwy, *A Critical Examination of the So-Called Moabite Inscription in the Louvre*, 3d ed. [London: Printed for private circulation, 1903], 8–18, 20–24, 26–29, 31–32; Charles Clermont-Ganneau, "The Moabite Stone," *Contemporary Review* 52 [1887]: 169–83). Löwy's views never had a scholarly consensus. During the 1940s, William F. Albright quickly refuted the last and perhaps weakest challenge to the authenticity of the Mesha Inscription, now regarded as fully established (Dearman, *Studies*, 78, n. 140).

[7] *WSS*, 372–86, nos. 1006–1047.

[8] Joseph Naveh, *The Development of the Aramaic Script* (Israel Academy of Sciences and Humanities Proceedings, vol. 5, no. 1; Jerusalem: Israel Academy of Sciences and Humanities, 1970), 8.

ries, in the Mesha Inscription its foot descends steeply to the reader's left at a very obtuse angle to the vertical shaft. This is clearly Hebrew/Moabite lapidary script, most likely from the ninth century.

**Language**: 2) The identity of this previously unknown or unrecognized language was deduced from the self-identification of the author in the inscription as the king of the realm whose people spoke that language: Moabite.

**Socio-political classification**: 3) Determined by explicit historical references, by theological statements, by the theophoric element "Kemosh-" in the name of Mesha's father, and by its provenance: Moabite. Permitted by what little is known of the Moabite onomasticon,[9] by the early Moabite script (see under "Date" above), and by language parameters.

### (3.3) How Mesha's Inscription correlates with the historical framework

In Egyptian sources, in the Temple of Luxor at Thebes, "along the outer face (north end) of the east wall of the Court of Ramses II"[10] (r. 1279–1213 B.C.E[11]), the texts of two palimpsests read, "Town which the mighty arm of Pharaoh, L.P.H.,[12] plundered in (the) land of Moab: B(w)trt"[13] and "The t[own, which] the mighty arm of Pharaoh, L.P.H., [plundere]d, of Tbniw (= Dibon)."[14]

---

[9] The number of Moabite names which are known is so small that low frequency or absence of any particular name or verbal root is insignificant. Nevertheless, the Moabite PN אהישע is derived from the root ישע / ושע (WSS, 376, no. 1017; cf. 380, no. 1031, 506), as is Mesha's name. (A Moabite seal of the first half of the sixth century, unearthed at Damascus and inscribed only with the five letters למשׁעא, is apparently derived from the root שׁעא, "to polish, cover" [SANSS, 157–58, no. 6, Fig. 75, no. 6; DNWSI, s.v. "šyʿ₁"], so it is not relevant.) PNs derived from the root ושע / ישע are found in Aramaic (Maraqten, 155–56, 173), Ammonite (Jackson, 96), Hebrew (Fowler, 348), and possibly Phoenician (WSS, 409, no. 1082); overall, see WSS, 506. If accurately preserved in 1 Chr 2:42, Mesha may also be a Hebrew PN, the name of a son of Caleb (LXX Μαρισα, Syriac ʾElišmî).

[10] Kenneth A. Kitchen, "Some New Light on the Asiatic Wars of Ramesses II," JEA 50 (1964): 47.

[11] Ibid., 69, n. 1.

[12] L.P.H. is an abbreviation for the Egyptian formula meaning "life, prosperity, health."

[13] Ibid., 49, Fig. 2, A.I, (A), 50, Pl. III.

[14] Ibid., 52, Fig. 3, B. IV, (A), 53, 55, Pl. IV.
Hence the reading *Ti-bw-iniw* [in which the dots over the letters *i* resemble apostrophes], syllabically *Tabunu* or *Tibunu*—surely none other than Dibon or Daibon (modern Dhiban), a famous Moabite town mentioned on the Moabite Stone and often in the Old Testament. This name has not hitherto been attested with certainty in any Egyptian text. (Ibid., 55; cf. *ANET*, 242–43)

In Assyrian sources, Moab is named in the inscriptions of Assyrian kings as early as 729[15] and as late as the mid-seventh century.[16] Moab is clearly a kingdom, and the name of its king is often given. Mesha, however, is not mentioned, despite the repeated campaigns of Shalmaneser III during the ninth century.[17] The Assyrian military threat from the north might have made it easier for Mesha to rebel against the Israelite yoke. The location of Moab is strongly implied by its usually being mentioned in the company of other kingdoms in southern Palestine or Transjordan, such as Judah, Edom, Philistine city-states, and Ammon.[18]

### (3.3) How Mesha's Inscription contributes to the historical framework

The interpretation and list of contributions of the Mesha Inscription to the historical framework regarding Moab are as follows:

At a political group level, this inscription documents the ninth-century existence of the kingdom of Moab between the Egyptian references to Moab as a nation in the thirteenth century and the references to the same kingdom of Moab in Assyrian sources of the eighth to mid-seventh century. The Mesha Inscription specifies Kemosh[yat] and his son Mesha as two of its ninth-century kings. Mesha's claim to be a "Daibonite" (lines 1–2) strongly implies that Dibon was located in Moab and suggests that Dibon was Moab's capital city.

At a religious group level, inscriptional data indicate that Kemosh was the primary deity of Moab. The Mesha Inscription refers to Moab as the land of the deity Kemosh ("his land," line 5). Moab's king attributes both the defeats before his reign and all his royal successes to Kemosh (lines 3–4, 5, 14, 19, 32, 33), the sole deity for whom he performs acts of religious devotion (lines 3, 11–12, 18), except ʿAshtar-Kemosh in line 17, who seems to be a divine consort of Kemosh. The theophoric element in the name of Mesha's father, King Kemosh[yat] (line 1), also testifies to the prominence of this deity among the Moabites.

---

[15] Summary Inscription 7 of Tiglath-pileser III (r. 744–727) from his seventeenth *palû* (regnal year), i.e., 729 or shortly thereafter (*ITP*, 154), reverse, line 10: "Sanipu the Ammonite, Salamanu the Moabite (ᵐ*sa-la-ma-nu* KUR *ma-ʾa-ba-a-a*) . . . ," line 11: "[Mi]tinti the Ashkelonite, Jehoahaz the Judahite, Qaushmalaka of Edom . . ." (*ITP*, 170–71; *ANET*, 282).

[16] Annals of Ashurbanipal (r. 668–627), Cylinder C, col. 1, line 25: ". . . Minsê (Manasseh), king of Judah," line 26: "Qausgabri, king of Edom, Muṣuri, king of Moab (KUR *ma-ʾ-ba*)" line 27: "Ṣilbel, king of Gaza, . . . " (Maximilian Streck, *Assurbanipal und die letzten assyrischen Könige bis zum Untergange Niniveh's* [3 vols.; VAB 7; Leipzig: J. C. Hinrichs, 1916], 2:138–39; *ANET*, 294).

[17] Dearman, *Studies*, 167, 169.

[18] See notes 15 and 16 above in this chapter as examples.

At an individual level, this inscription documents the existence in the ninth century of Kemosh[yat] and his son, Mesha, consecutive kings of Moab.

The Mesha Inscription supplies these historical data concerning Israel:

It makes clear that Omri's kingdom was Israelite. The inscriptions of the Assyrian conqueror Shalmaneser III (r. 858–824) refer to $^{m}a$-$ha$-$ab$-$bu$ KUR $sir$-$^{ʾ}a$-$la$-$a$-$a$, "Ahab the Israelite"[19] and to $^{m}ia$-$ú$-$a$ DUMU $^{m}$ $hu$-$um$-$ri$-$i$, "Jehu, son of Omri."[20] An inscription of Adad-nirari III (r. 810–783) refers to KUR $hu$-$um$-$ri$-$i$, "Omri-land;"[21] other Assyrian royal inscriptions also refer to that territory by using Omri's name.[22] The Mesha Inscription provides a clear link between the land of "Ahab the Israelite" and "Omri-land" in its statement that "Omri was the king of Israel" (lines 4–5). Thus, at a political group level, this inscription provides the link that certifies the ninth-century existence of Israel (lines 5, 7, 10–11, 14) *as the kingdom of Omri* and his dynasty.

At a religious group level in Israel, in referring to things that Mesha "dragged . . . before Kemosh," presumably as offerings from the spoils of war, the inscription names two things or kinds of things. The first, captured from Ataroth (lines 10–13), seems to have been a cultic object, the אראל דודה (on which see section E.2 in Appendix E, below). Second in the account are the "[ve]ssels of *Yhwh*" (lines 17–18), a deity whom the Israelites worshipped (see section 3.5 below). His ritual equipment became spoil taken by another deity, Kemosh, or, if viewed as in line 5, he abandoned it to Kemosh (cf. section 3.5

---

[19] The Kurkh Monolith of Shalmaneser III (BM118884), col. 2, lines 91–92; Grayson, *Assyrian Rulers (858–745 BC)*, 23, col. 2, lines 91–92 of A.0.102.2; RawlCu 3, Pl. 7–8; *ANET*, 279; Galil, *Chronology*, 15; see also Chapter 2, note 57, above.

[20] This is in the epigraph over relief B on the Black Obelisk (BM118885), depicting Jehu's tribute payment (Grayson, *Assyrian Rulers (858–745 BC)*, 149, A.0. 102.88). A long version of Shalmaneser's annals on a stone tablet (IM 55644) in the outer wall of the city of Aššur also refers to Jehu in col. 4, line 11: $^{m}ia$-$a$-$ú$ DUMU $^{m}hu$-$um$-$ri$-$i$, "Jehu son of Omri" (ibid., 54, col. 4, line 11 of A.0.102.10; cf. the parallel "fragment of an annalistic text published in Rawlinson, Vol. III, Pl. 5, No. 6" in *ANET*, 280 [See RawlCu 3 above in "Abbreviations"]). On the Kurba'il Statue, discovered at Fort Shalmaneser, Calah (British excavation no. ND10000; IM 60497) lines 29–30 also refer to $^{m}ia$-$ú$-$a$ DUMU $^{m}hu$-$um$-$ri$-$i$, "Jehu son of Omri" (Grayson, *Assyrian Rulers (858–745 BC)*, 60, lines 29–30 of A.0.102.12). See also Chapter 2, note 57, above.

[21] This inscription is on a broken stone slab discovered in 1854 by W. K. Loftus at Calah, line 12 (ibid., 213, line 12 of A.0.104.8; Hayim Tadmor, "The Historical Inscriptions of Adad-Nirari III," *Iraq* 35 [1973]: 148–49); RawlCu 1, Pl. 35, no. 1. It has no museum number. Grayson reports, "The location of the original broken slab is unknown and the text is known only from the published copy, which was based on paper squeezes which were subsequently destroyed" (Grayson, *Assyrian Rulers (858–745 BC)*, 212).

[22] See Chapter 2, note 57, above.

below regarding Hazael's booty, under the heading regarding correlation with the historical framework).²³

At an individual level, this inscription verifies the existence in the ninth century of Omri and his son or sons, consecutive kings of Israel.

### (3.3) Question 2: whether the setting of the inscription *permits* a match

**Date**: 4) Agrees with the biblical account; dated by historical references and by script (see on epigraphy above). All factors point to a ninth-century date; the historical content of the inscription in connection with the biblical period of the Omride dynasty indicates the mid-ninth century (see under singularity below). The Hebrew Bible presents Mesha as the contemporary of Jehoram (r. 851–842/1), a grandson of Omri.

**Language**: 2) The identity of the language of the inscription, unknown or unrecognized until this inscription was discovered, was deduced from the self-identification of the author of the inscription as the king of the realm whose people spoke this language. It agrees with the language expectation raised by the biblical account: Moabite.

**Socio-political classification**: 3) Agrees with the biblical account. Provenance, explicit historical references, theological statements, and the theophoric element in the name of Mesha's father combine to establish that the inscription and its author are Moabite (see on socio-political classification above).

It is worth noting that beyond the general setting established by the three criteria immediately above, there are several particular matters of agreement that link the Mesha Inscription and the biblical account in their separate descriptions of in the specific setting:

a. Mesha implicitly acknowledges Omri's military prowess in the reference to Omri's conquest and Israel's lengthy occupation of "the land of Mehadaba" (lines 7–8). The Bible also depicts Omri as a victorious military leader, initially as an army general (שַׂר־צָבָא, 1 Kgs 16:16) who besieged and conquered Tirzah (vv. 17, 18), thus overcoming Zimri's forces and succeeding him on the throne (vv. 21–22). During his reign, Omri became renowned for "his mighty military success which he achieved" (וּגְבוּרָתוֹ אֲשֶׁר עָשָׂה,²⁴ v. 27).

---

²³ It is interesting to compare Mesha's way of dedicating the spoils of war with that of the Philistines in 1 Sam 5:1 and David's dedication of spoils in 2 Sam 8:9–12.

²⁴ Hans Kosmala, "גָּבַר gabhar; גְּבוּרָה gebhûrah; גְּבִיר gebhîr; גִּבּוֹר gibbôr; גֶּבֶר gebher," *TDOT* 2:369.

b. Mesha refers to Omri's "son" as his successor. Whereas several kings of the northern kingdom of Israel were not succeeded by their sons, the Bible agrees, in that it says three of Omri's descendants succeeded him.

c. Mesha's statement that Omri had "oppressed" Moab (ויענו · את · מאב, line 5) for a long time. Such oppression apparently included the levying of a heavy tribute in wool as stated in 2 Kgs 3:4: "he rendered to the king of Israel the wool of a hundred thousand lambs and of a hundred thousand rams." Mesha's stele does not give specific information, likely because it could have been embarrassing, particularly to a monarch in the ancient Near East. Nevertheless, his mention of "sheep" in line 31, though preceded by a lacuna, could well be a Moabite reflection of the reality behind the Israelite statement in 2 Kgs 3:4, "Now Mesha, king of Moab, was a sheep-raiser."

d. Explicit reference to Moab as "his [i.e., Kemosh's] land" (line 5) and to Kemosh as the deity who either permitted enemies to conquer Moabite territory (line 5) or granted victory to Mesha and Moab (lines 4, 14–16, 19). The Bible likewise presents an Israelite judge expressing the view that Kemosh could grant territory to a ruler who acknowledged him as his god (Judg 11:24). Repeatedly, the Bible depicts the Moabites as the "people of Kemosh" (Num 21:29 and Jer 48:46; similar references are in 1 Kgs 11:7, 33; 2 Kgs 23:13; Jer 48:7, 13).

e. In a basic matter of geography, the location of "the land of Mehadabah" in lines 7–8 and that of the cities named in this inscription very clearly indicate that the territory of Moab was on the Mishor, i.e., the plateau east of the Dead Sea.[25]

**(3.3) Question 3: How strongly the specific data in [3] the Mesha stele from Dhiban count for or against an identification with the biblical (69) Mesha, king of Moab (2 Kgs 3:4; r. mid- to late ninth century)[26]**

√ **Name**: 2) Spelling has a negligible difference. In the inscription, מֹשע (line 1), is completely present, clearly legible, and although the spelling does not agree precisely with the consonants of the biblical spelling, מֵישַׁע (2 Kgs 3:4), the difference is negligible. In Hebrew, the vowel *sere* may or may not take a

---

[25] Yohanan Aharoni, *Land of the Bible* (trans. and ed. Anson F. Rainey; 2d rev. and emended ed.; London: Burns & Oates, 1979), 336–40, esp. 338, Map 26.

[26] The number of each person is indicated in parentheses ( ), and the number of each inscription is indicated in brackets [ ]. These numbers originate from the order of appearance in Appendix B.

*yodh*. The LXX Μωσα suggests the possibility that although the triconsonantal root of the name Mesha is cognate in Moabite and Hebrew, a Moabite name might not have been pronounced or written precisely the same way in Hebrew. In Moabite, the original proto-Semitic I-*waw* form of the verbal root וֹשׁע may have been retained, whereas in Hebrew, such forms became I-*yodh* verbs. The Hebrew oral preference for a *yodh*, combined with the possibility in the process of Hebrew textual transmission that a *waw* may easily have been read as a *yodh*, probably resulted in Hebrew vocalization of this Moabite name.

The defective spelling on the stele accords with its antiquity. In the inscription, /ō/ would not necessarily be represented. It does not appear, for example, in מאב (lines 1, 2, 5, 6, 12), where, in light of the many similarities between Moabite and Hebrew, it might have appeared. Internal *waw* appears as a vowel in the proper name חורנן (lines 31, 32).

**Relations**: 5) In the Bible, a patronymic is absent, therefore there is none to match or contradict the inscriptional patronymic. Mesha's father is named in the inscription as "Kemosh[yat],"²⁷ king of Moab, possibly also a "Daibonite," who "ruled over Moab thirty years" (lines 1–2).

√ **Title(s)**: 1) Title matches. Doubtless Mesha's title was מלך מאב (line 1; cf. מֶלֶךְ מוֹאָב in 2 Kgs 3:4), despite the syntactical ambiguity of the inscriptional appositive,²⁸ which can relate to either father or son. The immediate context in lines 1–2 states that they both ruled as king over Moab (using the verb מָלַךְ), and Mesha speaks of enemy kings as his counterparts, e.g., lines 18–19, "Now the king of Israel . . . . was fighting against me." His battles, building projects, and extension of his rule over cities which he annexed (lines 28–29) were all conventional royal activities for monarchs of his day.

**Other**: 5) Other identifying marks of the individual are absent.

√ **Singularity**: 1) The available data require an ID on grounds of both inscriptional singularity and biblical singularity. Although no extant ancient source gives a complete list of the kings of Moab, inscriptional discoveries have

---

²⁷ The lacuna in the name is filled in from a fragment of another Moabite inscription discovered at Kerak during or before 1958. The first of its three lines of text reads, "[k]*mšyt* | *mlk* | *m'b · h* . . . ." The initial publication is William L. Reed and Fred V. Winnett, "A Fragment of an Early Moabite Inscription from Kerak," *BASOR* 172 (December 1963): 1–9. See also David Noel Freedman, "A Second Mesha Inscription," *BASOR* 175 (October 1964): 50–51.

²⁸ Andersen observes, "Grammar alone does not indicate whether 'king of Moab' and 'the Dibonite' in S1 [i.e., sentence 1] refer to Meša or his father; the former is more likely, so that here four nouns are in apposition" (Francis I. Andersen, "Moabite Syntax," *Or* 35 (1966): 90). Cf. Chapter 1, note 102, above; the ambiguity of the appositives in Moabite syntax in this instance is not appreciably different from the same phenomenon in the syntax of biblical and inscriptional Hebrew.

revealed only one Moabite king named Mesha. The Hebrew Bible also knows only one Mesha, king of Moab. Nevertheless, there could have been other Moabite kings who bore the same name, and it is hazardous to build on an absence of evidence. There is, however, a way to establish the identity of the Mesha of the inscription as the biblical Mesha on the basis of historical circumstances. It was against Omri's descendant, Jehoram, that Mesha's revolt met with success (2 Kgs 3:5–27). This *successful rebellion against Omri's descendant*, which is expressed in lines 4–7a, repeated in lines 7b–9, and detailed in lines 10–11, 14–15, and 20, *is a singular identifying mark in common* which indicates that the Mesha who produced the Mesha stele and the Mesha of 2 Kgs 3:4–27 are one and the same person. The fact that this singular circumstance is present both in the inscription and in the Hebrew Bible gives this ID double grounds of singularity (abbreviated as SI + SB).

### (3.3) Remarks

The Bible and the Mesha Inscription confirm each other as to the *fact* of Mesha's successful revolt against the Omrides. A point of controversy, however, is at what time the rebellion occurred. Despite ambiguities and the uncertainties in our understanding of the Mesha Inscription, for reasons described in point 1 below, it is entirely possible, and perhaps likely, that it contradicts 2 Kgs 1:1 and 3:5 regarding the time of the revolt, for reasons described in point 3 below.

1. A *terminus ad quem* for the end of the Israelite occupation of the Medeba ("Mehadaba") territory cannot be clearly determined. Most commentators regard 2 Kgs 1:1 and 3:5, which place Mesha's revolt after the death of Ahab, as contradictory to lines 7–9 of Mesha's inscription, which they understand to refer to the reign of Omri and half of the reign of Ahab.

Ahab's northern wars might have made his reign an opportune time for Mesha's rebellion in the south to begin. This military assessment has led many scholars to think that the revolt occurred during Ahab's reign, while he was at war with the Aramaeans and/or later, as part of the coalition that included Aram when he fought Shalmaneser III of Assyria. It makes good military sense, because of the difficulties of fighting on two fronts. It also fits one interpretation of בנה in line 8, i.e., as singular (see point a below). Another opportune time for the revolt would have been soon after Ahab's death, when his relatively weak successor, Ahaziah, became king. Despite the good sense in both of these positions, ambiguities and uncertainties in lines 7–8 make it too unreliable to use the Mesha Inscription to support them. In fact, it is difficult to use this inscription to determine any *terminus ad quem* for the end of the Israelite occupation.

*Identifications in Provenanced Inscriptions* 107

a. In line 8, ‏וחצי · ימי · בנה · ארבען שת‎, "and half the days of his son(s), forty years," is ambiguous and imprecise. It is ambiguous, because in Moabite, ‏ה‎- (-*ôhu* or -*ôhi*), representing the complete third person masculine singular suffix, can be attached to *nouns which are either singular or plural*. Therefore, ‏בנה‎ can mean either "his son" or "his sons." That it can also represent the plural is evident in line 8, ‏ימה‎ (*yômôhu* or -*ôhi*), "his days," and in line 20, ‏רשה‎ (*rōšôhu* or -*ôhi*), "its chiefs."[29]

b. Even if ‏בנה‎ is singular, it need not refer to a descendant in the generation immediately following Omri, but can refer to any ruling son of Omri in later generations, including his sons Ahaziah and Jehoram.[30]

c. The phrase in line 8 is also imprecise, because, as with the English word "half," the word ‏חצי‎ does not always mean exactly "half." In Jer 17:11, ‏בַּחֲצִי יָמָו‎ (following the *qere* ‏ימיו‎) it is used very approximately to mean "in the middle of his days," i.e., only part of the way through a normal lifespan. In this inscription, it could simply mean only partway through the reign(s) of Omri's son(s). After Omri's twelve-year reign (1 Kgs 16:23), three of Omri's descendants followed: Ahab, who ruled 22 years (16:29), Ahaziah for two years (22:51), and Jehoram for twelve years (2 Kgs 3:1). A precise calculation of "half the days of his son(s)," then, arrives at a total of approximately eleven, twelve, or eighteen years, depending on whether the count ends with Ahab, Ahaziah, or Jehoram. The fact that when added to Omri's twelve-year reign, none of these totals "forty years" (line 8) indicates that the chronological terminology in the inscription is approximate or symbolic, rather than precise.

d. The "forty years" in line 8 are very difficult to pin down to specific years. The problems involved in such an attempt are that 1) it might be approximate or symbolic, just as Israel's "forty years" in the wilderness represented a generation, 2) it is not clear whether "forty years" stands for the days of Omri *and* "half" his son's (or sons') days or perhaps only "half" his son's (sons') days.

2. The *terminus a quo* from which Mesha counted is not certain. As an army general (‏שַׂר־צָבָא‎ in 1 Kgs 16:16) under the rule of his royal predecessors, Omri could have conquered and occupied the territory around Medeba

---

[29] Garr, *Dialect Geography of Syria-Palestine*, 108.
[30] E.g., Bright states that here "Omri's son, in view of 2 Kgs 3:4ff, . . . must be taken to mean 'grandson,' as frequently in the Bible" (John Bright, *A History of Israel*, 4th ed. [Louisville, Ky.: Westminster/John Knox, 2000] 248, n. 56).

even before he became king.[31] That Israelite kings did not always receive the credit for the victories of their armies is evident in the saying, "Saul has slain his thousands, and David his ten thousands" (1 Sam 18:7). Omri's acclaim (1 Kgs 16:16, 21) tends to support a similar possibility in Moab as well.

3. The two very different datings of the revolt probably reflect the difference in viewpoint between the inscriptional account and the biblical account. The Hebrew viewpoint is reflected in 2 Kgs 1:1, "Moab rebelled against Israel after the death of Ahab" (אַחֲרֵי מוֹת אַחְאָב), perhaps to imply that it was only at a point late in time that Mesha finally succeeded. The Israelites would tend to regard the plain of Medeba as that which was divinely apportioned to the tribe of Reuben (Josh 13:7–9, 15–23), and which therefore belonged to them until they were finally expelled in war. Mesha would likely have preferred to regard his earliest acts of rebellion as the beginning of his successful territorial conquests.

Human experience of military rebellion tends to support a view of Mesha's revolt as a lengthy process which each of the belligerent rulers was likely to portray in a temporal frame which was flattering to his own military image. The terms "Moab" and "Israel" in 2 Kgs 1:1 suggest full-scale, national involvement on each side. In slight contrast, the terms "king of Moab" and "king of Israel" in 2 Kgs 3:5 might suggest an earlier phase of the rebellion, initiated in Mesha's administrative decisions, probably including a refusal to pay tribute. Regardless of whether this difference in terminology actually reflects two different phases of the revolt, the chronological realities of mounting a successful revolt help to explain the difference between the Moabite and the Israelite viewpoints.

Although difficulties remain in dating Mesha's revolt, they are not sufficient to break the connection between the biblical Mesha and the Mesha of the inscription. The time frame from the latter part of Ahab's reign to the failed attempt by Joram's league with Judah and Edom to crush the Moabite revolt (2 Kgs 3:6–27), amounting to about two decades, remains much too short to try to fit in a different Moabite king named Mesha and a completely different revolt.

### 3.4 Is the biblical Omri, king of Israel, named in the Mesha Inscription?

On the inscription itself, the question of reliability of inscriptional data, the setting of the inscription apart from biblical data, and the relationship between the historical framework and the Mesha Inscription, see section 3.3 above.

---

[31] Julian Morgenstern, *Amos Studies* (Cincinnati: Hebrew Union College Press, 1941), 208–9, cited in Roland E. Murphy, "Israel and Moab in the Ninth Century," *CBQ* 15 (1953): 412.

## (3.4) Question 2: whether the setting of the inscription *permits* a match

The setting is described above in section 3.3. The Hebrew Bible presents only one Hebrew king with this name, the seventh king of the northern kingdom of Israel. The Mesha Inscription, a ninth-century document that refers to Omri and one or more of his descendants, corresponds well with the period to which the Hebrew Bible assigns Omri (see section 3.3, "Question 2"). As for Omri's name, the root ʿmr is attested among PNs in Aramaic, Nabatean, Palmyrene, Safaitic, and Arabic inscriptions, but not in Hebrew inscriptions.[32] Even in the Bible, only four persons bear this name. This apparently uncommon Hebrew PN might have been borrowed from another people.

## (3.4) Question 3: how strongly the specific data in [3] the Mesha stele from Dhiban count for or against an identification with the biblical (7) Omri, king of Israel (1 Kgs 16:16ff; r. 884–873)

√ **Name**: 1) The name is completely present (in lines 4–5 and 7), clearly legible, and in exact agreement with the consonants of 1 Kgs 16:16ff, עָמְרִי.

**Relations**: 5) In the inscription, filionymics are absent. The Mesha Inscription clearly implies that one or more of Omri's sons succeeded him as rulers of Israel, but it does not name them. This datum is compatible with the biblical account of Omri's dynasty, which covers four consecutive generations. It is not, however, specific enough to be an identifying mark, because there is no filionymic to match or contradict the biblical filionymics Ahab, Ahaziah, and Jehoram, kings of Israel.

√ **Title(s)**: 1) Title matches. Omri's title in the Mesha Inscription, line 5, is מלך ישראל. The placement of עמרי before מלך, as in Mesha's self-introduction in line 1, combined with the absence of על before ישראל, favors the reading of מלך in line 5 as a title, rather than a verb, whereas על is used with the verb מלך in line 2. Also, the direct object marker את does not appear in front of יראל, although admittedly it is used in only about half of the places where it might have appeared.[33] The Bible clearly implies that Omri bore the title of מלך by stating that his deeds were written in the book of the chronicles of the kings of Israel (1 Kgs 16:27), by using the verb מָלַךְ in vv. 16, 23, and by the formula used following the death of a king in the clause, "and Ahab his son reigned in his stead" (v. 28).

---

[32] Maraqten, 199.
[33] Andersen, "Moabite Syntax," 101–3.

√ **Other**: 1) Some of the inscriptional data agree explicitly and clearly with biblical account and 3) some data are vague or ambiguous. See section 3.3, "Question 2."

√ **Singularity**: 1) Available data require an ID on grounds of both inscriptional singularity and biblical singularity. Just as in section 3.3 above, Mesha is identified in a way that singles him out, so Omri is singled out as the progenitor of Mesha's opponent, *the founder of the dynasty against which Mesha successfully rebelled*. This pair of names, combined with the successful Moabite rebellion against Israel in the mid-ninth century, is a distinctive cluster of specific circumstances in both the inscriptional and the biblical accounts.

## 3.5 Is the biblical King David named in the Tel Dan stele?

### Description, transcription, and translation

There are currently three extant fragments of the Tel Dan stele.[34] Fragment A, discovered in 1993, is 32 cm. high by 22 cm. across at its widest point. Its face and the side at the reader's right are smoothed. Engraved on its face are thirteen lines of writing that are part of the (reader's) right side of the inscription.

Fragments B1 and B2, discovered a year later, clearly fit together, forming Fragment B with a single, flat writing surface. B1 is somewhat rectangular, about 20 cm. by 14 cm., and has a smoothed surface 15 cm. high by 11 cm. wide, on which six lines of writing are engraved. B2 is roughly trapezoidal, 10 cm. high by 9 cm. wide, and has a smoothed face 9 cm. high by 6 cm. wide containing four lines of writing. All three pieces are of local basalt with at least one smoothed side. All bear Aramaic words engraved very clearly in the same script and letter size, with dots used as word dividers. For these reasons, and because the words of both Fragment A and Fragment B suggest a memorial or victory stele, like that of the Mesha Inscription, most scholars agree that these fragments come from the same inscription.

---

[34] Fragments of the Aramaic stele from Tel Dan, alias "the 'house of David' inscription," discovered in the summers of 1993 and 1994, were first published in Avraham Biran and Joseph Naveh, "An Aramaic Stele from Tel Dan," *IEJ* 43 (1993): 81–98, and idem, "The Tel Dan Inscription: A New Fragment," *IEJ* 45 (1995): 1–18. On the earliest fragment, see also Avraham Biran, *Biblical Dan* (Jerusalem: Israel Exploration Society and Hebrew Union College, Jewish Institute of Religion, 1994), 274–78. The revision of a 1999 University of Sydney doctoral diss. by George Athas, *The Tel Dan Inscription: A Reappraisal and a New Interpretation* (JSOTSup 360; Copenhagen International Seminar 12; New York: Sheffield Academic Press, 2003), was published too late to permit anything more than mention here.

*Identifications in Provenanced Inscriptions* 111

In published photographs, the three fragments seem to be correctly positioned relative to each other.[35] Nevertheless, the original position of Fragments A and B relative to each other in the stele is not certain. They seem to have an "internal fit," i.e., below the original surface of the stele, but as Professor Biran

---

[35] Although some scholars think the internal fit is arbitrary, close inspection of the published photographs leads me to the tentative observation that it brings about four simultaneous physical alignments. Unable to physically examine the fragments themselves, but only photographs of them, I cannot verify my observations. Therefore, they are only noted here:

1. The writing surfaces are in the same plane, without forming a V-shaped ridge or "valley," and without forming a "plain and plateau" by being in two parallel planes.

2. The letters at the right and left edges of the X-shaped gap between Fragments A and B are *directly opposite* each other. They are not misaligned with respect to the letters on the opposite side of the gap.

3. When the letters at both edges of the gap are directly opposite each other, the lines of which they form a part continue across the face of the stele undisturbed, in *fairly* straight, horizontal lines, without exhibiting writing that goes "uphill," then "downhill" or "downhill," then "uphill" *at the break* on the writing surface. Even before the stele was broken, the horizontal lines of writing were *not perfectly* straight, as can be seen on Fragment A alone, especially in the upper right corner, where the lines begin to arch slightly upward. Schniedewind suggests that this arching may have been to suit an arched top of the Tel Dan stele, like that of the Mesha stele (William M. Schniedewind, "Tel Dan Stela: New Light on Aramaic and Jehu's Revolt," *BASOR* 302 [1996]: 78).

4. When the horizontal lines of writing are straight, the *broken edges also line up with each other*. The (reader's) upper right edge of Fragment B1 descends toward the reader's right. After the gap in the writing surface, the (reader's) lower left edge of Fragment A continues that line of breakage in a fairly straight alignment. This line is the upper-left-to-lower-right diagonal of the X-shaped gap between Fragment A and Fragment B. The other diagonal comes from the upper left edge of the front of Fragment A forming a line that continues, slightly offset, along the lower right edge of Fragments B1 and B2.

The resulting X-shaped gap suggests that the portion of the stele that included Fragments A and B was broken by the application of intense force at the narrowest point in the gap, i.e., at line 5. These four alignments, combined with the obliteration of the writing surface at that line, make the fit seem more likely than unlikely. It would be a rare coincidence for all four alignments and the precise obliteration spot to occur when Biran's and Naveh's fit is made, if it were not the original fit of the stele. Nevertheless, without intermediate fragments to guide the positioning of Fragments A and B, their original spatial relation to each other remains uncertain. According to Galil, Fragment B seems to precede Fragment A. He regards Biran's and Naveh's arrangement as impossible (Gershon Galil, "A Re-Arrangement of the Fragments of the Tel Dan Inscription and the Relations between Israel and Aram," *PEQ* 133 [2001]: 16–21).

admits, this fit is less clear than the sure fit between Fragments B1 and B2.[36] Biran's and Naveh's arguments for putting A and B side by side are:

1. With line 1 of Fragment A to the reader's right of line 1 of Fragment B1, a "meaningful and continuous text" resulted, "albeit with some difficulties."[37]

2. With the writing surfaces masked,[38] three experienced restorers, each acting independently, joined Fragments A and B side by side by using the inconclusive "fit" at the level of line 5 of Fragments A and B.[39]

3. Joining Fragments A and B at line 5 allowed restorers to proceed on the assumption that the (reader's) upper right edge of Fragment B and the (reader's) lower left edge of Fragment A "form a straight line of the same break."[40]

In view of the Mesha Inscription and other stelae of the ancient Near East, Biran and Naveh are correct in pointing out that "Fragment B preceding Fragment A . . . [would be] an unlikely possibility since the reference to the writer's father normally belongs to the beginning of the stele."[41] The remaining two options are 1) that Fragment B was originally below Fragment A, which would lead to largely separate treatments of text, or 2) that Fragment B was originally to the reader's left of Fragment A, since Fragment A includes part of the margin on the reader's right, whereas Fragment B does not include any margin. (The last is the most attractive option, because it offers the potential to gain more information and more textually grounded possibilities by considering the text on each fragment in closer relation to the text on the other.) On the basis of the geometric likelihood of the internal fit at line 5 as treated above, the following transcription and translation adopts the Biran-Naveh arrangement and much of the text they supply:

line
1    [ ]    [מר · ע]    ·[ןוגזר]
2    [ ] · אבי · יסקן    בה[ן]תלחמה · בא[ן ·]
3    וישכב · אבי · יהך · אל [·] אבהו[ן]ה · ויעל · מלכ[ין]ש[
4    ראל · קדם · בארק · אבי · ו[ן]יהמלך · הדדן [·] א[ן]יתי ·[
5    אנה · ויהך · הדד · קדמי · ו[ן]אפק · מן · שבע[ת]·[

---

[36] Biran and Naveh, "Tel Dan Inscription," 11.
[37] Ibid.
[38] Ibid.
[39] Ibid.
[40] Ibid.
[41] Ibid.

## Identifications in Provenanced Inscriptions

```
6  י · מלכי · ואקתל · מל[כן · שב]ען · אסרי · אן לפי · ר]
7  כב · ואלפי · פרש · [קטלת · אית ...]רם · בר · [ ·
8  מלך · ישראל · וקתל[ת · אית ...]יהו · ב[ ] · מל[
9  ך · ביתדוד · ואשם · [אית · קרית · הם · חרבת · ואהפך · א]
10 ית · ארק · הם · לישמן                             [
11 אחרן · ולהן                                       [מ]
12 לך · על · ישראל                                   ואשם · [
13 מזר · על · ]                                      [
```

line
1   [ ] . . . [  ] and cut [ ]
2   [ ] my father went up [ ] when he fought at '[ . . . ]
3   And my father lay down; he went to his [fathers]. Now the king of I[s] / rael had penetrated
4   into my father's land before. [But then] Hadad made me king,
5   and Hadad marched before me. So I went forth from [the] seven [ . . . ] / s
6   of my rule, and I killed [seve]nty kin[gs] who had harnessed thou[sands of cha] / riots
7   and thousands of cavalry. [And I killed . . . ]ram, son of [ . . . ,]
8   the king of Israel, and I kill[ed . . .]yahu, son of [ . . . , the ki] / ng of
9   the house of David. And I made [their towns into ruins and turned]
10  their land into [a desolation . . . ]
11  others and [ . . . . Then . . . became ki] / ng
12  over Is[rael. . . . And I laid]
13  siege against [ . . . ]

**(3.5) Question 1: reliability of the inscriptional data**

**Access**: 1) Excavated under controlled conditions.[42]
**Provenance**: 1) At Tel Dan, the three exact findspots are known.
**Authenticity**: 1) Regarded as authentic, because excavated.[43]

---

[42] Biran and Naveh, "Aramaic Stele," 81–98; Biran, *Biblical Dan*, 274–78; Biran and Naveh, "Tel Dan Inscription," 1–18.

[43] Some unfounded accusations of forgery have had little or no effect on the scholarly acceptance of this inscription as genuine. See Stephen A. Kaufman, "Recent Contributions of Aramaic Studies to Biblical Hebrew Philology and the Exegesis of the Hebrew Bible," 44, in André Lemaire, ed., *Congress Volume: Basel 2001*, VTSup 92 (Boston: Brill, 2002).

## Fig. 8

### A Portion of the Tel Dan Stele
### Bearing the Name of "the House of David"

(Drawing by the author)

David's name appears in a phrase that refers to his dynasty or the realm of his descendants. It appears to parallel a preceding reference to a king of the northern kingdom of Israel.

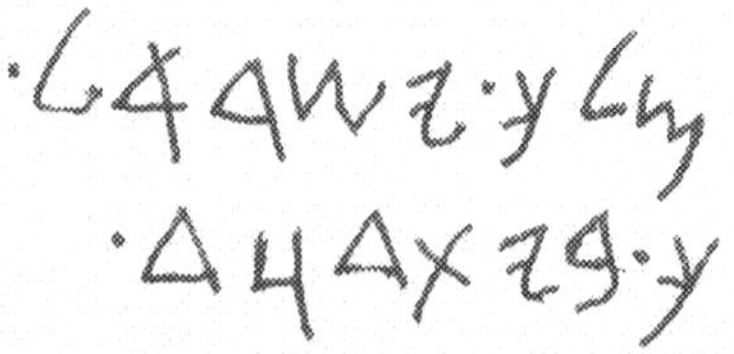

Fragment A line

·ᒷ𐤀𐤒𐤔𐤉·𐤉ᒷ𐤉    8a

·𐤃𐤉𐤃𐤕𐤉𐤁·𐤉    9a

## (3.5) The setting of the inscription, apart from biblical data

**Date**: 3) Dated by stratigraphy, ceramic typology, and epigraphy: mid-ninth to mid-eighth century.

The stele was inscribed by Aramaean conquerors, then broken by Israelites who captured it. Later, the fragments now extant were re-used by Israelites to help build a gate complex. The wall in which Fragment A was put to secondary use was covered by a destruction layer datable to the third quarter of the eighth century and attributed to Tiglath-pileser III's conquest of northern Israel in 733/732. This date stands as a firm latest possible date, if perhaps a distant one.[44] A small assemblage of pottery from the level beneath Fragment A contained nothing from later than the middle of the ninth century. Halpern observes that "seriation of ninth century B.C. wares remains uncertain,"[45] but in view of the knowledge and lengthy experience of the excavators, one may take their dating to be at least approximately correct. Fragment A was put to secondary use in the base of the wall that seems to be no earlier than the mid-ninth century.

The flagstone pavement containing Fragment B2 was also under rubble from the time of Tiglath-pileser III's conquest. The base of the wall containing Fragment B1, built upon that pavement, must also have been at least partly under the same rubble. Excavators examined the level *beneath* the flagstone pavement in the area where Fragment B2 was found. The most recent pottery from under this pavement came from the end of the ninth to the beginning of the eighth century. Therefore, this secondary use of Fragments B1 and B2 probably dates between approximately 825 and 775. It seems that the building of the gate complex progressed slowly and in gradual stages, and apparently Fragments B1 and B2 had lain unused until then.

Although stratigraphy normally takes precedence in dating,[46] this stratigraphy refers to the secondary use, therefore, it can only tell us that the date of writing is around the mid-ninth century and possibly earlier. The epigraphy provides an approximate earliest possible date which agrees with that of the overall stratigraphic picture and with the ceramic typology of the secondary use. The script is very close to the scripts of Phoenician, Ammonite, and Aramaic monumental inscriptions of the tenth, ninth, and eighth centuries. Five items in Fragments A and B are helpful in establishing a reasonable earliest date of writing:

---

[44] Biran and Naveh, "Aramaic Stele," 81, 85–86; Biran and Naveh, "Tel Dan Inscription," 5, 8.

[45] Baruch Halpern, "The Stela from Dan: Epigraphic and Historical Considerations," *BASOR* 296 (November 1994): 68.

[46] See section 1.25, criterion 4, fourth paragraph, above.

1. The form of the letter *tav* in Fragment A provides the clearest chronological line of demarcation. In inscriptions from the thirteenth through the tenth centuries, *tav* looks like a modern plus sign, a cross with all arms of equal or almost equal length, or else like a modern English letter X. In the ninth century, however, an innovation occurred: the lowest of the four arms became a tail three or four times the length of the shortest arm. The lowest arm also became a diagonal stroke descending toward the reader's lower left. Until the discovery of the stele fragments at Tel Dan, the earliest known Syro-Palestinian example of this long-tailed *tav* was in the Melqart stele of Bar-hadad, ca. 850, in which the tail tilts only slightly toward the reader's left as it descends. Outside of Syria-Palestine, the earliest known example of such a *tav* with a long tail descending leftward is in a grave inscription on Cyprus from the early to mid-ninth century.[47] It is therefore reasonable to say that the Tel Dan Aramaic stele was written no earlier than the early to mid-ninth century. (This form of *tav* continued in use for two more centuries.)

2. Fragments A and B1 both contain an *aleph* with a vertical stroke that extends below the lower horizontal stroke only about the length of the upper horn. Also, the triangular face of the *aleph* is rather broad, because the vertical stroke approximately bisects the other two strokes. The earliest known *aleph*s characterized by these traits appear in the Nora stone of Sardinia[48] and the aforementioned Cyprus grave inscription, both dated to the early to mid-ninth century.

3. The earliest known examples of *kaph* which are like those in Fragments A and B1, having a rather widely opened palm, tails, and the same length and direction of fingers are also from the Nora stone and the Cyprus grave inscription.

4. On Fragment A, the letter *waw* does not have the usual rounded U- or V-shaped head that is common in inscriptions from the tenth century onward. Instead, it has a sharply squared chin that gives it the appearance of a modern number four. Before this fragment was discovered, the earliest known example of the square-chinned *waw* was on the Kilamuwa orthostat of the late ninth century. The square-chinned *waw* appears occasionally for at least another four centuries. In view of the relatively small number of ninth-century inscriptions, however, and giving due weight to the earliest dates of the previous three letters, it is reasonable to say that the Tel Dan stele could be slightly earlier than the Kilamuwa orthostat. Epigraphic comparisons, then, point to an early to mid-ninth century *terminus a quo*.

---

[47] *KAI*, Nr. 30.
[48] *KAI*, Nr. 46.

5. Another line of epigraphic evidence points to a date no earlier than the ninth century. The word dividers in the Tel Dan stele are dots. The short vertical line used as a word divider in formal Northwest Semitic inscriptions of the later second and early first millennium "gradually became shorter, until it turned into a dot."[49] The short line of the tenth century continued in frequent use during the ninth and early eighth centuries, but in the ninth century the dot appeared, e.g., in the Mesha stele and the Kilamuwa orthostat, both from the second half of the ninth century. The dot became dominant mainly during the eighth century, e.g., in the inscriptions of Bar Rakab. Although there were some exceptions to this general trend, especially in informal inscriptions, such as graffiti, ostraca, and inscriptions on unbroken pottery vessels, single-dot word dividers apparently were not used before the ninth century.[50]

Because of the fragmentary state of the inscription, many of its historical data have been lost or are unclear. The historical content which has survived is only marginally useful for dating this inscription.

To summarize the range of possible years during which the stele was written, epigraphy indicates an earliest possible date of early to mid-ninth century, and stratigraphy with ceramics indicates that the earliest possible secondary use was in the mid-ninth century. Within the *terminus ante quem* of 733/732, the latest possible date of the writing of the inscription is less clear, but could hardly have been much later than 750. Attempts to narrow this range of roughly 870 to 750 on stratigraphic, ceramic, or epigraphic grounds are generally hazardous.[51]

**Language**: 5) Specifically determined by vocabulary, morphology, and syntax: Aramaic.[52]

---

[49] Joseph Naveh, "Word Division in West Semitic Writing," *IEJ* 23 (1973): 207.

[50] Ibid., 206–8.

[51] E.g., Puech's attempts to narrow the date of writing to the mid-ninth century by comparing the letter shapes with those of inscriptions on Hazael's ivories run the risk of possible differences in the rate of development of the script on stone monuments and that of carved ivory (Émile Puech, "La stèle araméenne de Dan: Bar Hadad II et la coalition des Omrides et de la maison de David," *RB* 101–2 [1994]: 215–41).

[52] On the language of the stele, which seems to be a relatively early southern dialect of Aramaic with grammatical remnants in common with Canaanite, see Frederick H. Cryer, "On the Recently-Discovered 'House of David' Inscription," *SJOT* 8/1 (1994): 9–13, 18; idem, "Of Epistemology, Northwest-Semitic Epigraphy and Irony: The '*bytdwd*/ House of David' Inscription Revisited," *JSOT* 69 (1996): 6; Halpern, "Stela from Dan," 64–68; Edward Lipiński, *Studies in Aramaic Inscriptions and Onomastics II*, OLA 57 (Leuven: Uitgeverij Peeters en Departement Oriëntalistiek, 1994), 97–101; Hans-Peter Müller, "Die aramäische Inschrift von Tel Dan," *ZAH* 8 (1995): 121–39; Takamitsu Muraoka, "Linguistic Notes on the Aramaic Inscription from Tel Dan," *IEJ* 45 (1995): 19–21; Schniedewind, "Tel Dan Stela," 81–82.

**Socio-political classification**: 4) Determined by explicit references to armed conflict with Israel, theological statements mentioning the Aramaean deity Hadad, recognizable language indicators, and provenance near the border of the territory ruled from ancient Damascus: Aramaean. Permitted by the rather broad script parameters. (Ninth-century Aramaic script, for example, had not yet developed significant differences from Phoenician script.[53])

### (3.5) How the inscription correlates with the historical framework

The existence of a mid-ninth century Aramaean kingdom whose capital was at Damascus is documented in Assyrian and Aramaean inscriptions of that century. These sources portray the kingdom of Damascus as a strong military power. The inscriptions of Shalmaneser III (r. 858–824) which mention the king of Damascus include the following:

1. The Kurkh Monolith Inscription, col. 2, lines 90–91, presents $^{md}$IŠKUR-*id-ri* [*ša* KUR.]ANŠE- *šú*, i.e., Adad-idri (Hadad-ezer), king of Damascus, as the leader of the largest force within the anti-Assyrian alliance at the battle of Qarqar in 853.[54]

2. The so-called "Baghdad Text," an edition of the annals on baked clay discovered at Ashur, describes the events of the first sixteen years of Shalmaneser's reign: in the sections for his tenth (849/48), eleventh (848/47), and fourteenth (845/44) regnal years, Adad-idri of Damascus is again named as one of the leaders of the anti-Assyrian alliance in col. 2, line 61, and col. 3, lines 3 and 27, respectively, each time as $^{md}$IŠKUR-*id-ri ša* KUR.ANŠE-*šú*.[55]

---

[53] "There is no basic difference between the Aramaic monumental script and that of the Phoenician inscriptions of the ninth century B.C.E. . . ." (Joseph Naveh, *The Development of the Aramaic Script* [The Israel Academy of Sciences and Humanities Proceedings, vol. 5, no. 1, preprint; Jerusalem: The Israel Academy of Sciences and Humanities, 1970], 8).

[54] Museum no. BM 118884; RawlCu 3, Pl. 7–8; Grayson, *Assyrian Rulers (858–745 BC)*, 23, A.0.102.2.

[55] Col. 2, line 61: Museum no. VAT 9553, Excavation no. Ass 14627. Otto Schroeder, *Keilschrifttexte aus Assur historischen Inhalts* (vol. 2; WVDOG 37; Leipzig: J. C. Hinrichs, 1922), nos. 109–10, 112–15; Grayson, *Assyrian Rulers (858–745 BC)*, 37–39, A.0.102.6. Col. 3, lines 3, 27: Museum no. K 3106, no excavation no., British Museum, Department of Egyptian and Assyrian Antiquities, *Catalogue of the Cuneiform Tablets in the Kouyunjik Collection of the British Museum* (ed. Carl Bezold; London: British Museum, 1891), 2:503.

3. The Kurbail Statue of Shalmaneser III, line 21, shows that ᵐḫa-za-ʾe-DINGIR šá- KUR.ANŠE-šú, i.e., Hazael of Damascus (r. ca. 844/42–ca. 800) carried on this tradition of Damascene military might, opposing Assyria in Shalmaneser's eighteenth year without the aid of a coalition. At the same time, however, ᵐia-ú-a DUMU ᵐḫu-um-ri-i, i.e., Jehu, king of Israel, paid tribute to Shalmaneser, as recorded on the same statue, also in the section for his eighteenth year, lines 29–30. Indications of opposition between the kingdoms of Damascus and Israel during the second half of the ninth century are the breakup of the military alliance (including the forces of "Ahab the Israelite") which the Damascene kingdom had led in 853 and the tribute paid by Jehu to Hazael's major enemy (on Ahab and Jehu, see Chapter 2, note 57, above).[56]

Aramaic inscriptions indicate that the ninth-century Damascene kingdom did not shrink from attacking its neighbors.[57] Perhaps Hazael was taking advantage of the fact that in the later years of the reign of Shalmaneser III, Assyrian military campaigns in Syria-Palestine were largely curtailed. Hazael's military penetration northward is revealed by two bronze, matching horse blinders which were discovered, each during a different part of this century, at a temple at Eretria on the Greek island of Euboea. One of them (Eretria Museum No. B 273) was excavated from a late eighth-century stratum, and the matching blinder (National Archaeological Museum, Athens, No. 15070), from an unknown stratum, bears a poorly preserved inscription in Phoenician style (i.e., ninth-eighth century) Aramaic letters: זי נתן הדד למראן חזאל מן עמק בשנת עדה מראן נהר, "That which Hadad gave our lord Hazael from ʿUmqi in the year that our lord crossed the river." This booty inscription understands these spoils of war to be rewards from the presumed patron deity of the kingdom to the king (cf. section 3.3, note 23). It seems to refer to the region of ʿUnqi in northern Syria (note

---

[56] For an overview of Assyria's relations with Syria-Palestine during the reign of Shalmaneser III, see Jeffrey K. Kuan, *Neo-Assyrian Historical Inscriptions and Syria-Palestine: Israelite/Judean-Tyrian-Damascene Political and Commercial Relations in the Ninth–Eighth Centuries BCE* (Jian Dao Dissertation Series 1; Bible and Literature 1; Hong Kong: Alliance Biblical Seminary, 1995), 5–68.

[57] Regarding the Melqart stele discovered by Dunand in the late 1930s near Aleppo (Maurice Dunand, "Stèle Araméene Dédiée à Melquart," *Bulletin du Musée de Beyrouth* 3 [1941]: 65–76; *DOTT*, 239–41), on the ambiguities of the identity and socio-political classification of its author, Bar-hadad, see Wayne T. Pitard, *Ancient Damascus: A Historical Study of the Syrian City-State from Earliest Times until its Fall to the Assyrians in 732 B.C.E.* (Winona Lake, Ind.: Eisenbrauns, 1987), 138–44; idem, "The Identity of the Bir-Hadad of the Melqart Stela," *BASOR* 272 (1988): 3–21.

the *mem* instead of *nun*), which is frequently attested in ninth- and eighth-century Assyrian inscriptions. The "river" is best interpreted as the Euphrates.[58]

More recently, a bronze ornament (frontlet) for a horse's forehead, whose iconography[59] is very similar to that of the blinders, was discovered at the Heraion on Samos.[60] On it is an inscription which duplicates that on the blinder. It was the legible inscription on this horse frontlet that enabled researchers to render intelligible the aforementioned, poorly preserved blinder inscription.

The Zakkur stele, discovered by Pognon in 1903, reveals in lines 4–5 of its front side that Hazael's son Bar-hadad (II or III, r. ca. 800–ca. 770) continued this tradition of military aggression against neighboring kingdoms into the eighth century: והוחד | עלי | ברהדד | בר | חזאל | מלך | ארם | ש[שת]ן | עשר . . . . מחנתה | ברהדד | מלכן |, "But Bar-hadad, son of Hazael, king of Aram, united against me s[ix]teen kings: Bar-hadad and his camp, [et al.] . . . ."[61]

The Tel Dan stele is an Aramaean, and most likely a Damascene, victory stele composed amid an ongoing conflict against the kingdom of Israel. The provenance of this stele at the extreme northern border of the kingdom of Israel near the kingdom of Damascus, plus its Aramaic language, its reference to armed conflict between the author's dynasty and the king of Israel, and its discovery in a fragmentary state in secondary use in an Israelite city all point to this conclusion. In light of the aggressive military posture of mid-ninth- to early eighth-century Damascus, one should interpret the Tel Dan stele as a record of

---

[58] Israel Eph'al and Joseph Naveh, "Hazael's Booty Inscriptions," *IEJ* 3–4 (1989): 192–200, Pl. 24A, 25A; François Bron and André Lemaire, "Les inscriptions araméennes de Hazaël," *RA* 83 (1989): 35–44. The engraved blinder in the museum in Athens was originally published in Elly Niki, "Sur une 'Potnia-Gorgone' d'Erétrie au Musée national d'Athènes," *RAr* 6me series, 1 (1933): 145–53. Its mate, discovered in 1973, has a stratigraphic context which furnishes a date for both pieces, i.e., the last quarter of the eighth century. This second, matching blinder was published in André Charbonnet, "Le dieu au lions d'Erétrie," *AION* 8 (1986): 117–73, Pl. 33–52. Pages 140–44 refer to this inscription.

[59] See Helene J. Kantor, "Oriental Institute Museum Notes, No. 13: A Bronze Plaque with Relief Decoration from Tell Tainat," *JNES* 21 (April 1962): 93–117, Pl. XI–XV. Cf. Eph'al and Naveh, "Hazael's Booty Inscriptions," Pl. 24A and 25A, with Kantor's very similar Figs. 13A and 13B on 108.

[60] Helmut Kyrieleis and Wolfgang Röllig, "Ein altorientalischer Pferdeschmuck aus dem Heraion von Samos," *MDAI, Athenische Abteilung* 103 (1988): 37–75, Pl. 9–15. The presence of these blinders and this horse frontlet in Greek temples suggests a new meaning in view of the different religious context. Were the Greek deities understood to be receiving Hadad's former spoils, which he had given to Hazael, as their spoils from defeating Hadad? Cf. note 23 above in this chapter.

[61] Henri Pognon, *Inscriptions sémitiques de la Syrie, de la Mésopotamie et de la Région de Mossoul* (Paris: Imprimerie Nationale, 1907), 156–78, no. 86, 209–11, Pl. IX–X, XXXV–XXXVI; *KAI*, Nr. 202.

*Identifications in Provenanced Inscriptions* 121

one of the conflicts that the kingdom of Damascus had with neighboring kingdoms.

### (3.5) How the inscription contributes to the historical framework

This inscription shows that in the shadow of the Assyrian threat, which at one point Jehu might have tried to use against Hazael, his northern neighbor, the kingdom of Israel and that of Damascus were involved in a seesawing military conflict that had probably begun by the mid-ninth century. It is clear that the northern extremity of what was sometimes Israel's territory fell into the hands of alternate sides at various times. The Damascans conquered the city of Dan and erected the stele, then the Israelites conquered and rebuilt the city, breaking the stele and putting some of its pieces to secondary use. The destruction brought about by Tiglath-pileser III in 733/732, used by the stele's discoverers as a latest possible date for the *secondary use* of the fragments,[62] closed this chapter in the history of the conflict between Israelites and the Aramaeans of Damascus.

As for ביתדוד in line 9, the following interpretive options exist:

1. דוד as an Aramaic common noun, either דּוּד, meaning "kettle," as in the term בית דודא, meaning "kitchen," attested over a millennium later at Palmyra,[63] or דּוֹד, meaning "uncle" or "friend." Mention of a kitchen obviously does not fit the context of a victory stele, nor does ביתדוד as "uncle's house."

2. דוד as the title of an official, perhaps a military leader. It may be speculated that such a title might derive from the PN דוד, David, just as the title of Roman emperors, Caesar, began as part of the PN of Caius Julius Caesar. This is

---

[62] Biran and Naveh, "Aramaic Stele Fragment," 85–86; idem, "Tel Dan Inscription," 1–2.

[63] An Aramaic Palmyrene inscription of 243 C.E., line 8, contains the phrase, וזבי בר שעדא די הוא על בית דודא, "and Zabbai, the son of Soʿada, who is over the kitchen," i.e., head cook (Harald Ingholt, "Un nouveau thiase à Palmyre," *Syria* 7 [1926]: 129, 138–39, 141, Pl. XXXIV; *DNWSI*, s.v. "dwd₂," 1:242). In this Palmyrene inscription, the determinative ending insures that this word is a common noun. The fact that there is no such determinative ending on ביתדוד in the Tel Dan stele inscription means that there דוד may be either a common noun in the absolute state or a proper noun. For an earlier, Hebrew attestation of דּוּד, "kettle, pot, jar," see 1 Sam 2:14. It also appears in four other places in the Hebrew Bible. On the analogy of Bethlehem, possibly meaning "bakery," it might be supposed that ביתדוד as "kitchen" could be a similar GN, but no such GN is known. This interpretation is listed as an option in Davies, "'House of David' Built on Sand," 55.

possible both here and in the Mesha Inscription, line 12, in הדוד אראל,⁶⁴ but since such a usage as a title has never been established, it remains speculative.⁶⁵

3. ביתדוד as a GN, rendered variously as Beth-david/BaytDawid, Beth-dōd/BaytDōd, or Beth-daud/BaytDaud.⁶⁶ Despite the use of real GNs as parallels, this possibility remains entirely speculative, because such a GN is completely unknown in the ancient Near East.⁶⁷

4. ביתדוד as a cultic object venerated at Dan.⁶⁸ This interpretation originates from a possible parallel with the Mesha Inscription, lines 3–4 and 12–13, but has no basis in the text of the Tel Dan stele, which is its context.

5. דוד as a DN, Dōd or Daud. There is no firm ground on which to establish the existence of such a deity, despite the fact that many nineteenth-century scholars thought there was a deity named Dōd.⁶⁹ Since then, acceptance of such a deity's existence has greatly decreased in the absence of clear evidence.⁷⁰ Al-

---

⁶⁴ See Appendix E, section E.2, below. For an overview of earlier interpretations of this phrase, see Jackson, "Language of the Mesha Inscription," in Dearman, *Studies*, 112–13.

⁶⁵ See, e.g., Eduard Lipiński, "Etymological and Exegetical Notes on the Meša 'Inscription,'" *Or* 40 (1971): 332–34. The term *dāwîdum* from Mari cannot be used as a basis for interpreting *dwd* as "chieftain" (Hayim Tadmor, "Historical Implications of the Correct Reading of Akkadian *dakû*?," *JNES* 17 [1958]: 129–31).

⁶⁶ E.g., Davies, "'House of David' Built on Sand," 54; Cryer, "On the Recently-Discovered," 17–19. Contra Davies, the absence of a word divider between ב־ית and ־דוד does not make his proposal any more likely, as several scholars have pointed out. The most broadly based case is in Gary A. Rendsburg, "On the Writing ביתדוד in the Aramaic Inscription from Tel Dan," *IEJ* 45 (1995): 22–25. Others include Anson F. Rainey, "The 'House of David' and the House of the Deconstructionists," *BAR* 20, no. 6 (November/December 1994): 47; David N. Freedman and Jeffrey C. Geoghegan, "'House of David' Is There!" *BAR* 21, no. 2 (March/April 1995): 78–79.

⁶⁷ E.g., Freedman and Geoghegan observe that such a GN is unknown in ibid., 79.

⁶⁸ Ernst A. Knauf, Alan de Pury, and Thomas Römer, "*BaytDawid ou *BaytDōd? Une relecture de la nouvelle inscription de Tel Dan," *BN* 72 (1994): 67.

⁶⁹ See Hans M. Barstad, "Dod דוד," in *DDD*, 259–62. For an example of the widespread nineteenth-century acceptance of such a deity's existence, which later was increasingly rejected, see Archibald H. Sayce, *Lectures on the Origin and Growth of Religion as Illustrated by the Religion of the Ancient Babylonians*, (London: Williams & Norgate, 1900), 53, 56–57.

⁷⁰ For examples of support for Dōd's existence set forth in the twentieth century, see Knauf, de Pury, and Römer, "*BaytDawid ou *BaytDōd?" 66–67; Gösta W. Ahlström, *Royal Administration and National Religion in Ancient Palestine*, SHANE 1 (Leiden, Brill, 1982), 14, n. 27; idem, *Psalm 89: Eine Liturgie aus dem Ritual des leidenden*

*Identifications in Provenanced Inscriptions* 123

though it is possible to hypothesize the presence of such a DN in line 12 of the Mesha Inscription[71] and other inscriptions,[72] the name itself *as a DN* remains a hypothesis brought in to explain these texts, rather than an independently known reality (cf. section 2.8). Because, in the inscriptional texts used as evidence, possible DNs are also possible epithets or else unknown terms, such inscriptions provide mere instances of ambiguity.[73] (Personal pronominal suffixes attached to the word דוד in some of these instances, as apparent in, e.g., הדוד in line 12 of the Mesha Inscription,[74] suggest, but only suggest, that in those places דוד might not be a proper noun.[75]) In any event, most scholars find no compelling reason to accept דוד as a DN.[76]

---

*Königs* (Lund: Älund, Haakan Ohlssons, 1959), 164–65; Johann J. Stamm, "Der Name des Königs David," in International Organization of Old Testament Scholars, *Congress Volume, Oxford 1959* (ed. George W. Anderson; VTSup 7; Leiden: Brill, 1960), 172–73, repr. in Johann J. Stamm, *Beiträge zur hebräischen und altorientalischen Namenkunde: Johann Jakob Stamm zu seinem 70. Geburtstag* (ed. Ernst Jenni and Martin A. Klopfenstein; OBO 30; Göttingen: Vandenhoeck & Ruprecht, 1980), 32–33.

[71] This possibility is recognized, e.g., in Jackson, "Language of the Mesha Inscription," 113.

[72] See *DNWSI*, s.v. "dd₁," "dd₄," "dwd₁," "dwd₃," and "dwd₄," 1:241–43; "dr₁," 1:258–59. Van den Branden finds *dd* to be the name of a Canaanite deity in Dedanite, Lihyanite, and Thamudic inscriptions (Albert van den Branden, *Les inscriptions Dédanites*, Publications de l'Université Libanaise, section des études historiques 8 [Beirut: Université Libanaise, 1962], 24, 33–34), corresponding to *dhd* in Minaean and to *dwd* as a DN in the Mesha Inscription, line 12 (on this last "DN," cf. Appendix E, section E.2, below). Such inscriptional names as *ntndd* and *sg'dd*, however, only permit, but do not establish, *dd* as a DN, since *dd* might only be an epithet, "(the) beloved," and almost any deity might receive it. His allegation that such a deity corresponds to *dwd* as a DN in the Mesha Inscription is only an educated guess, and establishes nothing.

[73] See the previous note and, in the same light regarding the ambiguity about possible DNs as possible epithets, the inscriptions listed in Ahlström, *Royal Administration*, 14, n. 27; idem, *Psalm 89*, 164–65; Stamm, "Der Name des Königs David," 32–33.

[74] According to *KAI* 2:175 on the Mesha Stele (Nr. 181), line 12, "The meaning of הדוד only leaves one to guess. The suffix (fem.) may refer to קר . . . ." Andersen and Segert agree that the last letter is a personal pronominal suffix (Andersen, "Moabite Syntax," 90, 93, 101; Stanislav Segert, "Die Sprache der moabitischen Königsinschrift," *ArOr* 29 [1961]: 213). Samuel I. Feigin, "The Origin of 'Elôh, 'God,' in Hebrew," *JNES* 3 (1944): 259, explains the final ה on הדוד in the Mesha Inscription, line 12, as related to the pronoun הוא. See Appendix E, section E.2, below, for Rainey's clear way to end the confusion.

[75] Nevertheless, perfectly acceptable, though rare, inscriptional examples of personal pronominal suffixes attached to proper nouns are found on two Kuntillet ʿAjrūd pithoi, which contain the following: "*brkt ʾtkm lyhwh . . . wlʿšrth*, "I bless you by Yahweh . . . and by his Asherah" (Joseph Naveh, "Graffiti and Dedications," *BASOR* 235

6. דוד as an epithet applied to a deity.⁷⁷ The epithet "beloved" could be applied to deities of the ancient Near East, and it is possible to speculate that in line 9 בהיתה might be used in connection with offering the spoils of war to a deity known by this epithet. There is no evidence, however, to show that among the Aramaeans in the region of Syria דוד was ever used as a divine epithet.⁷⁸ To argue that the identity of the "beloved" were somehow so obvious that it did not need to be stated would be to advance a modern theory without the benefit of ancient evidence.⁷⁹

The case for דוד as an epithet of Yahweh⁸⁰ in inscriptions is fraught with ambiguity. It is largely based on the use of this word in the Israelite inscriptional onomasticon.⁸¹ In theophoric names, however, which ordinarily use an element representing a DN in connection with common nouns or with adjectives and

---

[1979]: 28). On Asherah as a proper noun and a DN here bearing a personal pronominal suffix, see Freedman, "Yahweh of Samaria and his Asherah," 243, 246–49; for that instance and similar examples at Ebla and Ugarit, see Paolo Xella, "Le dieu et 'sa' déesse: l'utilisation des suffixes pronominaux avec des théonymes d'Ebla à Ugarit et à Kuntillet ʿAjrud," *UF* 27 (1995): 599–610.

⁷⁶ "It cannot be established clearly that *dwd* was used as a divine name in the East, West, or South Semitic region. In these areas, where it appears as a theophorous element in proper names (which is not always the case), it functions simply as the appellative of another deity. In the material presently at our disposal there is no evidence, then, that *Dwd* was a god" (Joaquin Sanmartin-Ascaso, "דוד dôdh," *TDOT* 3:148). The present scholarly consensus is that "*dwd* is not a divine name at all, hardly in the biblical *Umwelt* and most certainly not in the Bible itself" (Barstad, "Dod דוד," 260).

⁷⁷ It should be kept in mind that an epithet is not simply an adjective, but "a descriptive adjective, noun, or phrase, often complimentary, accompanying or occurring in place of the name of a person or thing" (*Webster's New Collegiate Dictionary*, s.v. "epithet," definition 1). E.g., in nature: the *rosy-fingered* dawn, in the animal kingdom: *man's faithful friend*, among humans: Frederick *the Great* and *Stonewall* Jackson (ibid.). Among deities, epithets include Zeus *the far-darter*, Adad, *canal-inspector of heaven and underworld*, and the Lord *of hosts*.

⁷⁸ E.g., in *DNWSI*, there are no such Aramaic usages under "*dd*" or "*dwd*."

⁷⁹ Cf. section 1.7, numbered paragraphs 1 through 5; section 1.9 numbered paragraph 5; and section 1.17, numbered paragraph 1.

⁸⁰ "The expression *bytdwd* may be read as . . . referring to the temple of Uncle Yahweh, i.e., an eponymic referent to Yahweh as Godfather . . ." (Schniedewind, "Tel Dan Stela," 80). Cf. Cryer, "On the Recently-Discovered," 17; Davies, "'House of David' Built on Sand," 55; Thomas L. Thompson, "'House of David': An Eponymic Referent to Yahweh as Godfather," *SJOT* 9 (1995): 59–74.

⁸¹ E.g., *KAI*, Nr. 181, 2:175; Sanmartin-Ascaso, "דוד dôdh," 3:150–51; Segert, "Sprache der moabitischen Königsinschrift," 241.

verbs in ordinary use, there is a real possibility that דוד is not an epithet, but simply one of these ordinary elements.⁸²

7. דוד as a PN. Regarding inscriptions that use the pattern בית plus proper noun, which is most common in Aramaic texts, Rendsburg observes, "Examples of X-בית, where X can stand either for a royal name or for a simple place name, but in most cases refers in some way to an independent political entity, are forthcoming from a variety of sources . . . ."⁸³

Assyrian inscriptions use the term É ḫu-um-ri-a (i.e., bît ḫu-um-ri-a) to refer the territory of the kingdom that belonged to the royal house of Omri. By this syntactical pattern, they imply that Omri was known as the founder of a dynasty which ruled the kingdom of Israel.⁸⁴ Rendsburg goes on to state,

> In Assyrian and Babylonian records Aramaean states are repeatedly referred to as *Bit-X*. Examples are *Bit-Adini* . . ., *Bit-Amukkani* . . ., *Bithyani*, *Bit-Dak-kuri*, *Bit-Garbaia*, *Bit-Halupe*, *Bit-Saʾalla*, *Bit-Sillani*, *Bit-Sin*, *Bit-Yahiri*, *Bit-Yakini* and *Bit-Zamani*, again in a disproportionate manner compared to other ethnic or linguistic groups. One might even venture that the Assyrian designation *Bit-Humri* "house of Omri" for the kingdom of Israel reached Assyrian scribes through Aramaean mediation.⁸⁵

In light of these parallels, in an Aramaean inscription which mentions at least one neighboring Hebrew kingdom and its ruler twice in thirteen lines (i.e., the king of Israel in lines 3–4 and 8), it makes sense to interpret a term following בית as a proper noun. Since דוד and ביתדוד have already been shown above not to be clearly identifiable as GNs or DNs, the remaining category of proper nouns is that of PNs. In the Aramaic and Assyrian pattern *bît ḫu-um-ri-a*, the PN designated the founder of a dynasty and the phrase בית plus PN was the term for that dynasty, which by extension became the term for the realm over

---

⁸² Barstad, "Dod דוד," 261. Regarding the subject of דוד as an epithet for Yahweh, see ibid., 260–61.

⁸³ Rendsburg, "On the Writing," 22. See also Kaufman, "Recent Contributions of Aramaic Studies," 44, n. 3.

⁸⁴ An inscription of Tiglath-pileser III (r. 744–727) makes it clear from the immediate context that É ḫu-um-ri-a (i.e., bît ḫu-um-ri-a) means the territory of the kingdom that belonged to the royal house of Omri, i.e., the territory of the northern kingdom of Israel: "[. . . the cities of . . .]-nite, Gil[ead, and] Abel-. . ., which are the border of KUR É ḫu-um-ri-[a]—the ent[ire] wide land of [Bit Hazaʾi]li, I annexed to Assyria." (Summary [alias Display; see *ITP*, 25] Inscription 4, discovered at Calah on a fragmentary slab and left *in situ*, lines 6–7 [*ITP*, 138–39, Pl. XLIX–LI; RawlCu 3, Pl. 10, no. 2]; *ANET*, 283; Galil, *Chronology*, 153).

⁸⁵Rendsburg, "On the Writing," 24.

which that dynasty ruled.[86] Therefore, these are geopolitical terms, not simply GNs. Following this inscriptional pattern, דוד could hardly be anything but a PN, and ביתדוד is the term used for that person's dynasty and realm.

The options of interpreting דוד or ביתדוד as a kitchen, as a cultic object, as the title of an official, as a GN, as a DN, and as a divine epithet have been eliminated, not in theory, but because of real, observable inappropriateness to context, lack of basis in the inscriptional text, and absence of unambiguous evidence of existence. The remaining interpretive option, a PN, fits the internal context of the inscription (as seen in its larger historical framework) and builds on clear indications in the syntactical structures in Aramaic inscriptions. Although it is not the only *potential* option, it has demonstrably existent bases, and it has the best grounding in Aramaic and other inscriptions. Therefore, דוד is best interpreted as a PN, and ביתדוד is best translated as "the house of David," meaning the dynasty of David or the territory it ruled. Although this interpretation is not necessarily final, it would take strong new evidence to overturn it.

This reference to David as the founder of a dynasty raises the question of what realm that dynasty ruled. Biblical data aside, clues in the inscription cannot lead to firm conclusions, because there are breaks in the text. They do, however, suggest the identity of the realm of the house of David. These clues reside in the apparent but unprovable parallel between רם בר ... מלך ישראל -in lines 7–8 and ב-... בר יהו- -in lines 8–9, which seems to make ביתדוד the dynastic "house" to which [ ]-yahu, the son of [ ], belonged. The indications and suggestions in the word sequence are traceable as follows:

1. The word בר, "son," which appears twice, is an indication that the word immediately preceding it is very likely a PN.

2. The מלך ישראל of line 7, whose name apparently ends in -רם, followed by בר, is not the same person as "-יהו," followed by בר, in line 8. This difference is observable in the difference between these two PNs and in the

---

[86] Cryer states,

This fact [i.e., that it is unlikely that -*k bytdwd* in line 9 means [Kin]g Bethdaud], plus the assumption that the parallelism [of *bytdwd* in line 9] with lines 6–8, with their reference to the "king of Israel" in line 8, is intentional and is carried on further in the inscription strongly suggests that the former possibility [i.e., "the king of Betdawd"] is the more likely. Hence it may be that ביתדוד was the author's designation for a geographical unit which may have been equivalent to all or some part of the region we regard as Judah. If so, then the title is comparable to such well-known Assyrian designations as *bit Humri, bit mittinti* [*sic*], and so forth. (Cryer, "On the Recently-Discovered," 17)

presence of the term ביתדוד instead of the corresponding term for a political entity, מלך ישראל.

3. The term מלך ישראל in line 8 and the term ביתדוד in line 9 seem to be parallel, each designating a ruler or a line of rulers of political entities. Since these two names are different from each other, and since the apparent parallelism seems to associate a different person (in point 2 immediately above) with each of them, respectively, it is reasonable to interpret מלך ישראל and ביתדוד as designations for the rulers of two *different* political entities.

4. The person "-יהו" (line 8), who, according to the apparent parallelism, is a member of the ביתדוד, has a theophoric name which designates him as a worshipper of Yahweh. As such, he was the ruler of another Yahwistic political entity besides the kingdom of ישראל (cf. the Mesha Inscription, lines 5, 7, 8).

5. Yahweh, whose name is commonly represented in PNs, including royal names, by the theophoric element *-yaw* or *-yahu*, was the primary, though not the exclusive, deity of two kingdoms: Israel and Judah, as evident from many inscriptional Hebrew PNs and from the Mesha Inscription. The very few inscriptional indications of Yahwism in Syria, compared to the many more indications of the worship of Hadad and Baal in Syria, indicate that there were little more than traces of the worship of Yahweh there.

6. Given the two Yahwistic kingdoms and the fact that Israel is named in a context suggesting that it was different from the "house of David," the Davidic ruler's Yahwistic name certainly seems to indicate that he is the ruler of Judah, where also names ending in *–yahu* were inscribed (see note 136 in this chapter).

7. The stele author's possible claim in lines 8–9 to have killed the king of the house of David and the mention of earlier incursions of the king of Israel into the author's father's land (lines 3–4) in a military context (lines 5–7) seem to point to the author of the stele as a common enemy of both Israel and the house of David. From within an ancient Near Eastern world view which viewed war as a conflict between deities (see section 3.3 under historical framework), opposition to a common enemy serves to support the identity of the house of David as the dynasty of Judah, because both Israel and Judah were largely, if nominally, Yahwistic. From the then-current supernatural point of view in Syria-Palestine and, indeed, in the ancient Near East, it was reasonable that the same deity, Yahweh, would marshal both his kingdoms against the forces of his rival deity, Hadad.

The term "the house of David" makes this inscription very significant for the historical framework. The suggestion in the stele that this dynasty ruled the kingdom of Judah, and the presence of what appear to be fragments of the names of a monarch of Israel (see section 2.8 above) and a monarch of Judah only add to the stele's historical interest (cf. section 2.8).

### (3.5) Question 2: whether the setting of the inscription *permits* a match

**Date**: 3) Agrees with the biblical text, as determined by stratigraphy, ceramic typology, and epigraphy. Dated to approximately 870–750 (see above), it agrees with the Bible in referring to David as a ruler in a previous generation.

**Language**: 1) Agrees with the expectation raised by the biblical text: Aramaic (on the inscriptional side, see above), as specifically determined by inscriptional vocabulary, morphology, and syntax. In light of the seesawing military conflict between the kingdom of Damascus and the kingdom of Israel, partly depicted in the books of Kings (e.g., 1 Kgs 15:20; 20:34; 2 Kgs 8:28; 13:3, 22, 24–25), the language of the inscription agrees with the language expectation raised in the Hebrew Bible for a non-Israelite victory stele at Israel's northernmost city.

**Socio-political classification**: 4) Agrees with the biblical account: Aramaean (see above), as specifically determined by the theological and non-theological references and statements in the inscription plus the language and provenance of the inscription, and as permitted by the script. Regarding the classification of דוד- as a Hebrew PN in ביתדוד, there is one other extant, potential use of the root דוד in the inscriptional Hebrew onomasticon, though it is debated.[87] Neither proven nor disproven, it offers potential support for such a Hebrew PN, which agrees with David's socio-political classification in the Bible. For whatever reason(s), Hebrew PNs based on the root דוד either never were common or else become unpopular among the Hebrews after the ninth century, both in inscriptional and in biblical materials.

---

[87] The name appears as a patronymic on an unprovenanced Hebrew seal of one Ḥilqiyahu, datable to the late seventh to early sixth century. *AHI*, 161–62, no. 100.325, offers both *ddyhw* and *ʿdyhw* as possible readings. The reading *ddyhw* (as *ddjhw*) appears in Nahman Avigad, "New Names on Hebrew Seals," *ErIsr* 12 (1975): 66, no. 2, Pl. 14:2; Vattioni, "I sigilli ebraici III," 242, no. 325; Fowler, 341. On the other hand, *ʿdyhw* finds support in Hestrin and Dayagi-Mendels, *Inscribed Seals*, 80, no. 56; *WSS*, 98, no. 156. The debated letter has the stance of a triangulated *ʿayin* but the short leg of a *daleth*. The root *dwd* is also the basis of some names in Ugaritic and Old Akkadian (Fowler, 292), and Aramaic (Maraqten, 151).

**(3.5) Question 3: How strongly the specific data in the [2] Tel Dan stele count for or against an identification with the biblical (2) King David (r. ca. 1010–970)**

√ **Name**: 1) The name of the person in the inscription is completely present, clearly legible, and in exact agreement with the consonants of one of two biblical spellings of the biblical candidate for identification: דוד.[88] Whether David's name is an element in ביתדוד in line 9 is the subject of ongoing debate, in which the following options have been proposed:

1. דוד as a DN, Dōd or Daud (cf. above, the first numbered paragraph 5 under contributions of the Tel Dan stele to the historical framework). There is no firm ground on which to establish the existence of such a deity in Amos 8:14,[89] where such a DN remains no more than a hypothesis. Further, the personal pronominal suffix in the emendation דֹּדְךָ in Amos 8:14 suggests that the supposed דוד would more likely be a common noun rather than a DN.[90]

2. דוד as a biblical epithet[91] of Yahweh (cf. above, the first numbered paragraph 6 under contributions of the Tel Dan stele to the historical frame-

---

[88] Freedman summarizes the biblical spellings: "The name David occurs 1073 times in the Hebrew Bible. Of these, approximately 788 have the standard three-letter orthography (*dwd*), while the remainder (c. 285) are spelled with four letters (*dwyd*) . . ." (David N. Freedman, "The Spelling of the Name 'David' in the Hebrew Bible," *Hebrew Annual Review* 7 (1983): 89).

> The books of the Bible, . . . generally speaking, . . . with the three-letter spelling belong to the First Temple period (or not later than the first part of the 6th century), while those with the four-letter spelling may be assigned to the Second Temple period. Those which have a mixed spelling may be assigned to the transitional period between the other two, or roughly the middle part of the 6th century. (Ibid., 102)

[89] A widely referenced emendation of דֹּדְךָ to דֹּדְךָ in Amos 8:14 (Knauf, de Pury, and Römer, "*BaytDawid ou *BaytDōd?" 66–67; Ahlström, *Royal Administration*, 14, n. 27; idem, *Psalm 89*, 164–65; Stamm, "Der Name des Königs David," 32–33, etc.) appears to have originated in Hugo Winckler, *Altorientalische Forschungen* (Leipzig: Eduard Pfeiffer, 1893–1905) 1:195. It is an ingenious attempt to explain the difference between the MT and the LXX᾽ ὁ θεός σου, but it must be admitted that᾽ ὁ θεός σου simply repeats the corresponding term from the previous clause in the verse. It does not explain why the LXX does not use᾽ ἀγαπητός or another word with a meaning similar to "beloved." Apparently the LXX translator, unable to make sense of דֹּדְךָ, simply substituted the parallel term from the preceding clause. On the text criticism and interpretation of this verse, see Shalom M. Paul, *Amos* (ed. Frank M. Cross; Hermeneia; Minneapolis: Fortress, 1991), 271.

[90] See notes 74 and 75 above.

[91] See note 77 above.

work). The case is based on the use of this word in Cant, Isa 5:1, emendation from דֹּרֶךְ to דֹּדְךָ in Amos 8:14, and the Israelite onomasticon of the Hebrew Bible. As Barstad correctly points out, in Cant, understood as love poetry, דוד refers to a lover, and in Isa 5:1, this term refers to Yahweh in a poetic metaphor and is not used as an epithet.[92] The emendation in Amos 8:14 is not necessarily correct and is not necessarily an epithet at all. It might just as easily indicate a common noun not used as an epithet. In theophoric names, whether inscriptional or biblical, there is a real possibility that דוד is not an epithet, but simply an ordinary, non-epithetical noun.[93] Attempts to read דוד as a biblical epithet fail.

3. דוד as a PN (cf. above, paragraph 7 under contributions of the Tel Dan stele to the historical framework). The biblical phrase "the house of [name of king]" is the characteristic term for a dynasty, and it is used of the hereditary lines of Saul, David, Ahab, Jehu, Jeroboam, and Baasha. Such usage is a specific extension of the broader use of the term "house of [name of ancestor]" to refer to a family, clan, tribe, or kingdom.[94] The term בֵּית דָּוִיד or בֵּית דָּוִד, "the house of David," which occurs 24 times in the Hebrew Bible,[95] is frequently used in the sense of the Davidic dynasty (e.g., Jer 21:11, 12).[96]

As far as can be observed, this biblical term seems synonymous with the dynastic meaning of the term ביתדוד in the Tel Dan stele. The apparent but unprovable parallelism between the word sequences רם בר ... מלך ישראל in lines 7–8 and -יהו בר ... ך- ביתדוד in lines 8–9 seems to make ביתדוד the dynastic "house" to which king [ ]-yahu, the son of [ ], belonged. This works especially well if the ך- before ביתדוד is the final letter of מלך.[97]

---

[92] Barstad, "Dod דוד," 260.

[93] Ibid., 261. On the subject of דוד as an epithet for Yahweh, see ibid., 260–61.

[94] Harry A. Hoffner, "בַּיִת bayith," TDOT 2:113–15.

[95] 2 Sam 3:1, 6; 19:11; 1 Kgs 12:19, 20, 26; 13:2; 14:8; 2 Kgs 17:21; Isa 7:2, 13; 22:22; Jer 21:12; Zech 12:7, 8, 10, 12; 13:1; Ps 122:5; Neh 12:37; 1 Chr 17:24; 2 Chr 8:11; 10:19; 21:7.

[96] Only twice does the Bible use this exact term to refer to the physical building in which David lived (1 Sam 19:11 and Neh 12:37).

[97] Some have objected to supplying מלך here on the grounds that "Indeed, never, neither in the biblical literature nor in the inscriptions of Syria-Palestine do we find the expression 'king of the house of NN,' ..." [Knauf, de Pury, and Römer, "*BaytDawid ou *BaytDōd?" 65]. Na'aman, however, finds this to be "a very strange argument" and points out six clear instances in Assyrian inscriptions in which a "*Bit* PN" construct combination is preceded by the word šar (i.e., "king"), by the name of a ruler, vel cetera. He also points out four biblical instances in which byt dwd is preceded by a word in the construct state (Nadav Na'aman, "Beth-David in the Aramaic Stela from Tel Dan," BN 79 [1995]: 20).

In a context of neighboring kingdoms at war, in which the Hebrews looked back upon David's and Solomon's reigns as the age of empire, it makes good interpretive sense, as Victor Sasson has observed, that an Aramaean conqueror would use "the occasion to brag about the devastation he had inflicted on Judah."[98] He most likely used the term ביתדוד, meaning "house of David," to magnify his victory over a once mighty dynasty.

**Relations**: 2) In the inscription, a patronymic is absent, therefore there is none for the Bible to match or contradict. Nevertheless, the Aramaic term ביתדוד indicates that דוד was the founder of a dynasty. This identifying mark in the area of relations registers under the category of singularity, treated below.

√ **Title(s)**: 2) The title as implied clearly indicates the position of the inscriptional candidate, even though there is no explicit title. In this instance, the title is implied in the Aramaic inscription and stated in the Hebrew Bible: מֶלֶךְ.

**Other**: 3) Other identifying information is vague in its meaning. The inscription suggests by apparent parallelism between "the king of Israel" and "the house of David" that the two are allied kingdoms, if only in their shared struggle against Damascene aggression. The apparent parallelism also suggests that the house of David was a dynasty *of Judah*; the Hebrew Bible, of course, asserts this connection very clearly in several books and in a large number of passages.[99]

√ **Singularity**: 1) The available data require an ID on grounds of both inscriptional singularity and biblical singularity. On the inscriptional side, just as the Assyrians apparently borrowed an Aramaic pattern and called the "house of Omri" by the name of its founder, so also the Aramaeans themselves called a contemporary dynasty, "the house of David," by the name of its founder. According to biblical dates, David's own reign ended approximately ninety years before Omri's reign began. In the single term, ביתדוד, two identifying criteria are met: the name of the individual and one other identifying mark: that he was the founder of the dynasty.

In fact, this last mark is more specific than most supplied in other inscriptions. Whereas the title עבד המלך, for example, is generic, because more than one individual held the office, there was *only one* founder of the house of David. It is impossible to answer question 3 more specifically. The combined evidence regarding David in this inscription supports the conclusion that the historical existence of the founder of the house of David is now evident both in an excavated inscription and in the Hebrew Bible. Knauf, de Pury, and Römer grasp what such a conclusion implies: "Certainly David is not mentioned there

---

[98] Victor Sasson, "The Old Aramaic Inscription from Tel Dan: Philological, Literary, and Historical Aspects," *JSS* 40 (1995): 22.

[99] E.g., 2 Sam 2:4; 5:4–5; 1–2 Kgs, passim; Isa 7:13.

as an individual, but how not to conclude from the mention of a 'dynasty of David' the historicity of its founder, indeed of his empire?"[100]

### (3.5) Remarks

The foregoing evidence and discussion allows the following conclusions (see the augmentation in the final section of Appendix E, under "Remarks"):

1. Although interpreters are free to favor possibilities for ביתדוד meaning something other than "the house of David," these other meanings remain largely theoretical, rather than demonstrable.

2. There was a dynasty called ב֯יתדוד, "the house of David," mentioned both in the Hebrew Bible and, according to the weight of the evidence, also in the inscription on the Tel Dan stele.

3. "The house of David" in this inscription and in the Bible was a dynastic and geopolitical entity referred to as such by the Aramaeans in the characteristic terminology they used for naming such entities of that era. The inscriptional suggestion that David's dynasty ruled Judah meets with biblical affirmation.

4. The house of David was important enough to be recognized internationally and was considered significant enough to be mentioned in a public monument, likely as an enemy whose military power was recognized, so that any leader who could defeat it could justly boast.

5. David's name is incorporated into a dynastic or territorial term in an Aramaean inscription sometime between just over a century and just over two centuries after his reign. David's existence and his status as the founder of a dynasty now stand documented both in an excavated inscription and in the Bible.

---

[100] Knauf, de Pury, and Römer, "*BaytDawīd ou *BaytDōd?" 60.

*Identifications in Provenanced Inscriptions* 133

## 3.6 Is the biblical Jeroboam II, king of Israel, named in the Megiddo seal of Shema, the minister of Jeroboam?

### Description, transcription, and translation

The original, unperforated jasper scaraboid seal,[101] measuring 37 mm. long, 26.5 mm. wide, and 17 mm. thick,[102] was lost in Istanbul. A bronze cast (IDAM, Copy No. 230) in the Rockefeller Museum, Jerusalem, remains the only reliably accurate copy. The magnificent, incised profile of a roaring lion facing left dominates the seal. In front of and behind the lion, two objects were not incised but rather painted in a pale color on the face of the original seal. Behind the lion was painted an Egyptian *ankh*, and in front of the lion was painted an object which could be interpreted as another *ankh* or as a palm tree.[103] Above the lion is engraved לשמע, "belonging to Shema."[104] Beneath a single line under the lion's feet is engraved עבד ירבעם, "Minister of Jeroboam."[105] Two lines surround the seal's face.

### (3.6) Question 1: reliability of the inscriptional data

**Access**: 1) Excavated under controlled conditions.
**Provenance**: 1) Within the site of the find, the exact findspot is known.[106]
**Authenticity**: 1) Regarded as authentic, because excavated.

### (3.6) The setting of the seal of Shema apart from biblical data

**Date**: 4) Dated by stratigraphy, whose ambiguity is resolved by the indications of epigraphy (normally, undisturbed stratigraphy takes precedence over

---

[101] The seal of Shema, discovered in 1904 in Gottlieb Schumacher's excavations at Tell el-Mutesellim (Megiddo), was first published in Emil Kautzsch, "Ein althebräisches Siegel vom Tell el-Mutesellim," *MNDPV* 10 (1904): 1–14; idem, "Zur Deutung des Löwensiegels," ibid., 81–83. See also *WSS*, 49, no. 2; *AHI*, 129, no. 100.068.

[102] Gibson 1:62, no. 13.

[103] Diringer, 225–26, no. 68.

[104] Shema is apparently a hypocoristicon for שְׁמַעְיָו, "Yaw has heard," i.e., has granted my prayer request.

[105] The name ירבעם is probably derived from רבב, and, if so, means, "Let the people increase."

[106] Gottlieb Schumacher, *Tell el-Mutesellim*, vol. 1: *Fundbericht*, B. *Tafeln* (Leipzig: Rudolf Haupt, 1908), Table XXIX, A. Plan des Palastes; Carl Watzinger, *Tell el-Mutesellim*, vol. 2: *Die Funde* (Leipzig: J. C. Hinrichs, 1929), 64; Ussishkin, "Gate 1567," 413, Fig. 24-1, 421.

epigraphy[107]). This seal was found within a meter of the inner face of the city wall, in debris lying about 1 m. west of Gate 1567 and above the courtyard of Palace 1723. Palace 1723 and its courtyard belong to Stratum VA/IVB, which is considered to be from what has been called the Solomonic period, ca. 970–931. Stratum IVA is considered to be from the period of the kingdoms of Israel and Judah before the Assyrian conquest of 732. Stratum IVA is the last phase of public architecture at Megiddo, and it includes City Wall 325 and the so-called stable compounds. Above that level, Strata III and II contained no remnants of public buildings, but only of private housing. The initial excavator, Gottlieb Schumacher, did not uncover the whole structure of Gate 1567. Later excavators Lamon and Shipton did not understand how six-chambered gates were constructed. They dated the upper part (i.e., the floor) of Gate 1567 to Stratum IVA, but they assigned the lower part (i.e., the foundation) of the very same gate to Stratum VA/IVB, misinterpreting it as an earlier gate that had been walled shut.

The seal of Shema was 0.5 m. (according to Lamon and Shipton) to 1.5 m. (according to Schumacher) above the elevation of the floor of Gate 1567.[108] Ussishkin observes that when this stratigraphic position is considered separately from other seals excavated at this site, it is "ambiguous."[109] That is, according to its stratigraphy alone, the seal of Shema could belong to the "divided kingdom" Stratum IV(A) or to the "Solomonic" Stratum VA/IVB. (The biblical context presented below will reveal that each of these periods has a different Jeroboam.)

Another beautiful Megiddo seal, made of lapis lazuli, decorated with a striding, winged griffin, and inscribed לאסף, "belonging to Asaph," was found inside Gate 1567, lying on the second-from-the-top row of foundational ashlars. The top row had been robbed out before the initial archaeological excavation. This seal most likely dates to the gate's destruction and fell into the robber trench from the floor of the gate. Ussishkin has opined that

> the stratigraphic context of the two seals should be considered together. The two seals are very similar typologically. Both of them are unpierced, a relatively unusual feature in Hebrew seals, and must have been mounted on rings. The rings were not found, and it must be assumed that the seals were torn from their mounts in antiquity. The seal of Asaph seems to have belonged to an official comparable to Shema. Both seals were uncovered in association with a single public building used in a single period and not replaced by similar structures in later periods. A priori it would seem an extraordinary coincidence that two similar seals would have been left in the same place under different circumstances. Hence, if the seal of Asaph

---

[107] See section 1.25, Criterion 4, fourth paragraph, above.
[108] Ussishkin, "Gate 1567," 421, based on calculations on 415 and 417.
[109] Ibid., 421.

### Fig. 9

**A Bronze Cast from the Megiddo Seal "of Shema, the Minister of Jeroboam"**

(Drawing by the author)

most likely belonged to the stratigraphic context of Gate 1567, so then did the seal of Shema, even if its stratigraphic position is ambiguous. It seems quite possible that the two seals were kept in the gatehouse, or even in Palace 1723, to be used there by government officials. At the time of the palace's destruction, someone took the seals; tore away the rings, which were probably of precious metal; and discarded the scaraboids before leaving the (already burning?) compound.[110]

The seals of Haman and Elamar, also unpierced and beautifully decorated, were discovered in the same vicinity, but they had been removed from their original stratigraphic context, probably during Schumacher's excavation and possibly from the locale of Gate 1567. All four of these seals are unperforated, elegant seals of semiprecious stone with animal iconography. None of the rings which provided settings were found. It is Ussishkin's view that "in summary, the circumstantial evidence suggests the possibility that all four Hebrew seals belonged to government officials and stemmed from the same context."[111]

He concludes that since the floor of Gate 1567 does not come from a stratum later than that of the tenth-century foundation, but from the same stratum, the seal of Asaph and hence the seal of Shema, the minister of Jeroboam, should be assigned to Stratum VA/IVB, late tenth to early ninth century. Therefore, according to Ussishkin, the Jeroboam named in the seal is Jeroboam I, king of Israel (r. 931/30–909). In this ID, he concurs with Yeivin and Ahlström.[112]

Ussishkin's dating of the seal of Shema is logical, plausible, and possible, but the connections on which it depends are not clear enough to be convincing. The similarities of the seal of Shema, with its lion, to that of Asaph, with its griffin, are no closer than its similarities to several other well-decorated seals of this and other locations and of other centuries. Although it was a common practice to perforate seals, this seal's lack of perforation is not rare. The seal of Asaph could have fallen onto the foundational ashlars of Gate 1567 from any of two or three stratigraphic levels which were above, and therefore later than, the gate when, "in a later period,"[113] the upper layer of ashlars were robbed out.

Epigraphy indicates a date within the eighth century. In archaic Hebrew script, the legless *daleth* and nearly circular *'ayin*s of this seal find similar forms in the Gezer Calendar (tenth century) and the Mesha Inscription (late ninth century). On the other hand, the *'ayin*s here are not perfectly circular, and the first two seem to be intermediate between a circular and an oval form, which is later,

---

[110] Ibid., 422.

[111] Ibid., 423.

[112] Shmuel Yeivin, "The Date of the Seal 'Belonging to Shemaʿ (the) Servant (of) Jeroboam," *JNES* 19 (1960): 205–12; Gösta W. Ahlström, "The Seal of Shema," *SJOT* 7 (1993): 208–15.

[113] Ussishkin, "Gate 1567," 422.

and which became triangular. A legless *daleth* is attested as late as the early eighth century Hebrew inscription ND.10150 of the Nimrud ivories.[114]

The *mem* in the upper register of this seal consists of a slightly angular U shape whose lower right edge appears to be tangent to an upside-down *lamedh* shape. This may be an early "double lamedh" form, datable to the eighth century. The *mem* in the lower register, whose head has separate strokes for the center and left verticals and a slanting right vertical that is abutted by the top of the vertical tail, finds a similar form in the seal impression לצדק / סמך, approximately of the late eighth century.[115] Both are eighth-century *mem*s, not ninth-century. Considered together, the epigraphic traits of this seal are mid-eighth century.

**Language**: 5) The language of the inscription cannot be specifically determined on linguistic grounds. If language parameters are set by vocabulary, morphology, and syntax, most Northwest Semitic languages of the day are options.

**Socio-political classification**: 3) The inscription's Hebrew character is determined by its script and provenance. It is permitted by the onomastic parameters,[116] broad language parameters, arrangement of text,[117] and material characteristics of the seal.[118] The northern provenance indicates that it is Israelite.

### (3.6) How the seal of Shema correlates with the historical framework

The Mesha Inscription documents the existence of Israel as a kingdom during a few decades leading to a point in the mid-ninth century. Assyrian inscriptions document the existence of kings of Israel here and there down to the eighth-century reign of Hoshea (see Chapter 2, note 57, above). This seal provides similar documentation between these two dates.[119]

---

[114] Alan R. Millard, "Alphabetic Inscriptions on Ivories from Nimrud," *Iraq* 24 (1962): 45–49, 51, Pl. 24a.

[115] *SANSS*, 109, no. 58, Fig. 57, no. 58, Fig. 71, no. 58.

[116] Both the PN שמע and its theophoric compounds are very common in Hebrew inscriptions. PNs formed from the root שמע appear in at least ten non-Hebrew socio-political classifications (Fowler, 284; *WSS*, 536, *SANSS*, 208).

[117] Animals between two lines of writing, all horizontally arranged and without horizontal lines demarcating registers also appear on at least one other excavated Hebrew seal (*WSS*, 63, no. 35, fish) and two marketed Hebrew seals (*WSS*, 84, no. 108, bird; ibid., 158, no. 374, quadruped).

[118] An unperforated, scaraboid Hebrew seal made of jasper is not unusual.

[119] It is worth noting that the city of Stratum VA/IVB may have been brought to an end by the conquest of Sheshonq I (r. 945–924) ca. 925, which is attested by his stele fragment at Megiddo (Robert S. Lamon and Geoffrey M. Shipton, *Megiddo I: Seasons of*

### (3.6) How the seal of Shema contributes to the historical framework

The eighth-century date of this seal adds it to the documentary evidence for the continuity of this kingdom between the reign of Omri and that of Hoshea.

The provenance of the seal of Shema, the minister of Jeroboam, indicates an Israelite socio-political classification, and its script exemplifies a Hebrew writing culture. Indeed, the royal ministers carried out the administrative functions of the kingdom using seals of notable refinement and beauty.

### (3.6) Question 2: whether setting of the seal of Shema, the minister of Jeroboam, *permits* a match with the biblical Jeroboam II

**Date**: 3) (see above) Agrees with the biblical account, especially by the match between the date of the seal and the second of two alternatives (i.e., Jeroboam I or Jeroboam II) offered by the Hebrew Bible.

**Language**: 3) The language of the inscription presents no known disagreement with the language expectation raised by the biblical account: Hebrew.

**Socio-political classification**: 3)[120] Agrees with the biblical account: Israelite, as determined by its provenance and script (see above).

### (3.6) Question 3: How strongly the specific data in [7] Megiddo seal לשמע עבד ירבעם count for or against an identification with the biblical (12) Jeroboam II, king of Israel (2 Kgs 13:13ff; r. 790–750/749)

√ **Name**: 1) Completely present, clearly legible, and in exact agreement with the consonants of all biblical spellings of the name of Jeroboam II.

**Relations**: 5) In the inscription, no patronymic appears, therefore there is none to match or contradict Jeroboam's biblical patronymic. In the Bible, no servant of King Jeroboam (I or II) named שמע is mentioned, therefore there is none to match or contradict that of the inscription.

√ **Title(s)**: 2) The title *ʿebed* preceding the PN of the inscriptional person to be identified implies that he is a king (see Appendix A).

---

*1925–34, Strata I–V*, [OIP 42; Chicago: University of Chicago Press, 1939], Fig. 70; Graham I. Davies, *Megiddo* [Cities of the Biblical World; Grand Rapids, Mich.: Eerdmans, 1986], Fig. 18, 89, 96.

[120] Regarding onomastic phenomena, such as the PN Shema, the root שמע, "to hear, obey" is too common in Semitic PNs to be a distinctive marker for any socio-political classification; Fowler finds it in eight language groups, including Hebrew (Fowler, 284). As for Jeroboam, similarly, the root רבב and the word עם are too common in Semitic PNs to be distinctive of Hebrew or any other language group in which it is found (ibid., 280, 294).

*Identifications in Provenanced Inscriptions* 139

**Other**: 3) Other identifying information is vague in its meaning. By itself, the lion iconography suggests that the seal owner may have been an official in the king's court,[121] but according to present knowledge does not guarantee it.

√ **Singularity**: 2) Once the combined stratigraphic and epigraphic evidence pointing to an eighth-century date is accepted, then it will be seen that the available data require an ID on grounds of biblical singularity. In the Hebrew Bible's list of Hebrew kings of the biblical era, only two bear that name, Jeroboam I (r. 931/30–909) and Jeroboam II (r. 790–750/49), both rulers of the northern kingdom of Israel.

### (3.6) Remarks

The preference above not to follow the circumstantial evidence offered by the seal of Asaph does not utterly eliminate the option to date Shema's seal to Stratum V/IVB and therefore to identify Shema's king as Jeroboam I of Israel. Those who take that option, however, have the difficulty of explaining epigraphic traits of the mid-eighth century in the seal of a tenth-century personage. From the other point of view, Ussishkin's date appears as an alternative option, rather than as an insurmountable difficulty, to the ID of Jeroboam II.

### 3.7 Is the biblical Shaphan the scribe, father of Gemariah, named in the city of David bulla of Gemaryahu?

### Description, transcription, and translation[122]

The bulla is approximately 14 mm. long and 12 mm. wide. It was discovered among a group of fifty-one bullae averaging between 2 and 6 mm. thick.[123] It is aniconic, with one line surrounding the smooth, inscribed face and two horizontal lines between the upper and lower register. A missing fragment from the lower right eliminated the first letter of the lower register. The inscription reads, לגמריהו [ב]ן שפן, "belonging to Gemaryahu, [so]n of Shaphan."

---

[121] Izak Cornelius, "The Lion in the Art of the Ancient Near East: A Study of Selected Motifs," *JNSL* 15 (1989): 53–85; Kautzsch, "Zur Deutung des Löwensiegels," 81–83; Yeivin, "Date of the Seal," 209–10, 212.

[122] The bulla of Gemariah, son of Shaphan, excavated in the summer of 1982, received its first scholarly publication in Yigal Shiloh, *Excavations at the City of David I, 1978–1982: Interim Report of the First Five Seasons* (Qedem 19; Jerusalem: The Hebrew University of Jerusalem, The Institute of Archaeology, 1984), 19–20, Pl. 35, no. 3. See also *WSS*, 191, no. 470; *AHI*, 233, no. 100.802.

[123] The length and width are according to the measurements of the sketch drawn to scale in Shiloh, "Group of Hebrew Bullae," 28, Fig. 8. The average thickness is mentioned in ibid., 27.

## (3.7) Question 1: reliability of the inscriptional data

**Access**: 1) Excavated under controlled conditions.[124]
**Provenance**: 1) Within the city of David, the exact findspot is known.[125]
**Authenticity**: 1) Regarded as authentic, because excavated.

## (3.7) The setting of the bulla of Gemaryahu, apart from biblical data

**Date**: 4) Dated by stratigraphy, ceramic typology,[126] and epigraphy. The bulla was in Stratum 10B. "Stratum 10 represents the second half of the seventh century . . . to the final destruction early in the sixth century."[127] The relevant ceramic assemblage, which includes a storage jar bearing the rosette seal impressions normally attributed to the latter half of the seventh century,[128] "is . . . paralleled at various Judean sites in the latest phase of the Iron Age II, which came to an end in 586."[129]

Epigraphic examination of the bulla of Gemaryahu reveals no letter traits that date it more precisely than the eighth to early sixth centuries. At least two of

---

[124] Shiloh, *Excavations I*, 18–20, 29; idem, "Group of Hebrew Bullae," 16–38, Pl. 4–7.

[125] Area G, Squares B–C 5–6, Locus 967, which is a 1 m. by 8 m. area called the "House of the Bullae," in its northern corner (Shiloh, *Excavations I*, 18–20, 29; idem, "Group of Hebrew Bullae," 17–21, 25, Pl. 4–6).

[126] "The house of the bullae," in which this bulla was found, is in Stratum 10B, which dates from the second half of the seventh century to 586 (Shiloh, *Excavations I*, 3, 19, 29). Regarding "the destruction layer of Stratum 10—the destruction of the entire city by Nebuchadnezzar in 586 BCE," Shiloh finds that "the pottery of the destruction stratum in all areas is identical with the corpus of pottery typifying the other sites in Judah of the very end of the Iron Age, such as at Lachish stratum II, En-Gedi stratum V, Arad stratum VI and Ramat Raḥel stratum V" (ibid., 29).

[127] Shiloh, "Group of Hebrew Bullae," 23.

[128] Scholars have usually dated the rosette seals of Judah to Josiah's reign (r. 640/39–609). But using stratigraphic evidence, Jane Cahill, 1980 to 1982 supervisor in Area G, where the 51 bullae were discovered, dates the earliest Judahite rosette seal impressions to 605/604, in the reign of Jehoiakim (Jane M. Cahill, "Comparing the *lmlk-* and Rosette-Stamped Vessels," paper presented at the Annual Meeting of the SBL and the ASOR, New Orleans, November 26, 1996); idem, "Rosette Stamp Seal Impressions from Ancient Judah," *IEJ* 45 (1995): 230–52; idem, "Rosette-Stamped Handles," in *Inscriptions* (ed. Donald T. Ariel; vol. 6 of *Excavations at the City of David 1978–1985 Directed by Yigal Shiloh*; City of David Final Report 6; Qedem 41; Jerusalem: The Hebrew University of Jerusalem, The Institute of Archaeology, 2000), 85–108; idem, "Royal Rosettes Fit for a King," *BAR* 23, no. 5 (September/October 1997): 48–57, 68–69.

[129] Shiloh, "Group of Hebrew Bullae," 23.

### Fig. 10

### The City of David Bulla
### "of Gemaryahu, Son of Shaphan"

(Drawing by the author)

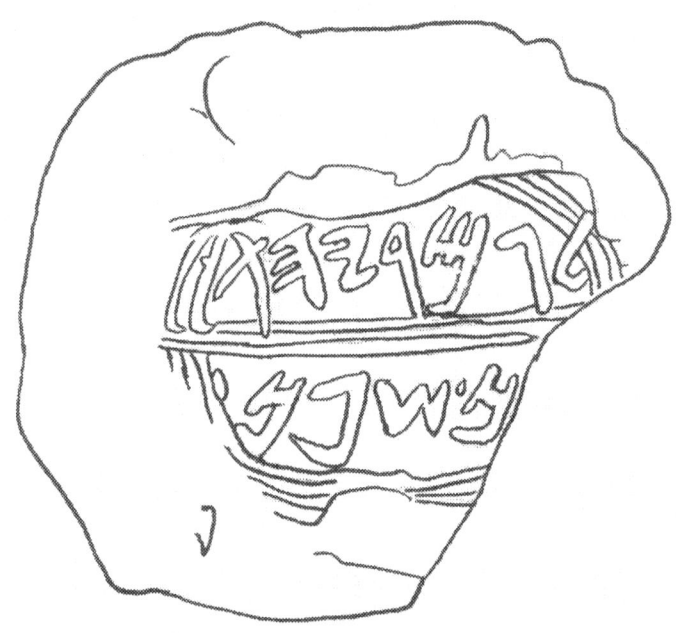

the other fifty bullae excavated from the same findspot, however, exhibit a letter *he* which indicates the late seventh to early sixth centuries. That is, the three crossbars of this *he* are not parallel, but converge toward the open (the reader's left) side of the letter, and its top crossbar extends beyond the vertical shaft.[130] These are the bulla "belonging to Benayahu, son of Hoshayahu"[131] and the bulla "belonging to ʿAzaryahu, son of Ḥilqiyahu."[132] They indicate that the archive was not closed until the late seventh or early sixth century. Therefore, the bulla should be assigned to the period 630–586, primarily on the basis of stratigraphy, with the consent of epigraphy.

**Language**: 5) The inscription's language cannot be specifically determined on linguistic grounds. If language parameters are set by vocabulary, morphology, and syntax, then Hebrew, Ammonite, Moabite, and Edomite are options.

**Socio-political classification**: 2) Determined by the theophoric element, i.e., *-yahu* in Gemaryahu's name, along with the Hebrew script and the provenance: Hebrew. Permitted by the onomasticon of inscriptional Hebrew,[133] the language parameters, the arrangement of the text on the bulla,[134] and the material characteristics of the bulla.[135] Both the theophoric element, *-yahu*, rather than *-yaw*,[136] and the city of David provenance indicate that it is specifically Judahite.

---

[130] Vaughn, "Palaeographic Dating of Judaean Seals," 47, 52–53.

[131] Shiloh, *Excavations I*, 19, Pl. 35, no. 2; idem, "Group of Hebrew Bullae," 29, no. 31, Pl. 7, no. C. The *he* in the upper register and the first of two *he*s in the lower register are diagnostic.

[132] Ibid., 19, 61, Fig. 26; idem, "Group of Hebrew Bullae," 28, Fig. 8, no. 6, and 29, no. 27. The diagnostic *he* appears in the lower register.

[133] The PN Shaphan occurs in four other Hebrew inscriptions, of which one is provenanced (*WSS*, 538; *AHI*, 505). This PN is also found in one unprovenanced Moabite seal (*WSS*, 538).The PN Gemaryahu is present in seven other Hebrew inscriptions, of which six are provenanced (*WSS*, 492; *AHI*, 327). PNs based on the root *gmr* appear in Ugaritic and Amorite inscriptions (Fowler, 285).

[134] It is common for Hebrew bullae of the late seventh to early sixth century to be aniconic, with the text running the length of the ringed, oval writing surface in two registers separated by two lines.

[135] Hebrew bullae are small, dark lumps of clay with a seal impression on the front, sometimes with indentations from papyrus fibers and string on the otherwise flat back.

[136] Describing the discovery in Jerusalem of a Hebrew seal impression reading "Belonging to Neri son of Shebanio," i.e., "for . . . the first time . . . a name terminating in the shortened theophoric element *-io* . . . found in Judah in a clear archaeological context" (Nahman Avigad, *Discovering Jerusalem* [Oxford: Basil Blackwell, 1984], 44), Avigad summarizes the phenomena of the endings as follows:

## (3.7) How Gemaryahu's bulla correlates with the historical framework

In light of the historical framework, this bulla is to be interpreted as that of a man in the kingdom of Judah during the late seventh to early sixth century. He must have been actively involved as a witness in the process of official documentation in the city of Jerusalem during that time. The presence of his bulla accompanying records in the capital city of Judah suggests that he might have

---

While names ending in the *-io* [i.e., the *-yw*] form were common in the northern Kingdom of Israel—as evidenced by the Samaria Ostraca of the 8th century B.C., in names such as Abio, Gadio, Obadio, Shemario—in the Kingdom of Judah the theophoric element was given a fuller form, *-iahu* [i.e., *-yhw*]—as seen in the Arad Letters of the 8th–7th centuries B.C., and the Lachish Letters of the early 6th century B.C., in names such as Abiahu, Berechiahu, Gemariahu, Obadiahu, and Shemariahu. It has been suggested—and quite properly—that the names Amario, Obadio, and Shemaio occurring in the Hebrew inscriptions of the 9th and early 8th centuries B.C. recently discovered at Kuntillet ʿAjrud, in northern Sinai, represent persons who may well have been from the northern kingdom. But our new discovery in Jerusalem [i.e., of the *-yw* form] supports the view that names ending in *–io* occurred in Judah as well as in Israel in the 9th and 8th centuries B.C., under northern influence. After the fall of Samaria in 722 B.C., the *-io* form ceased to be used in Judah, as in the north. It is of note that names such as Urio and Aḥio reappear again in Judah in the post-exilic period [ibid.].

Here Avigad represents a scholarly consensus that Hebrew names ending in *-yahu* which can be dated between the fall of the northern kingdom of Israel near the end of the eighth century and the late-sixth-century beginning of the post-exilic period must be from Judah. Cross takes the same position:

... There is the use in these seals of the syncopated form of the divine name *-yaw*. So far as our evidence goes, this form does not appear in Judah in the age of monarchy after the 8th century. All Hebrew seals from Northern Israel use *-yaw-*, and the same is true of ostraca of northern provenience. In Judah *-yhw-* /yahû/ was used in the 8th century, and as well, in a small group of seals, including seals of officials of Jerusalem, the syncopated form *-yaw-* appears: ʾbyw ʿbd ʿzyw, šbnyw bd ʿzyw, mqnyw ʿbd yhwh, ʾyqm n ʾr ywkn, ʿšyw bn ywqm, and ʿzryw hgbh. In Judah in the 7th–6th centuries *-yhw-* /yahû/ is used exclusively. That the form *-yhw-* /yahû/ was pronounced with the *h* sounded (and hence not merely historical spelling) is clear from Babylonian transcriptions of the early 6th century B.C.E. (Cross, "The Seal of Miqnêyaw, Servant of Yahweh," in *Ancient Seals and the Bible* [ed. Gorelick and Williams-Forte], 57)

Thus, theophoric endings may be of use in discerning the northern or southern origin of preexilic Hebrew inscriptions. Cf. H. L. Ginsberg, "Lachish Notes," *BASOR* 71 (1938): 24–25; Sara Japhet, "The Supposed Common Authorship of Chronicles and Ezra-Nehemia Investigated Anew," *VT* 18 (1968): 338–41; Zevit, *Matres Lectionis in Ancient Hebrew Epigraphs*, 12–13, n. 14.

been a government official. For Shiloh's interpretation of the archive in which it was discovered as a public archive, see "Question 3, Other, 3," below in this section.

### (3.7) How Gemaryahu's bulla contributes to the historical framework

The bulla of Gemaryahu, son of Shaphan, develops the historical framework by providing the name and patronymic of an official witness in the documentation process at Jerusalem, capital of the kingdom of Judah, during the late seventh to early sixth century.

### (3.7) Question 2: whether setting of Gemaryahu's bulla *permits* a match

**Date**: 3) The date of 630–586 permits a match.
**Language**: 3) The language of the inscription, although not specifically determined by vocabulary, morphology, and syntax, presents no known disagreement with the language expectation raised by the biblical account: Hebrew.
**Socio-political classification**: 2) Agrees with the biblical account: Judahite Hebrew, according to the theophoric ending, script, and provenance (see above).

### (3.7) Question 3: How strongly the specific data in [48] the city of David bulla לגמריהו / ]בן[ שפן count for or against an identification with the biblical (36) Shaphan the scribe, son of (34) Azaliah, son of (33) Meshullam, and father of (50) Gemariah (2 Kgs 22:3ff, Jer 36:10ff)

√ **Name**: 1) The name of Shaphan is completely present, clearly legible, and in exact agreement with the consonants of the biblical spelling: שפן.

√ **Relations**: 1) The inscriptional filionymic matches the biblical one with only a negligible difference in spelling: inscriptional *-yahu* and biblical *-yah*.

**Title(s)**: 7) An inscriptional title is absent. Some biface stamp seals have the owner's name, but no title, on one side and the owner's name and title on the other side of the same carved stone. One example which is reliable, because it was acquired long before knowledge of appropriate epigraphy was available to forgers, is the seal obv. לשבניו rev. לשבניו ע / בד עזיו (see section 4.3 below). We may speculate that perhaps the side with the title was reserved for royal documents, whereas the side with only the owner's name but no title was used to impress bullae on more ordinary documents, such as records of land bought and sold by commoners. This bulla of Gemaryahu might represent an instance in which the side of a seal without a title was used by a titled official.

√ **Other**: 1) Three other inscriptional facts tend to make this ID agree with the biblical data:

1. The provenance of the bulla is strikingly close to the most likely location of two of the three biblical scenes in which Shaphan appears: the temple and the royal palace.[137] The bulla was discovered well within three hundred meters south of and downhill from the presumed site of the First Temple in Jerusalem, in the city of David.[138] The fact that Micaiah, the son of Gemariah, "went down" (וַיֵּרֶד, Jer 36:12) from the temple to the royal palace probably means that the place where this bulla was discovered was even closer to the palace[139] than to the temple. The findspot, "the house of the bullae," Locus 967 in Area G of Shiloh's excavations, is only about 250 meters[140] south of the southern edge of the modern Ḥaram esh-Sharif. This area is also called the Temple Mount, and it is the traditional site of the First Temple. The bulla's findspot is too close to the most likely locations of the biblical scenes to be ignored.

Because of the chance that another seal owner named Gemaryahu, with the same patronym, might have lived in Jerusalem at the same time, the provenance of this bulla, seen as an identifying mark, might not be regarded with quite the same degree of confidence as, for example, a title. But observe two other facts:

2. The name Shaphan is attested relatively infrequently; it occurs in only four other Hebrew inscriptions. One of these is provenanced: a seal that reads only "שפן," from a Jerusalem cave, ca. 700; the others are unprovenanced: a seal, "לשפן ב / מתן," a seal, "לשפן / פדיהו" (late seventh or early sixth century), and [47] bulla "לא[חיקם / [ב]ן שפך]."[141] In view of the more than

---

[137] 2 Kgs 22:3–10; par. 2 Chr 34:8–9, 14–18.

[138] As the highest point in the city of David, it was the culturally appropriate location for a temple. Tradition agrees by placing the location of Solomon's Temple within the bounds of the present-day Haram esh-Sharif. The Western Wall of the Second Temple as rebuilt by Herod the Great, which was presumably built in the same location as that of the First Temple, is visible today.

[139] According to ancient Near Eastern culture, as revealed in many sites, the royal palace was located near the temple in the highest part of the city.

[140] I.e., approximately 230 meters when depicted from directly overhead, as on a map. The vertical dimension of the mountain slope adds somewhat to this distance.

[141] The first is an inscription discovered by Kenyon's excavators in the Jerusalem cave labeled Cave I, item no. 127 (Jean Prignaud, "Scribes et Graveurs à Jérusalem vers 700 av. J.-C.," in *Archaeology in the Levant: Essays for Kathleen Kenyon* [ed. P. Roger S. Moorey and Peter J. Parr; Warminster: Aris and Phillips, 1978], 136; *AHI*, 67, no. 4.108, 505). For the three unprovenanced seals, see *WSS*, 162, nos. 387, 388, and 181–82, no. 431.

All in all, the infrequency of the name Shaphan among the Judahite populace militates against any supposition that more than one Shaphan served in the royal administration—or was the father of others who served therein—during the late monarchic period from the reign of King Josiah onward.

1,200 preexilic Israelites whose names are known from inscriptions,[142] this is not a common name. There are only three or four Shaphans in the Hebrew Bible besides the scribe in 1 Kgs 22:3ff.[143] Of the Shaphans in Jerusalem, who were probably few at most, how many would have had a son named Gemaryahu?

On duplicate pairs of name and patronymic, Shiloh and Tarler observe,

> Surprisingly, although there are 45 cases [among 51 bullae in this hoard] in which both the personal name and the patronymic survive, there are no bullae that have identical mates with the hundreds of inscriptions, seals, seal impressions, or other bullae comprising the written archaeological source material of ancient Israel. One name, however, "ʿAzaryahu son of Ḥilkiyahu," also appears on a seal found in Jerusalem and published by Avigad . . . [cf. section 3.9 below].[144]

3. The fact that this bulla was discovered in what was most likely a government archive strongly suggests that it belonged to a government official. Although some government officials owned several seals and used them for administrative tasks, as at Arad,[145] there was very little repetition of names in the archive that contained this bulla. Shiloh interprets the immediate context of this bulla, i.e., the hoard of fifty-one bullae, as follows: "The fact that the names do not overly repeat themselves, as would be expected in a private or family archive, . . . would indicate that this find may represent a public archive, located in some bureau close to the administrative centre in the City of David."[146]

**Singularity**: 3) An ID on grounds of singularity is not required.

### (3.7) Remarks

Since this grade 3 ID is of a scribe, rather than a king, we have here a rare, documented detail of a high administrator in Judah's government, ca. 600. Provenance by itself is usually too general to be an identifying mark. In this instance, it is the *combination* of the following that creates specificity: the PN Gemaryahu, the infrequent PN Shaphan, the findspot very near the locations specified in the biblical narrative, and the indication that the seal owner was most likely a government official, as the biblical Shaphan's son Gemariah was.

---

[142] Tigay, *You Shall Have No Other Gods*, 9.

[143] I.e., the father of Ahikam in 2 Kgs 22:12, who seems to be the same as the scribe in vv. 3ff, the father of the Elasah who served as Jeremiah's messenger in Jer 29:3, and the father of Jaazaniah in Ezek 8:11.

[144] Yigal Shiloh and David Tarler, "Bullae from the City of David: A Hoard of Seal Impressions from the Israelite Period," *BA* 49 (1986): 204.

[145] E.g., Eliashib, commandant of the fortress at Arad, three of whose seals have been discovered (Aharoni, *Arad Inscriptions*, 119–20, nos. 105–7, 142–43, 149–50).

[146] Shiloh, *Excavations I*, 20.

## 3.8 Is the biblical Gemariah, son of Shaphan the scribe, named in the city of David bulla of Gemaryahu?

On the inscription itself, its authenticity, its relationship to the historical framework, and its setting, see section 3.7 above.

**(3.8) Question 3: How strongly the specific data in |48| the city of David bulla שפן ן|בן / לגמריהו count for or against an identification with the biblical (50) Gemariah, son of (36) Shaphan the scribe, son of (34) Azaliah, son of (33) Meshullam (Jer 36:10ff)**

√ **Name**: 2) The spelling has a negligible difference: inscriptional -*yahu* rather than the biblical -*yah*.
√ **Relations**: 1) The inscriptional patronymic matches the consonants of the biblical one: שפן.
**Title(s)**: 7) An inscriptional title is absent. On the absence of a title in what might be the seal of a titled official, see under "Title(s)," question 3 in section 3.7 above.
√ **Other**: 1) Other facts regarding the bulla agree with the biblical account. See "Other" under question 3 in section 3.7 above.
It is observable here that a person with an unusual patronym, found also in the Bible, left behind some of his finished work within about 250 meters of where the Bible depicts him with his colleagues. He was doing the work of a civil servant, as the Bible designates him, and his work was left in what was very likely a public archive. When combined, these facts are even more specific than a title.
**Singularity**: 3) An ID on grounds of singularity is not required.

### (3.8) Remarks

Whereas the names of rulers, which are more common in provenanced inscriptions, provide an overall structure and sequence, this grade 3 ID is not of a monarch, but of one of several שָׂרִים (Jer 36:12), officials[147] of the royal administration. By giving us a glimpse of this person, this ID documents a detail about the government of Judah in its twilight years. (Cf. Chapter 2, note 18).

---

[147] Fox, *In the Service of the King*, 158 63.

148  *Identifying Biblical Persons in Northwest Semitic Inscriptions*

## 3.9 Is the biblical Hilkiah the high priest, father of Azariah, named in the city of David bulla of Azaryahu?

### Description, transcription, and translation

This bulla[148] is about 14.5 mm. long and 13.5 mm. wide. It was discovered in the same group of fifty-one city of David bullae as that of Gemaryahu (see section 3.7), which averaged between 2 and 6 mm. thick.[149] Like Gemaryahu's bulla, it is aniconic, with one line circumscribing its face and two registers separated by two horizontal lines. On its face is impressed, לעזריהו ב / ן חלקיהו, "belonging to Azaryahu, son of Hilqiyahu." This ID was first made by a Hebrew University library staff member, Tsvi Schneider.[150]

### (3.9) Question 1: reliability of the inscriptional data

**Access**: 1) Excavated under controlled conditions; this bulla's Registry No. is G.11652. On the provenance and authenticity, see section 3.7 above.

### (3.9) The setting of the bulla of Azaryahu, apart from biblical data

Date:4) Dated by stratigraphy, ceramic typology,[151] and epigraphy. For stratigraphic and ceramic dating, see section 3.7, "Date," above. The bulla of Azaryahu has a diagnostic *he* in the lower register. Its converging horizontals, of which the top one crosses the vertical shaft, indicate a late seventh- to early sixth-century date.[152]

---

[148] The bulla of ʿAzaryahu, son of Ḥilqiyahu, excavated in the summer of 1982, received its first scholarly publication in 1984 in Shiloh, *Excavations I*, 19, 61, Fig. 26. See also Shiloh, "Group of Hebrew Bullae," 28, Fig. 8, no. 6, and 29, no. 27; *WSS*, 224, no. 596; *AHI*, 235, no. 100.827.

[149] The average thickness is mentioned in ibid., 27. These measurements are from the scale drawing in Shiloh, "Group of Hebrew Bullae," 28, Fig. 8.

[150] Tsvi Schneider, "Azariahu, Son of Hilkiahu (High Priest?) on a City of David Bulla," *IEJ* 38 (1998): 139–41; idem, "Six Biblical Signatures: Seals and Seal Impressions of Six Biblical Personages Recovered," *BAR* 17, no. 4 (July/August 1991)): 30–33.

[151] "The house of the bullae," in which this bulla was found, is in Stratum 10B, which dates from the second half of the seventh century to 586 (Shiloh, *Excavations I*, 3, 19, 29). Regarding "the destruction layer of Stratum 10—the destruction of the entire city by Nebuchadnezzar in 586 BCE," Shiloh finds that "the pottery of the destruction stratum in all areas is identical with the corpus of pottery typifying the other sites in Judah of the very end of the Iron Age, such as at Lachish stratum II, En-Gedi stratum V, Arad stratum VI and Ramat Raḥel stratum V" (ibid., 29).

[152] Vaughn, "Palaeographic Dating of Judaean Seals," 47, 52–53.

### Fig. 11

**The City of David Bulla
"of Azaryahu, Son of Ḥilqiyahu"**

(Drawing by the author)

On the language and socio-political classification, see section 3.7 above. This bulla, discovered in the same hoard as that of Gemaryahu, bears two names with the Judahite theophoric ending *yahu* (see note 136 in this chapter). As for the onomasticon, Azaryahu and Ḥilqiyahu are very common Hebrew PNs.[153]

On the correlation of this bulla with the historical framework, see section 3.7 above.

This bulla provides the same sort of glimpse of the priests as the one described in section 3.7 does of royal officials. Also as in that section, under question 2, the general setting of this bulla permits a match.

**(3.9) Question 3: How strongly the specific data in [50] the city of David bulla לעזריהו ב / ן חלקיהו count for or against an identification with the biblical (37) Hilkiah the high priest, father of (38) Azariah (2 Kgs 22:4ff)**

√ **Name**: 1) The name is completely present, clearly legible, and in exact agreement with the consonants of one of two biblical spellings: חלקיהו.

√ **Relations**: 1) The inscriptional filionymic matches the biblical one with only a negligible difference in spelling: inscriptional -*yahu* and biblical -*yah*.

**Title(s)**: 7) No inscriptional title is present. On the absence of a title in what might be the seal of a titled official, see under question 3 in section 3.7. Also, as Elayi has observed, the unprovenanced seal ring לחנן ב / ן חלקיהו הכהן / has a number of epigraphic traits that indicate the same date and even the same engraver as that of the seal that made this bulla; see "Date" under question 2 in section 4.7 below. If this seal ring proves to be authentic, then the title *hkhn*, meaning not just "the priest," but "the high priest" (see "Title(s)" under "Question 3" in section 4.7) will be seen to apply to the חלקיהו of this bulla, as well, because both will be identifiable with the same person in the Bible.

√ **Other**: 1) The provenance of the bulla agrees well with the biblical settings, i.e., the First Temple and the royal palace, because, strikingly, it is within about 250 meters of what are certainly to be regarded as the ancient sites of both; see "Other" under question 3 in section 3.7 above.

Although the provenance is the same, this bulla is different from that of Gemaryahu, son of Shaphan in that both of its names, Azaryahu and Ḥilqiyahu, were very common in eighth- to sixth-century Judah. No rarity of one name can be combined with the provenance to achieve specificity. Nevertheless, the fact that among all fifty-one bullae in its group, this is the only one whose combina-

---

[153] It is only the theophoric ending that makes them distinctively Hebrew. PNs based on the root חלק are found in Phoenician and Aramaic (Fowler, 280); those based on עזר (or Amorite חזר) appear in Phoenician, Aramaic, and Amorite (Fowler, 289).

tion of name and patronymic is duplicated elsewhere, and only in one unprovenanced seal, is evidence that this *combination* of names cannot be regarded as very common.[154] In any event, the provenance, supported slightly by the combination of names, should be taken into account as a factor in evaluating this potential ID. Although this ID is not virtually certain, like those of Shaphan and of Gemariah in sections 3.7 and 3.8 above, it is still a reliable grade 3 ID.

**Singularity**: 3) An ID on grounds of singularity is not required.

## (3.9) Remarks

This is the only excavated Hebrew inscription in which any high priest(s) of the First Temple can be identified. In this reliable ID, the father can safely be considered the illustrious Hilkiah, who served as high priest during the reign of Josiah and who "discovered the book of the law in the house of the Lord" (2 Kgs 22:8). It is evidence that a Yahwistic priesthood was functioning in Jerusalem in the late seventh to early sixth century.

## 3.10 Is the biblical Azariah, son of Hilkiah the high priest, named in the city of David bulla of Azaryahu?

On the inscription itself, its authenticity, and its relationship to the historical framework, see section 3.9 above. On its setting, see sections 3.7 and 3.9 above. These sections account for questions 1 and 2.

---

[154] In section 3.7, above, Question 3, under "Other," just after numbered paragraph 2, see the quotation from Shiloh and Tarler.

The seal, לעזריהו / חלקיהו, contains in its upper register a diagnostic *he*, which, by its converging horizontals and top horizontal bar crossing the vertical shaft, indicates a late seventh- to early sixth-century date (Vaughn, "Palaeographic Dating of Judaean Seals," 47, 52–53.). That seal did not produce the bulla under consideration, but if this seal is authentic, there is some possibility that it might have belonged to the same Azaryahu, since we know of examples in which one person owned and used more than one seal (e.g., Eliashib, commandant of the fortress at Arad during the seventh century until 609, three of whose seals have been discovered [Aharoni, *Arad Inscriptions*, 119–20, nos. 105–7. 142–43, 149–50]). Azaryahu's seal was in the Shlomo Moussaieff collection when published (Nahman Avigad, "Six Ancient Hebrew Seals" [in Hebrew], in *Shmuel Yeivin Volume* [ed. Shmuel Abramsky et al.; Jerusalem: Kiryat Sefer, 1970], 305, n. 1, no. 4, 307, no. 4). Since this seal contains only a name and a patronymic and is unprovenanced, it cannot provide more than a conditional grade 2 ID; therefore, it is not treated in this chapter or the next.

**(3.10) Question 3: How strongly the specific data in [50] the city of David bulla of Azaryahu count for or against an identification with the biblical (38) Azariah, son of (37) Hilkiah the high priest (1 Chr 5:39;[155] 9:11; Ezra 7:1)**

√ **Name**: 2) There is a negligible difference in spelling: inscriptional -*yahu* compared to the biblical -*yah*.

√ **Relations**: 1) The inscriptional patronymic exactly matches the consonants of a spelling of the biblical one.

**Title(s)**: 7) An inscriptional title is absent. On the absence of a title in what might be the seal of a titled official, see under question 3 in section 3.7 above. See also under "Title(s)" in question 3, section 4.7 below, on the unprovenanced seal ring לחנן ב ן חלקיהו / הכהן.

√ **Other**: 1) The provenance of the bulla agrees well with the biblical settings, i.e., the First Temple and the royal palace, because it is within about 250 meters of what are arguably the ancient sites of both; see "Other" under question 3 in section 3.9 above.

**Singularity**: 3) An ID on grounds of singularity is not required.

**(3.10) Remarks**

This is a grade 3 ID of the same degree of strength as that in section 3.9 above; in this instance, a father and son, both high priests, can be identified reliably. Therefore, this bulla provides an example of a high priest serving as a witness in a documented transaction.

---

[155] 1 Chr 6:13 in English versions.

# Chapter 4

# Identifications in Unprovenanced Inscriptions

## 4.1 The scope of potential identifications evaluated in this chapter

The corpus of inscriptions treated in Chapters 3 and 4 is defined in section 3.1 above. Since the deadline at the beginning of October 1997, several publications of relevant "new," unprovenanced inscriptions have appeared.[1]

## 4.2 Is the biblical Uzziah, king of Judah, named in the seal of Abiyaw?

### Description, transcription, and translation

This unpierced agate seal,[2] which was probably used in a ring, measures 16.1 mm. long by 12 mm. wide by 3.8 mm. thick, and its reverse side is nearly flat. Down the center of its ellipsoid face, in a vertical or "portrait" orientation, is a carved figure variously identified as the Egyptian sun god,[3] the Egyptian in-

---

[1] See Appendixes B and C below, which are updated through July 2002. In these appendixes, footnotes frequently mark the addition of updates (post-deadline items).

[2] The seal of Abiyaw, minister of Uzziyaw, purchased on the antiquities market, was first published in Ernst Otto F. H. Blau, "Bibliographische Anzeigen," *ZDMG* 12 (1858): 726. Its last published location is La Bibliothèque Nationale, Paris, specifically in "le Cabinet des Médailles, la collection François Chandon de Briailles, no. 156" (*CSOSI*, 45). It is listed in *AHI*, 129, no. 100.065, and in *WSS*, 51, no. 4.

[3] G. A. D. Tait, "The Egyptian Relief Chalice," *JEA* 49 (1963): 113, Fig. 4, 115, no. 16, 134–36, 135, Fig. 7.

fant solar deity Nefertum,[4] the newly born Horus,[5] or as Harpocrates.[6] Wearing an Egyptian wig or hairstyle topped by an Egyptian crown, he is kneeling on his right knee atop a lotus blossom between two lotus buds. In impressions produced by this seal, he is facing the reader's left and has his right hand raised, palm forward, as if in a gesture conferring blessing, while his left hand covers his solar plexus. Below his head, his only discernible clothing seems to be a belt. Vertically, behind the figure's crown and back, is engraved לאביו עבד, "belonging to Abiyaw, the minister (of)," which reads downward. In front of the figure and the lotus blossom the name עזיו, "Uzziyaw," is also engraved vertically but reads upward.[7] A single line surrounding the face of the seal is broken by three minor chips which do not interfere with the text or image.

### (4.2) Question 1: reliability of inscriptional data

**Access**: 3) Purchased on the antiquities market in 1858 or earlier.
**Provenance**: 4) Unknown.
**Authenticity**: 2) Presumable, because when it was purchased in the mid-nineteenth century, knowledge of epigraphy was not sufficient to forge letters that would fit in with the typology of letter shapes that developed later.[8] The authenticity of this seal is virtually certain, because the specific letter shapes consistent both with each other and with the date of the biblical Uzziah certainly could not have been known by forgers when the seal was purchased, ca. 1858.

### (4.2) The setting of the seal of Abiyaw, apart from biblical data

**Date**: 5) Dated by epigraphy: mid- to late eighth century. Among the diagnostic letters are the two *waw*s; the fact that in them the right stroke does

---

[4] *CSOSI*, 45.

[5] Max E. L. Mallowan, *Nimrud and Its Remains* (New York: Dodd, Mead, & Co., 1966), 475.

[6] Diringer, 221, no. 65.

[7] The PN Abiyaw means, "Yaw is my father." Uzziyaw means, "Yaw is my might."

[8] This concept is not original with this study and perhaps not with the source used here, which is the following statement regarding the authenticity of the Mesha Inscription: "The form of the letters is consistent with other inscriptions of the 9th cent. B.C. and could not have been known when the stone was discovered" (Patrick D. Miller Jr., "Moabite Stone," *ISBE* 3:396).

*Identifications in Unprovenanced Inscriptions* 155

**Fig. 12**

**The Seal "of Abiyaw, the Minister of Uzziyaw"**

(Reversed to appear as an impression. Drawing by the author)

not cross over to the left side of the vertical shaft is a reliable indicator of an eighth-century date (All but one of the extant examples of such a form of *waw* are early to mid-eighth century; the one exception is late eighth century).[9] The form of the *aleph* has parallels as early as the second half of the eighth century.[10] The *zayin* with its cursive-style ticks on both horizontals is found on exemplars as early as the late eighth century.[11] The ligatured *beth* and *daleth* in עבד find close parallels in the late eighth-century seal לאשנא ·ע / בד · אחז (treated below in section 4.4). A date in the second half of the eighth century best accommodates these paleographic traits.[12]

**Language**: 5) The language of the inscription cannot be specifically determined on linguistic grounds. If language parameters are set solely by vocabulary, morphology, and syntax, most Northwest Semitic languages of the day are viable alternatives.

**Socio-political classification**: 3) Determined by the two theophoric elements -*yaw*[13] and the Hebrew script. Permitted by the onomasticon of inscriptional Hebrew,[14] the language parameters, the arrangement of the text on the face of the seal,[15] and the material characteristics of the seal:[16] Hebrew.

### (4.2) How the seal of Abiyaw correlates with the historical framework

Although two texts of Tiglath-pileser III (r. 744–727) refer to a man named Azriyau, it does not appear demonstrable that he is to be identified with the bib-

---

[9] See Chapter 2, note 3, second paragraph, above.

[10] *SANSS*, 89, no. 14, 127, no. 102, Hebrew Seal Script Fig. 64, nos. 14, 102.

[11] Ibid., 136, no. 127, Hebrew Seal Script Fig. 67, no. 127.

[12] Bordreuil proposes a date between 780 and 740 (*CSOSI*, 45); Cross dates it "ca. 768–734" (Cross, "Seal of Miqnêyaw, Servant of Yahweh," in *Ancient Seals and the Bible*, [ed. Gorelick and Williams-Forte], 56).

[13] See Chapter 3, note 136, above.

[14] The PN Abiyaw occurs in three or four other Hebrew inscriptions, of which one or two are Samaria ostraca (ca. second quarter of the ninth century to mid-eighth century), one is an undated seal from Carthage, and one is an unprovenanced seal dated to the eighth century (*AHI*, 266; *WSS*, 475). The forms Abiyah and Abiyahu also appear in Hebrew inscriptions (*AHI*, 266; *WSS*, 475). PNs formed from אב, "father," are found also in at least nine other socio-political classifications (Fowler, 280; *WSS*, 475).

The PN Uzziyaw is present in only one other Hebrew inscription, the seal of Shubnayaw (see section 4.3 below), which is also unprovenanced (*WSS*, 522; *AHI*, 458). There are four other Hebrew theophoric compounds and hypocoristica based on the root עזז (*WSS*, 521–22; *AHI*, 457–58). PNs based on the root עזז appear in inscriptions of at least six other socio-political classifications (Fowler, 288; *WSS*, 521–22).

[15] See sections 2.2 above and 4.3 below.

[16] Several Hebrew seals are unperforated, iconic, and made of semiprecious stone.

lical Azariah/Uzziah.[17] The Hebrew script, the two theophoric elements, and the use of the term *'ebed* as a title on a seal, however, make it evident that the seal owner's master was a Hebrew monarch. It is not possible on purely inscriptional grounds to say which kingdom he ruled. Extant inscriptions of the northern kingdom of Israel exhibit the syncopated suffix, /-*yaw*/, spelled י-, to the exclusion of /-*yahu*/ (written as יהו-). But until the late eighth century, the seals and bullae of Judah display both of these theophoric endings.[18] Therefore, the inscriptional evidence reveals only that Uzziah was a mid-eighth-century Hebrew king, not which kingdom he ruled.

Assyrian and Babylonian inscriptions mention four kings of Judah: Jehoahaz (see section 4.4 below), Hezekiah (see section 4.6 below), Manasseh,[19] and Jehoiachin,[20] but not Uzziah/Azariah.

---

[17] For a discussion of Azriyau, whose ID as Azariah/ Uzziah, king of Judah, was once widely accepted, see Na'aman, "Sennacherib's 'Letter to God,'" 25–39 (contra *ANET*, 282); cf. Hayim Tadmor, "Azriyau of Yaudi," *Scripta Hierosolymitana* 8 (1961): 232–71; *ITP*, 273–74. Tadmor observes that "had it been the name of an Aramean, or had it been transmitted to Assyria through Aramaic, the name would probably have been rendered *Idri-yau* in Akkadian transcription . . ." (ibid., 273, n. 1). His current position seems to be that the question of this potential ID cannot be resolved without new evidence (ibid., 274). For bibliography of works for and against this ID, see Becking, *Fall*, 3, n. 9.

[18] See Chapter 3, note 136, above.

[19] "Manasseh (ᵐ*me-na-si-i*), king of Judah (KUR *ia-ú-di*)," according to Prism B of Esarhaddon (r. 680–669), was among those who paid tribute to the latter (Esarhaddon's Prism B, column 5, line 55; R. Campbell Thompson, *The Prisms of Esarhaddon and Ashurbanipal* [London: Trustees of the British Museum, 1931], 25; *ANET*, 291; Galil, *Chronology*, 154). Also, Ashurbanipal (r. 668–627) records that "Manasseh, king of Judah (ᵐ*mi-in-si-ešar* KUR *ia-ú-di*)" paid tribute to him (Ashurbanipal's Cylinder C, col. 1, line 25; Maximilian Streck, *Assurbanipal und die letzten assyrischen Könige bis zum Untergang Niniveh's*, [Vorderasiatische Bibliothek 7; Leipzig: J. C. Hinrichs, 1916], 2:138–39; *ANET*, 294; Galil, *Chronology*, 154).

[20] Jehoiachin is named in four Babylonian administrative tablets regarding oil rations or deliveries. Discovered at Babylon, they are dated from the tenth to the thirty-fifth year of Nebuchadnezzar II. One tablet calls Jehoiachin ᵐ*ia-ʾ-u-kin* and applies the title "king" to him. (Text Babylon 28122, obverse, line 29; William J. Martin, "The Jehoiachin Tablets," *DOTT*, 86, Text [a], first line; *ANET*, 308). A second mentions "[ᵐ*ia*]-ʾ-*kin*, king of KUR *ia*[ . . . ]" in an immediate context that refers to "[ . . . so]ns of the king of Judah (KUR *ia-a-ḫu-du*)" and "Judahites (LÚ *ia-a- ḫu-da-a-a*)" (Text Babylon 28178, obverse, col. 2, lines 38–40; Martin, "Jehoiachin Tablets," 86, Text [b], second through fourth lines; *ANET*, 308). The third tablet calls him "ᵐ*ia-ku-ú-ki-nu*, the son of the king of Judah (KUR *ia-ku-du*)" and refers to "the five sons of the king of Judah (KUR *ia-ku-du*)" (Text Babylon 28186, reverse, col. 2, lines 17–18; Martin, "Jehoiachin Tablets," 86, Text [c], third and fourth lines; *ANET*, 308). It is unknown whether the language back-

158   *Identifying Biblical Persons in Northwest Semitic Inscriptions*

**(4.2) How the seal of Abiyaw contributes to the historical framework**

This seal provides inscriptional information about an eighth-century Hebrew king, a ruler of the kingdom of Israel or the kingdom of Judah, who is not known from Egyptian, Assyrian, or Babylonian inscriptions. His name reveals a Yahwistic religious background.

**(4.2) Question 2: whether the setting of Abiyaw's seal *permits* a match**

**Date**: 5) Agrees with the biblical account (see "Date" above).
**Language**: 3) The language of the inscription presents no known disagreement with the language expectation raised by the biblical account: Hebrew (see above).
**Socio-political classification**: 3) Agrees with the biblical account: Hebrew (either Israelite or Judahite; see "How the seal of Abiyaw correlates . . ." above), permitting a match.

**(4.2) Question 3: how strongly the specific data in [17] the seal לאביו עבד עזיו count for or against an identification with the biblical (20) Uzziah, king of Judah (2 Kgs 15:13ff; r. 788/7–736/5)**

√ **Name**: 2) Spelling has a negligible difference. On the spelling of the theophoric element as *-yw* rather than the biblical *-yhw* or its biblical alternative *-yh*, which are both used in Uzziah's name in the Hebrew Bible, see Chapter 3, note 136, above.
**Relations**: 5) Both an inscriptional patronymic and a biblical servonymic are absent, so neither source can match or contradict a counterpart in the other.
√ **Title(s)**: 2) The inscriptional title of Abiyaw's master, which is implicit in the servant's title of *'ebed*, matches the biblical title *melek* (see Appendix A).

---

ground, writing skills, or attitude of the scribe led to the latter spelling of Jehoiachin's name. The fourth text, the most fragmentary of all, confirms "Judah" and part of Jehoiachin's name, but contributes no data that is not found in the other texts (Martin, "Jehoiachin Tablets," 86, Text [d]).

On these four tablets, see Ernst F. Weidner, "Jojachin König von Juda in babylonischen Keilschrifttexten," in *Mélanges Syriens offerts à M. René Dussaud* (Bibliothéque archéologique et historique 30; Paris: P. Guenther for Haut-commissariat de la Republique francaise en Syrie et au Liban, Service des antiquites, 1939), 2:923–35; William F. Albright, "King Joiachin in Exile," *BA* 4 (1942): 49–55, repr. in *The Biblical Archaeologist Reader, Volume I* (ed. G. Ernest Wright and David N. Freedman; Missoula, Mont.: Scholars Press, for ASOR, 1959), 106–12; Abraham Malamat, "Jeremiah and the Last Two Kings of Judah," *PEQ* (1951): 81–87; Donald J. Wiseman, *Chronicles of Chaldean Kings (626–556 B.C.) in the British Museum* (London: Trustees of the British Museum, 1956), 33–35; Martin, "Jehoiachin Tablets," 84–86; *ANET*, 308.

*Identifications in Unprovenanced Inscriptions* 159

**Other**: 3) Other information is vague in its meaning. The iconography of the seal is Egyptianizing, depicting an Egyptian deity on a lotus blossom. Artistic borrowing from Egypt is common on Northwest Semitic seals of officials, but the iconography used here does not seem to indicate any specific office.

√ **Singularity**: 2) The available data require an ID on grounds of biblical singularity. According to the Hebrew Bible, there was only one Hebrew king named Uzziah. Although he fits into the historical framework as an eighth-century king of Judah or of Israel, no ID can be made on any grounds of *inscriptional* singularity.

**(4.2) Remarks**

The virtually certain authenticity of this seal (see "Question 1" above in section 4.2) places its ID in a class with the inscriptions of the previous chapter.

## 4.3 Is the biblical Uzziah, king of Judah, named in the seal of Shubnayaw?

### Description, transcription, and translation

This reddish carnelian seal[21] with white veins is an elliptical scaraboid. It measures 21 mm. long, 16 mm. wide, and 10 mm. thick, and it is perforated longitudinally. Both of its slightly convex faces are iconic and inscribed, and both are encompassed by a border of two lines, between which is a ring of dots. On impressions made by face A, a man strides toward the right upon a single ground line. He is apparently bare-chested and wearing an ankle-length skirt and a wig, perhaps representing Egyptian or Assyrian clothing. Behind him, reading downward, is the word לשבניו, which can be vocalized as לְשֻׁבְנָיָו, "belonging to Shubnayaw."[22] His left hand grasps a scepter, and his right hand is raised,

---

[21] The seal of Shubnayaw, the servant of Uzziyaw, was acquired on the antiquities market during or before 1863, and its last published location is the Musée de Louvre, Paris, where it bears the numbers Antiquités Orientales 6216 and Acquisition 1147. It was first published in Henri Adrien P. de Longpérier, "Cachet de Sébénias, fils d'Osias," in *CRAI* 6 (1863): 288. It is listed in *AHI*, 129, no. 100.067, and in *WSS*, 50, no. 3.

[22] Another alternative is Shebanyaw, following the example of vocalization of the first two syllables in Neh 9:4, 5, etc. If derived from the root ישב, this name, vocalized as Shebnayaw, means, "Please stay [or be enthroned], O Yaw" or the like. E. g., in Akkadian, it was appropriate to use this root when speaking of a deity (*CAD* 1/2:387–89, s. v. ašābu; Manfred Görg, "יָשַׁב yāšab̲; מוֹשָׁב môšāb̲," *TDOT* 6:420–22); so also in Hebrew (ibid., 6:432–38). If derived from the root שוב (so *CSOSI*, 46), the name, vocalized as Shubnayaw, means, "Please turn [or "return" or "relent"], O Yaw." Bordreuil (in ibid.) is probably correct to prefer the latter root on the basis of the LXX rendering Σοβνία,

palm forward, perhaps in a gesture of conferring blessing. On face B, there are four registers to be viewed in "portrait" orientation. A single, horizontal line separates each register from the adjacent one. The upper and lower registers each contain a winged solar disc. The outspread, drooping vulture wings of the upper disc clearly follow the Egyptian style. The raised, shorter wings of the lower disc, seemingly charged with energy, are reminiscent of the winged Assyrian disc. The two middle registers contain the text, לשבניו ע / בד עזיו, "Belonging to Shubnayaw, the minister of Uzziyaw."

### (4.3) Question 1: reliability of inscriptional data

**Access**: 3) Purchased on the antiquities market.
**Provenance**: 4) Unknown.
**Authenticity**: 2) Presumable. Because the seal was purchased during or before 1863, its authenticity may be regarded as a virtual certainty; see above, section 4.2, "Question 1, Authenticity."

### (4.3) The setting of the seal of Shubnayaw, apart from biblical data

**Date**: 5) Dated by epigraphy: early to mid-eighth century. As in the seal of Abiyaw (section 4.2 above), among the significant diagnostic letters are the *waw*s. Again, the fact that the right stroke does not cross to the left side of the vertical shaft indicates an eighth-century date.[23] The *waw* in לשבניו in the second register of face B has a curved head, which is a slightly earlier form than the V-shaped head made with straight lines.[24] The other two *waw*s, one in the third register and one on face A, have just such V-shaped heads. The fact that they display no tick to the right attached to the left stroke of the head also indicates an eighth century date, although this observation is somewhat qualified by the partial indistinctness of the latter two *waw*s. The *yodh*s are shorter and shorter-tailed than those of the mid- and late-eighth century, but they are not from the seventh century. The short-legged *daleth*, nearly circular *ayin*, and *zayin* without cursive-style ticks are all early forms that call for a date in the first half of the eighth century.[25]

---

which uses an o-class vowel in the first syllable, rather than an e-class vowel. See also note 27 below in this chapter.

[23] See Chapter 2, note 3, second paragraph, above.

[24] At the reading of his paper, "Methodological Issues," Vaughn reasoned orally that *waw* with a head composed of straight lines was slightly later than *waw* with a round head. The form in question is intermediate between the earlier semicircular head and the later forms, all of which are made with straight lines.

[25] *SANSS*, 84, no. 4.

*Identifications in Unprovenanced Inscriptions* 161

### Fig. 13

### The Seal "of Shubnayaw, the Minister of Uzziyaw"

(Reversed to appear as an impression. Drawing by the author)

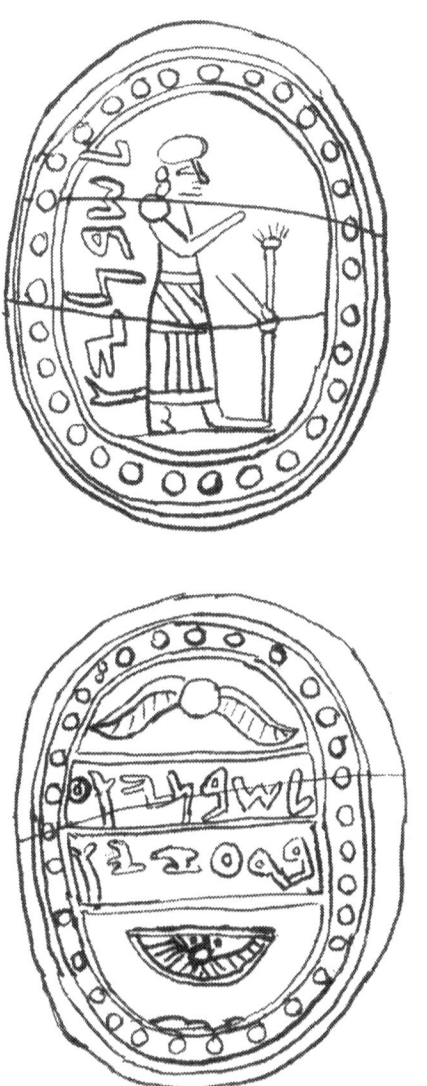

**Language**: 5) The language of the inscription cannot be specifically determined. If language parameters are set solely by vocabulary, morphology, and syntax, then most Northwest Semitic languages are possibilities.

**Socio-political classification**: 3) Determined by the two theophoric elements -*yaw*[26] and the Hebrew script. Permitted by the onomasticon of inscriptional Hebrew,[27] the language parameters, the arrangement of the text on the face of the seal,[28] and the material characteristics of the seal:[29] Hebrew.

### (4.3) How Shubnayaw's seal correlates with the historical framework

As in the instance of the seal of Abiyaw, the minister of Uzziyaw (section 4.2 above), the Hebrew script, the two theophoric elements, and the use of the term *ʿebed* as a title in a seal lead to the conclusion that Uzziyaw was a Hebrew monarch. The seals of Abiyaw and Shubnayaw, however, do not tell us whether he ruled the northern kingdom of Israel or the southern kingdom of Judah. As in the seal of Abiyaw, the theophoric element in its syncopated form, /-*yaw*/, spelled י-, places this seal either in the southern kingdom before the beginning of the seventh century or in the northern kingdom during the whole period of its existence (see Chapter 3, note 136). The date in the first half of the eighth century also permits the possibility that Uzziyaw ruled Israel or Judah.

### (4.3) How Shubnayaw's seal contributes to the historical framework

This seal provides a second inscription for identifying Uzziah, king of Israel or Judah, as in section 4.2 above. Using inscriptional data alone, the fact that the script of the seal of Shubnayaw is recognizably older than that of the seal of Abiyaw, the difference being as much as fifty or sixty years, may indicate either that Uzziyaw had a very long reign or that there was more than one Hebrew monarch named Uzziyaw during the early to mid-eighth century. Also, based on inscriptional data alone, conceivably one might have ruled Israel and the other Judah, or there might have been two in either of those kingdoms.

---

[26] See Chapter 3, note 136, above.

[27] The PN Shubnayaw (possibly Shubnayah) occurs in one other Hebrew inscription, the jar-handle seal impression of Neri, excavated in the Jewish Quarter of Jerusalem in 1975 (*AHI*, 490; *WSS*, 534). As many as eight other PNs based on שוב (but some possibly on ישב) appear in Hebrew inscriptions (*AHI*, 489–91; *WSS*, 533–34). PNs formed from שוב are found also in at least four other socio-political classifications (Fowler, 291; *WSS*, 533–34). On the PN Uzziyaw, see note 14 above in this chapter.

[28] See sections 2.2 and 4.2 above.

[29] Among perforated, iconic seals made of semiprecious stone, several are Hebrew.

## (4.3) Question 2: whether the setting of this seal *permits* a match

**Date**: 5) Agrees with the biblical account; dated by epigraphy (see above).
**Language**: 3) The language of the inscription presents no known disagreement with the language expectation raised by the biblical account: Hebrew (see under "The setting of the seal" above).
**Socio-political classification**: 3) Agrees with the biblical account: Hebrew (see under "The setting of the seal" above).

## (4.3) Question 3: how strongly the specific data in [18] the seal obv. לשבניו rev. עזיו בד / ע לשבניו count for or against an identification with the biblical (20) Uzziah, king of Judah (2 Kgs 15:13ff; r. 788/7–736/5)

√ **Name**: 2) Spelling has a negligible difference. See section 4.2, "Name."
**Relations**: 5) Neither an inscriptional patronymic nor a biblical servonymic is present, therefore neither can match or contradict a counterpart in the other.
√ **Title(s)**: 2) The inscriptional title of Shubnayaw's master, which is implicit in the servant's title of *ʿebed* (see Appendix A), matches the biblical title *melek*.
**Other**: 3) Other information is vague in its meaning. The iconography of the seal seems both Assyrianizing and Egyptianizing. The dress of the carved figure appears to be Assyrian. No specific office is indicated.
√ **Singularity**: 2) Available data require an ID on grounds of biblical singularity. According to the Bible, there was only one Hebrew king named Uzziah.

For "Remarks," see section 4.2 above.

## 4.4 Is the biblical Ahaz, king of Judah, named in the seal of Ushna?

### Description, transcription, and translation

This orange carnelian scarab[30] measures approximately 11.5 mm. wide by 15.5 mm. long by 6 mm. thick, and it is perforated longitudinally.[31] On its face

---

[30] The seal of Ushna, the minister of Ahaz, was first published in Charles C. Torrey, "A Hebrew Seal from the reign of Ahaz," *BASOR* 79 (October 1940): 27–29 (stated dimensions inaccurate). Formerly in the Edward T. Newell Collection, New York (*SANSS*, 83), it is now reported to be in the Yale Babylonian Collection, New Haven Conn., where its number is NCBS 883. It is listed in *WSS*, 51, no. 5, and *AHI*, 137, no. 100.141.

164    *Identifying Biblical Persons in Northwest Semitic Inscriptions*

are three registers, whose iconography and writing call for a "portrait" orientation. The top register occupies the upper half of the face, and it contains only iconography: a solar disc flanked by two uraei supports an Egyptian crown on which rest three pomegranates, flanked by two smaller uraei. All of this iconography is in an Egyptianizing style. The middle and lower registers contain only letters in archaic Hebrew script: אחז · בד / ע · לאשנא, "belonging to Ushna, the minister of Ahaz."[32] A pair of oval lines rings the face, and the registers are separated from each other by pairs of straight lines. A single straight line appears at the bottom of the lowest register.

### (4.4) Question 1: reliability of inscriptional data

**Access**: 3) Purchased on the antiquities market during or before 1940.
**Provenance**: 4) Unknown.
**Authenticity**: 4) A consensus of expert opinion favors authenticity.

### (4.4) The setting of the seal of Ushna, apart from biblical data

**Date**:  5) Dated by epigraphy: late eighth century. In modern impressions made by this seal, the horizontals of the three *aleph*s meet at the vertical shaft or very slightly to its left, but show no uninscribed space between them on the left

---

[31] The location of small chips at the top center and bottom center of the face and their well-defined U shape, all of which are observable in the photograph in ibid., Fig. 2, indicate a longitudinal perforation.

[32] The name 'Aḥaz means, "He [i.e., Yahweh] has seized," taken hold, or the like. The meaning of the name 'Ušna' is not easy to determine. Gibson offers the possibilities of a derivation from אשן in Aramaic, with the meaning "be hard, firm," or a relationship to the Ugaritic *'ušn*, "gift" (Gibson 1:62, 63, n. 12). Another verbal element, אשה, "to support," e.g., in the name of Josiah, 2 Kgs 21:24 ff, might be present in 'Ušna'. There are sufficient grounds for following Albright's suggestion in his editorial note attached to Torrey's *editio princeps*:

I favor connecting the name with the verbal element in the names "Josiah," "Joash," and *Yā'oš* . . . , all from the stem *'wš*, "to give," familiar in Arabic and North Canaanite. The name may represent *Ušna'* for * *Ušna-Yahu* (lit., "Give, pray, O Yahweh["]), like *Šubna'* (MT *Šebna'*) for *Šûb-na-Yahu* (MT *Šĕbanyahû*), "Turn, pray, O Yahweh," the original form and sense of which are established by East-Canaanite names like *Šûb-na-ilu* (common between 2000 and 1600 B.C.), and the vocalization of which is approximately fixed by the Neo-Babylonian transliteration *Šû-bu-nu-ia-a-ma* (fifth century B.C.), reflecting a pronunciation something like *Šûbnyau*. (W. F. A.) (Torrey, "Hebrew Seal," 28–29, n.1)

*Identifications in Unprovenanced Inscriptions* 165

### Fig. 14

### The Seal "of Ushna, the Minister of Aḥaz"

(The inscription is in retrograde, i.e., mirror-image, script.
Drawing by the author)

side of the shaft. Such open space between the horizontals appears only to the right of the vertical shaft. Nevertheless, the lower horizontal is not simply parallel to the upper, but rather, it curves downward from the point where they meet. This form is almost seventh-century in the transition from the broad-muzzled *aleph*s of the tenth and ninth centuries, e.g., in the Mesha Inscription, to the form which became predominant in the seventh century, in which the lower stroke is a separate, straight line beginning at the vertical shaft.[33] This form of *nun*, along with the oval *ayin* (transitional between the circular and the triangulated forms, and the *zayin*, with its cursive-style ticks (though the upward tick on the lower horizontal is unusual), all appear in the eighth, seventh, and sixth centuries. Still, the forms of the latter two letters represent a transition *toward* seventh-century forms which has almost reached them. The ligatured *beth* and *daleth* in the word ʿ*ebed* find a parallel to the same letters ligatured in the same word in the seal of Abiyaw of the second half of the eighth century (section 4.2 above). A date in the late eighth century seems best.

**Language**: 5) The language of the inscription cannot be specifically determined on linguistic grounds. If language parameters are set solely by vocabulary, morphology, and syntax, then most Northwest Semitic languages are possible.

**Socio-political classification**: 4) Determined by the Hebrew script. Permitted by the onomasticon of inscriptional Hebrew,[34] language parameters, the arrangement of the text,[35] and the material characteristics of the seal:[36] Hebrew.

## (4.4) How the seal of Ushna correlates with the historical framework

The Hebrew script and the use of the term ʿ*ebed* as a title in a seal lead to the conclusion that Ahaz, the master of Ushna, was a Hebrew monarch (see Appendix A). On the basis of the historical framework thus far constructed, one

---

[33] See *SANSS*, 83, no. 2, and Figs. 46, 64.

[34] The PN Ushna occurs in two other unprovenanced Hebrew seals. One is from the eighth century and the other from the eighth/seventh century (*AHI*, 293; *WSS*, 478). As many as eight other PNs based on אשׁ appear in Hebrew inscriptions, but some of these may be based on the root אשׁ, "man" (*WSS*, 477–78). PNs formed from אשׁ appear in at least nine other socio-political classifications (Fowler, 285; *WSS*, 477–78).

Eight other Hebrew inscriptions contain the PN Ahaz: two eighth-century Samaria Ostraca, one Jericho seal (*AHI*, 273), and five others listed in Appendixes B and C under person (22). At least two other Hebrew PNs are based on the root אחז (ibid.). PNs formed from the root אחז appear also in Aramaic inscriptions (Maraqten, 119–20).

[35] Other seals of titled Hebrew individuals exhibit iconography above the text, which occupies two registers, e.g., *WSS*, 53, no. 11, 55, no. 16, 58, no. 25, 60, 30, all unprovenanced.

[36] Among perforated, iconic seals made of semiprecious stone, several are Hebrew.

can say that the Ahaz of this seal was a late eighth-century king of Israel or of Judah and that he ruled after Uzziah.

A summary inscription of Tiglath-pileser III (r. 745–727) records the payment of tribute by many kings, each of whom is described by the gentilic corresponding to his kingdom. This list includes "Jehoahaz," ($^{m}ia$-$ú$-$ḫa$-$zi$) the Judahite (KUR $ia$-$ú$-$da$-$a$-$a$).[37] "Jehoahaz" is an alternative form of the name of the biblical king Ahaz, king of Judah, Hezekiah's immediate predecessor.

The fact that over 94% of theophoric Hebrew names in inscriptions of this period are Yahwistic constitutes very strong presumptive evidence that the royal name on the seal is a hypocoristicon for either Ahaziah or Jehoahaz.[38] Based on inscriptional data alone, one can only tentatively identify the Jehoahaz of the Assyrian inscription with Ahaz, the Hebrew king whose name appears in this official seal. Therefore, this potential ID makes a reasonable hypothesis, especially within the limited, late eighth-century period to which the Assyrian and Hebrew inscriptions are dated.[39]

## (4.4) How the seal of Ushna, if authentic, would contribute to the historical framework

This seal would document the fact that a Hebrew king named Ahaz ruled in Israel or Judah, during the late eighth century. If the reasonable possibility stated in the preceding paragraph is correct, then this Hebrew seal would confirm the existence of a Hebrew king who is already named in an Assyrian inscription.

---

[37] Summary (alias Display; see *ITP*, 25) Inscription 7 of Tiglath-pileser III, (K 3751), which represents about half of a large clay tablet used in the building of the royal palace at Calah (modern Nimrud), reverse, lines 10–12; *ITP*, 170–71, reverse, line 11, Pl. LV; *ANET*, 282, labeled continuously with the obverse as lines 56–63; Galil, *Chronology*, 153. Tadmor observes that the tablet "has a Kouyunjik number [K 3751], but . . . correctly . . . the tablet is marked . . . 'S.E. Palace, Nimroud'" (*ITP*, 154).

[38] Tigay summarizes his calculations as follows:
Theophoric names of 592 individuals are known from inscriptions and from the Bible 466 pre-exilic individuals with theophoric names are known. The ratio of Yahwistic names to pagan names is 94.1% to 5.9% in the inscriptions and 89% to 11% for all pre-exilic periods represented in the Bible. For the periods from which inscriptional names are known—those of the Divided Monarchy and Late Judah—the ratio in the Bible is 96% to 4%. (Tigay, *You Shall Have No Other Gods*, 17–18)

[39] Assyriologists have assigned the date of Ahaz's payment of tribute to Tiglath-pileser III within the years 735–732 (*ITP*, 277).

**(4.4) Question 2: provided the seal of Ushna were authentic, whether its setting would *permit* a match**

**Date**: 5) Agrees with the biblical account (see above). The late eighth-century date permits a time near the end of the reign of Ahaz, son of Jotham, king of Judah.

**Language**: 3) The language of the inscription presents no known disagreement with the language expectation raised by the Bible: Hebrew (see above under the heading on setting).

**Socio-political classification**: 4) Agrees with the biblical account: Hebrew (see above under the heading on setting).

**(4.4) Question 3: provided the seal were authentic, how strongly the specific data in [23] the seal לאשנא · ע / בד · אחז would count for or against an identification with the biblical (22) Ahaz, king of Judah, son of Jotham (2 Kgs 15:38ff; r. 742/1–726)**

√ **Name**: 1) Is complete, fully legible, and in exact agreement with the consonants of all biblical occurrences of the name of the eighth-century Ahaz, king of Judah.

**Relations**: 5) Neither an inscriptional patronymic nor a biblical servonymic is present, therefore neither can match or contradict any counterpart in the other source.

√ **Title(s)**: 2) The inscriptional title of Ushna's master, which is implicit in the servant's title of *ʿebed*, matches the biblical title *melek* (see Appendix A).

**Other**: 3) Other information is vague in its meaning. The iconography of the seal is Egyptianizing. Artistic borrowing from Egypt is common on Northwest Semitic seals of officials, but no specific office seems to be indicated.

√ **Singularity**: 2) The available data would require this ID on grounds of biblical singularity. That there *was* such a Judahite king at that time is evident from the identifying mark in common between the biblical account and the Assyrian inscription (not the Hebrew seal): that (Jeho)ahaz, king of Judah, was a tributary of Tiglath-pileser III.[40] (The biblical hypocoristicon Ahaz matches the full name Jehoahaz in the Assyrian inscription.) Second, since the biblical account presents its list of the kings of Israel and Judah as complete, there is unequivocal linkage; the Hebrew Bible knows only one eighth-century Hebrew

---

[40] Since the Assyrians certainly were not averse to receiving tribute any number of times, this ID does not need to be tied to a particular instance of payment common to both the Assyrian inscription and the Bible. Tadmor is convinced that the specific instance of payment to which the inscription of Tiglath-pileser III refers took place in 734. It should be kept in mind that "the payment of tribute by Ahaz in 734 [allegedly] is not necessarily identical with the 'bribe' (שחד) of II Kings xvi:8 . . . ." (ibid).

King Ahaz, and he was king of Judah. Provided this bulla is authentic, there is no escaping the ID of Ahaz, king of Judah, on grounds of *biblical* singularity.[41]

The ID of Ahaz cannot be made on grounds of inscriptional singularity, because inscriptions provide no list of Hebrew kings which purports to be complete. An ID on inscriptional grounds alone would be grade 2.

**4.5 Is the biblical Hoshea, king of Israel, named in the seal of Abdi?**

See sections 2.2 and 2.13 above.

**4.6 Is the biblical Hezekiah, king of Judah, named in the bulla of Yehozaraḥ?**

**Description, transcription, and translation**

When purchased, this bulla[42] consisted of three fragments glued together. It is 16 mm. long, 14 mm. wide, and 5 mm. thick. The aniconic seal impression on its face is 12 mm. long and 9 mm. wide. On the edges are fingerprints. The reverse side shows the imprint of string and papyrus fibers. The text is:

| line 1 | ליהוזר | "Belonging to Yehozara /ḥ,[43] |
| line 2 | ח בן · חלק | son of Ḥilqi / [y]ahu,[44] |
| line 3 | [י]הו עבד ח · | the minister of Ḥi / zqiyahu"[45] |
| line 4 | זקיהו | |

**(4.6) Question 1: reliability of inscriptional data**

**Access**: 3) Purchased on the antiquities market during or before 1974.
**Provenance**: 4) Unknown.
**Authenticity**: 4) A consensus of expert opinion favors authenticity.

---

[41] There is no tenable ancient alternative for such an ID, i.e., no known Aramaean or other non-Hebrew ruler with a Yahwistic name based on the root אחז, let alone one in the late eighth century. Further, any servants having Yahwistic names who served Gentile rulers would have had seals inscribed in Aramaic script or another non-Hebrew script.

[42] The bulla of Yehozaraḥ, son of Ḥilqiyahu, the minister of Ḥizqiyahu, was first published in Ruth Hestrin and Michal Dayagi, "A Seal Impression of a Servant of King Hezekiah," *IEJ* 24 (1974): 27–29, Pl. 2, B, C. Its last published location is the Israel Museum, Jerusalem. It is listed in *AHI*, 161, no. 100.321, and in *WSS*, 172–73, no. 407.

[43] The name Yehozaraḥ means, "Yahweh has come forth in brilliance" or dawned.
[44] The name Ḥilqiyahu means, "My portion [or share] is Yahweh."
[45] Ḥizqiyahu means, "My strength is Yahweh."

170    *Identifying Biblical Persons in Northwest Semitic Inscriptions*

### Fig. 15

### The bulla "of Yehozarah, Son of Hilqiyahu, the Minister of Hizqiyahu"

(Drawing by the author)

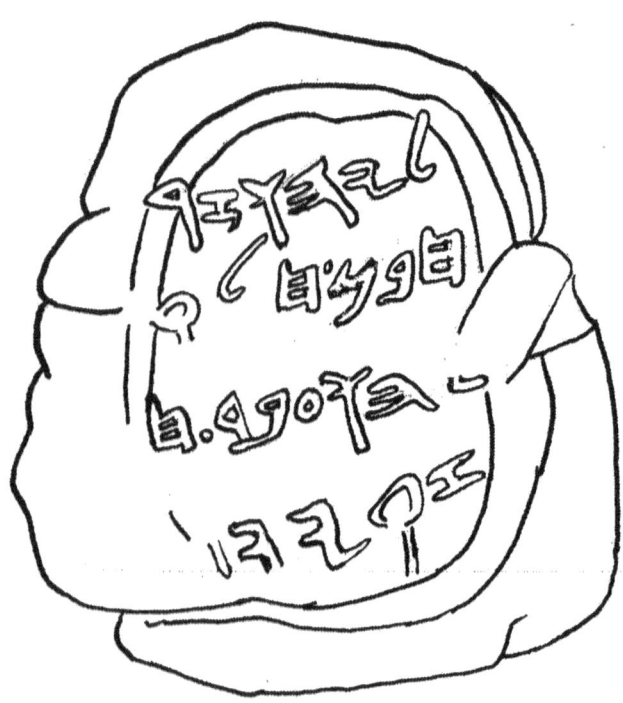

*Identifications in Unprovenanced Inscriptions* 171

**(4.6) The setting of the bulla of Yehozaraḥ, apart from biblical data**

**Date**: 5) Dated by epigraphy: late eighth to early seventh century. The potentially diagnostic letters are *waw, he, nun,* and *qoph*. Although the heads of the *waw*s in lines 1 and 4 are not visible, the fact that the right stroke of the head of the *waw* in line 3 crosses the vertical shaft indicates a broad range of possible dates from the eighth to the late seventh century.[46] This is not a diagnostic form.

The *he* of line 1 has a top horizontal bar that crosses the vertical shaft, but since its horizontal bars are parallel, it is not a diagnostic form.[47]

The *nun* of line 2 appears to be transitional toward a distinctive late seventh-century form.[48] The left stroke of its head is parallel to the vertical shaft on the right, and this left vertical extends slightly below the point at which the middle stroke meets it. The middle stroke is a horizontal bar that is not quite perpendicular to the left vertical stroke, but because the left vertical stroke is tilted from the upper right to the lower left, the middle horizontal bar can be seen as forming an acute angle with the lower tip of the left vertical stroke. Where the horizontal bar touches the vertical shaft on the right, however, the horizontal bar is rounded upward, producing a V shape with the upper end of the right vertical and preventing a perpendicular from forming. If the middle, horizontal stroke had been perpendicular to the verticals on both sides, this *nun* would have fit Vaughn's description of a late seventh- to early sixth-century form. This letter as it is found on the bulla is transitional, not diagnostic.

The forms of the *qoph*s in lines 2 and 4 are not entirely clear in any published photograph or in sketches, presumably because the bulla itself either was never clear or was damaged. The sketch in the initial publication[49] shows both *qoph*s with a complete, circular head which is bisected by a vertical shaft extending downward from the very top of the head to a point below the head. The

---

[46] Vaughn, "Palaeographic Dating of Judaean Seals," 53, Table 6. In a sketch by Herr, the form of the *waw* in line 3 approaches but does not quite match a form of *waw* which Vaughn later identified as a distinctive form of the late seventh to early sixth century (*SANSS*, Hebrew Seals Fig. 54, no. 3; Vaughn, "Palaeographic Dating of Judaean Seals," 53, Table 6, col. labeled "First peg," the two upper forms of three "Developed, distinctive" forms found in the city of David). The head of this form of *waw* pointed out by Vaughn consists of a small V with a third, bottom bar *starting* from the upper tip of the right bar of the V and descending to the lower left to form a laterally reversed Z shape that is oriented on a downward, left slant. The vertical shaft of the *waw* descends from a point in the middle of that bottom bar of the head. In Herr's sketch of the *waw* in the bulla of Yehozaraḥ, the bottom bar of the head does not start at the upper tip of the right bar of a V.

[47] Vaughn, "Palaeographic Dating of Judaean Seals," 47, 52–53.

[48] Ibid., 54–55. See the photograph in Benjamin Mazar and Gaalyahu Cornfeld, *The Mountain of the Lord* (Garden City, N.Y.: Doubleday, 1975), 179.

[49] Hestrin and Dayagi, "Seal Impression," 27, Fig. 1.

vertical shaft in the *qoph* in יהזקיהו is only faintly visible; without it, the letter would be an *ayin*. This reading of *qoph* is incidentally supported by the fact that there is no extant root חזע in any Northwest Semitic language of that era.⁵⁰ This form of the letter *qoph* is distinctively of the late eighth century,⁵¹ and in fact the paleography of the seal as a whole fits the late eighth century.

**Language**: 5) The bulla's vocabulary, morphology, and syntax are not a large enough sample to reveal the language of the inscription. Several Northwest Semitic languages are viable alternatives, but the word *ben* eliminates Aramaic.

**Socio-political classification**: 3) Determined by the three theophoric elements -*yahu*⁵² and the Hebrew script. Permitted by the onomasticon of inscriptional Hebrew,⁵³ the language parameters, the arrangement of the text,⁵⁴ and the material characteristics of the bulla:⁵⁵ Hebrew, and specifically Judahite.

---

⁵⁰ *DNWSI*, 1:361. Palmyrene inscriptions reveal a compound word חזעין, but it seems to have been formed from the roots חזי and עין (*DISO* 1:85, lines 22–24). In addition, it may be noted that the Hebrew Bible, the Targumim, the Talmud, Midrashic literature, and the Syriac language contain no such root as חזע.

⁵¹ Vaughn, "Palaeographic Dating of Judaean Seals," 57–58.

⁵² See chapter 3, note 136. The theophoric element -*yahu* indicates Judahite origin.

⁵³ The PN Yehozaraḥ occurs in one other unprovenanced Hebrew inscription, a bulla of the late seventh to early sixth century from a burnt archive (*AHI*, 367; *WSS*, 503). The name Zeraḥ appears in two other Hebrew inscriptions, another unprovenanced bulla from the same burnt archive and a Kuntillet ʿAjrūd plaster inscription (*AHI*, 345; *WSS*, 496). PNs formed from the root זרח do not seem to be found in any other socio-political classifications besides Hebrew (Fowler, 283; *WSS*, 496; Maraqten, 161; Jackson, 96; *SANSS*, 206).

The PN Ḥilqiyahu is present in at least fifteen other Hebrew inscriptions, of which two are provenanced (*AHI*, 352; *WSS*, 498). Other Hebrew hypocoristica based on the root חלק are found in six other Hebrew inscriptions (*AHI*, 351; *WSS*, 498). PNs based on the root חלק appear in inscriptions of two other socio-political classifications: Aramaic and Phoenician (Fowler, 280; *WSS*, 498; Jackson, 96; *SANSS*, 206).

The PN Ḥizqiyahu probably occurs in two provenanced Hebrew inscriptions, both of somewhat uncertain reading (*AHI*, 348). Hebrew PNs based on the root חזק are present in two other Hebrew inscriptions, both unprovenanced (*WSS*, 497). Although it appears that only Hebrew PNs are formed from the root חזק, there nevertheless exists in Aramaic the root חזן, a parallel of חזק, from which, in a neo-Assyrian setting, two Aramaic PNs are formed (Maraqten, 163).

⁵⁴ Over a dozen aniconic, Hebrew seals and bullae contain three to five lines of writing across the face in vertical or "portrait" orientation. One of these displaying three lines of writing was excavated at Arad (*WSS*, 85, no. 111). One other such seal, unprovenanced, contains four lines of writing without any lines drawn between them (*WSS*, 64,

## (4.6) How Yehozaraḥ's bulla correlates with the historical framework

The data presented by the bulla itself, i.e., the Hebrew script, the Judahite spelling of three Yahwistic names, and the title ʿebed, lead to the conclusion that Ḥizqiyahu was the king of Judah sometime during the late eighth to early seventh centuries. The inscriptions of Sennacherib (r. 704–681) name KUR ia-ú-di (Judah) and ḫa-za-qi-a-a-a (Hezekiah) its king,[56] ᵐḫa-za-qi-a-ú (Hezekiah) LÚia-ú-da-ai (the Judahite) and URUur-sa-li-im-mu (Jerusalem), his royal residence.[57] Evidently, then, Hezekiah was king of Judah and Jerusalem was his capital city during Sennacherib's reign. Earlier inscriptions of Sargon II (r. 722–705) reveal that Assyria had put an end to the kingdom of Israel by conquest, exile, repopulation, and annexation early in the fourth quarter of the eighth century,[58] leaving Judah the only surviving Hebrew kingdom. This event, combined

---

no. 40). Two unprovenanced fiscal bullae contain four registers and five registers of writing, respectively (*WSS*, 177–78, nos. 421 and 422).

[55] Some Hebrew bullae to have the impressions of papyrus fibers and string on their reverse side. A few have fingerprints on the edges beside the inscribed face, e.g., the bulla "belonging to Yishmaʾel, the king's son" (Gabriel Barkay, "A Bulla of Ishmael, the King's Son," *BASOR* 290–91 [1993]: 109).

[56] The Bull Inscription published as nos. 1, 2, and 3 in George Smith, *History of Sennacherib, Translated from Cuneiform Inscriptions* (London: Williams and Norgate, 1878), 3–89, line 21; Luckenbill, *Annals of Sennacherib*, 77; *ANET*, 288.

[57] This prism mentions "Hezekiah the Judahite" (col. 2, line 76 and col. 3, line 1; Luckenbill, *Annals of Sennacherib*, 31, 32) and "Jerusalem, his royal city" (col. 3, lines 28, 40; ibid., 33; *ANET*, 287, 288; Galil, *Chronology*, 153). The Bull Inscription from the palace at Nineveh also mentions "Hezekiah the Judahite" (lines 23, 27; Luckenbill, *Annals of Sennacherib*, 69, 70) and "Jerusalem, his royal city" (line 29; ibid., 33).

[58] Sargon II (r. 721–705) records that he removed over 27,000 Israelites from Samaria:

    (line 25) [The inhabitants of Sa]merina, who ... with a king
    (26) [hostile (?) to] me, not to endure servitude
    (27) [and not to br]ing tribute
    (28) [to Ashur (?)], did battle.
    (29) [Wit]h the power of the great gods, my [lord]s
    (30) [aga]inst them I foug[ht].
    (31) [2]7,280 people, together with [their] chariots,
    (32) and the gods, in which they trusted, as spoil
    (33) I counted. With 200 chariots for [my] royal force
    (34) from them I formed a unit.
    (35) The rest of them
    (36) I settled in the midst of Assyria.
    (37) I repopulated Samerina more than before.
    (38) People from countries, conquered by my hands,
    (39) I brought in it. My commissioner

with the apparently narrow time frame during which Sennacherib's and Hezekiah's reigns overlapped, a few years before and after 700, suggests that the Hezekiah of Yehozarah's bulla and the Hezekiah of the Assyrian inscriptions are probably the same person. The incompleteness of the list of Hebrew kings which could be compiled from inscriptions, however, makes it impossible to say on purely inscriptional grounds that such an ID is certain.

The earliest and most thorough extant copy of the account of Sennacherib's third campaign, which was against Syria-Palestine during his fourth year, is in the Rassam Prism Inscription:

> As for Hezekiah, the Judaean, who had not submitted to my yoke, I besieged forty-six of his fortified walled cities and surrounding small towns, which were without number. Using packed-down ramps and by applying battering rams, infantry attacks by mines, breeches, and siege machines, I conquered (them). I took out 200,150 people, young and old, male and female, horses, mules, donkeys, camels, cattle, and sheep, without number, and counted them as spoil. Himself, I locked him up within Jerusalem, his royal city, like a bird in a cage. I surrounded him with earthworks, and made it unthinkable (lit. "taboo") for him to exit by the city gate. His cities which I had despoiled, I cut off from his land and gave to Mitinti, king of Ashdod, Padi, king of Ekron and Ṣillibel, king of Gaza, and this diminished his land. I imposed upon him in addition to the former tribute, yearly payment of dues and gifts for my lordship.

---

(40) I appointed as Governor over them.
(41) I counted them as Assyrians
(Nimrud Prism of Sargon II, col. 4, lines 25–41, found in Texts D and E, which are both partial copies of the same text. Text D comprises fragments ND 2601, 3401, and 3417. Text E comprises fragments ND 3400, 3402, 3408, and 3409; Cyril J. Gadd, "Inscribed Prisms of Sargon II from Nimrud," *Iraq* 16 (1954): 173–201, Pl. 45 and 46; translation slightly adapted from that of Bob Becking in Becking, *Fall*, 29, 31].

Sargon II also states that he ended Samaria's home rule and, by implication, its kingdom, by conquest and exile: "I besieged and conquered Samaria (URU*sa-me-ri-na*). 27,290 people, who lived in its midst, I carried away. Fifty chariots I gathered from their midst. The bereaved I taught proper behavior. I appointed my commissioner over them. The levy of the former king I laid upon them" (Lines 23–24 of the Display Inscription of Sargon II, which "stood on the wall slabs of Salons IV, VII, VIII, and X of the palace at Khorsabad. It was a résumé of the events from the year of accession to the fifteenth year of the reign" of Sargon II [Luckenbill, *ARAB*, 2:25; Winckler, *Keilschrifttexte Sargons*, 1:100–101; Becking, *Fall*, 26; Luckenbill, *ARAB*, 2:27, section 55; *ANET*, 285]).

This last quotation implies that the last time Samaria had paid tribute it was to his predecessor, Shalmaneser V, therefore the exile seems to have been early in the reign of Sargon II. Only a few years before this, Hoshea (r. 732/1–722) was the last king of Israel mentioned in Assyrian records (see section 2.13, note 57, above). The king and kingdom of Israel disappear from Assyrian inscriptional references to the years after ca. 720.

He, Hezekiah, was overwhelmed by the awesome splendor of my lordship, and he sent me after my departure to Nineveh, my royal city, his elite troops and his best soldiers, which he had brought into Jerusalem as reinforcements, with 30 talents of gold, 800 talents of silver, choice antimony, large blocks of carnelian, beds (inlaid) with ivory, armchairs (inlaid) with ivory, elephant hides, ivory, ebony-wood, boxwood, garments with multicolored trim, garments of linen, wood (dyed) red-purple and blue-purple, vessels of copper, iron, bronze and tin, chariots, siege shields, lances, armor, daggers for the belt, bows and arrows, countless trappings and implements of war, together with his daughters, his palace women, his male and female singers. He (also) dispatched his personal messenger to deliver the tribute and to do obeisance.[59]

### (4.6) How this bulla of Yehozaraḥ, if authentic, would contribute to the historical framework

This bulla documents, from the Hebrew side, the existence of Hezekiah, king of Judah, to whom Sennacherib's inscriptions refer, as a ruler of the late eighth to early seventh century. It also tells the names of a father and son, one of whom was a titled, high official of Hezekiah, king of Judah.

### (4.6) Question 2: provided the bulla of Yehozaraḥ were authentic, whether its setting would *permit* a match

**Date**: 5) Agrees with the biblical account: late eighth century (see above). This date matches the regnal years of the biblical Hezekiah, king of Judah.
**Language**: 3) The inscription's language presents no known disagreement with the language expectation raised by the Bible: Hebrew (see above).
**Socio-political classification**: 3) Agrees with the Bible: Judahite (see above).

---

[59] Rassam Prism Inscription, col. 3, lines 18–49; Luckenbill, *Annals of Sennacherib*, 32–34; translation of Mordechai Cogan and Hayim Tadmor, *II Kings: A New Translation with Introduction and Commentary* (Anchor Bible 11; N.p.: Doubleday, 1988), 338–39. It is noteworthy that Sennacherib states only that he besieged Hezekiah in Jerusalem. He does not claim to have conquered it, but only to have forced the payment of lavish tribute.

This account was composed several months after the campaign in 700 B.C.E. (Eponym year of Metunu) and is extant in a copy inscribed on the "Rassam cylinder." Every successive edition of Sennacherib's annals copied this text, with slight abbreviations—e.g., the unusually long list of booty received from Judah is not repeated in the later texts. (Ibid., 246)

**(4.6) Question 3: provided the bulla were authentic, how strongly the specific data in [28 group] the bulla** / ח · חלק / ]י[הו עבד · ח / ליהוזר  
וזקיהו **would count for or against an identification with the biblical (23) Hezekiah, king of Judah (2 Kgs 16:20ff; r. 726–697/6)**

√ **Name**: 1) A Completely present, clearly legible, and in exact agreement with the consonants of the most common biblical spelling of this name.

**Relations**: 5) In the inscription, a patronymic is absent, therefore there is none to match or contradict the king's biblical patronymic, אָחָז. (Seals and bullae do not usually include royal patronymics.) The syntax of the text on the bulla makes it ambiguous whether the father or the son is the ʿebed. In the Bible, the potential servonymic Yehozaraḥ is absent, therefore there is none to match or contradict that of the inscription. If Ḥilqiyahu is the ʿebed of the seal, such verses as 2 Kgs 18:18, 37 and Isa 36:3, 22 do not provide another clear identifying mark; they might refer to a different Hilkiah.

√ **Title(s)**: 2) The inscriptional title of the ʿebed's master, which is implicit in the servant's title, matches the biblical title *melek*. See Appendix A.

**Other**: 3) Other information: the significance of the aniconism is ambiguous. It might reflect biblical content regarding Hezekiah's reforms, but not necessarily, since aniconism could also result from individual aesthetic preference, the limits of the engraver's skills, etc.

√ **Singularity**: 2) Available data require an ID on grounds of biblical singularity. The Hebrew Bible's presentation of a complete list of kings of Israel and Judah includes only one monarch named Hezekiah. The biblical chronology placing his rule during the late eighth to the beginning of the seventh century fits with the inscriptions of Sennacherib. Hezekiah's withstanding of Sennacherib's siege is the identifying mark in common between the Assyrian record and the biblical account (2 Kgs 18:13–19:37) but not the Hebrew bulla. Therefore, this ID is made on grounds of biblical singularity but not inscriptional singularity. (Since inscriptions provide only an incomplete list of Hebrew kings, they allow no more than a grade 2 ID, "a reasonable supposition.")

**(4.6) Remarks**

Few IDs have better complementary documentation, yet without verification (section 1.25, Criteria 4), this bulla's authenticity remains questionable.

## 4.7 Is the biblical Hilkiah, the high priest, to be identified in the seal ring of Ḥanan?

### Description, transcription, and translation

The seal ring of Ḥanan[60] is a well-preserved silver ring that encases an inscribed, dark blue agate scaraboid seal. A vein of light blue arcs across its face.

The bezel, in which the seal was set, is surrounded by a double cable circle (*000*). The base of the bezel is decorated with a dotted line composed of granules, bordered with two cable-circle lines. On both sides of the ring, adjacent to the bezel, is a triangular area in which there are five knobs, surrounded by a cable circle, in the local tradition. This description must be considered somewhat provisional because unfortunately the ring has not been cleaned—and the owner will not permit it to be cleaned.[61]

The exterior diameter of the seal ring is 23 mm., and its interior diameter measures 19 mm. The inscribed face of the seal, slightly convex, measures 11 mm. long and 10 mm. wide; its thickness cannot be determined because of the fact of its insertion into the setting. The inscribed surface bears three lines of writing, each separated by two parallel horizontal lines . . . .[62]

The meticulously executed inscription, carved in paleo-Hebrew letters, is:

line 1    לחנן · ב    "Belonging to Ḥanan,[63] so / n
line 2 · ן · חלקיהו ·    of Hilqiyahu,[64]
line 3          הכהן    the priest"

According to published reports, the seal has not been removed from the ring, so it is not known whether the reverse side of the stone is inscribed.

---

[60] The seal ring "of Ḥanan, son of Hilqiyahu, the priest," was first published in Josette Elayi, "Le sceau du prêtre Ḥanan, fils de Hilqiyahu," *Sem* 36 (1986): 43–46. The last published location of this seal ring is Paris, where it was reported to have been in the possession of an anonymous collector. It is listed in *AHI*, 223, no. 100.734, and in *WSS*, 59–60, no. 28.

[61] Josette Elayi, "Name of Deuteronomy's Author Found on Seal Ring," *BAR* 13, no. 5 (September/October 1987): 54–56.

[62] Idem, "Le sceau du prêtre," 44, translation mine.

[63] The name Ḥanan is a hypocoristicon, in this instance, presumably, of Ḥananyahu, meaning, "Yahweh has shown favor" or has been gracious.

[64] On the meaning of the name Hilqiyahu, see note 44 above in this chapter.

178    *Identifying Biblical Persons in Northwest Semitic Inscriptions*

### Fig. 16

**The seal ring of Ḥanan, Son of Ḥilqiyahu, the Priest"**

(The inscription is in retrograde, i.e., mirror-image, script.
Drawing by the author)

*Identifications in Unprovenanced Inscriptions* 179

**(4.7) Question 1: reliability of inscriptional data**

**Access**: 3) Purchased on the antiquities market, reportedly in 1980.
**Provenance**: 4) Unknown.
**Authenticity**: 4) Expert opinion substantially supports authenticity.

**(4.7) The setting of the seal ring of Ḥanan, apart from biblical data**

**Date**: 5) Dated by epigraphy: late seventh to early sixth century. The diagnostic letters are *nun*, *he*, *yodh*, and *waw*. Of the four *nun*s on the seal, the only one which is diagnostic is the one in הכהן. It consists of a vertical shaft joined to a shorter, parallel stroke by a horizontal stroke that is perpendicular to both. As observed above, this form is also a clear indication of a late seventh- to early sixth-century date.[65]

In all three *he*s on the seal, the top horizontal bar crosses the vertical shaft. Only in the two *he*s in הכהן, the three horizontal bars are not parallel. Again, as noted above, these two traits in combination clearly indicate a date of late seventh to early sixth century.[66]

Further, there is a very close resemblance between the paleography of this seal and that of a hoard of fifty-one late seventh- to early sixth-century bullae excavated from the city of David.[67] Elayi's comparison of each letter on this seal of Ḥanan with the same letter in the city of David bulla no. 27 "of Azaryahu, son of Ḥilqiyahu" (treated in section 3.9 above) reveals significant paleographic similarities in the letters *he*, *yodh*, and *waw*.[68] In both of these inscriptions, the top, slanting horizontal bar of the *he* always crosses over the top of the vertical shaft, and the horizontal bars of the *he* are "parallel or slightly convergent."[69] In both the seal of Ḥanan and the bulla of Azaryahu, the *he*s with parallel horizontal bars *precede* those whose horizontal bars are not parallel, as if by a formula or habit of the engraver. As Elayi also observes, "When a letter is repeated, it is

---

[65] Vaughn, "Palaeographic Dating of Judaean Seals," 54–55.
[66] Ibid., 47, 52–53.
[67] The excavations conducted by Shiloh during the summer of 1982 brought to light fifty-one bullae in Area G, Locus 967, "the House of the Bullae," at Stratum 10, which dates between the reign of Josiah, king of Judah (r. 640/39–609) and the destruction of Jerusalem in 586, and specifically from Stratum 10B, the corresponding destruction layer, in which the final conflagration consumed the papyri but fired the bullae that sealed them (Shiloh, "Group of Hebrew Bullae," 16–38; Shiloh and Tarler, "Bullae from the City of David," 196–209; Shiloh, *Excavations I*, 18–20, 29, 58, Fig. 22, 61, Figs. 25, 26, Pl. 29:1, 35:1–3).
[68] Elayi, "New Light on the Identification of the Seal of Priest Ḥanan, son of Ḥilqiyahu (2 Kings 22)," cols. 681–83.
[69] Ibid., col. 682.

never exactly reproduced in the same way; such is the case for *h*, *ḥ*, and *n* on the seal, and *h*, *w*, *y*, and *l* on the bulla."⁷⁰

On the bulla, the *yodh* in "Azaryahu" is almost identical to the shape of the seal's *yodh* in "Ḥilqiyahu."⁷¹ It may be added that the *yodh*'s position with respect to the head of the preceding *resh* in "Azaryahu" on the bulla is precisely the same as the *yodh*'s position with respect to the head of the preceding *qoph* in "Ḥilqiyahu" on the seal. There is also a close similarity in the relative position of *he* with respect to a following *waw*: "the way of binding the letters *h* and *w* which can be conceived in different ways, is identical on the seal and on the bulla."⁷² As a result, the letter sequence -*yhw* in "Azaryahu" on the bulla and the letter sequence -*yhw* in "Ḥilqiyahu" on the seal are very similar in appearance.

Perhaps most importantly, two forms of *waw* which closely resemble each other and which seem to be very infrequently attested appear both on the city of David bulla "of Azaryahu, son of Ḥilqiyahu," and on this seal ring "of Ḥanan, son of Ḥilqiyahu, the priest." The two *waw*s in the PNs on the bulla of Azaryahu consist of a short, slanting horizontal stroke that intersects a slightly leaning vertical shaft that extends well below the bottoms of shorter letters. Only an extremely short, diagonal tick extends above the slanting horizontal stroke, and it is only one-half to one-third as long as that horizontal stroke.⁷³ On the seal of Ḥanan, the single *waw* is precisely the same, except that there is no tick at all above the short, slanting horizontal stroke, which simply rests atop the vertical shaft. These forms of *waw* are so similar and so infrequent that they tempt the observer to regard them as stages in the development of an idiosyncratic form of *waw* used by one and the same engraver.

Indeed, Elayi regards the eight letters on the seal of Ḥanan as "identical" to their counterparts on the bulla of Azaryahu, even stating, "Letter *q* has the same shape in both cases . . . ," although the head of the *qoph* on Ḥanan's seal seems more curved than the head of the *qoph* on Azaryahu's bulla.⁷⁴ Nevertheless, her paleographic conclusion that "all seems to indicate that the seal and the bulla are not only contemporary but also from the hand of the same engraver . . ." does not overstate the facts of the case. The close similarities between the two greatly strengthen the case for a Judahite provenance and a late seventh- to early sixth-century date of the seal ring of Ḥanan, son of Ḥilqiyahu, the priest.

The striking paleographic similarities, however, can also serve as grounds for healthy skepticism. The city of David bullae were excavated in 1982, and Elayi first heard about this seal ring in June 1984,⁷⁵ the same year in which Shi-

---

[70] Ibid., col. 683.
[71] Ibid., col. 682.
[72] Ibid., col. 683.
[73] Ibid., col. 682.
[74] Ibid., col. 683.
[75] Elayi, "Name of Deuteronomy's Author," 54.

loh's *Excavations at the City of David I, 1978–1982* was published.[76] Did a forger use Shiloh's publication of several bullae, including that of Azaryahu the son of Hilqiyahu, as a pattern? Unfortunately, Elayi's excellent initial article on the seal ring, its *editio princeps*, was not published until 1986. Since the ring was reportedly purchased in 1980, proof of the date of purchase could be crucial to establishing its authenticity. Granted that such paleographic similarities could not be an accident, are they to be attributed to the habits of an ancient engraver, or the skillful duplication of a modern forger? A demonstrably genuine bill of sale, dated before Shiloh's discovery of the city of David bullae in 1982, could settle the question.

**Language**: 5) The language of the inscription cannot be specifically determined on linguistic grounds. If language parameters are set solely by vocabulary, morphology, and syntax, then several Northwest Semitic languages of the day are viable alternatives. Nevertheless, Aramaic is eliminated, because of the definite article *h-*, the use of *bn* rather than *br*, and the word *khn*, rather than the Aramaic priestly title *kmr*.[77]

**Socio-political classification**: 3) Determined by the Hebrew script and the theophoric element *-yahu*. Permitted by the onomasticon of inscriptional Hebrew,[78] the language parameters, the arrangement of the text on the seal,[79] and

---

[76] See section 3.7, note 122, above.

[77] Before the fifth century, Aramaic inscriptions which are currently extant did not use *khn*, but rather *kmr* (*DNWSI*, s.v. khn$_1$, 1:491, kmr$_2$, 1:515–16). The only potential exception is *khnh*, "priestess," in Combination I, line 11, of the plaster inscription from Deir ʿAlla (ca. 700), which is arguably more a South Canaanite dialect than Aramaic (Hackett, *Balaam Text from Deir ʿAllā*, 124).

[78] The PN Ḥanan occurs in eleven other Hebrew inscriptions, including five whose provenance is in the northern kingdom of Israel and three whose provenance is in Judah (*AHI*, 354). Hebrew PNs based on the root חנן are present in at least forty-two other Hebrew inscriptions, of which most are provenanced (*AHI*, 354–56). PNs formed from the root חנן appear in the inscriptions of at least seven other socio-political classifications (Fowler, 290; *WSS*, 499).

The PN Ḥilqiyahu is present in at least fifteen other Hebrew inscriptions, of which two are provenanced (*AHI*, 352; *WSS*, 498). Other Hebrew hypocoristica based on the root חלק are found in six other Hebrew inscriptions (*AHI*, 351; *WSS*, 498). Only the theophoric ending makes the PN Ḥilqiyahu distinctively Hebrew. PNs based on the root חלק are found in Phoenician and Aramaic (Fowler, 280; *WSS*, 498; Jackson, 96; *SANSS*, 206).

[79] Over a dozen aniconic, Hebrew seals and bullae contain three to five lines of writing across the face in vertical or "portrait" orientation. One of these displaying three lines of writing was excavated at Arad (*WSS*, 85, no. 111).

its material characteristics:[80] Hebrew. Both the theophoric element, -*yhw*,[81] and the date of the inscription, which is about a century after the exile of the northern kingdom of Israel,[82] indicate a Judahite nationality.

### (4.7) How Ḥanan's seal ring correlates with the historical framework

Most inscriptional, theophoric Hebrew PNs, as well as the theological references of the Mesha inscription, indicate that the primary deity of the Hebrews was *Yhwh*. By the analogy of excavated cities in other kingdoms of the ancient Near East, it is to be expected that this primary deity should have at least one temple in each of the capital cities of Israel and Judah and perhaps other temples or sanctuaries in these kingdoms, as well. Arad ostracon 18 refers to a temple (בית יהוה), presumably at Arad, in lines 9–10: בית יהוה / הו ישב, i.e., someone "is staying in the temple of *Yhwh*."[83] A combination of inscriptional and non-inscriptional, archaeological discoveries also tends to support the existence of more than one sanctuary dedicated to this deity.[84]

---

[80] Hebrew seals are commonly made of semiprecious stone. On seals in metal housings, including rings or ringlike mounts not designed to be worn on a finger, see W. Culican, "Seals in Bronze Mounts," *RSF* 5 (1977): 1–4, Tables. I–III; André Lemaire, "Sept nouveaux sceaux nord-ouest sémitiques inscrits," *Sem* 41–42 (1993): 78–80; idem, "Name of Israel's Last King," 52 (box); *BAR* 21, no. 6 (November/December 1995): cover photograph. The seal "belonging to Shaphat" was recovered still mounted in its original gold ring (Adolf Reifenberg, *Ancient Hebrew Seals* [London: East and West Library, 1950], 29, Fig. 5, 53, Fig. 51, nos. 1 and 2; *WSS*, 160–61, no. 381). Unperforated Hebrew seals are assumed to have been worn in jewelry settings, especially rings (e.g., Ussishkin, "Gate 1567," 422).

[81] See Chapter 3, note 136.

[82] See section 4.6, note 58, above.

[83] Aharoni, *Arad Inscriptions*, 35–38; Pardee, *Handbook*, 54–57. An additional letter *beth* prefixed to the first word in this phrase could have been rubbed or chipped off of the lower right corner of the ostracon, which has room for it, or the *beth* that begins the first word of this phrase could be doing "double duty" as both a preposition and the first letter of the object of the preposition.

[84] On the plurality of Yahwistic sanctuaries in Judah, see especially Aharoni, *Land of the Bible*, 378–79. Excavated remains at various sites in Palestine show that before the sixth century, this deity certainly seems to have been worshipped in more than one sanctuary in Palestine:

1. Most notably, the Yahwistic temple at Arad (Yohanan Aharoni, "Arad: Its Inscriptions and Temple," *BA* 31 [1968]: 2–32; idem, "Excavations at Tell Arad: Preliminary Report on the Second Season, 1963," *IEJ* 17 [1967]: 233–49; idem, "The Israelite Sanctuary at Arad," in *New Directions in Biblical Archaeology* [ed. David N. Freedman and Jonas C. Greenfield; Garden City, N.Y.: Doubleday, 1969], 25–33; Yohanan Aharoni, *Arad Inscriptions* [Jerusalem: Israel Exploration Society, 1981], 148–49).

*Identifications in Unprovenanced Inscriptions* 183

The priesthood of Ḥanan and/or Ḥilqiyahu was carried out in a Hebrew and specifically a Judahite context.⁸⁵ As at Arad, the Yahwistic theophoric element in the PN of a priest (or the PN of one of his family members) testifies to the Yahwistic character of the temple at which one or both of these men ministered. That a temple of Yahweh was functioning in Jerusalem, the capital, may be presumed. On purely inscriptional grounds, however, it cannot be demonstrated that Jerusalem was the location of the temple in which either of these men served as priests. Even if the late seventh-century demolition of the temple of Yahweh at Arad⁸⁶ were due to a domestic reform movement, rather than wartime destruction, it still has not been demonstrated that Judah had only one functioning temple or that there was ever only one high priest of Yahweh in the kingdom of Judah.

Unfortunately, inscriptions reveal little about priesthood itself in Western Semitic regions.⁸⁷ Hebrew inscriptional material from before the year 100 B.C.E. that mentions the word *khn* is extremely limited in quantity and of little use in understanding the term *hkhn*.⁸⁸ Although the meaning of *hkhn* in the text of this

---

2. Beersheba, where a large horned altar was unearthed (idem, *Land of the Bible*, 378).

3. Possibly Lachish, from which Sennacherib's reliefs depict two soldiers carrying two decorated incense burners (ibid.).

4. The sacred precinct at Dan. It includes what has been dubbed a *bamah*, but its complex of buildings, horned altar, and other excavated structures may have included a temple (Avraham Biran, *Biblical Dan* [Jerusalem: Israel Exploration Society and Hebrew Union College, Jewish Institute of Religion, 1994], 159–214; Menahem Haran, *Temples and Temple-Serviced in Ancient Israel: An Inquiry into Biblical Cult Phenomena and the Historical Setting of the Priestly School* [Oxford: Clarendon Press, 1978; repr. with corrections, Winona Lake, Ind.: Eisenbrauns, 1985], 30–31).

For biblical evidence and partial archaeological evidence supporting Haran's claim of more than a dozen temples outside of Jerusalem, see ibid., 26–42.

⁸⁵ Although priests of Yahweh conducted Samaritan worship at Mount Gerizim after 722, this seal is thoroughly Judahite in its paleography.

⁸⁶ Under the heading "Stratum VI (end of the seventh, beginning of the sixth century B.C.E.)," Aharoni summarizes, "The general plan of the fortress was not changed in this stratum except for two things: the sanctuary ceased to exist, most of it being buried under the wall; and the gate was moved to the north side" (Aharoni, *Arad Inscriptions*, 8; above in this chapter see also note 84, numbered paragraph 1). Elsewhere, he states, "The sanctuary fell into disuse with the religious reformations of Hezekiah and Josiah, and was not rebuilt in Stratum VI" (ibid., 149).

⁸⁷ Helmer Ringgren, "כֹּהֵן *kōhēn*," *TDOT* 7:64–65.

⁸⁸ Not counting the seal of Ḥanan, there are only three extant Hebrew inscriptions from before ca. 100 that contain the word *khn* (*AHI*, 383). Of these, only two are seals of individuals. The first of these is a limestone seal whose reverse side reads: [לזכריו / כהן דאר / (obverse: מכא / בן לצדק). This seal was first published in Nahman Avi-

seal cannot be decided on the basis of ancient usage among the *Hebrews*, inscriptions from neighboring peoples may be used to show general tendencies. Although at least in Egypt, priesthood was not originally an inherited office, both Egyptian and Mesopotamia priests were commonly succeeded by their sons for many generations.[89] "This tendency increased with the passage of time."[90]

By religious convention in the ancient Near East, the priesthood of a given temple was headed by one of the priests, who bore various titles in Egypt, Mesopotamia, and among Western Semites.[91] Ugaritic, Phoenician, and Neo-Punic inscriptions use the term *khn* among other terms for "priest," and Ugaritic and Phoenician designate the head of a priesthood by the term *rb khnm*.[92] From the standpoint of inscriptional data, the most that can be said about the Hebrew inscriptional title *hkhn* is that there is neither any reason why it *cannot* designate the high priest, nor is there any compelling reason why it should.[93]

---

gad, "The Priest of Dor," *IEJ* 25 (1975): 101–5, Pl. 10:C, D. Although this seal is said to have been a surface find from near Sebaste, the site of ancient Samaria (ibid., 101), the fact that it was purchased on the antiquities market makes this provenance uncertain. Further, its authenticity is called into question by a form of *nun* which, at least in Judahite paleography, would be considered from the late seventh to early sixth century, in the same inscription which contains a distinctively eighth-century form of *waw*. (Paleographic criteria for establishing a more accurate date of this form of *nun* were not available in 1975, when Avigad dated it to the mid-eighth century.)

The second is a Hasmonean-era bulla, probably of Alexander Janneus (ca. 103–76), which reads, ם / ירשלם / גדל ן כה / יָנתן, "Jonathan, high priest; Jerusalem; 40." Since it is chronologically distant from the seal of Ḥanan and because it uses the term *khn gdl* instead of *hkhn*, it is not very relevant to the seal under discussion.

The third pre-100 inscription containing the word *khn* is also not very relevant to the seal of Ḥanan. It is inscribed on an ivory pomegranate, apparently from a priest's scepter. It reads: לבית יהוֹה קדש כהנם, "belonging to the tem[ple of Yahwe]h; sacred to priests." It was first published in André Lemaire, "Une inscription paléo-hébraïque sur grenade en ivoire," *RB* 88 (1981): 236–39. See also [Hershel Shanks], "The Pomegranate Scepter Head—From the Temple of the Lord or from a Temple of Asherah?" *BAR* 18, no. 3 (May/June 1992): 42–45 and its bibliographic citations.

[89] Jan Bergman and Helmar Ringgren, "כֹּהֵן *kōhēn*," *TDOT* 7:62–63.

[90] Ibid., 7:62.

[91] Ibid., 7:61–65.

[92] Ibid., 7:64–65.

[93] Elayi recognizes the ambiguity of the syntax, but on the basis of other seals thinks that the title applies to the son, rather than to the father.

In the English translation of the inscription—"(Belonging) to Ḥanan. son of Ḥilqiyahu, the priest"—it is unclear whether the priest is Ḥanan or Ḥilqiyahu. From other seals, however, we know that it is Ḥanan, the seal's owner, not his father Ḥilqiyahu, who is being identified as a priest. The last word, *kohen*, "the priest," designates the function of the owner of the seal, Ḥanan, and not of his father,

**(4.7) How the seal ring of Ḥanan, if authentic, would contribute to the historical framework**

This seal would be evidence of a functioning, Yahwistic priesthood in a temple or other sanctuary in Judah during the late seventh to early sixth century. It would also strengthen the inscriptional evidence for the identification of high priests Hilkiah and Azariah in the city of David bulla of Azariah (see sections 3.9 and 3.10 above), both by providing additional inscriptional evidence of Hilkiah's existence and by suggesting a paleographic indication of a high-priestly identity of the seal owner and/or his father, which would be evident both in this seal ring and in the city of David bullae (see on "The Setting" after "Question 1" above in this section).

**(4.7) Question 2: provided the seal ring of Ḥanan were authentic, whether its setting would *permit* a match**

**Date**: 5) A late seventh- to early sixth-century date agrees with the biblical chronology regarding Hilkiah, the high priest, who served in the First Temple in Jerusalem during the reign of Josiah (r. 640/39–609) (see above).

**Language**: 3) The language of the inscription presents no known disagreement with the language expectation raised by the biblical account: Hebrew (see above in this section under "Language").

**Socio-political classification**: 3) Agrees with the biblical account: Hebrew, and specifically Judahite (see above).

**(4.7) Question 3: Provided the seal ring were authentic, how strongly the specific data in [49] the seal ring לחנן ב · ן · חלקיהו · / הכהן would count for or against an identification with the biblical (37) Hilkiah, the High Priest, father of (38) Azariah (2 Kgs 22:4ff)**

√ **Name**: 1) Completely present, clearly legible, and in exact agreement with eleven of twenty biblical occurrences of this name. Nine end in -*yah*.

**Relations**: 5) Ḥanan as a biblical filionymic for Ḥilqiyahu is absent, and therefore neither can Ḥilqiyahu *as the patronymic of Ḥanan* match or contradict any counterpart in the Bible.

√ **Title(s)**: 2) Inscriptional data do not prohibit the title from being defined as "high priest," but neither do they provide the meaning (see above under correlation with the historical framework). The only biblical *title* applied to the earliest high priests, i.e., Aaron, Eleazar, and Phinehas, is simply *hakkohen*, "the

---

Ḥilqiyahu. (Josette Elayi, "Name of Deuteronomy's Author Found on Seal Ring," *BAR* 13, no. 5 [September/October 1987]: 55)

priest."[94] This title is also ascribed to the high priests in the books of Joshua, Samuel, and Kings. During the monarchic period, four high priests are called by this title: Azariah (1 Kgs 4:2), Jehoiada (2 Kgs 11:9), Uriah (2 Kgs 11:9), and Hilkiah (2 Kgs 22:10, 12, 14). In biblical sources referring to the preexilic period, when *hakkohen* is used *as a title*, there is no clear instance of it referring to an ordinary priest. This usage is exclusive in *the only extant Hebrew usages* of this title from before ca. 100 (except in three unhelpful inscriptions in note 88). It should be recognized, *but only provisionally*, that in a Hebrew inscriptional context, this designation more likely than not served as an official title of high priests.[95] To avoid circular reasoning in interpreting this title, any new inscriptional evidence regarding its meaning should be immediately applied to this ID.

In the absence of clear indications from Northwest Semitic inscriptions, Egyptian and Mesopotamian inscriptional sources suggest that the office was

---

[94] The phrase *hakkohen haggadol me'eḥaw*, "the greatest priest among his brothers," in Lev 21:10, is not a title, but simply a descriptive phrase, as is *hakkohen hammašiaḥ* (Lev 3:4, 5, 16; 6:15). The title *hakkohen haggadol*, "the high priest," appears in only seven verses which describe preexilic times (Num 35:25, 28 [bis]; Josh 20:6; and the four references immediately below in the de Vaux quotation). Cogan and Tadmor comment on this phrase in 2 Kgs 12:11:

> The accepted view (e.g., de Vaux, *Ancient Israel*, 377–79; 397–98) is that "high priest" is a Second Temple title; during the pre-exilic era, the head of the Temple bureaucracy was simply "the priest" or "head priest." Accordingly, the titles in 2 Kgs 12 and 22 are seen as accretions from the hand of a later copyist. Yet it cannot be excluded that both titles coexisted in late First Temple time; they were still interchangeable in the days of the Chronicler, when in the opinion of all, the title was *kōhēn gādôl*. . . . (Cogan and Tadmor, *II Kings*, 138)

Indeed, de Vaux showed that the substitution of *kohen gadol* for *hakkohen* might *possibly* have taken place, but he does not demonstrate that it did.

> The term 'high priest' (*hakkohen haggadôl*) is found only four times in pre-exilic texts (2 K 12: 11; 22: 4, 8; 23: 4); but in the parallels to these texts, 2 Ch 24: 11 (=2 K 12:11) has *kohen harôsh* ('the head priest'), 2 Ch 34: 14, 18 (=2 K 22: 4, 8) has merely *kohen* and the Greek version of 2 K 23: 4 also presumes the reading *kohen*. Thus all four references to the 'high priest' before the exile seem to be later modifications. Since the title 'high priest' did not exist before the Exile, . . . (Roland de Vaux, *Ancient Israel*, vol. 2: *Religious Institutions* [London: Darton, Longman, and Todd, 1961; repr., New York: McGraw Hill Book Company, 1965], 378)

Werner Dommershausen follows de Vaux's view in his portion of the article, "כֹּהֵן *kōhēn*," *TDOT* 7:71. On the significance of the title *hakkohen haggadol* in post-exilic times, see Eric M. Meyers, "The Shelomith Seal and the Judean Restoration: Some Additional Considerations," *ErIsr* 18, Nahman Avigad Volume (1985), 35*–37*.

[95] Elayi does not commit herself to this significance of the title *hkhn*: "Since the sacerdotal function (*hkhn*) of Ḥanan, the owner of the seal, is hereditary in this veterotestamentary context, his father was necessarily a priest or a high priest" (Elayi, "New Light," col. 681).

*Identifications in Unprovenanced Inscriptions* 187

likely inherited (see above under correlation with historical framework) and the Bible specifies that it was.[96] Although the title is syntactically ambiguous (see Chapter 1, note 102, above), the expectation that the office should be hereditary makes it much safer to say that the title applies to Hilqiyahu, rather than Hanan, because if the father were high priest, not every son of his would succeed him in that office, whereas if Hanan held that office, then Hilqiyahu would also normally have been the high priest before him. On this basis, it is certainly more secure to regard Hilqiyahu as *hkhn*.

Hanan is not mentioned in the Hebrew Bible. His father Hilqiyahu, however, is named as one of the high priests who served in Judah during the reign of Josiah (r. 639–609), and who, in ca. 621, discovered "the book of the law," now thought to be a portion of Deuteronomy, "in the house of the Lord" (2 Kgs 22:8). The inscriptional title matches the shorter biblical title *hakkohen*, which is applied to Hilkiah in 2 Kgs 22:10, 12, and 14. The fuller title *hakkohen haggadol* is applied to him in verses 4 and 8.

√ **Other**: 2) Other information is implicit in its significance for the ID. If this seal ring could be shown to have existed before the discovery of the city of David bullae in 1982, then the match between the script of this seal ring and the script of the city of David bulla of Azariah, son of Hilkiah, would imply a very likely connection to the high-priestly family which was functioning at the temple in Jerusalem. Since such a connection would be based on likelihood, rather than singularity, it would serve as a basis for a grade 3 ID at most.

**Singularity**: 3) The available data do not require an ID on grounds of singularity. The date of this seal indicates that it was probably used after Josiah's reforms of ca. 628–622, which, given Josiah's zeal for razing the temple of Yahweh at Arad, for example, *probably* left only one temple of Yahweh functioning in Judah, the one in Jerusalem. If that were known to be true, then at that time, only one high priest would have carried out his duties at that temple: Hilkiah. The available ancient data would then require that the Hilqiyahu of this seal be identified with the biblical Hilkiah. But that has not been demonstrated beyond a degree of probability, so there is no ground of clear-cut singularity.

### (4.7) Remarks

This grade 3 ID, conditional as it is on verification of the seal ring's authenticity, has the potential to lend plausible support to the IDs of Hilkiah the high priest and of his son Azariah in sections 3.9 and 3.10 above, as well as to provide a second ID (besides the grade 3 ID in section 3.9 above) of the same

---

[96] It is an uncontroversial biblical datum that succession to the high priestly office was normally hereditary (e.g., Num 20:26; Ezra 7:1–5).

high priest Hilkiah whose discovery of the law scroll in the temple at Jerusalem is prominent in 2 Kgs 22.

### 4.8 Is the biblical Baruch the scribe, son of Neriah, named in the bullae of Berekyahu?

On the first-known bulla itself, the question of its authenticity, and its setting apart from biblical data, in which six factors indicate its socio-political classification, see section 2.3 above.

### (4.8) How Berekyahu's bullae correlate with the historical framework

In light of the historical frameworks presented thus far, these bullae, if genuine, would be interpreted as a late seventh- to early sixth-century bulla of a scribe of Judah. The Hebrew script, the epigraphically determined date of the bullae, and the theophoric ending -*yahu* on both names (rather than -*yaw*, as it might have been before the end of the kingdom of Israel),[97] all support such a setting of the seal owner.

### (4.8) How the bullae of Berekyahu, if authentic, would contribute to the historical framework

These bullae of Berekyahu would develop the historical framework by specifying the name, title, and patronymic of a scribe in the twilight years of the kingdom of Judah. Along with other inscriptions of this period in Judah which have the same theophoric ending, they would also verify its Yahwistic religious orientation.

### (4.8) Question 2: provided the bullae of Berekyahu were authentic, whether their setting would *permit* a match

The match would be permitted. See section 2.3 above for a comparison of the inscriptional and the biblical setting (Criteria 4, 5, and 6: date, language, socio-political classification) related to matching the inscriptional person and the biblical person.

---

[97] See Chapter 3, note 136, and section 4.6, note 58, above.

*Identifications in Unprovenanced Inscriptions* 189

**(4.8) Question 3: provided the bullae were authentic, how strongly the specific data in [57 group[98]] the two bullae לברכיהו / בן נריהו / הספר would count for or against an identification with the biblical (47) Baruch the scribe, son of (46) Neriah and likely the brother of (49) Seraiah (Jer 32:12ff)**

The specific identifying criteria are exactly the same as those listed above in section 2.3, which shows that the criteria of name, relations, and title are met, along with one other criterion met under "Other." Provided the inscription is authentic, it is a grade 3, virtually certain ID.

**(4.8) Remarks**

The fact that the contemporary, late seventh- to early sixth-century bullae of Gemaryahu, son of Shaphan, and of Azaryahu, son of Ḥilqiyahu, were excavated in the city of David (see sections 3.7 through 3.10 above) makes the authenticity of this inscription very plausible. Expert opinion also stands strongly on the side of authenticity. *Demonstration* of authenticity, however, remains the condition that must be met to resolve any uncertainty. The most reliable technical means should be used to test the age of one or both of these two bullae of Berekyahu (see section 1.25, Criterion 4, third paragraph, "Other means of dating," above, and the article by Rollston in Chapter 1, note 106).

**4.9 Is the biblical Neriah, father of Baruch, named in the bullae of Berekyahu?**

On the inscription itself, the question of its authenticity, and its setting apart from biblical data, see section 2.3 above. On the correlation and contribution of the bullae to the historical framework, again see section 4.8 above.

**(4.9) Question 2: provided the bullae of Berekyahu were genuine, whether their setting would *permit* a match**

Yes, it would. See section 2.3 above for a comparison of the inscriptional and the biblical setting (Criteria 4, 5, and 6: date, language, socio-political classification).

---

[98] For the sake of convenience and clarity, bullae which are made by the same seal and inscriptions which are very similar to each other are given the same inscription number with the word "group" added.

**(4.9) Question 3: provided the inscription were authentic, how strongly the specific data in [57 group⁹⁹] the two bullae לברכיהו / בן נריהו / הספר would count for or against an identification with the biblical (46) Neriah, son of Maḥseiah and father of (47) Baruch the scribe and probably of (49) Seraiah (Jer 32:12ff)**

√ **Name**: 1) The spelling agrees with the less frequent spelling of the full form of the name of Baruch's father in the Hebrew Bible, e.g., in Jer 36:32.

√ **Relations**: 5) The inscriptional filionymic matches the biblical one, which in all 23 biblical occurrences (Jer 32:12ff) is the hypocoristicon, בָּרוּךְ, of the full name on the bullae, where it is complete and clearly legible.

**Title(s)**: 7) A title for Neriyahu seems be absent; see next paragraph.

√ **Other**: 4) The inscriptional title, which is complete and clear in the bullae, is syntactically ambiguous in its application. It could apply to patronymic or to the filionymic. Nevertheless, it does match the title of the son in the Hebrew Bible, who is the seal owner. If seal owners had a title, they lent the weight of their official authority to sealed documents by including their title on the seal (cf. Elayi's view in note 93 above in this chapter).

3) Other information is vague in its meaning. The city of David bullae reveal that it was common for bullae of Judahite officials of this period to be aniconic,¹⁰⁰ but aniconism does not correlate with any specific office.

**Singularity**: 3) An ID on grounds of singularity is not required.

**(4.9) Remarks**

As with the biblical Baruch (section 4.8 above), this is a near-certain, grade 3 ID which is conditional upon the authenticity of at least one of the two bullae of Berekyahu.

---

⁹⁹ See preceding note.

¹⁰⁰ Of the fifty-one bullae of this archive, four contain only iconographic representations and forty-seven contain writing (Shiloh and Tarler, "Bullae from the City of David," 202).

Those impressions containing personal names are aniconic, with only occasional geometric floral designs employed in the horizontal dividers separating the bulla into registers. This would appear to support the view that Hebrew seals without pictorial decoration characterize the final stage in the morphological and iconographical development of that glyptic art during the last century of the Judean Monarchy. On the other hand, the seals of the ninth to eighth centuries B.C. (which, in addition to the owner's name, were accompanied by floral and geometric motifs or mythological creatures, such as the griffin) were influenced by the northern, Israelite kingdom. It is noteworthy that only 4 bullae out of 51 in this assemblage were iconographic *and*, in addition, totally anepigraphic. (Ibid., their italics)

## 4.10 Is the biblical Jerahmeel, the king's son, named in the bulla of Yeraḥmeʾel?

### Description, transcription, and translation

The bulla of Yeraḥmeʾel,[101] 12 mm. long and 10 mm. wide, contains an irregular, oval seal impression 9 mm. long and 7 mm. wide. Its aniconic face contains two lines of writing separated by two parallel lines and surrounded by a single line. A dot follows the last letter.

line 1    לירחמאל    "Belonging to Yeraḥmeʾel,[102]
line 2    בן המלך·    the king's son"

### (4.10) Question 1: reliability of inscriptional data

**Access**: 3) Purchased on the antiquities market.
**Provenance**: 4) Unknown.
**Authenticity**: 4) A consensus of expert opinion favors authenticity.

### (4.10) The setting of the bulla of Yeraḥmeʾel, apart from biblical data

**Date**: 5) Dated by epigraphy: the latter part of the seventh century. The letter *he* points to a late seventh- to early sixth-century date, in that its three crossbars are not parallel, but converge toward the open (the reader's left) side of the letter, and its top crossbar extends beyond the vertical shaft.[103] As Herr points out, the *yodh* and *heth*, which have enough vertical space to be taller, as the *aleph* is, are instead "squat" forms, indicating a date in the late mid-seventh century.[104] Overall, the script seems to fit best within the last third of the seventh century.

**Language**: 5) The language of the inscription cannot be specifically determined on linguistic grounds. If language parameters are set solely by vocabulary, morphology, and syntax, several Northwest Semitic languages are possibilities. The word *bn* rather than *br* and the definite article *h-* exclude Aramaic.

---

[101] The bulla of Yeraḥmeʾel was first published in Avigad, "Baruch the Scribe," 52–56. It is listed in *AHI*, 186, no. 100.508, and in *WSS*, 175, no. 414.
[102] The name Yeraḥmeʾel means, "God will have compassion," show mercy, or the like.
[103] Vaughn, "Palaeographic Dating of Judaean Seals," 47, 52–53.
[104] Herr, "Paleography and the Identification of Seal Owners," 67.

192    *Identifying Biblical Persons in Northwest Semitic Inscriptions*

**Fig. 17**

**The bulla "of Yeraḥmeʾel, the King's Son"**

(Drawing by the author)

**Socio-political classification**: 3) Determined by the Hebrew script. Permitted by the theophoric element -*el*, the onomasticon of inscriptional Hebrew,[105] the language parameters, the arrangement of the text on the seal,[106] and its material characteristics:[107] Hebrew. The theophoric element, -*el*, could be Hebrew but is not distinctively so. The date of the inscription, however, in combination with its Hebrew script, are evidence for a Judahite nationality; since the kingdom of Israel had ceased to exist for at least a century,[108] Judah was the only Hebrew kingdom left.

### (4.10) How Yeraḥmeʾel's bulla correlates with the historical framework

This bulla's setting in the kingdom of Judah during the latter part of the seventh century and the title "the king's son" make it clear that Yeraḥmeʾel was an official in the royal administration of Judah during that period.

### (4.10) How the bulla of Yeraḥmeʾel, if authentic, would contribute to the historical framework

This seal would provide the PN of a particular royal official in the administration of the kingdom of Judah during the latter part of the seventh century. It would also testify to the existence of the title and office of "the king's son" in that setting.

### (4.10) Question 2: provided the bulla of Yeraḥmeʾel were authentic, whether its setting would *permit* a match

**Date**: 5) A date within the last third of the seventh century (see above) agrees with the biblical chronology regarding Jerahmeel, which places his one biblical appearance in an episode during "the fourth year of Jehoiakim the son of Josiah, king of Judah" (r. 609–598; Jer 36:1), i.e., 606/605.

---

[105] Although the PN Yeraḥmeʾel has not yet been found in any other Hebrew inscription (*AHI*, 378; *WSS*, 531), a Hebrew PN apparently based on the root רחם is found in one other Hebrew inscription, a bulla from the city of David (*WSS*, 531). Unfortunately, the third root letter is missing in an incomplete seal impression (*WSS*, 221, no. 586). PNs based on the root רחם are also found in Aramaic (Maraqten, 211).

[106] Many aniconic Hebrew seals and bullae contain two lines of writing across the face in horizontal or "landscape" orientation (*WSS*, 49–263, passim).

[107] See note 55 above in this chapter.

[108] See section 4.6, under "How the bulla of Yehozaraḥ correlates with the historical framework" and note 58, above.

**Language**: 3) The language of the inscription presents no known disagreement with the language expectation raised by the biblical account: Hebrew (see above).

**Socio-political classification**: 3) Agrees with the biblical account: Hebrew, and specifically Judahite (see above), which is the setting of Jer 36.

**(4.10) Question 3: provided the inscription were authentic, how strongly the specific data in [59] the bulla לירחמאל / בן המלך would count for or against an identification with the biblical (48) Jerahmeel, the king's son (Jer 36:26)**

√ **Name**: 1) Completely present, clearly legible, and in exact agreement with the consonants of the only reference to this man in the Bible: Jer 36:26.

**Relations**: 6) The family information apparently in the inscription includes no names. Whether the title, בן המלך, signifies a physical descendant of the king or simply an appointee to the post who was not necessarily of royal descent, is not clear.[109] Even if the title were known to apply only to blood descendants of the king, a particular "king's son" would not necessarily be a son of the currently reigning king, but could be a *previous* king's immediate son, retained as a royal official after the end of his father's reign. Yeraḥmeʾel's title designates him as a physical descendant of "the king," yet that king might not

---

[109] Avigad candidly states,
The present writer has in the past been inconsistent in the interpretation of this title, but he is now inclined to return to his original opinion, that the bearers of the title 'son of the king' were indeed members of the royal family. This interpretation finds support in the biblical reference to 'Jotham, the king's son, (who was) over the house, judging the people of the land' (2 Kings 15:5). Here the title is definitely applied to the crown prince who was the son of King Uzziah. In the other cases cited above the bearers of this title probably were among the many princes who were entrusted by kings with various functions, among them also the important office of maintaining security at the royal court. They were high officials of royal descent. (Avigad, "Baruch the Scribe," 55)
On the significance of this title, see also idem, "A Seal of 'Manasseh, Son of the King,'" *IEJ* 13 (1963): 133–36; idem, "A New Seal of a 'Son of the King,'" *Michmanim* 6 (1992): 27*–31*; Barkay, "Bulla of Ishmael,"109–14; Gershon Brin, "The Title בן (ה)מלך and its Parallels: The Significance and Evaluation of an Official Title," *AION* 29 (1969): 433–65; André Lemaire, "Note sur le titre *bn hmlk* dans l'ancien Israël," *Sem* 29 (1979): 59–65; James Muilenburg, "Baruch the Scribe," in *Proclamation and Presence: Old Testament Essays in Honour of Gwynne Henton Davies* (ed. John I. Durham and J. Roy Porter; Richmond: John Knox Press, 1970), 231; Anson F. Rainey, "*Bn hmlk* in Ugarit and among Hittites" (in Hebrew), *Lešonenu* 33 (1969): 304–8; idem, "The Prince and the Pauper," *Ugarit-Forschungen* 7 (1975): 427–32; Sass, "Pre-Exilic Hebrew Seals," 242.

have been Jehoiakim, but possibly Josiah (r. 640/39–609). An earlier paternity might also provide a more suitable fit for the date of the bulla.[110]

√ **Title(s)**: 2) The inscriptional title exactly matches the consonants of the biblical phrase: ךלמה ןב לאמחרי (Jer 36:26). On the meaning of the title, see the preceding paragraph.

√ **Other**: 2) Other information is implicit, and it agrees with the biblical account in its indication that Berekyahu and Jerahmeel were contemporaries and colleagues in the same royal administration. The bulla of Yeraḥmeʾel and the first-known bulla of Berekyahu were from the same hoard. Avigad states, ". . . the fact is that both of them are mentioned in the same biblical account and their bullae were found together."[111] Avigad's knowledge of the way in which these two bullae appeared on the antiquities market gave him enough confidence to use their appearance together as a datum for identification. After giving an account of a possible place where the bullae might have been illegally dug, Avigad tells why he believes that these two bullae came from the same large hoard:

> . . . Bullae were brought to me in small batches, and I had only a brief opportunity to examine and photograph them. There was no reason to suspect their authenticity, and I seriously doubt whether it would be possible to forge such burnt and damaged bullae. Despite the delay in the appearance of subsequent batches of bullae, *there was no doubt that all of them belonged to a single assemblage; identical impressions often occurred in different batches, and occasionally two fragments of a single bullae* [sic], *from different batches, could be joined.* This was revealed only by means of enlarged photographs.[112]

Such interpolation is not utterly secure, but the observations on which it is based are reasonably convincing evidence that these two bullae were found together in a large hoard(s) totaling over 250 bullae. These bullae were illegally excavated, apparently all at about the same time, around October 1975.[113] It is now impossible to reconstruct all of the details of the process by which Avigad reached his conclusion.

**Singularity**: 3) An ID on grounds of singularity is not required.

---

[110] In the context of Jer 36, if the circumstances suggested here were in effect, then Jerahmeel might have been a well-seasoned member of the royal security force—perhaps the most experienced person who could have been sent to arrest Baruch and Jeremiah—and probably able to recognize them both. The meaning of Jerahmeel's name might be ironically reflected in the last statement of Jer 36:26, "But the Lord hid them."

[111] Avigad, "On the Identification," 236, translation mine.

[112] Idem, *Hebrew Bullae*, 13; italics mine.

[113] Ibid., 12.

### (4.10) Remarks

This grade 3 ID, which is conditional on verification of the bulla's authenticity, also depends on the bulla's accompanying that of Berekyahu as an indication that they were discovered together. In Avigad's judgment, based on his knowledge of the way two hoards of bullae appeared on the Jerusalem antiquities market, this accompaniment was "fact."[114]

---

[114] Avigad, "On the Identification," 236, translation mine. He describes the discovery of four entirely different hoards of bullae, two of which were excavated under controlled conditions, in idem, *Hebrew Bullae*, 11–12.

# Chapter 5

# Conclusions

### 5.1 Tabulation of identifications of individuals

Chapter 3 evaluated eight potential IDs in five provenanced inscriptions published before October 1997, producing the following results:

| Grade of ID | Person(s) identified in which inscription(s) | Number of IDs |
|---|---|---|
| Certain on inscriptional & biblical grounds SI + SB | **Mesha** and **Omri** in the Mesha Inscription<br>**David** in the Tel Dan stele | 2<br>1 |
| Certain on biblical grounds SB | **Jeroboam** (II), son of Jehoash, in the Megiddo seal "belonging to Shema, minister of Jeroboam" | 1 |
| Virtually certain to reliable 3 | **Shaphan** the scribe, father of Gemariah, and<br>**Gemariah**, son of Shaphan the scribe, both in the city of David bulla, "belonging to Gemaryahu, son of Shaphan"<br>**Hilkiah**, the high priest, father of Azariah, and | 1<br>1<br>1 |

| | |
|---|---|
| **Azariah**, son of Hilkiah the high priest, both in the city of David bulla, "belonging to Azaryahu, son of Hilqiyahu" | 1 |

Total IDs in provenanced inscriptions: 8

Of the eight marketed, unprovenanced inscriptions evaluated in Chapter 4, the two seals relating to Uzziah appeared long before any forger could have known the appropriate details of Hebrew epigraphy for the time of Uzziah (see "Question 1, Authenticity", in sections 3.3, 4.2, and 4.3 above). These are the seal of Abiyaw, published in 1858, and the seal of Shubnayaw, published in 1863. Consequently, they should be considered to be as authentic as any excavated seals, and they contain two more IDs:

| Grade of ID | Person(s) identified in which inscription(s) | Number of IDs |
|---|---|---|
| Certain on biblical grounds SB | **Uzziah** in the seal of Shubnayaw, minister of Uzziyaw | 1 |
| | **Uzziah** in the seal of Abiyaw, minister of Uzziyaw | 1 |

Total IDs in provenanced inscriptions, listed above: + 8

Total instances of identification in inscriptions of known authenticity: 10
Total number of persons identified (Uzziah being identified twice) 9

These ten IDs of nine persons include five kings, two high government officials, and two high priests. It is noteworthy for the study of the sources used by the biblical writers that the names of almost half of these identified persons would not be found in a king list.[1]

As with most ancient archaeological evidence used in historical inquiry, the published material is what remains after a step-by-step reduction of evidence and availability of evidence. As a result, only a small part remains of what might

---

[1] The usual range of content in an ancient Near Eastern king list can be seen, e.g., in Babylonian King List A, museum no. BM 33332 (Theophilus G. Pinches, *Proceedings of the Society of Biblical Archaeology* [London: Society of Biblical Archaeology, 1884], 6:193–94; Hugo Winckler, *Untersuchungen zur Altorientalischen Geschichte* [Leipzig: E. Pfeiffer, 1889], 146–47; *ANET*, 272) and in Babylonian King List B, museum no. BM 38122, previously numbered 80, 11-12-3 (Winckler, *Untersuchungen zur altorientalischen Geschichte*, 145; *ANET*, 271). See also section 5.3 and note 4 below.

otherwise have been currently accessible.² It is most significant that these results come from *only a tiny part* of the available Northwest Semitic inscriptional evidence: pre-Persian-era Hebrew inscriptions, the Mesha Inscription, and the Tel Dan stele. Lack of space prohibits detailed treatment of *many* other inscriptions offering additional potential IDs, both from the whole biblical period in languages besides Hebrew and in Hebrew from the Persian era (see section 5.5).

---

² The fullest description of this reduction of evidence is in Edwin M. Yamauchi, *The Stones and the Scriptures* (New York: J. B. Lippincott, A Holman Book, 1972), 146–57. Several processes of elimination, most of which are linked in a series, destroy, ignore, or otherwise reduce the amount of ancient data that is actually available.

Of the fraction of the evidence which survives, successive fractions are surveyed and excavated under controlled conditions. In 1963, Lapp stated, "Roughly only 2 per cent of potentially good archaeological sites in Palestine have been touched, and only in rare instances is more than 5 per cent of a site excavated" (Paul W. Lapp, *Biblical Archaeology and History* [New York: World Publishing, 1969], 83–84; cf. idem, "Palestine: Known but Mostly Unknown," *BA* 26 [1963]:121–34).

The limitations of the site and limits of the processes of controlled excavation and analysis, as actually carried out, can also detract from the quantity and trustworthiness of whatever data are eventually published. " . . . Of the material from excavated sites . . . perhaps 5 to 10 per cent has a reliable stratigraphic, typological, and analytic base, [so that] the amount of trustworthy data available to the historian is an extremely limited sample" (Lapp, *Biblical Archaeology and History*, 84).

On recognizing bullae during an excavation, Philip J. King has commented, " . . . The real reason few bullae have been found is that bullae are small, and sieving is not yet widely practiced. Also, to the uninitiated, an unbaked clay bulla looks like an ordinary lump of clay if it is not carefully examined" (King, *Jeremiah*, 93).

With regard to ostraca, he added,

Aharoni . . . introduced the practice of soaking and dipping sherds in water and then inspecting them carefully for possible inscriptions before proceeding with the more vigorous washing process. The traditional procedure of scrubbing the pottery with a brush without dipping in advance may have obliterated countless inscriptions from ostraca [ibid., 100].

Of course, illegal digging, forgeries, and fakes have led to precautions which can disqualify not only fraudulent material, but also a certain amount of authentic material on the antiquities market; as a result, some authentic data is ruled out of consideration.

Finally, only a fraction of the excavated material is ever published, and a smaller fraction is published or otherwise made available in a timely manner. Lapp estimated that "perhaps half of the material from excavated sites has actually been published" (Lapp, *Biblical Archaeology and History*, 84). See Hershel Shanks, ed., *Archaeology's Publication Problem* (Washington, D.C.: Biblical Archaeology Society, 1996) and the review essay on the issues it raises: Giorgio Buccellati, "Review/Essay: *Archaeology's Publication Problems*," *Near Eastern Archaeology* 61 (1998): 118–20. The matter of promptness in publication, not only in the instance of the Dead Sea Scrolls, is a perennial problem (see, e.g., Donald J. Wiseman, "The Bottleneck of Archaeological Publication," *BAR* 16, no. 5 [September/October 1990]: 60–63).

## 5.2 Conclusion in relation to the thesis

This study has demonstrated that, on the basis of a systematic identification process, a number of persons named in the Hebrew Bible are indeed to be identified with persons named in extant inscriptions, most of which were once contemporary with them. Inscriptions discovered between 1858 and 1904 refer to Mesha, Omri, Jeroboam II, and in two inscriptions, Uzziah. Inscriptions unearthed in 1982 and 1993 refer to Shaphan, Gemariah, Hilkiah, Azariah, and David.

## 5.3 Conclusions as they would be developed if unprovenanced inscriptions were demonstrated to be authentic

This discussion has thus far avoided most of the results in Chapter 4, i.e., those besides the two seals of ministers of King Uzziah tabulated above, until after reaching the conclusion based on provenanced materials. The following IDs are conditional, because their authenticity is not beyond question, yet in some instances it is very widely accepted. As in section 5.1, these inscriptions were published before October 1997:

| Grade of ID | Person(s) identified in which inscription(s) | Number of IDs |
|---|---|---|
| Certain on biblical grounds SB | **Ahaz** in the seal of Ushna, minister of Aḥaz | 1 |
| | **Hoshea** in the seal of Abdi, minister of Hoshea | 1 |
| | **Hezekiah** in the bulla of Yehozarah, son of Ḥilqi-yahu, minister of Ḥizqiyahu | 1 |
| | **Hilkiah** the high priest, father of Azariah, in the seal ring of Ḥanan, son of Ḥilqiyahu, the priest | 1 |
| Virtually certain to reliable 3 | **Neriah**, father of Baruch the scribe, and | 1 |
| | **Baruch** the scribe, son of Neriah, in the two bullae of Berekyahu, son of Neriyahu, the scribe | 1 |
| | **Jerahmeel**, the king's son, in the bulla of Yeraḥme-'el, the king's son | 1 + |

Total conditional IDs in six unprovenanced inscriptions: 7
Total number of persons conditionally identified in these inscriptions: 7

This section describes *potential* results, provided all six of these unprovenanced inscriptions should be shown to be genuine. The total number of IDs in inscriptions would then rise to seventeen, instead of ten. Three more kings, the same high priest Hilkiah, two more royal officials, and Baruch's father Neriah, who might have been a commoner, would be identified in Hebrew inscriptions.

For the kings of the northern kingdom of Israel, in addition to the previous IDs of Omri and Jeroboam II, there would be a Hebrew seal in which one could identify Israel's last king, Hoshea, who is already mentioned in the Assyrian royal inscriptions (Chapter 2, note 57, above). For the kings of Judah, besides the previous ID of David, there would be IDs of Ahaz and Hezekiah, consecutive monarchs in the Hebrew Bible who are also both mentioned in Assyrian inscriptions (sections 4.4 and 4.6, historical frameworks, above). The effect of identifying these three Hebrew kings in the inscriptions of their ministers would be to confirm the Assyrian and the biblical evidence of their existence.

Among non-royals, Hilkiah the high priest already has a reliable ID in one of the city of David bullae listed in section 5.1. But there would also be added IDs of Neriah, Baruch, and Jerahmeel.

These systematically established yet conditional IDs uphold the second part of the thesis as stated above in section 0.2, regarding *conditional* IDs in unprovenanced Hebrew inscriptions.

## 5.4 Nine biblical episodes which include more than one individual identified or conditionally identifiable in an inscription

Beyond the consideration of the identified persons taken one by one, as above, several biblical persons identified or conditionally identifiable in inscriptions appear in small clusters within specific biblical episodes. These clusters of IDs are of interest to researchers seeking to ascertain the historical background of these biblical passages. In order not to exclude any potentially relevant inscriptions, the list of materials that name or might name persons in each episode below includes both provenanced and unprovenanced items.

As stated in section 3.1, IDs below grade 3 and inscriptions published *after* the beginning of October 1997 are not treated above. "Latecomer" inscriptions all appear in Appendixes B and C, rather than above. They include about a dozen of the IDs and inscriptions mentioned in connection with the following nine episodes. All person numbers and inscription numbers are taken from Appendixes B and C, where their bibliographic references appear.

It is important to keep in mind that in seals and bullae, there is no indication as to whether the identified persons carried out the actions which the biblical narratives attribute to them in these episodes. Regarding the *activities* of identified individuals, usually the most that can be said is that persons named both in the Bible and in inscriptions were at one time *in a position* (usually indicated by setting and title or lineage) to do what the Bible says they did. From a purely inscriptional standpoint, compatibility between the person's position as observable in inscription(s) and his or her biblical actions can do nothing more than make the biblical narratives plausible.[3]

Episode 1: Mesha, king of Moab, vs. the dynasty of Omri, king of Israel (2 Kgs 1:1; 3:4–27). Three sources place Mesha and/or the dynasty of Omri in the early to mid-ninth century: 1) the Mesha Inscription, with its IDs of Mesha and Omri on grounds of both inscriptional and biblical singularity, 2) Assyrian inscriptions, including those that mention "the house of Omri," "Jehu, son of Omri," and "Ahab the Israelite" (Chapter 2, note 57, and section 3.3, historical framework, above), and 3) the biblical books of 1–2 Kings and 2 Chronicles.[4]

Episode 2: the deliverance of Hezekiah's Jerusalem (2 Kgs 18:13–19:37). Person (75), Sennacherib, king of Assyria, is known from the Bible, from his own inscriptions (see, e.g., section 4.6, historical framework, above) and from a Neo-Babylonian chronicle regarding his having been assassinated by his son (*ABC*, 81, Chronicle 1, lines 34–35). The Ashur ostracon offers an ID of Sennacherib that is certain on both inscriptional and biblical grounds. As for (23) Hezekiah, king of Judah, the unprovenanced bulla of Jehozarah yields a conditional grade SB ID of him (section 4.6 above), as do other unprovenanced bullae in Appendixes B and C under person (23). The Silwan epitaph [34] offers a grade 2 ID of (25) Shebna which complements the conditional grade 2 ID of (28) Eliakim, the overseer of Hezekiah's palace (Isa 22:20–25), and of his father, (27) Hilkiah, in unprovenanced bulla [40]. Four provenanced jar handles [41 group] bearing the impression of the seal of Eliakim, steward of Yokan, offer a grade 1 ID of the same overseer of Hezekiah's palace, possibly at an earlier stage in his career. The seal of Shubnayaw, minister of Uzziyaw (section 4.3 above), as good as provenanced (see section 5.1 between totals), offers a dubious grade 1 ID of an official who was an overseer of Hezekiah's palace (Isa 22:15–19; Appendixes B and C, person (25) and possibly (26), below).

---

[3] Becking mentions an instance of plausibility in that the biblical narrative is consistent with Babylonian governmental practice. "That, however, does not imply that the acts pursued by these individuals as reported or narrated in later narratives are thus historical" (Bob Becking, "Inscribed Seals as Evidence for Biblical Israel? Jeremiah 40.7–41 *par exemple*," in Lester L. Grabbe, ed., *Can a 'History of Israel' Be Written?* JSOT Supplement Series 245, European Seminar in Historical Methodology 1 [Sheffield, England: Sheffield Academic Press, 1997], 83).

[4] I.e., 1 Kgs 16:16–33; 22:39–40, 52–54; 2 Kgs 1:1; 3:1–9, 21–27; 8:26; 2 Chr 22:2; cf. Mic 6:16. It may be noted that the biblical data extend beyond the customary range of a king list, i.e., names of successive monarchs, to include annalistic information. See note 1 above in this chapter.

## Conclusions

Episode 3: the replacement of Shebna with Eliakim as the royal minister *śr 'l hbyt*, "who is in charge of the palace." Two persons included in Episode 2 (in 2 Kgs 18:18, 26, 37; 19:2) also seem to appear in Isa 22:15–23, which, on the basis of the titles they had, seems to be previous to Episode 2. The [34] Silwan epitaph's grade 2 ID of (25) and possibly (26) Shebna and the conditional grade 2 IDs of (28) Eliakim and his father (27) Hilkiah mentioned in the preceding paragraph are also relevant here (see all in Appendixes B and C).

Episode 4: Hilkiah's discovery of the book of the law and the events which stem from it (2 Kgs 22). The city of David bullae offer reliable grade 3 IDs both of (36) Shaphan the scribe and of (37) Hilkiah the high priest in the same excavated archive. These discoveries suggest, on inscriptional and archaeological grounds, that they were contemporaries. The fact that the names of both Shaphan and Hilkiah are inscribed only as patronymics seems to support this suggestion (in published lists, they both occur only once in the bullae of this archive[5]). It must still be kept in mind, however, that these bullae appear to include persons from three generations, because six of the names in Shiloh's list of the thirty most legible appear both as patronymics and as filionymics.[6] Although not enough data are available to know whether any of these six in the patronymics are really the same persons as in the filionymics, one must reckon with the possibility that some are. Using the published names, however, it is not possible to construct any potential sequence of *more* than three generations. Hence, it may be assumed that the names on the bullae represent three generations.

Within a three-generation framework, since both names appear only as patronymics, Shaphan and Hilkiah must either have been from the same generation or from consecutive generations, and since the lives of fathers and sons usually

---

[5] The fifty-one discovered bullae of this archive include four which contain only iconographic representations and forty-seven which contain writing. On forty-five of these forty-seven, both the filionymic and patronymic survive. Of these forty-five, forty-one are legible. These "41 were very well-preserved because the conflagration that destroyed the bullae house (along with the rest of Jerusalem) fired them, thus hardening and preserving them for future generations" (Shiloh and Tarler, "Bullae from the City of David," 202). The list of thirty bullae in Shiloh, "Group of Hebrew Bullae," 29, covers the most significant inscriptions. Summary statements about the bullae, their paleography, and the names on them, along with pictures (photographs or drawings) of sixteen bullae, are found in Shiloh and Tarler, "Bullae from the City of David," 202–205. The latest description is found in Yair Shoham, "Hebrew Bullae" in *Inscriptions* (ed. Donald T. Ariel; vol. 6 of *Excavations at the City of David 1978–1985 Directed by Yigal Shiloh*, City of David Final Report 6, Qedem 41; Jerusalem: The Hebrew University of Jerusalem, The Institute of Archaeology, 2000), 29–57.

[6] 'Afraḥ, 'Elišamaʿ, Bilgay, Ḥananyahu (Ḥananiah), Yaʾazanyahu, and Mikayahu.

overlap chronologically, it is likely that they would still be contemporaries. (Of course, even grandfathers and grandchildren could be contemporaries, but the hazards of life make that somewhat less likely.) This is rough reckoning, not an incontrovertible case. Nevertheless, apart from biblical IDs, *inscriptional data* lend some reasonable support to a case for Shaphan the scribe and Hilkiah the priest being contemporaries, as they are depicted in 1 Kgs 22.[7]

Episode 5: the readings of an early scroll of Jeremiah (Jer 36). The reliable grade 3 IDs of the biblical (36) Shaphan and his son (50) Gemariah in city of David bulla [48] testify to the existence of two persons named in Jer 36. If the [57 group] bullae of Baruch and [59] bulla of Jerahmeel are demonstrated to be authentic (though even now, most experienced epigraphers are convinced of their genuineness), then these bullae will offer virtually certain IDs of three more persons: (46) Neriah, (47) Baruch, and (48) Jerahmeel. Three other IDs appear in Appendixes B and C but not above. Unprovenanced bulla [61] offers conditional grade 2 IDs of (51b) Zedekiah and his father, (51a) Hananiah, and [56] Lachish ostracon 3 offers a grade 1 ID of (44) Elnathan, son of Achbor.

Four other episodes, listed below in chronological order, offer mostly grade 2 IDs (reasonable but uncertain) along with some that are weaker:

Episode 6: Jehu's assassination of Jehoram, Ahaziah, and Jezebel (2 Kgs 9). Despite affinities with the Tel Dan stele, *systematic* identification of the assassinated trio is not currently possible. See section 2.8 above on (10) Jehoram and Appendixes B and C, persons (8) Jezebel (grade 1), (10) Jehoram (grade 0.2), and (17) Ahaziah (grade 0). This triad is a warning against facile IDs.

Episode 7: Jeremiah's conflict with Hananiah the false prophet, son of Azzur of Gibeon (Jer 28). Seal [65] offers conditional grade 2 IDs of (58)

---

[7] See Appendixes B and C for these IDs: a grade SB certain match with (37) Hilkiah the high priest that awaits authentication of seal ring [49] (see "Title(s)" under "Question 3" in sections 3.9 and 4.7) and, at grade 2, (37) Hilkiah the high priest in unprovenanced seals [51] and [52], as well as (36) Shaphan in unprovenanced bulla [47].

Avigad suggested that unprovenanced seal [46] might relate to (36) Shaphan of 2 Kgs 22, although the relationships cannot be demonstrated. This seal, *l'ṣlyhw bn mšlm*, i.e., "belonging to Azaliah, son of Meshullam," last reported in the possession of a private collector, was published by Avigad ("On the Identification," 237, including Fig. 5). It is also mentioned, but not pictured, in Schneider, "Six Biblical Signatures," 30, 32, box. It might refer to ancestors of Shaphan, (34) Azaliah, the son of (33) Meshullam, the scribe, both named in 2 Kgs 22:3. Without specific grounds for a connection to Shaphan besides the matching pair of names, these two conditional grade 2 IDs remain unresolved.

Hananiah and his father, (57) Azzur. Seven jar-handle inscriptions from Gibeon, [66 group], offer a grade 2 ID of the same Azzur.

Episode 8: the assassination of Gedaliah (2 Kgs 25; Jer 40). The Tell el-Umeiri seal impression [89] of Milkomʾur has a grade 2 ID of (77) Baalis, king of Ammon.[8] An unprovenanced seal [55] offers a conditional grade 2 ID of (42) Elishama, father of Nethaniah, father of (62) Ishmael. An unprovenanced bulla [71] offers a conditional grade 2 ID of this same Ishmael.[9] A Tell en-Naṣbeh seal [70] has a grade 2 ID of (61) Jaazaniah, the Maacathite's son.

Episode 9: The apostasy of leaders in Jerusalem (Ezek 11:1). An unprovenanced accounting ostracon [63] offers conditional grade 2 IDs of Jaazaniah and his father Azzur (in Appendixes B and C, persons (55) and (54), respectively).

## 5.5 Promising directions for further investigation

The starting point established in the five provenanced and eight marketed inscriptions treated above is the reliable identification of nine to sixteen biblical persons, depending on demonstration of authenticity of the marketed inscriptions. In order to gain a more complete picture, Appendixes B and C take a first step in further investigation. They include the findings above and also provide a preliminary survey of all (or almost all) other promising extant, pre-Persian-era, Northwest Semitic inscriptions, listing verdicts of evaluations of potential IDs of a total of seventy-nine persons in ninety-one inscriptions. Appendix C takes the evaluations of Appendix B and arranges them in descending order of strength.

Appendix F summarizes all of these evaluations numerically. In Table 4, it finds that fifteen persons can be identified, from reliably to certainly, in fourteen provenanced inscriptions (this finding includes those treated above). In Table 5, marketed inscriptions, if authenticity were to be demonstrated, could potentially add as many as nine other persons identified reliably to certainly in eighteen other inscriptions. Counting both provenanced and marketed inscriptions in Table 6, then, the total number of persons who *might* conceivably be identified, from reliably to certainly, is from fifteen to twenty-four,[10] depending on demonstration of authenticity of the marketed inscriptions.

---

[8] The seal [90] "of Baʾalyašaʿ / Baʾališaʿ king of the sons of Ammon," published in 1999, is another inscription that contains a grade 2 ID of the biblical Baalis, person (77).

[9] See Becking, "Inscribed Seals," 65–83; Peter van der Veen, "Beschriftete Siegel als Beweis für das biblische Israel? Gedalja und seine Mörder *par exemple* (Ein Antwort an Bob Becking)," in *Wort und Stein: Festschrift Udo Worschech* (ed. Friedbert Ninow; Beiträge zur Erforschung der antiken Moabitis (Ard el-Kerak); Frankfurt: Peter Lang Verlag, 2004), 114–35.

[10] See Appendix F, the underlined items in Tables 4, 5, and 6, as well as note 12.

Shifting to the Persian era, a rough estimate is that approximately thirty additional Northwest Semitic inscriptions name fifteen or more additional persons whose potential IDs as biblical persons would be worth evaluating. Considering the entire period of the Hebrew Bible, Persian-era IDs could bring the number of biblical persons reliably to certainly identified in Northwest Semitic inscriptions to an approximate total of thirty or forty, depending on demonstration of authenticity of unprovenanced inscriptions. Encounters with "new" conditions in inscriptions not treated in this volume could also lead to further development of the identification system.

# Appendix A

# The Significance of the Title *'Ebed* in Northwest Semitic Seals and Seal Impressions

The following quotation characterizes the Old Babylonian use of the title "servant" in seals and seal impressions:

> Seal inscriptions of the O[ld] B[abylonian] period from Mari show that men who owned seals proclaimed themselves servants of the king . . . or of a deity, but never the servant of anyone less than the king. The same is true, as far as the publication of seal inscriptions allows a conclusion, at Chagar Bazar. Jacobsen has fully published seal inscriptions from Eshnunna, showing how OB seal inscriptions developed from those of the Ur III period, in which the seal itself was dedicated to a deity. Weidner took the principle for granted in a study of OB seal inscriptions.[1]

Northwest Semitic seals and seal impressions reveal a similar use of the corresponding term, עבד (*'bd* in the chart below). In these materials, it is always the title of a high-ranking official of a monarch or the title of a cult functionary of a deity. Comparison of the names that follow this title with inscrip-

---

[1] Stephanie Dalley, Christopher B. F. Walker, and J. David Hawkins, *The Old Babylonian Tablets from Tell al Rimah* (N.p.: British School of Archaeology in Iraq, 1976), 32.

tions that indicate the names of kings and deities yields consistent evidence that in Northwest Semitic *seals and seal impressions*, as distinguished from narratives, this title is always followed either by the name of a monarch, by the word המלך (*hmlk* in the chart below), meaning "the king," or a DN. This phenomenon is familiar to epigraphers, paleographers, and archaeologists.[2] *It is most significant that among Northwest Semitic seals and seal impressions of the monarchic and exilic periods, there is no clear, provenanced example of an* עבד *being the servant of anyone but a deity or a monarch* (cf. note 20).

Below is a partial sample of such Northwest Semitic usage. For eleven examples of עבד המלך (including two Edomite seal impressions) and three of עבד plus DN in seals and bullae, see *WSS*, 466–67; see also *AHI*, 453.

| Northwest Semitic seal or bulla | Inscriptional verification of RN |
|---|---|
| **Ammonite: King Pado'el** Seal: obv.: *lbyd'l\| 'bd pd'l* rev.: *lbyd'l\| 'bd pd'l*.[3] Between 701 and 635 (Assyrian chronology)[4] | Oriental Institute Prism of Sennacherib: "As to all the kings of Amurru, . . . Buduili from Beth-Ammon . . ." Prism B of Esarhaddon: "Puduil, king of Beth-Ammon."[5] |
| **Ammonite: King Amminadab I** Seal: *l'dnplt 'bd 'mndb*[6] Seal: *l'dnnr '/ bd 'mndb*[7] mid-7th c. (Assyrian chronology)[9] | Cylinder C of Ashurbanipal: "Amminadbi, king of Beth-Ammon;"[8] Tell Siran bottle, line 3: "*'mndb mlk bn 'mn*," "Amminadab, king of the sons of Ammon."[10] |

---

[2] E.g., Deutsch and Heltzer, *New Epigraphic Evidence from the Biblical Period*, 75, no. (74) 19.

[3] *CSOSI*, 63–64, no. 69; *WSS*, 321, no. 857; Charles Clermont-Ganneau, "Sceaux et cachets israélites, phéniciens et syriens," *JA* 8 (February–March 1883): 135–36, no. 10.

[4] Frank Moore Cross, "An Ammonite King List," *BA* 48 (1985): 171.

[5] *ANET*, 287, 291.

[6] Charles C. Torrey, "A Few Ancient Seals," *AASOR* 2–3 (1921–1922): 104; *WSS*, 321, no. 858.

[7] G. Lankester Harding, "The Seals of Adoni Nur, Servant of the Ammonite King: New Finds from a Seventh-Century B.C. Jordanian Tomb," *Illustrated London News* 5759 (September 3, 1949): 351; idem, "Four Tomb Groups from Jordan," *Annual of the Palestine Exploration Fund* 6 (1953): 48–53, Pl. VI: 1; *WSS*, 322. no. 859.

[8] *ANET*, 294.

[9] Cross, "Ammonite King List," 171.

[10] Henry O. Thompson and Fawzi Zayadine, "The Tell Siran Inscription," *BASOR* 212 (1973): 5–11.

**Aramaean: King Barṣur**
Seal: *l ʾzb ʾl / ʿbd brṣr*[11] (ca. 750)

(Other Aramaean examples are *WSS*, 281–82, nos. 752 and 753.)

The Panamuwa monumental inscription from near Zenjirli, written by Barrakkab to honor his father, Panamuwa II, mentions *brṣr* (line 1) as the father of Panamuwa and the rightful king of the same realm, identified in the inscription as Ya'di. This Barṣur reigned before Tiglath-pileser III's conquest of Damascus in 733.[12]

**Israelite: (16) King Hoshea**[13]
[15] Seal: *l ʿbdy. / ʿbd hwšʿ* (8th c.; see 2 Kgs 17:1ff; sections 2.2 and 2.13 above)

A fragmentary, annalistic text of Tiglath-pileser III names Hoshea (ᵐ*A-ú-si- ʾi*) as the king of Israel who immediately succeeded Pekah during the reign of this Assyrian monarch.[14]

**Judahite: (22) King Ahaz**[15]
[23] Seal *l ʾšnʾ. ʿ/ bd ʾḥz* (late 8th c.; see 2 Kgs 15:38ff; section 4.4 above), etc.

Summary inscription of Tiglath-pileser III: ᵐ*Ia-ú-ha-zi* KUR*Ia-ú-da-a-a*, "Jehoahaz the Judahite."[16]

**Judahite: (23) King Hezekiah**
[28 group] Bulla *lyhwzr / ḥ bn ḥlq / yhw ʿbd . ḥ / zqyhw* (late 8th to early 7th c.; see

Inscriptions of Sennacherib name KUR*ia-ú-di* (Judah) and *ḫa-za-qi-a-a-a* (Hezekiah) as its king,[17] ᵐ*ḫa-za-qi-a-ú* LÚ*ia-ú-da-ai* (Heze-

---

[11] Deutsch and Heltzer, *New Epigraphic Evidence from the Biblical Period*, 75–76, no. (74) 1; Robert Deutsch and André Lemaire, *Biblical Period Personal Seals in the Shlomo Moussaieff Collection* (Tel Aviv: Archaeological Center Publications, 2000), 112, no. 105.

[12] Ibid., 76; *KAI*, Nr. 215.

[13] Numbers in parentheses refer to persons in Appendixes B and C. Numbers in brackets refer to inscriptions listed there.

[14] Summary Inscriptions from Calah, Summary Inscription 4, lines 17'–18', *ITP*, 140–41; *ANET*, 284; Galil, *Chronology*, 153.

[15] See previous note. Other inscriptions which name this King Ahaz are listed below in Appendixes B and C under (22) Ahaz.

[16] *ITP*, 170–71, Summary Inscription 7, reverse, line 11; *ANET*, 282. On the variation between Ahaz and Jehoahaz, see section 4.4 under "How the seal of Ushna correlates . . . ," third paragraph.

[17] See section 4.6, note 56, above.

2 Kgs 16:20ff; section 4.6 above), etc.[18]

ah the Judahite) and URU*ur-sa-li-im-mu* (Jerusalem, his royal residence.[19]

**Philistine: Kings Mitinti and Ṣidqa**

Seal: *l ʿbd ʾlʾb / bn šbʿt / ʿbd mtt bn / ṣdq*[20] (7th c.)

A building inscription of Tiglath-pileser III: "Mitinti of Ashkelon." Oriental Institute Prism of Sennacherib: "As to all the kings of Amurru . . . Mitinti from Ashdod;" "Mitinti, king of Ashdod;" "Ṣidqa, . . . king of Ashkelon."[21]

---

[18] Other bullae which name King Hezekiah are listed below in Appendixes B and C under (23) Hezekiah.

[19] See section 4.6, note 57, above.

[20] Joseph Naveh, "Writing and Scripts in Seventh-Century B.C.E. Philistia: The New Evidence from Tell Jemmeh," *IEJ* 35 (1985): 9, Pl. 2:A. In accordance with seal usage, Naveh and *WSS* (399–400, no. 1066) interpret *ʿbd ʾlʾb* as the PN of the seal owner, contra the perception that the seal owner's name is absent, as in example (ii) of Michael Heltzer, "Eighth Century B.C. Inscriptions from Kalakh (Nimrud)," *PEQ* 110 (1978): 6. In ibid., example (i), after [ ]*kl*, which is the name of the seal owner, *ʿbd ʾbrm* can be correctly read as a PN (a patronymic), rather than as a title plus PN. Cf. the parallel examples in Pierre Bordreuil and André Lemaire, "Nouveaux sceaux hébreux, araméens et ammonites." *Sem* 26 (1976): 57. Heltzer's interpretation in example (i) should not be used in making judgments regarding other inscriptions, because the inscription is unprovenanced (Clermont-Ganneau, "Sceaux et cachets," 138, no. 12).

[21] *ANET*, 282, 287–88 In the seal, the nun in Mitinti is assimilated into the tav.

# Appendix B

# Evaluations of Potential Identifications in Socio-Political, then Chronological Order, Updated through July 2002

*Scope and relation to other appendixes*

*Biblical persons listed here are not necessarily to be identified in the inscriptions at all!* The chart treats potential and former identifications (IDs) and non-IDs of biblical persons in Northwest Semitic inscriptions from before the Persian Era. Coverage is complete or almost complete (see Appendix C, note 54). Footnotes mention potential IDs in other inscriptions. The term *potential* applies to possible IDs before systematic evaluation. Included are: 1) biblical persons who, according to a scholar's published statement or suggestion, might be named in an inscription; 2) biblical persons whom inscriptions bring to mind; and 3) biblical persons for whom there seemed enough inscriptional evidence to warrant investigation. Appendix C rearranges Appendix B's data in descending order of ID strength. Appendix D indexes the biblical names in Appendixes B and C. Appendix E treats an ID that was not discussed in the 1998 dissertation. Appendix F tabulates all IDs and non-IDs in this book numerically.

*Key to the chart below*

"Means of access" listed on the right side of each entry: ***Excavated*** means dug up under controlled conditions, i.e., provenanced. ***Observed*** means that the inscribed object was not buried but visible, e.g., a cliff inscription. ***Marketed*** means unprovenanced, so that evaluations must be considered conditional upon demonstration of authenticity.

"Grade of ID or non-ID"[1] listed on the left side of the entry lists the verdict on each potential match in terms of one of the six grades. These are assigned whether authenticity has been established or not, therefore *grades in unprovenanced inscriptions carry an implicit conditionality* (see preceding paragraph). The following chart classifies the six grades according to their reliability:

| Reliable IDs (if the inscription is authentic): | Reasonable but uncertain IDs (if the inscription is authentic): | Completely unreliable IDs & non-IDs (even though the inscription may be authentic): |
| --- | --- | --- |
| Certain = grade **S**, including SI + SB, SI, and SB | Reasonable but uncertain = grade **2** | Doubtful = grade **1** |
|  |  | Without a clear basis = grade **0** (zero) |
| Virtually certain to Reliable = grade **3** |  | Disqualified = grade **D** |

Grade S indicates that, provided the inscription is authentic, the ID is certain, because *singular* circumstances require it (hence the abbreviation S). SI indicates that these singular circumstances are grounded in inscriptional data; SB indicates that they are grounded in biblical data. SI+SB means that inscriptional data considered alone and biblical data considered alone each indicate singular circumstances that match or fit together in such a way as to require the ID.

Grade 3 indicates IDs based on likelihood, ranging from virtually certain to reliable, provided the inscription is authentic. The 3 signifies that a common date and a common socio-political setting permit a match and that there are three or more identifying marks of the individual, each of which is found both in inscriptional and in biblical data.

Grade 2, also based on likelihood, indicates no certain or reliable ID, yet enough evidence to make a reasonable hypothesis, provided the inscription is authentic. This evidence consists of two identifying marks of the individual, each of which is found both in inscriptional and in biblical data. A common date and socio-political setting permit a match.

Grade 1 means the ID is doubtful. Even if the inscription is authentic, and although the date and socio-political setting may permit a match, still there is

---

[1] For more information on grades S (including SB and SI), 3, 2, 1, 0, and D, see section 2.1 above and the examples in Chapter 2. On "decimals" beside grade numbers, see below in this key and section 2.8 above regarding explanatory hypotheses.

only one identifying mark of the individual found both in inscriptional and in biblical data.

Grade 0 means that there is no clear basis for an ID. Even if the inscription is authentic and its date and socio-political setting match, any possible identifying marks of the individual are not clear.

Grade D means disqualified, because an ID is known to be impossible (or virtually so). Misidentifications that are well known may have **quotation marks** (" ") around the mistaken name.

"**Decimals**" attached to the grade acknowledge details which seem to favor an ID but which only provide a point(s) of entry for a separate explanatory hypothesis (see section 2.8). Because such hypotheses are extraneous to inscriptional data, "decimals" do not count under established identification criteria. They are not true decimals but integers to the right of grades 2, 1, and 0. Because grades S, 3 and D are clear enough without "decimals," they have none.

The **number of a person** is in **parentheses ( )**. The **number of an inscription** is in **square brackets [ ]**. Within brackets, the word *group* means that two or more impressions made from one seal, or similar inscriptions, are considered together (the first paragraph of Appendix F explains why). The **ff** includes mention later in the Hebrew Bible. Section numbers are those above.

*AHI* means G. I. Davies, *Ancient Hebrew Inscriptions*. *WSS* means Avigad and Sass, *Corpus of West Semitic Stamp Seals*. **Regnal chronology** follows Galil, *Chronology of the Kings of Israel and Judah*, 147; Pitard, *Ancient Damascus*, 144, 189; and for Mesopotamian rulers, *CAH* 3/2: 748.

*The pattern of the entries below*

**(Person number) name** and description of the person potentially to be identified, with a biblical reference:

| Grade of ID or non-ID | [Inscription number] name and/or text of inscription containing ID or non-ID, with whole or partial transcription and translation (or transliteration); perhaps references to other part(s) of this book and citations | Means of access |
|---|---|---|

*B.1 A Hebrew person of the pre-monarchic period*

**(1) "Hophni,"** son of Eli the priest; 1 Sam 1:3ff:

| No clear basis 0 | [1] ʿIzbet Ṣarṭah ostracon, line 4 . . . ח . . . , ". . . ḥ . . ." section 2.6 | Excavated |
|---|---|---|

## B.2 Persons of the united kingdom of Israel[2]

**(2) David**,[3] son of Jesse and king of Israel (r. ca. 1010–970); 1 Sam 16:13ff:

| | | |
|---|---|---|
| Certain SI+SB | [2] Tel Dan stele, Fragment A, line 9 ביתדוד, "the house of David,"[4] section 3.5. | Excavated |
| Certain SI+SB | [3] Mesha stele from Dhiban, line 31 בת[ד]וד, "the "house of David";[5] line 12 אראל דודה, "its Davidic lion,"[6] Appendix E; cf. section 3.3 | Observed |

**(3) Solomon**, son of (2) David, king of Israel (r. ca. 970–931/930); 2 Sam 5:14ff:

| | | |
|---|---|---|
| Disqualified D | [4] seal שלם, "Šallum"[7] cf. persons (14), (43), (45) | Marketed |

---

[2] Hezir the priest of Davidic times (1 Chr 24:15) appears to be named in a first-century-B.C.E. Kidron Valley mausoleum epitaph, line 3: כהנים מבני חזיר, "priests, of the sons of Hezir" (Nahman Avigad, *Ancient Monuments in the Kidron Valley* [in Hebrew] [Jerusalem, 1954], 61; Israel Museum, *Inscriptions Reveal: Documents from the Time of the Bible, the Mishna and the Talmud* [ed. Efrat Carmon; trans. Rafi Grafman; rev. 2d ed.; Israel Museum Catalogue 100; Jerusalem: Israel Museum, 1973], 78–79, no. 173, 174, no. 173). Observable above ground, it was partly transcribed as early as Daniel A. Chwolson, *Corpus Inscriptionum Hebraicarum* (St. Petersburg and Leipzig, 1882); repr., New York: Olms, 1974. For early bibliography, see Lidzbarski's *NE* 1:485, no. 3.

[3] The biblical David might also be named in an inscription of Pharaoh Shoshenq I (the biblical Shishak) on the exterior south wall of the Temple of Amun at Karnak in Thebes (Kenneth A. Kitchen, "A Possible Mention of David in the Late Tenth Century B.C.E., and Deity *Dod as Dead as the Dodo?" *JSOT* 76 [1997]: 39–41).

[4] The phrase "the house of David" is part of an Aramaic ossuary inscription dated ca. 50 B.C.E. to ca. 70 C.E., found in a burial cave discovered within the city limits of present-day Jerusalem. Amos Kloner excavated it on behalf of the Israel Department of Antiquities and Museums during 1971–1972. The complete text of the inscription is של בי דוד. The preliminary report is Amos Kloner, "A Burial Cave of the Second Temple Period at Giv'at Hamivtar, Jerusalem" (in Hebrew) *Qadmoniot* 19–20 (1972): 108–9. Treatments in English include David Flusser, "'The House of David' on an Ossuary," *The Israel Museum Journal* 5 (Spring 1986): 37–40. For bibliography, see ibid., 40, n. 1.

[5] André Lemaire, "La dynastie Davidique (*byt dwd*) dans deux inscriptions ouest-sémitiques du IXe s. av. J.-C.," *SEL* 11 (1994): 17–19; idem, "'House of David' Restored in Moabite Inscription," *BAR* 20, no. 3 (May/June 1994): 30–37. See Appendix E below.

[6] This translation makes use of the grammatical insight of Anson F. Rainey, "Syntax, Hermeneutics and History," *IEJ* 48 (1998): 244–51, who translates this Moabite phrase as "its Davidic altar-hearth." See Appendix E, section E.2, below.

**(4) Mikneiah**, a Levitical singer and lyrist in the procession of the ark of the covenant into Jerusalem; 1 Chr 15:18, 21:

| | | |
|---|---|---|
| Reasona- ble but un- certain 2 | [5] seal obv. יהוה עבד מקניו rev. עבד למקניו, יהוה rev. "belonging to Mikneyaw, the servant of the LORD"[8] | Mar- keted |

**(5) Semachiah**, son of Shemaiah, son of Obed-edom and temple gatekeeper; 1 Chr 26:7:

| | | |
|---|---|---|
| Doubtful 1 | [6] Tell el-Hesi ostracon, לסמך (or ?להמך?), "be- longing to Samak"[9] | Exca- vated |

### B.3 Persons of the northern kingdom of Israel

**(6) Jeroboam I**, son of Nebat and king of Israel (r. 931/30–909); 1 Kgs 11:26ff:

| | | |
|---|---|---|
| Disquali- fied D[10] | [7] Megiddo seal ירבעם עבד / לשמע, "belonging to Shemaʿ, the minister of Jeroboʿam" *AHI*, no. 100.068; *WSS*, no. 2; see person (12) and section 3.6 | Exca- vated |

---

[7] Deutsch and Lemaire, *Biblical Period Personal Seals*, 19, no. 13; Manfred R. Lehman[n?], "On My Mind: Sensational Find: King Solomon's Own Seal," *Miami Newspaper*, September 10, 1993; Hershel Shanks, "Magnificent Obsession: The Private World of an Antiquities Collector," *BAR* 22, no. 3 (May/June 1996): 34, colored photograph labeled "Solomon's Seal" with comments in caption, 64. On page 64, Shanks reports that "Manfred Lehmann" (-man?) published the seal "in an obscure New York Jewish newspaper named the *Algemeiner Journal*." Epigraphers Deutsch and Lemaire list the eighth century as their date "to be considered." In any event, it is certainly not a tenth-century inscription.

[8] Cross, "The Seal of Miqneyaw, Servant of Yahweh," in *Ancient Seals and the Bible* (ed. Gorelick and Williams-Forte), 55–63, Pl. IX–X.

[9] John A. Paine, "Critical Note: Not Lachish, but Gath," *BSac* 47, nos. 185–188 (October 1890): 690–91, referring to a report published later by Sir William M. Flinders Petrie, *Tell el Hesy (Lachish)* (London: Alexander P. Watt, for the Committee of the Palestine Exploration Fund, 1891), 50, drawing labeled, "Inscribed fragment of pottery from Tell el Hesy." In this drawing, the second letter resembles *he* more than *samekh*, yet there is no discussion. For this reference I am indebted to Jeffrey A. Blakely of the University of Wisconsin-Madison, private communication, February 26, 2000.

[10] Ussishkin's case for the ID of Jeroboam I has merit but has not attracted a scholarly consensus (Ussishkin, "Gate 1567," 410–28). Others who identify Jeroboam I in this seal are Yeivin, "Date of the Seal 'Belonging to Shemaʿ (the) Servant (of) Jeroboam,'" 205–12; Ahlström, "Seal of Shema," 208–15.

**(7) Omri**, king of Israel (r. 884–873); 1 Kgs 16:16ff:

| No clear basis 0 | [2] Tel Dan stele, Fragment A, line 1 [?רמ?]ע, "'O[?mri?]"[11] cf. section 3.5 | Excavated |
|---|---|---|
| Certain SI+SB | [3] Mesha stele from Dhiban, lines 4–5, 7 עמרי, "'Omri" section 3.3 | Observed |

**(8) Jezebel**, daughter of (70) Ethbaal, king of the Sidonians, and queen of Israel (r. ca. 873–852); 1 Kgs 16:31ff:

| Doubtful 1 | [8] seal יזבל or יזבל[?א?], "Yezebel" or "[?'I?]yzebel" (א possibly chipped off) WSS, no. 740 | Marketed |
|---|---|---|

**(9) Obadiah**, overseer of the palace of Ahab, king of Israel (r. 873–852); 1 Kgs 18:3ff:

| Disqualified D | [9] seal לעבדיהו / עבד המלך, "Belonging to 'Obadyahu, the king's minister" AHI, no. 100.070; WSS, no. 9 | Marketed |
|---|---|---|

**(10) J(eh)oram**, son of Ahab, king of Israel (r. 851–842/1); 2 Kgs 1:17ff:

| No clear basis 0.2[12] | [2] Tel Dan stele, Fragment B2, line 3 (= line 7 in Biran-Naveh arrangement of Fragments A and B) [?יהו?]רם, "[?Yeho?]ram" section 2.8 | Excavated |
|---|---|---|

**(11) J(eh)oash**, son of Jehoahaz, king of Israel (r. 805–790); 2 Kgs 13:9ff:

| Possibly certain | [10] "three shekels" ostracon, lines 1–2 אשיהו ... ... המלך, "... 'Ašyahu the king ..."[13] one of three | Marketed |
|---|---|---|

---

[11] Puech, "Stèle araméenne de Dan," 218–21, 233–34, Fig. 1, Pl. 4.

[12] The "decimal" acknowledges the two root letters of a PN appearing on the stele.

[13] Pierre Bordreuil, Felice Israel, and Dennis Pardee, "Deux ostraca paléo-hébreux de la collection Sh. Moussaïeff: I) Contribution financière obligatoire pour le temple de YHWH, II) Réclamation d'une veuve auprès d'un fonctionnaire," *Sem* 46 (1997): 49–76, Pl. 7, 8; ET, "King's Command and Widow's Plea: Two New Hebrew Ostraca of the Biblical Period," *NEA* 61 (1998): 2–13; Hershel Shanks, "Three Shekels for the Lord: Ancient Inscription Records Gift to Solomon's Temple," *BAR* 23, no. 6 (November/December 1997): 28–32. Some suggest that 'Ešyahu ('Ašyahu) might be a local governor in Arad or a non-Israelite king (Bob Becking and Jan A. Wagenaar, "Het 'Huis van JHWH' en het 'Verzoek van de weduwe': Enkele opmerkingen bij twee recent gepubliceerde oud-Hebreeuwse inscripties," *NedTT* 52 [1998]: 177–93).

| | | |
|---|---|---|
| SB | alternatives; see also persons (18) and (35). Selection to be determined by date and whether Judahite or Israelite. | |

**(12) Jeroboam II**, son of Joash, king of Israel (r. 790–750/49); 2 Kgs 13:13ff:

| | | |
|---|---|---|
| Certain SB[14] | [7] Megiddo seal לשמע / עבד ירבעם, "Belonging to Šemaʿ, the minister of Jeroboam" section 3.6; *AHI*, no. 100.068; *WSS*, no. 2 | Excavated |

**(13) Zechariah**, son of (12) Jeroboam II, king of Israel (r. 750–749); 2 Kgs 14:29ff:

| | | |
|---|---|---|
| Doubtful 1 | [11] Tel Dan jar handle seal impression זכר / יו, "Zekaryaw" section 2.5; *AHI*, no. 100.882; *WSS*, no. 669 | Excavated |

**(14) Shallum**, son of Jabesh and king of Israel (r. 749); 2 Kgs 15:10ff:

| | | |
|---|---|---|
| Doubtful 1.1 | [4] seal שלם, "Šallum"[15] cf. persons (3), (43), (45) | Marketed |

**(15) Pekah**, king of Israel (r. 750?–732/1); 2 Kgs 15:25ff:

| | | |
|---|---|---|
| Doubtful 1.1 | [12] seal פקח, "Peqaḥ" *AHI*, no. 100.004; *WSS*, no. 1170 | Marketed |
| Doubtful 1.1 | [13] bulla פקח with winged uraeus, "Peqaḥ"[16] | Marketed |
| Doubtful 1 | [14] Hazor storage jar inscription · סמדר · לפקח, "Belonging to Peqaḥ, grape blossom wine [?]" *AHI*, no. 24.007 | Excavated |

**(16) Hoshea**, son of Elah and king of Israel (r. 732/1–722); 2 Kgs 15:30ff:

| | | |
|---|---|---|
| Certain SB | [15] seal עבד הושע / לעבדי, "Belonging to ʿAbdi, the minister of Hošeaʿ"[17] sections 2.2 and 2.13 | Marketed |

---

[14] See note 10.
[15] See note 7.
[16] Robert Deutsch and Michael Heltzer, *West Semitic Epigraphic News of the 1st Millennium B.C.E.* (Tel Aviv: Archaeological Center Publications, 1999), 75–76, no. 156 (41). A better grasp of iconographic usage might someday improve this evaluation.

### B.4 Persons of the southern kingdom of Judah before 539 B.C.E.

Reign of AHAZIAH, son of Jehoram, son of Jehoshaphat

**(17) Ahaziah**, son of Jehoram, king of Judah (r. 843/2–842/1); 2 Kgs 8:25ff:

| No clear basis 0.1[18] | [2] Tel Dan stele, Fragment B2, line 4 (= Biran and Naveh's arrangement of Fragments A and B, line 8) יהו[?אחז?], "[?ʾAḥaz?]yahu" section 2.8 | Excavated |
|---|---|---|
| Disqualified D[19] | [16] seal לְיהואחז / בן המלך, "Belonging to Yehoʾaḥaz, the king's son" AHI, no. 100.252; WSS, no. 13; cf. persons (22), (43) | Marketed |

Reign of J(EH)OASH

**(18) J(eh)oash**, son of (17) Ahaziah, king of Judah (r. 842/1–802/1); 2 Kgs 11:2ff:

| Possibly certain SB | [10] "three shekels" ostracon, lines 1–2 אשיהו ... ... המלך, "... ʾAšyahu the king..."[20] one of three alternatives; see also (11) and (35). Selection to be determined by date and whether Judahite or Israelite. | Marketed |
|---|---|---|

**(19) Zechariah**, son of Jehoiada, the priest, during the reign of (18) J(eh)oash, son of Ahaziah, king of Judah; 2 Chr 24:20:

| Doubtful 1.1 | [10] "three shekels" ostracon, line 3 [ז]כריהו, "[Ze]-karyahu"[21] | Marketed |
|---|---|---|

---

[17] Deutsch and Lemaire, *Biblical Period Personal Seals*, 7, no. 1.

[18] The "decimal" registers the matching theophoric ending of a PN on the stele.

[19] See person (43) and accompanying note 69.

[20] See note 13.

[21] See note 13. I thank Gary N. Knoppers of Pennsylvania State University, private communication, 20 July 1999, for indicating this potential ID. [Me]karyahu is also possible; "P. Kyle McCarter, Jr., reads the first letter as a *mem*, rather than a *zayin* . . ." (Shanks, "Three Shekels," 31, note at asterisk). The latter full form is unattested in the Bible and Hebrew inscriptions (Clines, *Dictionary*, 5:274; *WSS*, 511), but cf. PNs Machir (Gen 50:23; Num 26:29; *WSS*, 119, no. 232) and Michri (1 Chr 9:8). The ostracon suggests [Ze]karyahu *might* be a priest.

## Reign of UZZIAH/AZARIAH

**(20) Uzziah/Azariah,** son of Amaziah, king of Judah[22] (r. 788/7–736/5); 2 Kgs 14.21ff.

| | | |
|---|---|---|
| Certain SB | [17] seal עזיו / לאביו עבד, "Belonging to ʾAbi-yaw, the minister of ʿUzziyaw" section 4.2; *AHI*, no. 100.065; *WSS*, no. 3 | Marketed[23] |
| Certain SB | [18] seal obv. לשבניו rev. בד עזיו / ע לשבניו, obv. "Belonging to Šubnayaw, rev. "Belonging to Šubnayaw, the minister of ʿUzziyaw" section 4.3; *AHI*, no. 100.067; *WSS*, no. 4 | Marketed[24] |
| Doubtful 1.1 | [19 group] Tell ej-Judeideh *lmlk* jar handle seal impressions שבניה / עזריה, "Šubnayah (son of) ʿAzariyah"[25] *AHI*, no. 100.455; *WSS*, no. 702 | Excavated |
| Doubtful 1.1 | [20 group] Tell ej-Judeideh *lmlk* jar handle seal impressions שבניהו / [ע]זריהו "Shubnayahu (son of) [ʿA]zaryahu"[26] *AHI*, no. 100.270; *WSS*, no. 703 | Excavated |

## Reign of JOTHAM

**(21) Jotham,** son of (20) Uzziah, king of Judah (r. 758/7–742/1); 2 Kgs 15:5ff:

| | | |
|---|---|---|
| Certain SB | [21] bulla לאחז י · / הותם · מלך · / יהדה, "Belonging to ʾAḥaz (son of) Yehotam, king of Judah"[27] | Marketed |

---

[22] King Uzziah is named in a Second-Temple-era, secondary burial inscription in Aramaic discovered "in the collection of the Russian Orthodox convent on the Mount of Olives" ([Greenfield, Jonas C.], "Professor Nahman Avigad, 1905–1992: In Memoriam," *IEJ* 42 [1992]: 2). See Eleazar L. Sukenik, "Funerary Tablet of Uzziah, King of Judah," *PEQ* (1931): 217–21, Pl. I and II; Israel Museum, *Inscriptions Reveal*, Hebrew section, 252, no. 255, with photograph on 253, and English section, 120, no. 255; Giovanni Garbini, "L'iscrizione del re Uzzia," *OrAnt* 24 (1985): 67–75.

[23] Published in 1858, long before any forgers could have known the appropriate paleographic details.

[24] Found in an 1863 publication, which appeared long before any forgers could have known the appropriate paleographic details.

[25] Vaughn observes (25) Shebna might be King Uzziah's son. See notes 45 and 46.

[26] See preceding note and notes 45 and 47.

| | | |
|---|---|---|
| Disqualified D | [22] Tel el-Kheleifeh seal ring ליתם, "Belonging to Yatom" sections 1.9 and 2.7 | Excavated |

## Reign of AHAZ

**(22) Ahaz**, son of (21) Jotham, king of Judah (r. 742/1–726); 2 Kgs 15:38ff:

| | | |
|---|---|---|
| Disqualified D[28] | [16] seal ליהואחז / בן המלך, "Belonging to Yeho'aḥaz, the king's son" *AHI*, no. 100.252; *WSS*, no. 13; cf. persons (17), (43) | Marketed |
| Certain SB | [21] bulla לאחז ‎· י‎ / הותם ‎·‎ מלך / ‎·‎ יהדה, "Belonging to ʾAḥaz (son of) Yehotam, king of Judah"[29] | Marketed |
| Certain SB | [23] seal לאשנא ‎·‎ ע / בד אחז; "Belonging to ʾUšna, the minister of ʾAḥaz" section 4.4 | Marketed |
| Certain SB | [24 group] bulla לחזקיהו אחז מלך / יהדה with one line on upper part of scarab's wing, "Belonging to Ḥizqiyahu, (son of) ʾAḥaz, king of Judah"[30] | Marketed |
| Certain SB | [25 group] bulla לחזקיהו אחז מלך / יהדה with two lines on upper part of scarab's wing, "Belonging to Ḥizqiyahu, (son of) ʾAḥaz, king of Judah"[31] | Marketed |
| Certain SB | [26 group] bulla לחזקיהו אחז מלך / יהדה with winged solar disc and two ankh symbols, "Belonging to Ḥizqiyahu, (son of) ʾAḥaz, king of Judah"[32] | Marketed |

---

[27] Robert Deutsch, *Messages from the Past* (in Hebrew) (Tel Aviv: Archaeological Center Publications, 1997), 49–51, no. 1, 170, Pl. 16, upper half, 171, Pl. 17, upper half, and color photograph on book jacket; ET, Robert Deutsch, *Messages from the Past* (trans. Robert Deutsch; Tel Aviv: Archaeological Center Publications, 1999), 61–63, no. 1, 204, Pl. 16, upper half, 205, Pl. 17, upper half, and color photograph on book jacket. From this point onward, only the ET will be cited.

[28] See person (43) and accompanying note 69.

[29] Deutsch, *Messages*, 61–63, no. 1, 204, Pl. 16, upper half, 205, Pl. 17, upper half, and color photograph on book jacket; idem, "First Impression: What We Learned from King Ahaz's Seal," *BAR* 24, no. 3 (May/June 1998): 54–56, 62.

[30] See notes 33 and 34.

[31] See note 35.

Appendix B 221

Reign of HEZEKIAH

**(23) Hezekiah,** son of (22) Ahaz, king of Judah (r. 726–697/6); 2 Kgs 16:20ff:

| | | |
|---|---|---|
| Certain SB | [24 group] bulla לְ[חזקיהו אחז מלך / יהדה] with one line on upper part of scarab's wing "[Belonging to] Ḥizqiyahu, (son of) ʾAḥaz, king of Judah"[33] | Marketed |
| Certain SB | Another exemplar in [24 group] bulla [לחז]קיהו] א[חז מ]לך / י[הדה] with one line on upper part of scarab's wing "[Belonging to Ḥiz]qiyahu, (son of) A[ḥaz, k]ing of J[udah]"[34] | Marketed |

---

[32] Robert Deutsch, "New Bullae Reveal Egyptian-Style Emblems on Judah's Royal Seals," *BAR* 28, no. 4 (July/August 2002): 42 (color photograph and drawing), 46, cover (color photograph).
  [33] Ibid., 45 (box), nos. 3 and 4, 46. The text that is legible on bulla no. 3 as numbered by Deutsch appears on this chart; the text of bulla no. 4 as numbered by Deutsch is more fragmentary.
  [34] Originally published in Avigad, *Hebrew Bullae from the Time of Jeremiah*, 110, no. 199, with a small, black-and-white photograph. Reading *-nyhw*, Avigad suggested restoring it as [ ʾAdo]niyahu. It also appears in Deutsch, *Messages*, 204, Pl. 16, lower half (large color photograph), 205, Pl. 17, lower half (drawing). There is also a small, black-and-white photograph with a drawing, both by Robert Deutsch, in Frank M. Cross, "A Bulla of Hezekiah, King of Judah," in *Realia Dei: Essays in Archaeology and Biblical Interpretation in Honor of Edward F. Campbell, Jr., at His Retirement* (ed. Prescott H. Williams Jr., and Theodore Hiebert; Atlanta: Scholars Press, 1999), 66, Fig. 2.
  At first, Deutsch and Cross thought that the same seal made both this first-known bulla in [22 group], originally published by Avigad, and the first-known bulla in [23 group], first published in ibid., 65, Fig. 1, previously mentioned in Deutsch, *Messages*, 41–42, no. A199. "Actually the bulla is the second extant example of a sealing from the king's seal, but the first that is fully legible. A more or less unreadable bulla published by the late Nahman Avigad proves to be made by the same seal as the bulla published here" (Cross, "Bulla of Hezekiah," 62). Later, however, based on a slight difference in iconography, Deutsch states that two different seals made these two bullae (Deutsch, "New Bullae Reveal Egyptian-Style Emblems," 44, box, under no. 2). The bulla originally published by Avigad and two bullae newly published in that article portray a two-winged scarab with a *single* line in the upper part of its wings (ibid., 44–45, box, nos. 1, 3, 4), whereas the bulla first published by Cross and one other exemplar have a two-winged scarab with a *double* line in the upper part of its wings (ibid., 44–45, box, nos. 2, 5).
  Both bullae are also published in Frank M. Cross, "King Hezekiah's Seal Bears Phoenician Imagery," *BAR* 25, no. 2 (March/April 1999): 42–45, 60, with a large, color photograph of each bulla (two-line, p. 42; one-line, p. 45) and the larger versions of the aforementioned two drawings by Deutsch (two-line, p. 43; one-line, p. 45).

| | | |
|---|---|---|
| Certain SB | [25 group] bulla ליחזקיהו אחז מלך / יהדה with two lines on upper part of scarab's wing, "Belonging to Ḥizqiyahu, (son of) ʾAḥaz, king of Judah"[35] | Marketed |
| Certain SB | [26 group] bulla לחזקיהו אחז / מלך יהדה with winged solar disc and two ankh symbols, "Belonging to Ḥizqiyahu, (son of) ʾAḥaz, king of Judah"[36] | Marketed |
| Certain SB | [27] bulla לעזריהו · בן יהו[א]ח · עבד · חזקיהו, "Belonging to ʿAzaryahu, son of Yeho-[ʾa]ḥ, the minister of Ḥizqiyahu"[37] | Marketed |
| Certain SB | [28 group] bulla ליהוזר / ח בן · חלק / יהו עבד / ח · זקיהו, "Belonging to Yehozaraḥ, son of Ḥilqiyahu, the minister of Ḥizqiyahu" section 4.6; *AHI*, no. 100.321; *WSS*, no. 407 | Marketed |
| Certain SB | Another exemplar in [28 group] bulla [ליה[וז]ר] / ח בן חלק / יהו · עבד · ח / זקיהו, "[Belonging to Yeh]oza[ra]ḥ, son of Ḥilqiyahu, the minister of Ḥizqiyahu"[38] | Marketed |
| Certain SB | [29] bulla עבד חזקיהו . . . , ". . . the minister of Ḥizqiyahu"[39] | Marketed |
| Certain SB | [30] bulla לעמריהו / חנניהו עבד / חזקיהו, "Belonging to ʿAmaryahu, (son of) Ḥananyahu, the minister of Ḥizqiyahu"[40] | Marketed |
| Certain SB | [31] bulla לדמלא / חזק · עבד / יהו, "Belonging to Domlaʾ, the minister of Ḥizqiyahu"[41] | Marketed |

---

[35] On two-line-wing bullae, see the second and third paragraphs of preceding note.
[36] See note 32.
[37] Deutsch, *Messages*, 64–66, no. 3.
[38] Ibid., 63–64, no. 2; made by the same seal as the preceding bulla in [28 group].
[39] Ibid., 66–67, no. 4.
[40] Deutsch, "New Bullae Reveal Egyptian-Style Emblems," 48–49 (box), no. A.
[41] Ibid., 48–49 (box), no. B.

| | | | |
|---|---|---|---|
| Certain SB | [32] bulla לדמלא עבד / חזקיהו, "Belonging to Domla', the minister of Ḥizqiyahu"[42] | | Marketed |

**(24) Hilkiah** (= (27)?), minister of (23) Hezekiah, king of Judah; 2 Kgs 18:18ff:

| | | | |
|---|---|---|---|
| Reasonable but uncertain 2 | [28 group] bulla ליהוזר / ח בן חלק / יהו · עבד זקיהו / ח ·, "Belonging to Yehozarah, son of Hilqiyahu, the minister of Ḥizqiyahu" *AHI*, no. 100.321; *WSS*, no. 407; cf. section 4.6 | | Marketed |
| Reasonable but uncertain 2 | Another exemplar in [28 group] bulla [ליה[וזר] / ח בן חלק / יהו · עבד · ח / זקיהו, "[Belonging to Yeh]oza[ra]ḥ, son of Ḥilqiyahu, the minister of Ḥizqiyahu"[43] | | Marketed |

**(25) Shebna**, the overseer of the palace; Isa 22: 15–19, who might be the same person as **(26) Shebna**, the scribe of (23) Hezekiah, king of Judah; 2 Kgs 18: 18ff, during a different royal assignment. Both are considered together here:

| | | | |
|---|---|---|---|
| Doubtful 1.1[44] | [18] seal obv. לשבניו rev. בד עזיו / לשבניו ע, obv. "Belonging to Šubnayaw," rev. "Belonging to Šubnayaw, the minister of ʿUzziyaw"[45] *AHI*, no. 100.067; *WSS*, no. 3; cf. section 4.3 | | Marketed |

---

[42] Ibid., 48–49 (box), no. C.

[43] Ibid., 63–64, no. 2; made from the same seal as the preceding bulla in [28 group].

[44] The "decimal" acknowledges that both the biblical and the inscriptional Shebna filled high-level positions in the royal Judean administration, with the possibility of promotion, demotion, or transfer from one position to another. See section 2.8 above.

[45] Given the possibility of having various titles during a career in royal service, this inscription might refer to the same person as שבניהו בן המלך, whose PN occurs on the *lmlk* jars. "Since we know of two additional seals belonging to שבניהו / (בן) עזריהו from the official seal impressions on *lmlk* jar handles, it is possible that the impression of לשבניהו / בן המלך was owned by this same official, who might have been the son of King Uzziah/Azariah" (Vaughn, *Theology, History and Archaeology*, 128–29). For details on these particular *lmlk* jar handle seal impressions and their publication, see ibid., 212–13, nos. XXXI, XXXIIIa, and XXXIIIb. The Bible nowhere reveals the lineage of the biblical royal administrator, Shebna. On the authenticity of seal [18], see note 24.

| | | |
|---|---|---|
| Doubtful 1.1 | [19 group] Tell ej-Judeideh *lmlk* jar handle seal impressions שבניה / עזריה, "Šubnayah (son of) ʿAzariyah"[46] *AHI*, no. 100.455; *WSS*, no. 702 | Excavated |
| Doubtful 1.1 | [20 group] Tell ej-Judeideh *lmlk* jar handle seal impressions שבניהו / [ע]זריהו, "Šubnayahu (son of) [ʿA]zaryahu"[47] *AHI*, no. 100.270; *WSS*, no. 703 | Excavated |
| Doubtful 1.1 | [33] *lmlk* jar handle seal impression with four-winged symbol (uraeus or beetle) at top לשבניהו / בן המלך, "Belonging to Šubnayahu, the king's son"[48] *AHI*, no. 100.784; *WSS*, no. 662 | Marketed |

---

Although Vaughn's suggestion is indeed possible, the general semantic range of בן also makes it possible for the seal owner to be a descendant of any earlier king of Judah. Perhaps *in seals and bullae*, בן המלך might refer only to the immediate father of the seal owner, but this is unproven. Cf. the narrowed significance of עבד in seals and bullae (Appendix A).

[46] Frederick Jones Bliss and Robert A. Stewart Macalister, *Excavations in Palestine During the Years 1898–1900* (London: Committee of the Palestine Exploration Fund, 1902), 120, no. 23, listed in Vaughn, *Theology, History and Archaeology*, 213, XXXIIIb, no. 188. The second example of a *lmlk* jar handle seal impression in which Vaughn finds this reading (ibid., 213, XXXIIIb, no. 189) is indistinct in the drawing in Tufnell, *Lachish III*, 341, Pl. 47B, no. 5; see Diringer's publications of it listed in *AHI*, no. 100.476. Vaughn's note seems to indicate that it is located at the University of Leeds, with the designation D/X. "The letters D/X indicate that the object concerned was found on the surface of the mound" [Tufnell, *Lachish III*, 25). The third such example is in the collection of H. Kaufman of Tel Aviv (Vaughn, *Theology, History and Archaeology*, 213, XXXIIIb, no. 190). Is this third example the unprovenanced seal impression *WSS*, no. 702 (B), which remains unpublished, except for Avigad's drawing in ibid.?

[47] Bliss and Macalister, *Excavations in Palestine*, 119–120, no. 21. Bliss and Macalister found three impressions from the same seal there, each of which is listed in Vaughn, *Theology, History and Archaeology*, 213, XXXIIIa, nos. 185–187.

[48] Nahman Avigad, "Titles and Symbols in Hebrew Seals" (in Hebrew), *ErIsr* 15 (Y. Aharoni Memorial Volume, 1981) 304, no. 2, Pl 57, no. 2, English summary 85*; listed in Vaughn, *Theology, History and Archaeology*, 212, XXXI, no. 175. See note 45, second paragraph.

| | Appendix B | 225 |
|---|---|---|
| For (25), reasonable but uncertain 2; For (26), doubtful 1[50] | [34] Silwan epitaph, line 1 [?שבנ]יהו אשר על הבית, "[?Šubna?]yahu, overseer of the palace"[49] *AHI*, no. 4.401 | Observed |
| Disqualified D | [35] Lachish bulla עבד[ המלך] or [בן] / [לשבניהו], "[Belonging to] Šubnayahu, the king's [son, or, minister]" *AHI*, no. 100.257 "late 7th cent."; *WSS*, no. 416 | Excavated |
| Doubtful 1 | [36] Ramat Raḥel seal impression on *lmlk* jar handle לנרא / שבנא, "Belonging to Nera', (son of) Šubna'"[51] *AHI*, no. 100.196; *WSS*, no. 686 | Excavated |
| Doubtful 1 | [37 group] Jerusalem, Lachish, unprovenanced (and unpublished Beth Shemesh) seal impressions on *lmlk* jar handles לנרא / שבנא, "Belonging to Nera', (son of) Šubna'"[52] *AHI*, no. 100.789; *WSS*, no. 687 | Excavated |

---

[49] Yigael Yadin suggested this potential ID (Nahman Avigad, "The Epitaph of a Royal Steward from Siloam Village," *IEJ* 3 [1953]: 150). The title matches that in Isa 22:15, and the rock-cut tomb in a hillside near Jerusalem, dated paleographically to ca. 700, answers to Isa 22:16 (ibid., 137–52). Avigad noted "certain affinities between this passage and the archaeological evidence" (ibid., 151), but he made no ID. Though the biblical Shebna was likely *one of* the successive palace overseers during Hezekiah's ca. thirty-year reign, still *the absence of all root letters of the PN* makes it possible that the PN is that of another man who held that office. What if the biblical Shebna's tomb is discovered elsewhere? Over the millennia, earthquakes could have covered it or caused it to collapse. This ID, based only on title and provenance, can be no more than grade 2, a reasonable hypothesis. (See also David Ussishkin, *The Village of Silwan: The Necropolis from the Period of the Judean Kingdom* [trans. Inna Pommerantz; Jerusalem: Izhak Ben-Zvi for the Israel Exploration Society, 1993]; 1986 title: *Kefar-ha-Shiloah*.)

[50] This inscription might refer to (26) Shebna the scribe of Hezekiah with a different title at another point in his career. But the resulting lack of a match in title reduces the grade of the ID to 1.1. The "decimal" acknowledges this career possibility.

[51] Vaughn, *Theology, History and Archaeology*, 209, XXIIb, no. 136. "Aharoni suggested that the official, Nera son of Shebna, may well have been the son of the high-ranking official Shebna in King Hezekiah's administration . . . ." (Gabriel Barkay, "The King of Babylonia or a Judaean Official?" *IEJ* 45 [1995]: 45, n. 18).

[52] Vaughn, *Theology, History and Archaeology*, 208–9, XXIIa, nos. 130–35. For no. 135, see Deutsch and Heltzer, *Forty New*, 33, no. (9) 2a, 34, Fig. 9a.

| | | |
|---|---|---|
| Doubtful 1 | [38] seal impression on *lmlk* jar handle לנרא [. . .] / שבנא, "[. . .] Belonging to Neraʾ, (son of) Šubnaʾ"[53] | Marketed |
| Doubtful 1 | [39] Jerusalem seal impression on the handle of a *lmlk*-type jar לנרי ב / ן שבניו, "Belonging to Nerî, son of Šubnayaw"[54] *AHI*, no. 100.787; *WSS*, no. 688 | Excavated |

**(27) Hilkiah**, ( = (24)?) father of (28) Eliakim the overseer of the palace of (23) Hezekiah, king of Judah; 2 Kgs 18:18ff:

| | | |
|---|---|---|
| Reasonable but uncertain 2.1 | [40] bulla לאיקם / חלקיהו, "Belonging to [E]lyaqim, (son of) [Hi]lqiyahu"[55] cf. section 4.6 | Marketed |

**(28) Eliakim**, son of (27) Hilkiah and the overseer of the palace of (23) Hezekiah; 2 Kgs 18:18ff; Isa 22:20–25:

| | | |
|---|---|---|
| Reasonable but uncertain 2.1 | [40] bulla לאיקם / חלקיהו, "Belonging to [E]lyaqim, (son of) [Hi]lqiyahu"[56] | Marketed |
| Doubtful 1.1 | [41 group] seal impression לאליקם / נער יכן on 4 jar handles: 2 from Tell Beit Mirsim, 1 from Beth Shemesh, 1 from Ramat Rahel, "Belonging to Elyaqim, steward of Yokan" *AHI*, no. 100.486; *WSS*, no. 663/ cf. section 1.10 | Excavated |
| Doubtful 1.1 | [42] seal לאליקם / עבד המלך, "Belonging to Elyaqim, the king's minister" *WSS*, no. 6 | Marketed |

**(29) Asaph**, father of (30) Joah the recorder of (23) Hezekiah, king of Judah; 2 Kgs 18:18, 37; Isa 36:3, 22:

---

[53] Vaughn, *Theology, History and Archaeology*, 209, XXIId, no. 138.
[54] Ibid., 209, XXIIe, no. 139.
[55] Deutsch, *Messages*, 96–97, no. 30.
[56] See preceding note.

| Disquali- | [43] Megiddo seal לאסף, "Belonging to Asaph" *AHI*, | Exca- |
| fied D | no. 100.007; *WSS*, no. 85 | vated |

**(30) Joah**, son of (29) Asaph and the recorder of (23) Hezekiah, king of Judah; 2 Kgs 18:18, 26, 37; Isa 36:3, 11, 22:

| Doubtful | [27] bulla · לעזריהו · בן יהו[א]ח · עבד · חזקיהו, | Mar- |
| 1.1 | "Belonging to ʿAzaryahu, son of Yeho[ʾa]ḥ, the minister of Ḥizqiyahu"[57] | keted |

**(31) Amariah**, an overseer of distribution of freewill offerings under (23) Hezekiah, king of Judah, during the chief priesthood of Azariah; 2 Chr 31:15:

| Doubtful | [30] bulla לעמריהו / חנניהו עבד / חזקיהו, "Be- | Mar- |
| 1.1 | longing to ʿAmaryahu, (son of) Ḥananyahu, the minister of Ḥizqiyahu"[58] | keted |

Reigns of MANASSEH and AMON

**(32) Manasseh**, son of (23) Hezekiah, king of Judah (697/6– 642/1); 2 Kgs 20:21ff:

| Disquali- | [44] seal למנשה בן / המלך with star and crescent, | Mar- |
| fied D | "Belonging to Manašeh, the king's son"[59] *WSS*, no. 1006 | keted |

| Reasona- | [45] seal למנשה ב / ן המלך with two-winged sca- | Mar- |
| ble but un- | rab beetle, "Belonging to Manašeh, the king's son" | keted |
| certain 2[60] | *WSS*, no. 16 | |

---

[57] Deutsch, *Messages*, 64–66, no. 3.

[58] See note 40.

[59] Deutsch and Lemaire, *Biblical Period Personal Seals*, 194, no. 187 (Moabite).

[60] Paleographic dating at 700 would make this seal owner Hezekiah's successor (Larry G. Herr, "Paleography and the Identification of Seal Owners," *BASOR* 239 [1980]: 69), but only if we knew that King Hezekiah were his father. This ID is not certain, because this seal does not name this Manasseh's father. The seal owner could be descended from any earlier king of Judah; e.g., he might have been King Manasseh's uncle. See note 45, second paragraph. Cf. note 69.

**(33) Meshullam**, father of (34) Azaliah, father of (36) Shaphan the scribe, father of (50) Gemariah and of (39) Ahikam, father of (60) Gedaliah; 2 Kgs 22:3ff:

| Reasonable but uncertain 2 | [46] seal לאצליהו / בן משלם, "Belonging to ʾAṣalyahu, the son of Mešullam" *AHI*, no. 100.853; *WSS*, no. 90 | Marketed |
|---|---|---|

**(34) Azaliah**, son of (33) Meshullam and father of (36) Shaphan the scribe, father of (50) Gemariah and of (39) Ahikam, father of (60) Gedaliah; 2 Kgs 22:3ff:

| Reasonable but uncertain 2 | [46] seal לאצליהו / בן משלם, "Belonging to ʾAṣalyahu, the son of Mešullam" *AHI*, no. 100.853; *WSS*, no. 90 | Marketed |
|---|---|---|

Reign of JOSIAH

**(35) Josiah**, son of Amon, king of Judah (r. 640/39–609); 2 Kgs 21:24ff:

| Possibly certain SB | [10] "three shekels" ostracon, lines 1–2 אשיהו ... ... המלך, "... ʾAšyahu the king ..."[61] one of three alternatives; see also (11) and (18). Selection to be determined by date and whether Judahite or Israelite. | Marketed |
|---|---|---|

**(36) Shaphan** the scribe, son of (34) Azaliah, son of (33) Meshullam, and father of (50) Gemariah and of (39) Ahikam, father of (60) Gedaliah; 2 Kgs 22: 3ff:

| Reasonable but uncertain 2 | [47] bulla ל[א]חיקם / [ב]ן שפן, "[Belonging to ʾA]ḥiqam, the [so]n of Šaphan" [62] *WSS*, no. 431; cf. section 3.7 | Marketed |
|---|---|---|
| Virtually certain 3 | [48] city of David bulla לגמריהו / [ב]ן שפן, "Belonging to Gemaryahu, the [so]n of Šaphan" section 3.7; *AHI*, no. 100.802; *WSS*, no. 470 | Excavated |

---

[61] See note 13.
[62] Deutsch, *Messages*, 91–92, no. 25.

*Appendix B*

**(37) Hilkiah** the high priest, father of (38) Azariah; 2 Kgs 22:4ff:

| Certain SB | [49] seal ring לחנן ב / ן חלקיהו / הכהן, "Belonging to Ḥanan, the son of Ḥilqiyahu, the priest" section 4.7; *AHI*, no. 100.734; *WSS*, no. 28 | Marketed |
| Reliable 3 | [50] city of David bulla לעזריהו ב / ן חלקיהו, "Belonging to ʿAzaryahu, the son of Ḥilqiyahu" section 3.9; *AHI*, no. 100.827; *WSS*, no. 596 | Excavated |
| Reasonable but uncertain 2 | [51] seal עזריהו / חלקיהו,[63] ʿAzaryahu, (the son of) Ḥilqiyahu" *AHI*, no. 100.496; *WSS*, no. 307; cf. section 3.9 | Marketed |
| Reasonable but uncertain 2.1 | [52] seal לעזריהו / חלקא, "Belonging to ʿAzarya-hu, (the son of) Ḥilqaʾ" *AHI*, no. 100.728; *WSS*, no. 306; cf. section 3.9 | Marketed |

**(38) Azariah**, son of (37) Hilkiah the high priest; 1 Chr 5:39; 9:11; Ezra 7:1:

| Reliable 3 | [50] city of David bulla לעזריהו ב / ן חלקיהו, "Belonging to ʿAzaryahu, the son of Ḥilqiyahu" section 3.10; *AHI*, no. 100.827; *WSS*, no. 596 | Excavated |
| Reasonable but uncertain 2 | [51] seal עזריהו / חלקיהו,[64] ʿAzaryahu, (the son of) Ḥilqiyahu" *AHI*, no. 100.496; *WSS*, no. 307; cf. section 3.10 | Marketed |
| Reasonable but uncertain 2.1 | [52] seal לעזריהו / חלקא, "Belonging to ʿAzarya-hu, (the son of) Ḥilqaʾ" *AHI*, no. 100.728; *WSS*, no. 306; cf. section 3.10 | Marketed |

**(39) Ahikam**, father of (60) Gedaliah and brother of (50) Gemariah and son of (36) Shaphan the scribe, son of (34) Azaliah, son of (33) Meshullam; 2 Kgs 22:12ff:

| Reasonable but uncertain 2 | [47] bulla לא[ח]יקם / [ב]ן שפן, "[Belonging to] ʾAḥiqam, the [so]n of Šaphan"[65] *WSS*, no. 431 | Marketed |

---

[63] Deutsch and Lemaire, *Biblical Period Personal Seals*, 80, no. 74.
[64] Ibid.

230    *Identifying Biblical Persons in Northwest Semitic Inscriptions*

**(40) Asaiah**, minister of (35) Josiah, king of Judah; 2 Kgs 22:12ff:

| Reasona-ble but un-certain 2 | [53] seal לעשיהו / עבד המלך, "Belonging to 'Asa-yahu, the king's minister" section 2.4 | Mar-keted |

**(41) Nathan-melech** the eunuch; 2 Kgs 23:11:

| Reasona-ble but un-certain 2.1[67] | [54] bulla לנתנמלך / עבד המלך, "Belonging to Natanmelek, the king's minister"[66] | Mar-keted |

**(42) Elishama**, father of Nethaniah, father of (62) Ishmael of royal descent; 2 Kgs 25: 25; Jer 41:1:

| Reasona-ble but un-certain 2 | [55] seal לאלשמע ב / ן המלך, "Belonging to 'Eli-šamaʿ, the king's son" *AHI*, no. 100.072; *WSS*, no. 11 | Mar-keted |

Reign of JEHOAHAZ

**(43) Jehoahaz**, alias Shallum, son of (35) Josiah, king of Judah (r. 609); 2 Kgs 23:30ff; see Chapter 1, note 115:

| Disquali-fied D | [4] seal שלם, "Šallum"[68] cf. persons (3), (14), (45) | Mar-keted |

| Reasona-ble but un-certain 2[69] | [16] seal ליהואחז / בן המלך, "Belonging to Yeho-ʾaḥaz, the king's son" *AHI*, no. 100.252; *WSS*, no. 13; cf. persons (17), (22) | Mar-keted |

---

[65] Deutsch, *Messages*, 91–92, no. 25.

[66] P. Kyle McCarter Jr., "The Bulla of Nathan-melech, the Servant of the King," in Williams and Hiebert, *Realia Dei*, 142–53; Deutsch, *Messages*, 73–74, no. 9.

[67] This grade 2 evaluation follows McCarter in understanding Nathan-melech's biblical designation, הַסָּרִיס, "the eunuch," to fall within the scope of the inscription's broad title, עבד המלך which was given to high-ranking royal servants (McCarter, "Bulla of Nathan-melech," 146–47). Among the 1,217 Northwest Semitic seals and bullae of *WSS*, only one contains the title סרס: an Aramaic bulla of a eunuch of Sargon excavated at Khorsabad (bulla [67] below; *WSS*, 283, no. 755). If later it becomes clear that these two titles were mutually exclusive in the kingdom of Judah, then this ID should be grade 1. The .1 "decimal" registers the rarity of the seal owner's name in the Bible and in inscriptions, as observed in McCarter, "Bulla of Nathan-melech," 145–46.

[68] See note 7.

Reign of JEHOIAKIM

**(11) Elnathan**, son of Achbor and an official of Jehoiakim, king of Judah; Jer 26:22; 36:12:

| | | |
|---|---|---|
| Doubtful 1.2[70] | [56] Lachish ostracon 3, line 14b ירד שר הצבא line 15 בא / אלנתן בן כני[הו] line 16a מצרימה "the army general went down, / Koniya[hu], the son of ʾElnatan, to enter / Egypt"[71] *AHI*, no. 1.003 | Excavated |

**(45) Shallum**, father of Maaseiah the keeper of the temple threshold; Jer 35:4; cf. persons (3), (14), (43):

| | | |
|---|---|---|
| Disqualified D | [4] seal שלם, "Šallum"[72] | Marketed |

**(46) Neriah**, son of Mahseiah, father of (47) Baruch the scribe and likely of (49) Seraiah; Jer 32:12ff; 51:59:

| | | |
|---|---|---|
| Virtually certain 3[73] | [57 group] 2 bullae from the same seal לברכיהו / בן נריהו / הספר, "Belonging to Berekyahu, the son of Neriyahu, the scribe" section 4.9; *AHI*, no. 100.509; *WSS*, no. 417 | Marketed |

---

[69] Paleographic dating would make this seal owner Josiah's successor (Herr, "Paleography and the Identification of Seal Owners," 69), but only if we knew that King Josiah were his father. This ID, however, is not certain, because this seal does not name this Yehoʾaḥaz's father. The seal owner could be descended from any earlier king of Judah. See note 45, second paragraph. Cf. note 60.

[70] The "decimal" acknowledges 1) that sons of officials tend to have an advantage in becoming officials and 2) retrieval from Egypt of fleeing persons was a task assigned to Elnathan, son of Achbor (Jer 26:20–23) and to army general Koniyahu, son of Elnathan, (Lachish ostracon 3, lines 14–16). That it was the same Elnathan is doubtful.

[71] I thank Nili S. Fox of Hebrew Union College-Jewish Institute of Religion for indicating this potential ID (Fox, *In the Service of the King*, 301, no. 272, 300, n. 39). She also mentions a "dubious" relationship to Jehoiachin's grandfather Elnathan (2 Kgs 24:8; ibid., 39); the PN is the only identifying mark in common, so the ID is grade 1, doubtful.

[72] See note 7.

[73] As pointed out above in section 2.3, under Question 3, "Remarks," the first-known bulla of Baruch meets not just three, but four specific identifying criteria. It would, therefore, actually provide grade 4 IDs of Baruch and Neriah if this study had included a separate grade for them. Although Grade 3 IDs are strong enough to make it unnecessary to create a grade 4, others might choose to develop the system in that way.

| | | |
|---|---|---|
| Reasona-<br>but un-<br>certain 2 | [58] seal לשריהו / נריהו, "Belonging to Śerayahu, (the son of) Neriyahu" section 4.9; AHI, no. 100.780; WSS, no. 390 | Mar-<br>keted |

**(47) Baruch**, son of (46) Neriah, the scribe and possibly the brother of (49) Seraiah; Jer 32:12ff:

| | | |
|---|---|---|
| Virtually<br>certain<br>3[74] | [57 group] 2 bullae from the same seal לברכיהו / בן נריהו / הספר, "Belonging to Berekyahu, the son of Neriyahu, the scribe" sections 2.3 and 4.8; AHI, no. 100.509; WSS, no. 417 | Mar-<br>keted |

**(48) Jerahmeel**, the king's son; Jer 36:26:

| | | |
|---|---|---|
| Virtually<br>certain<br>3 | [59] bulla לירחמאל / בן המלך, "Belonging to Yeraḥme'el, the king's son" section 4.10; AHI, no. 100.508; WSS, no. 41 | Mar-<br>keted |
| Disquali-<br>fied D | [60] seal לירן[ח]מאל / בן [ה]מלך, "Belonging to Yera[ḥ]me'el, [the] king's son"[75] | Mar-<br>keted |

**(49) Seraiah**, son of Neriah (= (46) Neriah?) and possibly the brother of (47) Baruch the scribe; Jer 51:59, 61:

| | | |
|---|---|---|
| Reasona-<br>ble but un-<br>certain 2 | [58] seal לשריהו / נריהו, "Belonging to Śerayahu (the son of) Neriyahu" AHI, no. 100.780; WSS, no. 390 | Mar-<br>keted |

**(50) Gemariah**, brother of (39) Ahikam and son of (36) Shaphan the scribe, son of (34) Azaliah, son of (33) Meshullam; Jer 36:10ff:

| | | |
|---|---|---|
| Virtually<br>certain<br>3 | [48] city of David bulla לגמריהו / [בן] שפן, "Be-<br>longing to Gemaryahu, the [so]n of Šaphan" section 3.8; AHI, no. 100.802; WSS, no. 470 | Exca-<br>vated |

**(51a) Hananiah**, father of Zedekiah *śar* of Judah; Jer 36:12
AND
**(51b) Zedekiah**, son of Hananiah and a *śar* of Judah; Jer 36:12:

---

[74] See preceding note.

[75] This seal is classified as Moabite and dated to the eighth or seventh centuries in Deutsch and Lemaire, *Biblical Period Personal Seals*, 193, no. 186. The same seal was published in Michael Heltzer, "Two Ancient West Semitic Seals," *SEL* 16 (1999): 45, no. 1, and 47, Fig.1–2, where it is misclassified as "Judaean" (ibid., 45, no. 1).

| Reasonable but uncertain 2 | [61] bulla לצדקיהו / בן חנני, "Belonging to Ṣedeq-yahu, the son of Ḥanani"[76] | Marketed |

Reign of JEHOIACHIN

**(52) "Jehoiachin"/Jeconiah/Coniah**, son of Jehoiakim, king of Judah; 2 Kgs 24:6ff:

| Disqualified D | [41 group] seal impression לאליקם / נער יכן on 4 jar handles: 2 from Tell Beit Mirsim, 1 from Beth Shemesh, 1 from Ramat Rahel, "Belonging to ʾElya-qim, steward of Yokan" section 1.10; *AHI*, no. 100.486; *WSS*, no. 663 | Excavated |

**(53) Pedaiah**, son of (52) Jehoiachin, king of Judah; 1 Chr 3:16–19:

| Reasonable but uncertain 2 | [62] seal לפדיהו בן / המלך, "Belonging to Peda-yahu, the king's son" *WSS*, no. 19 (see note 45, second paragraph) | Marketed |

Reign of ZEDEKIAH

**(54) Azzur**, father of (55) Jaazaniah; Ezek 11:1:

| Reasonable but uncertain 2 | [63] accounting ostracon, line 3, יאזניהו בן עזר II צ III נ, "Yaʾazanyahu, the son of ʿAzzur, n III ṣ II"[77] | Marketed |

---

[76] André Lemaire, "Nouvelles donées épigraphiques sur l'époque royale israélite," *REJ* 156 (1997): 445–61; idem, "Nouveaux sceaux et bulles paléo-hébraïques," in *ErIsr* 26 (Frank Moore Cross Volume, 1999): 108* and 111*, no. 10, photograph on 110*, no 22. Numberings (51a) and (51b) are due to an earlier, accidental omission of Hananiah.

[77] Robert Deutsch and Michael Heltzer, *New Epigraphic Evidence from the Biblical Period* (Tel Aviv: Archaeological Center Publication, 1995), 83–88, no. 77, 84, Fig. 77, and 85, Fig. 77a). They date the ostracon to "the first quarter of the VI cent." (ibid., 83) but allow "no possibility" (ibid., 85) of this ID. Major commentaries date Ezek 8:1 and 11:1 to the same year, which Greenberg affirms is 592 (Moshe Greenberg, *Ezekiel 1–20* [Anchor Bible 22; Garden City, N.Y.: Doubleday, 1983], 166, 186), and both passages imply that the men named (in Ezek 8:11; 11:1, 13) are recognizable public figures.

**(55) Jaazaniah**, son of (54) Azzur; Ezek 11:1:

| Reasonable but uncertain 2 | [63] accounting ostracon, line 3, יאזניהו בן עזר ג III צ II, "Ya'azanyahu, the son of 'Azzur, n III ṣ II"[78] | Marketed |

**(56) Malchiah**, the king's son; Jer 38:6:

| Reasonable but uncertain 2 | [64] seal למלכיהו / בן המלך, "Belonging to Malkiyahu, the king's son"[79] *WSS*, no. 15 | Marketed |

**(57) Azzur** of Gibeon, father of (58) Hananiah the false prophet; Jer 28:1ff:

| Reasonable but uncertain 2 | [65] seal לחנניהו / בן עזריהו, "Belonging to Hananyahu, the son of 'Azaryahu" *AHI*, no. 100.024; *WSS*, no. 165 | Marketed |
| Reasonable but uncertain 2 | [66 group] 7 Gibeon jar handle inscriptions (only 1 is complete) גבען / גדר / עזריהו, "Gibe'on. Wall of 'Azaryahu" *AHI*, nos. 22.001 through 22.007 (but 22.012 is doubtful) | Excavated |

**(58) Hananiah** the false prophet, son of (57) Azzur of Gibeon; Jer 28:1ff:

| Reasonable but uncertain 2 | [65] seal לחנניהו / בן עזריהו, "Belonging to Hananyahu, the son of 'Azaryahu" *AHI*, no. 100.024; *WSS*, no. 165 | Marketed |
| Disqualified D | [67 group] 16 Gibeon jar handle inscriptions (only 5 complete) חנניהו / נרא, "Ḥananyahu, (the son of) Nera'" *AHI*, 22.038, 22.050, 22.057, plus 11 incomplete inscriptions on jar handles (see *AHI*, 355–356) | Excavated |

---

[78] See preceding note.

[79] Deutsch and Lemaire, *Biblical Period Personal Seals*, 29, no. 23. The letter *he* in the upper register is from the late seventh century (Vaughn, "Palaeographic Dating of Judaean Seals," 47, 52–53).

## Appendix B

Governorship of GEDALIAH under Babylonian rule

**(59) Gedaliah**, son of Pashhur; Jer 38:1:

| Doubtful 1 | [68] Tell ed-Duweir bulla לגדליהו / אשר על הבית, "Belonging to Gedalyahu, the overseer of the palace" *AHI*, no. 100.149; *WSS*, no. 405 | Excavated |
| Doubtful 1 | [69] burnt-archive bulla לגדליהו / עבד המלך, "Belonging to Gedalyahu, the king's minister" *AHI*, no. 100.505; *WSS*, no. 409 | Marketed |

**(60) Gedaliah**, governor of Judah and son of (39) Ahikam, son of (36) Shaphan the scribe, son of (34) Azaliah, son of (33) Meshullam; 2 Kgs 25: 22ff:

| Disqualified D[80] | [68] Tell ed-Duweir bulla לגדליהו / אשר על הבית, "Belonging to Gedalyahu, the overseer of the palace" *AHI*, no. 100.149; *WSS*, no. 405 | Excavated |
| Doubtful 1.1 | [69] burnt-archive bulla לגדליהו / עבד המלך, "Belonging to Gedalyahu, the king's minister" *AHI*, no. 100.505; *WSS*, no. 409 | Marketed |

**(61) Jaazaniah**, the son of the Maacathite; 2 Kgs 25:23; Jezaniah in Jer 40:8 is probably a hypocoristicon referring to the same person:

| Reasonable but uncertain 2.1 | [70] Tell en-Naṣbeh seal ליאזניהו / עבד המלך, "Belonging to Yaʾazanyahu, the king's minister" *AHI*, no. 100.069; *WSS*, no. 8 | Excavated |

**(62) Ishmael** of royal descent, son of Nethaniah, son of (42) Elishama; 2 Kgs 25:23; 25; Jer 40:8ff:

| Reasonable but uncertain 2 | [71] bulla לישמעאל / בן המלך, "Belonging to Yišmaʿʾel, the king's son"[81] | Marketed |

---

[80] "The seal of 'Gedaliah who is over the house' is from the middle of the 7th cent. and thus most likely does not belong to the Gedaliah who ruled Judah from 586 to 582" (Larry G. Herr, "Seal," *ISBE* 4:374; in accordance with *SANSS*, 91, no. 18).

[81] Gabriel Barkay, "A Bulla of Ishmael, the King's Son," *BASOR* 290–291 (1993): 109–14.

## B.5 Gentiles before the beginning of the Persian era in 539 B.C.E.

**(63) Beor**, father of (64) Balaam; Num 22:5ff:

| Virtually certain 3 | [72] Tell Deir ʿAllā inscription on plaster, combination 1, lines 2, 4: ברבער, "son of Beʿor"[82] | Excavated |

**(64) Balaam**, son of (63) Beor; Num 22:5ff:

| Virtually certain 3 | [72] Tell Deir ʿAllā inscription on plaster, combination 1, lines 3, 4: בלעם, "Bileʿam"[83] | Excavated |

**(65) Achish**, king of Gath (r. late eleventh to early to mid-tenth century); 1 Sam 21:11ff:

| Disqualified D | [73] Ekron stone, lines 1–3: אכיש · בן · פדי · בן שר עק [. . .] / · , "ʾAkiš, the son of Padi,[84] the son of [. . .], ruler of Ekron" | Excavated |

**(66) Hiram**, king of Tyre (r. mid-tenth century) 2 Sam 5:11ff:

| Disqualified D | [74] Byblos sarcophagus inscription of ʾAḥiram line 1: ארן · ז פעל · [א]תבעל · בן אחירם · מלך · גבל · לאחירם · אבה, "The sarcophagus which [ʾE]tbaal, the son of ʾAḥiram, king of Gebal, made for ʾAḥiram, his father."[85] | Excavated |

---

[82] Hackett, *Balaam Text from Deir ʿAllā*, 33–34, 36; idem, "Some Observations on the Balaam Tradition at Deir ʿAllā," 216; Joseph A. Fitzmyer and Stephen A. Kaufman, *An Aramaic Bibliography, Part I: Old, Official, and Biblical Aramaic* (Baltimore: Johns Hopkins University Press, 1992), 23–24, section B.1.19. Many scholars accept the ID of the *literary* figures in the Deir ʿAllā inscription and Num 22–24, but this inscription of ca. 700 is of questionable *historical* value in identifying the biblical Balaam (ca. 1400).

[83] See preceding note.

[84] Seymour Gitin, Trude Dothan, and Joseph Naveh, "A Royal Dedicatory Inscription from Ekron," *IEJ* 47 (1997): 1–16; Joseph Naveh, "Achish-Ikausu in the Light of the Ekron Dedication," *BASOR* 310 (1998): 35–37; Anson F. Rainey, "Syntax, Hermeneutics and History," *IEJ* 48 (1998): 242–44; idem, "Following Up on the Ekron and Mesha Inscriptions," *IEJ* 50 (2000): 116–17.

[85] *KAI*, Nr. 1, Table 1; John C. L. Gibson, *Phoenician Inscriptions* (vol. 3 of *Textbook of Syrian Semitic Inscriptions*; New York: Oxford University Press, 1982), 12–16,

Appendix B 237

| | | |
|---|---|---|
| Disqualified D | [75] fragments of 1 of 2 Cyprus bowls with similar inscriptions, in the longer inscription: סכן קרתחדשת עבד חרם מלך צדנם, "the Governor of Carthage, the minister of Ḥiram, the king of the Sidonians[86] | Excavated |

**(67) Hadadezer**, son of Rehob and king of Zobah (r. early to mid-tenth century); 2 Sam 8: 3ff:

| | | |
|---|---|---|
| Disqualified D | [76] Saqqarah (Egypt) quartz scaraboid seal להדדעזר, "Belonging to Hadadʿezer"[87] *WSS* no. 785 | Excavated |

**(68) Ben-hadad I or II**, king of Aram at Damascus (r. early ninth century to 844/842); 1 Kgs 15:18ff:

| | | |
|---|---|---|
| No clear basis 0.3 | [2] Tel Dan stele, Fragment A, traces of letters along bottom edge of line 2;[88] cf. section 3.5; in [2]: | Excavated |
| Disqualified D | [77] Melqart stele from near Aleppo, lines 1–3: נצבא · זי · שם בר[ה] / דד · בר · עתרהמך / מלך ארם, "The stele that Bar-[h]adad, the son of Atarhamak, king of Aram, erected."[89] | Excavated |

---

no. 4; Frank L. Benz, *Personal Names in the Phoenician and Punic Inscriptions* (Studia Pohl 8; Rome: Biblical Institute Press, 1972), 318, s.v. "ḤRM;" Donald R. Vance, "Literary Sources for the History of Palestine and Syria: The Phoenician Inscriptions, Part I," *BA* 57 (1994): 6–8; Edward M. Cook, "On the Linguistic Dating of the Phoenician Ahiram Inscription (*KAI* 1)," *JNES* 53 (1994): 33–36.

[86] *KAI*, Nr. 31; Gibson, *Phoenician Inscriptions*, 66–68, no. 17; Donald R. Vance, "Literary Sources for the History of Palestine and Syria: The Phoenician Inscriptions, Part II," *BA* 57 (1994): 113–14. This Carthage was on Cyprus.

[87] Eighth- to seventh-century seal in the Egyptian Museum, Cairo, item no. given variously as JdE 25225 or J. 25225. Of its five registers, the second is re-cut and contains text only; the other four contain Egyptian or Egyptianizing iconography, most of which is apparently royal. "Though found in Saqqarah, the earliest one [i.e., this seal] apparently made its way there from abroad" (Bezalel Porten and Ada Yardeni, *Ostraca & Assorted Inscriptions* [vol. 4 of *Textbook of Aramaic Documents from Ancient Egypt*; Texts and Studies for Students; Jerusalem: Hebrew University, Department of History of the Jewish People, 1999], 228, inscr. 14.1).

[88] Puech, "La stèle araméenne de Dan," 215–21, 231–33.

[89] Fitzmyer and Kaufman, *Aramaic Bibliography, Part I*, 11, section B.1.1; *KAI*, Nr. 201; John C. L. Gibson, *Aramaic Inscriptions* (vol. 2 of *Textbook of Syrian Semitic*

**(69) Mesha**, king of Moab (r. early to mid-ninth century); 2 Kgs 3:4:

| Certain | [3] Mesha stele from Dhiban, line 1 מלך . . . משע, | Ob- |
| SI+SB | מאב, "Meša'. . . king of Moʾab" section 3.3 | served |

**(70) Ethbaal**, king of the Sidonians (r. early to mid-ninth century) and father of (8) Jezebel, queen of Israel; 1 Kgs 16:31[90]:

| Disquali- | [74] Byblos sarcophagus inscription of ʾAḥiram, line | Exca- |
| fied D | 1: ארן · ז פעל · [א]תבעל · בן אחירם · מלך · | vated |
| | גבל · לאחירם · אבה, "The sarcophagus which | |
| | [ʾE]tbaal, the son of ʾAḥiram, king of Gebal, made | |
| | for ʾAḥiram, his father."[91] | |

**(71) Hazael**, king of Aram at Damascus (r. 844/842–ca. 800, father of (72) Benhadad II or III; 1 Kgs 19:15ff:

| Certain | [78] Zakkur stele from near Afiz, near Aleppo, line 4: | Exca- |
| SI+SB | ברהדד | בר | חזאל | מלך | ארם |, "Bar-hadad, the | vated |
| | son of Hazaʾel, the king of ʾAram"[92] cf. section 3.5 | |

| Reliable | [79] a pair of horse blinders from Eretria, on the Greek | Exca- |
| 3.2 | island Euboea זי נתן הדד למראן חזאל מן עמק | vated |
| | בשנת עדה מראן נהר, "That which Hadad gave to | |

---

*Inscriptions*; New York: Oxford University Press, 1975), 1–4, no. 1, Fig. 1 (a, b, c); *DOTT*, 239–41. On the ambiguities of the identity of Bar-hadad, see Pitard, *Ancient Damascus*, 138–44; idem, "The Identity of the Bir-Hadad of the Melqart Stela," *BASOR* 272 (1988): 3–21. The transcription here follows ibid.

[90] Josephus calls Jezebel's father "Ethbaal, king of the Tyrians and Sidonians" (*Ant.* 8.13.1 [317]), and says Menander the Ephesian gleaned from the records of the Tyrian kings that Ἰθόβαλος (Ethbaal, spelled Ἰθωβαλος in *C.Ap.* 1.21 [156]), "the priest of Astarte," assassinated Pheles and thus succeeded him as the Tyrians' king (*C.Ap.* 1.18 [123]). Josephus also quotes Menander regarding a year-long drought during the reign of Ethbaal over the Tyrians, then comments that "By these words he designated the lack of rain . . . in the days of Ahab [cf. 1 Kgs 17:1–7; 18:1–2, 41–45], for it was at that time that Ethbaal also reigned over the Tyrians, as Menander informs us" (*Ant.* 8.13.2 [324]).

[91] *KAI*, Nr. 1, Table 1; Benz, *Personal Names*, 281, s.v. "[ʾ]TBʿL;" Vance, "Literary Sources," 6–8.

[92] Fitzmyer and Kaufman, *Aramaic Bibliography, Part I*, 13–14, section B.1.6; *KAI*, Nr. 202, Table 13, 14; Gibson, *Aramaic Inscriptions*, 6–17, no. 5, Pl. 1 (A), Fig. 2 (B,C); *DOTT* 242–50.

| | | |
|---|---|---|
| | Lord Ḥazaʾel from ʿUmqi in the year (the) Lord crossed the river."[93] | |
| Reliable 3.2 | [80] Samos horse frontlet זי נתן הדד למראן חזאל מן עמק בשנת עדה מראן נהר, "That which Hadad gave to Lord Ḥazaʾel from ʿUmqi in the year (the) Lord crossed the river."[94] | Excavated |
| Reasonable but uncertain 2 | [81] Arslan Tash (ancient Hadattah) ivory piece זֹ] קֹרב עמא · למראן · חזאל · בשנת · (break) ], אֹ[ח]זֹ[ת · ח]ו[ר?]?] "[That which] the people [pre]sented to Lord Ḥazaʾel in the year [ (break) sie]zed H[?oron?][95] | Excavated |
| Certain SI+SB | [82] Nimrud (biblical Calah) ivory piece ND 11310 [למר]אן חזאל], "[Belonging to Lo]rd Ḥazaʾel"[96] | Excavated |

---

[93] Fitzmyer and Kaufman, *Aramaic Bibliography, Part I*, 22–23, section B.1.17. Two matching bronze horse blinders or bridle pieces were discovered, each during a different part of the twentieth century, at the same temple. The engraved blinder in the museum in Athens was originally published in Elly Niki, "Sur une 'Potnia-Gorgone' d'Érétrie au Musée national d'Athènes," *RAr* 6me series, 1 (1933): 145–53. The second, matching blinder, kept at the Eretria Museum, was published in André Charbonnet, "Le dieu au lions d'Erétrie," *AION--Annali del Dipartimento di Studi del Mondo Classico e del Mediterraneo Antico, Sezione di Archeologia e storia antica* 8 (1986): 140–44. Pl. 33–39 do not make the inscription clearly visible. On the decipherment of both, see Ephʿal and Naveh, "Hazael's Booty Inscriptions," 192–200, Pl. 24A, 25A; François Bron and André Lemaire, "Les inscriptions araméennes de Hazaël," *RA* 83 (1989): 35–44.

[94] Helmut Kyrieleis and Wolfgang Röllig, "Ein altorientalischer Pferdeschmuck aus dem Heraion von Samos," *Mitteilungen des Deutschen Archäologischen Instituts, Athenische Abteilung* 103 (1988): 37–75, Pl. 9–15. On the iconography, see Kantor, "Oriental Institute Museum Notes, No. 13: A Bronze Plaque with Relief Decoration from Tell Tainat," 93–117, Pl. 11–15. Cf. Ephʿal and Naveh, "Hazael's Booty Inscriptions," Pl. 24A and 25A, with Kantor's very similar Figs. 13A and 13B on 108.

[95] Fitzmyer and Kaufman, *Aramaic Bibliography, Part I*, 12–13, section B.1.4; *KAI*, Nr. 232; Gibson, *Aramaic Inscriptions*, 4–5, no. 2, Fig. 6; Émile Puech, "L'ivoire inscrit d'Arslan Tash et les rois de Damas," *RB* 88 (1981): 544–62, Pl. 12, 13; Max E. L. Mallowan, *Nimrud and Its Remains* (New York: Dodd, Mead, 1966), 2:507–508, 598–99, 654 n. 84; Richard D. Barnett, *Ancient Ivories in the Middle East and Adjacent Countries* (Qedem 14; Jerusalem: The Hebrew University, Institute of Archaeology, 1982), 48.

[96] Mallowan, *Nimrud and Its Remains*, 2:477–78, 506, 508, 598–99, 598 Fig. 582; in relation to dating by associated finds (ibid., 2:472, 474), see Richard D. Barnett, "Hamath and Nimrud: Shell Fragments from Hamath and the Provenance of the Nimrud Ivories," *Iraq* 25 (1963): 81–85, Pl. 15–18; idem, *Ancient Ivories*, 53.

**(72) Ben-hadad II or III**, son of (71) Hazael, king of Aram at Damascus (r. early eighth century); 2 Kgs 13:3ff:

| | | |
|---|---|---|
| Certain SI+SB | [78] Zakkur stele from near Afīz, near Aleppo, lines 4–5: . . . \| ארם \| מלך \| חזאל \| בר \| ברהדד, "Bar-hadad, the son of Ḥazaʾel, the king of ʾAram . . . Bar-hadad"[97] | Excavated |

**(73) Tiglath-pileser III**, king of Assyria (r. 744–727); 2 Kgs 15:19ff:

| | | |
|---|---|---|
| Certain SI | [83] Aramaic monumental inscription from near Zenjirli honoring Panamu II, lines 13, 15, and 16 תגלתפלסר, "Tiglatpileser"[98] | Excavated or Observed |
| Certain SI | [84] Aramaic monumental inscription 1 of Bar Rekub from near Zenjirli, now in Istanbul, lines 3, 6 תגלתפליסר, "Tiglatpileyser"[99] | Excavated |
| Certain SI | [85] Aramaic monumental inscription 8 of Bar Rekub from near Zenjirli, now in Berlin, lines 1–2 [תגלתפ], ליסר / "[Tiglatpi]leyser"[100] | Excavated |
| Certain SI | [86] the Ashur ostracon, line 15 תכלתפלסרמן, "Tikultupilesarman"[101] | Excavated |

**(74) Sargon II**, king of Assyria (r. 721–705);[102] Isa 20:1:

---

[97] See note 92.

[98] Fitzmyer and Kaufman, *Aramaic Bibliography, Part I*, 14, 16–17; *KAI*, Nr. 215; Gibson, *Aramaic Inscriptions*, 76–86, Pl. 4.

[99] Fitzmyer and Kaufman, *Aramaic Bibliography, Part I*, 20–21, section B.1.14, inscr. 1; *KAI*, Nr. 216, Table XXXII; Gibson, *Aramaic Inscriptions*, 87–92, no. 15 (i).

[100] Fitzmyer and Kaufman, *Aramaic Bibliography, Part I*, 20–21, section B.1.14, inscr. 8; *KAI*, Nr. 217, Table XII; Gibson, *Aramaic Inscriptions*, 92–93, no. 16 (ii), Fig. 11.

[101] Fitzmyer and Kaufman, *Aramaic Bibliography, Part I*, 42, section B.2.13; *KAI*, Nr. 233, Table 26; Gibson, *Aramaic Inscriptions*, 98–110, no. 20, Pl. 5.

[102] The name Sargon (*srgwn*), with no other identifying data, appears in a Jewish Babylonian Aramaic incantation (line 2 of five) discovered in Iraq, dated linguistically to the Sassanian period, third through seventh centuries C.E. (Edward M. Cook, "An Aramaic Incantation Bowl from Khafaje," *BASOR* 285 [February 1992]: 79–81).

| No clear basis 0 | [83] Aramaic monumental inscription from near Zenjirli honoring Panamu II, line 18: שר[גון], "Šar-[gon]"[103] | Excavated or Observed |
| --- | --- | --- |
| Certain SI | [86] the Ashur ostracon, line 15: סרכון, "Sarkon[104] | Excavated |
| Certain SI or Doubtful 1; SI if kings alone had eunuchs | [87] Khorsabad bulla / [לפנאסר] / [למר סרס ז] / סרגן ['], "[Belonging to] Pan'aššur-[la]mur, eunuch o[f] Sargon" WSS, no. 755 | Excavated |

(75) **Sennacherib**, king of Assyria (r. 704–681);[105] 2 Kgs 18:13ff:

---

[103] See note 98. The supplied consonants appear in *An Aramaic Handbook* (ed. Franz Rosenthal; 2 vols. in 4; Porta Lingua Orientalium, n.s. 10; Wiesbaden: Harrassowitz, 1967), 1/1:8, no. 3.

[104] See note 101.

[105] The Words of Aḥiqar, of which the oldest extant version is the fragmentary fifth-century papyrus from Elephantine, mentions Sennacherib in lines 50, 51, and 55 (*Aramaic Papyri of the Fifth Century B.C.* (ed. Arthur E. Cowley; Oxford: Clarendon Press, 1923; repr., Osnabrück: Zeller, 1967), 213. Porten and Yardeni find more occurrences of Sennacherib's name in this ancient tale (Bezalel Porten and Ada Yardeni, eds. and trans., *Literature, Accounts, Lists* [vol. 3 of *Textbook of Aramaic Documents from Ancient Egypt*; ed. and trans. Bezalel Porten and Ada Yardeni; Texts and Studies for Students; Jerusalem: The Hebrew University, Department of the History of the Jewish People, 1993], 24–59). This ID can be regarded as certain on grounds of singularity in inscriptional materials and also in the Bible. On the historical aspect of the story of Aḥiqar, see Cowley, *Aramaic Papyri*, 204–9; Emil G. Kraeling, "Aḥiqar, Book of," *IDB* 1:68–69. For bibliography on The Words of Aḥiqar, see Fitzmyer and Kaufman, *Aramaic Bibliography, Part I*, 59–60, section B.3.c.3.

The name of Esarhaddon, son of Sennacherib and king of Assyria (r. 680–669), whom the Bible mentions in 2 Kgs 19:37; Isa 37:38; and Ezra 4:2, appears in The Words of Aḥiqar, lines 5, 10, 11, 13, 14, 32, 47, 53, 60, 64, 65, 75, and 78 (Cowley, *Aramaic Papyri of the Fifth Century B.C.*, 212–14). Esarhaddon can be identified there with certainty, on grounds of singularity in inscriptional materials (SI) from after 539 B.C.E.

Porten and Yardeni find Esarhaddon also mentioned as אסחדן in the fifth century Aramaic Cave Inscription observed near Sheikh Fadl, Egypt, panel XII, line 12 (Bezalel Porten and Ada Yardeni, eds. and trans., *Ostraca & Assorted Inscriptions* [vol. 4 of *Textbook of Aramaic Documents from Ancient Egypt*; ed. and trans. Bezalel Porten and Ada

| Certain SI+SB | [86] the Ashur ostracon, line 16: חרב[סנ], "[Senna-]ḥerib [106] | Excavated |

**(76) Nebuchadnezzar II**, king of Babylon (r. 604–562); 2 Kgs 24:1ff.

| Certain SI+SB | [88] [Sfire?] clay tablet, lines 5–6: [נ]בוכדרצר מלך [בב]ל /, "[Ne]bukadreṣṣar, king of [Baby]lon"[107] | Marketed |

**(77) Baalis**, king of the Ammonites (r. early sixth century); Jer 40:14:

| Reasonable but uncertain 2[108] | [89] Tell el-Umeiri ceramic cone (bottle stopper?) with seal impression למלכמאור / עב / ד בעל ישע, "Belonging to Milkomʿur, the minister of of Baʿalyašaʾ" (or Baʿalîšaʿ) *WSS*, no. 860 | Excavated |

---

Yardeni; Texts and Studies for Students; Jerusalem: The Hebrew University, Department of the History of the Jewish People, 1993], 286–98, inscr. D23.1, foldout 5–8). Their treatment contains a brief overview of the content, drawings of what remains of the inscriptions, a transcription, and an English translation. Porten and Yardeni date the inscription to the first quarter of the fifth century (ibid., 287); Joseph Naveh dates it paleographically to the second quarter of the fifth century (Naveh, *Development of the Aramaic Script*, 41). Lemaire finds no mention of Esarhaddon in the inscription (André Lemaire, "Les inscriptions araméens de Cheikh-Fadl (Égypte)," in *Studia Aramaica: New Sources and New Approaches: Papers Delivered at the London Conference of the Institute of Jewish Studies, University College, London, 26th–28th June 1991* [ed. Markham J. Geller, Jonas C. Greenfield, and Michael P. Weitzman; Journal of Semitic Studies Supplement 4; New York: Oxford University Press, on behalf of the University of Manchester, 1995], 77–132, which includes thorough background, transcription, French translation, commentary, a paleographic chart, and photographs of the panels). This inscription, too, is dated too late to be listed in this chart.

The Sheikh Fadl inscription also mentions Pharaoh Neco (I, to whom the Bible does not refer) in several places and Taharqa (*thrqʾ*), king of the Nubians (r. Egypt ca. 690–664), in panel VA, lines 8 (bis) and 9, panel VIII, line 10, panel XI, line 8, and panel XII, line 9. The latter, called "Tirhakah, King of Nubia [or Ethiopia]" in 2 Kgs 19: 9 and in its parallel in Isa 37:9, can be identified in the Sheikh Fadl Cave Inscription on grounds of singularity in inscriptional materials. Although this inscription seems to be a tale, it refers to real rulers and deities much as historical fiction does in our day.

[106] See note 101.

[107] *KAI*, Nr. 227. The inscriptional spelling, using *resh* after the *daleth*, is more accurate than the conventional English spelling.

[108] Current knowledge of the kings of Ammon does not permit us to say that there was only one king who bore this name; for a current list, see Robert Deutsch, "A Royal Ammonite Seal Impression," in *Michael: Historical, Epigraphical and Biblical Studies in Honor of Prof. Michael Heltzer* (ed. Yitzhak Avishur and Robert Deutsch; Tel Aviv:

| Reasonable but uncertain?[110] | [90] seal [לבעל יש]ע / מלך / בנעמן] , "Belonging to] Baʿalyašaʿ[ʿ], the king of the so[ns of ʿAmmon]"[109] (or Baʿališa[ʿ]) | Marketed |

(78)[111] **Belshazzar** (Bel-šarra-uṣur), son and coregent of Nabonidus, king of Babylon (coregency ca. 553–539); Dan 5:1ff:

| Disqualified D | [91] Egyptian granite statuette with Aramaic engraving בלסרעצר, "Belsarraʿuṣur"[112] | Uncertain |

---

Archaeological Center Publications, 1999), 124. Cf. repeated RNs in both Hebrew kingdoms: Jeroboam, Pekah/Pekahiah, Ahaz/Ahaziah/Jehoahaz; (65) Philistine Achish; (66) Phoenician ʾAḥiram/Ḥiram; and Damascene (68), (72) Bar-Hadad.

[109] Robert Deutsch, "Seal of Baʿalis Surfaces: Ammonite King Plotted Murder of Judahite Governor," *BAR* 25, no. 2 (March/April 1999): 46–49, 60, color photograph on front cover; Deutsch and Heltzer, *West Semitic Epigraphic News*, 53–57, no. 145 (47).

[110] See note 108.

[111] The total number of persons listed is seventy-nine, because of (51a) and (51b).

[112] Dated to the first half of the seventh century (Porten and Yardeni, *Ostraca & Assorted Inscriptions*, 234–35, inscr. D16.1, Egyptian museum in Cairo, item J. 31919).

# Appendix C

# The Corpus and the Remainder: Evaluations of Potential Identifications in Descending Order of Strength, Updated through July 2002

*The Corpus: The First Four of Eight Sections Below*

Sections C.1 through C.4 below contain the first extensive corpus of pre-Persian-era, Northwest Semitic inscriptions that name biblical persons. The reliable identifications (IDs) are found there, i.e., those in grades S (including SI and SB) through 3,. This appendix includes and goes beyond the IDs in Chapters 3 and 4—which cover pre-Persian-era *Hebrew* inscriptions—to cover all, or almost all, that are Northwest Semitic (see note 54 near the end of this appendix). It also updates Chapters 3 and 4, which are limited to publications before October 1997. Sections C5 through C8 contain the remainder: uncertain and doubtful IDs (grades 2 and 1) plus non-IDs (grades 0 and D).

*Location of Key and Relation to Other Appendixes*

The key to the chart below is at the beginning of Appendix B. The chart below simply rearranges most of Appendix B's text and notes and deletes whatever notes are not most directly relevant (since that appendix casts a wider net than this one). For peripheral information, such as potential IDs in inscriptions from the Persian era onward or from Egyptian inscriptions, see Appendix B, footnotes 2, 3, 4, 90, 102, and 105. For various exemplars in the same group of inscriptions and for "decimals" attached to the grade, see Appendix B under the same person and inscription numbers.

Appendix F provides a numerical tabulation of IDs in all sections of this appendix, then goes on to pay particular attention to sections C.1 through C.5 below, i.e., grades SI and SB down to 2. Appendix D is an alphabetical index of all biblical persons in Appendixes B and C.

*The Pattern of the Entries Below*

**(Person number) name and description of the person potentially to be identified, with a biblical reference:**

| [Inscription number] name and/or text of inscription containing ID or non-ID, with whole or partial transcription and translation or transliteration); references to other part(s) of this book and citations | Means of access |
|---|---|

**C.1 In the Corpus: Identifications That are Certain, Based on Singular Circumstances Both according to Inscriptional Data and, Separately, according to Biblical Data: Grade SI+SB**

**(2) David, son of Jesse and king of Israel (r. ca. 1010–970); 1 Sam 16:13ff:**

| | |
|---|---|
| [2] Tel Dan stele, Fragment A, line 9: ביתדוד, "the house of David"; section 3.5 | Excavated |
| [3] Mesha stele from Dhiban, line 31: בת[ד]וד, "the house of David"[1]; line 12: אראל דודה, "its Davidic lion"[2]; Appendix E | Observed |

**(7) Omri, king of Israel (r. 884–873); 1 Kgs 16:16ff:**

| | |
|---|---|
| [3] Mesha stele from Dhiban, lines 4–5, 7: עמרי, "'Omri"; section 3.3 | Observed |

---

[1] Lemaire, "La dynastie Davidique (*byt dwd*) dans deux inscriptions.," 17–19; idem, "'House of David' Restored in Moabite Inscription," 30–37. See the first part of Appendix E, section E.1, below.

[2] This translation makes use of the grammatical insight of Rainey, "Syntax, Hermeneutics and History," 244–51, who translates this Moabite phrase as "its Davidic altar-hearth." See Appendix E, section E.2, below.

## (69) Mesha, king of Moab (r. early to mid-ninth century); 2 Kgs 3:4:

[3] Meshaʿ stele from Dhiban, line 1: מלך מאב ... משע, "Mešaʿ ... king of Moʾab"; section 3.3

Observed

## (71) Hazael, king of Aram at Damascus (r. 844/842–ca. 800, father of (72) Ben-hadad II or III; 1 Kgs 19:15ff:

[78] Zakkur stele from near Afiz, near Aleppo, line 4: ברהדד | בר | חזאל | מלך | ארם |, "Bar-hadad, the son of Hazaʾel, the king of ʾAram"[3] cf. section 3.5, "How the inscription correlates..."

Excavated

[82] Nimrud (biblical Calah) ivory piece ND 11310 [למר]אן חזאל, "[Belonging to Lo]rd Hazaʾel"[4]

Excavated

## (72) Ben-hadad II or III, son of (71) Hazael, king of Aram at Damascus (r. early eighth century); 2 Kgs 13:3ff:

[78] Zakkur stele from near Afiz, near Aleppo, line 4: ברהדד | בר | חזאל | מלך | ארם | ... ברהדד, "Bar-hadad, the son of Hazaʾel, the king of ʾAram ... Bar-hadad"[5] cf. section 3.5, "How the inscription correlates..."

Excavated

## (75) Sennacherib, king of Assyria (r. 704–681); 2 Kgs 18:13ff:

[86] the Ashur ostracon, line 16: [סנ]חרב, "[Senna]ḥerib"[6]

Excavated

## (76) Nebuchadnezzar II, king of Babylon (r. 604–562); 2 Kgs 24:1ff:

[88] (Sfire?) clay tablet, lines 5–6: [נ]בוכדרצר מלך / [בב]ל, "[Ne]bukadreṣṣar, king of [Baby]lon"[7]

Marketed

---

[3] Fitzmyer and Kaufman, *Aramaic Bibliography, Part I*, 13–14, section B.1.6; *KAI*, Nr. 202, Table 13, 14; Gibson, *Aramaic Inscriptions*, 6–17, no. 5, Pl. 1 (A), Fig. 2 (B,C); *DOTT* 242–50.

[4] Mallowan, *Nimrud and Its Remains*, 2:477–78, 506, 508, 598–99, 598 Fig. 582; in relation to dating by associated finds (ibid., 2:472, 474), see Barnett, "Hamath and Nimrud," 81–85, Pl. 15–18; idem, *Ancient Ivories*, 53.

[5] See note 3.

[6] Fitzmyer and Kaufman, *Aramaic Bibliography, Part I*, 42, section B.2.13; *KAI*, Nr. 233, Table 26; Gibson, *Aramaic Inscriptions*, 98–110, no. 20, Pl. 5.

## C.2 In the Corpus: Identifications That are Certain, Based on Singular Circumstances according to Inscriptional Data Only: Grade SI

**(73) Tiglath-pileser III, king of Assyria (r. 744–727); 2 Kgs 15:19ff:**

[83] Aramaic monumental inscription from near Zenjirli honoring Panamu II, lines 13, 15, 16 תגלתפלסר, "Tiglatpileser"[8] — Excavated or observed

[84] Aramaic monumental inscription 1 of Bar Rekub from near Zenjirli, now in Istanbul, lines 3, 6: תגלתפליסר, "Tiglatpileyser"[9] — Excavated

[85] Aramaic monumental inscription 8 of Bar Rekub from near Zenjirli, now in Berlin, lines 1–2: [תגלתפ] / ליסר, "[Tiglatpi]leyser"[10] — Excavated

[86] the Ashur ostracon, line 15: תכלתפלסרמן, "Tikultupilesarman"[11] — Excavated

**(74) Sargon II, king of Assyria (r. 721–705); Isa 20:1:**

[86] the Ashur ostracon, line 15: סרכון, "Sarkon"[12] — Excavated

## C.3 In the Corpus: Identifications That are Certain, Based on Singular Circumstances according to Biblical Data Only: Grade SB

An ID of only one of the following three kings, i.e., person (11), (18), or (35), may be determined by date and whether the inscription is Judahite or Israelite:
**(11) J(eh)oash, son of Jehoahaz, king of Israel (r. 805–790); 2 Kgs 13:9ff; OR**

---

[7] *KAI*, Nr. 227. The inscriptional spelling, using *resh* after the *daleth*, is more accurate than the conventional English spelling.

[8] Fitzmyer and Kaufman, *Aramaic Bibliography, Part I*, 14, 16–17; *KAI*, Nr. 215; Gibson, *Aramaic Inscriptions*, 76–86, Pl. 4.

[9] Fitzmyer and Kaufman, *Aramaic Bibliography, Part I*, 20–21, section B.1.14, inscr. 1; *KAI*, Nr. 216, Table XXXII; Gibson, *Aramaic Inscriptions*, 87–92, no. 15 (i).

[10] Fitzmyer and Kaufman, *Aramaic Bibliography, Part I*, 20–21, section B.1.14, inscr. 8; *KAI*, Nr. 217, Table XII; Gibson, *Aramaic Inscriptions*, 92–93, no. 16 (ii), Fig. 11.

[11] Fitzmyer and Kaufman, *Aramaic Bibliography, Part I*, 42, section B.2.13; *KAI*, Nr. 233, Table 26; Gibson, *Aramaic Inscriptions*, 98–110, no. 20, Pl. 5.

[12] See preceding note.

**(18) J(eh)oash, son of (17) Ahaziah, king of Judah (r. 842/1–802/1); 2 Kgs 11:2ff;**
OR
**(35) Josiah, son of Amon, king of Judah (r. 640/39–609); 2 Kgs 21:24ff.**

[10] "three shekels" ostracon, lines 1–2: המלך אשיהו, "ʾAšyahu the king"[13]     Marketed

**(12) Jeroboam II, son of Joash, king of Israel (r. 790–750/49); 2 Kgs 13:13ff:**

[7] Megiddo seal ירבעם / לשמע עבד, "Belonging to Šemaʿ, the minister of Jeroboam" section 3.6[14]; *AHI*, no. 100.068; *WSS*, no. 2     Excavated

**(16) Hoshea, son of Elah and king of Israel (r. 732/1–722); 2 Kgs 15:30ff:**

[15] seal הושע עבד / לעבדי, "Belonging to ʿAbdi, the minister of Hošeaʿ"[15] sections 2.2 and 2.13     Marketed

**(20) Uzziah/Azariah, son of Amaziah, king of Judah (r. 788/7–736/5); 2 Kgs 14:21ff:**

[17] seal עזיו / לאביו עבד, "Belonging to ʾAbiyaw, the minister of ʿUzziyaw" section 4.2; *AHI*, no. 100.065; *WSS*, no. 3     Marketed[16]

[18] seal obv. לשבניו rev. עזיו בד / לשבניו ע, obv. "Belonging to Šubnayaw," rev. "Belonging to Šubnayaw, the minister of ʿUzziyaw" section 4.3; *AHI*, no. 100.067; *WSS*, no. 4     Marketed[17]

---

[13] Bordreuil, Israel, and Pardee, "Deux ostraca paléo-hébreux," 49–76, Pl. 7, 8; ET, "King's Command and Widow's Plea," 2–13; Shanks, "Three Shekels for the Lord," 28–32.

[14] Ussishkin's case for the identification of Jeroboam I has considerable merit, but it does not seem to have attracted a scholarly consensus (Ussishkin, "Gate 1567," 410–28). Others who identify Jeroboam I in this seal are Shmuel Yeivin, "Date of the Seal," 205–12; Gösta W. Ahlström, "Seal of Shema," 208–15.

[15] Deutsch and Lemaire, *Biblical Period Personal Seals*, 7, no. 1, and color photograph on book jacket.

[16] Published in 1858, long before any forgers could have known the appropriate paleographic details.

[17] Found in an 1863 publication, which was decades before the appropriate paleographic details were known by anyone, including potential forgers.

## Appendix C

**(21) Jotham, son of (20) Uzziah, king of Judah (r. 758/7–742/1); 2 Kgs 15:5ff:**

[21] bulla יהדה / · מלך · הותם / · · לאחז, "Belonging to ʾAḥaz (son of) Yehotam, king of Judah"[18]    Marketed

**(22) Ahaz, son of (21) Jotham, king of Judah, (r. 742/1–726); 2 Kgs 15:38ff:**

[21] bulla יהדה / · מלך · הותם / · · לאחז, "Belonging to ʾAḥaz (son of) Yehotam, king of Judah"[19]    Marketed

[23] seal אחז בד / ע · לאשנא, "Belonging to ʾUšna, the minister of ʾAḥaz" section 4.4    Marketed

[24 group] bulla יהדה / מלך אחז לחזקיהו with one line on upper part of scarab's wing, "Belonging to Ḥizqiyahu, (son of) ʾAḥaz, king of Judah"[20]    Marketed

[25 group] bulla יהדה / מלך אחז לחזקיהו with two lines on upper part of scarab's wing, "Belonging to Ḥizqiyahu, (son of) ʾAḥaz, king of Judah"[21]    Marketed

[26 group] bulla יהדה מלך / אחז לחזקיהו with winged solar disc and two ankh symbols, "Belonging to Ḥizqiyahu, (son of) ʾAḥaz, king of Judah"[22]    Marketed

**(23) Hezekiah, son of (22) Ahaz, king of Judah (r. 726–697/6); 2 Kgs 16:20ff:**

[24 group] bulla יהדה / מלך אחז לחזקיהו with one line on upper part of scarab's wing, "Belonging to Ḥizqiyahu, (son of) ʾAḥaz, king of Judah"[23]    Marketed

---

[18] Deutsch, *Messages* (ET), 61–63, no. 1, 204, Pl. 16, upper half, 205, Pl. 17, upper half, and color photograph on book jacket.

[19] Ibid.; idem, "First Impression," 54–56, 62.

[20] See Appendix B, notes 33 and 34.

[21] See Appendix B, the second and third paragraphs of note 34, regarding the two-line-wing bullae.

[22] Deutsch, "New Bullae Reveal Egyptian-Style Emblems," 42 (color photograph and drawing), 46, cover (color photograph).

[23] Ibid., 45 (box), nos. 3 and 4, 46. The text that is legible on bulla no. 3 (as numbered by Deutsch) appears on this chart; the text of bulla no. 4 is more fragmentary.

[25 group] bulla לחזקיהו אחז מלך / יהדה with two lines on upper part of scarab's wing, "Belonging to Ḥizqiyahu, (son of) ʾAḥaz, king of Judah"[24] — Marketed

[26 group] bulla לחזקיהו אחז מלך / יהדה with winged solar disc and two ankh symbols, "Belonging to Ḥizqiyahu, (son of) ʾAḥaz, king of Judah"[25] — Marketed

[27] bulla לעזריהו · בן יהו[אה]ח · עבד · חזקיהו, "Belonging to ʿAzaryahu, son of Yeho[ʾa]ḥ, the minister of Ḥizqiyahu"[26] — Marketed

[28 group] bulla ליהוזר / ח בן חלק / יהו · עבד · ח / זקיהו, "Belonging to Yehozaraḥ, son of Ḥilqiyahu, the minister of Ḥizqiyahu" section 4.6; *AHI*, no. 100.321; *WSS*, no. 407 — Marketed

[29] bulla עבד חזקיהו . . . , ". . . the minister of Ḥizqiyahu"[27] — Marketed

[30] bulla לעמריהו / חנניהו עבד / חזקיהו, "Belonging to ʿAmaryahu, (son of) Ḥananyahu, the minister of Ḥizqiyahu"[28] — Marketed

[31] bulla לדמלא / חזק · עבד / יהו, "Belonging to Domlaʾ, the minister of Ḥizqiyahu"[29] — Marketed

[32] bulla לדמלא עבד / חזקיהו, "Belonging to Domlaʾ, the minister of Ḥizqiyahu"[30] — Marketed

### (37) Hilkiah the high priest, father of (38) Azariah; 2 Kgs 22:4ff:

[49] seal ring לחנן ב / ן חלקיהו / הכהן, "Belonging to Ḥanan, the son of Ḥilqiyahu, the priest" section 4.7; *AHI*, no. 100.734; *WSS*, no. 28 — Marketed

---

[24] Regarding the two-line-wing bullae, see the second and third paragraphs of Appendix B, note 34.
[25] See Appendix B, note 32.
[26] Deutsch, *Messages*, 64–66, no. 3.
[27] Ibid., 66–67, no. 4.
[28] Deutsch, "New Bullae Reveal Egyptian-Style Emblems," 48–49 (box), no. A.
[29] Ibid., 48–49 (box), no. B.
[30] Ibid., 48–49 (box), no. C.

## C.4 In the Corpus: Virtually Certain to Reliable Identifications: Grade 3

**(36) Shaphan the scribe, son of (34) Azaliah, son of (33) Meshullam, and father of (50) Gemariah and of (39) Ahikam the father of (60) Gedaliah; 2 Kgs 22:3ff:**

[48] city of David bulla לגמריהו / [ב]ן שפן, "Belonging to Gemaryahu, the [so]n of Šaphan" section 3.7; *AHI*, no. 100.802; *WSS*, no. 470 — Excavated

**(37) Hilkiah the high priest, father of (38) Azariah; 2 Kgs 22:4ff; AND**
**(38) Azariah, son of (37) Hilkiah the high priest; 1 Chr 5:39; 9:11; Ezra 7:1:**

[50] city of David bulla לעזריהו ב / ן חלקיהו, "Belonging to ʿAzaryahu, the son of Ḥilqiyahu" section 3.10; *AHI*, no. 100.827; *WSS*, no. 596 — Excavated

**(46) Neriah, son of Mahseiah, father of (47) Baruch the scribe and possibly of (49) Seraiah; Jer 32:12ff; 51:59:**

[57 group] 2 bullae from same seal לברכיהו / בן נריהו / הספר, "Belonging to Berekyahu, the son of Neriyahu, the scribe"[31] section 4.9; *AHI*, no. 100.509; *WSS*, no. 417 — Marketed

**(47) Baruch the scribe, son of (46) Neriah, and possibly a brother of (49) Seraiah; Jer 32:12ff:**

[57 group] 2 bullae from same seal לברכיהו / בן נריהו / הספר, "Belonging to Berekyahu, the son of Neriyahu, the scribe"[32] sections 2.3 and 4.8; *AHI*, no. 100.509; *WSS*, no. 417 — Marketed

**(48) Jerahmeel, the king's son; Jer 36:26:**

[59] bulla לירחמאל / בן המלך, "Belonging to Yeraḥmeʾel, the king's son" section 4.10; *AHI*, no. 100.508; *WSS*, no. 41 — Marketed

---

[31] As pointed out above in section 2.3, under Question 3, "Remarks," the first-known bulla of Baruch meets not just three, but four specific identifying criteria. It could, therefore, provide grade 4 IDs. Although, in my judgment, Grade 3 IDs are strong enough to make a grade 4 unnecessary, others might choose to create one.

[32] See preceding note.

**(50) Gemariah, brother of (39) Ahikam and son of (36) Shaphan the scribe, son of (34) Azaliah, son of (33) Meshullam; Jer 36:10ff:**

[48] city of David bulla לגמר[י]הו / [ב]ן שפן, "Belonging to Gemaryahu, the [so]n of Šaphan" section 3.8; *AHI*, no. 100.802; *WSS*, no. 470 — Excavated

**(63) Beor, father of (64) Balaam; Num 22:5ff:**

[72] Tell Deir ʿAlla inscription on plaster, combination 1, lines 2, 4: ברבער, "son of Beʿor"[33] — Excavated

**(64) Balaam, son of (63) Beor; Num 22:5ff:**

[72] Tell Deir ʿAlla inscription on plaster, combination 1, lines 3, 4: בלעם, "Bileʿam"[34] — Excavated

**(71) Hazael, king of Aram at Damascus (r. 844/842–ca. 800, father of (72) Ben-hadad II or III; 1 Kgs 19:15ff:**

[79] pair of horse blinders from Eretria, on the Greek island Euboea זי נתן הדד למראן חזאל מן עמק בשנת עדה מראן נהר, "That which Hadad gave to Lord Hazaʾel from ʿUmqi in the year (the) Lord crossed the river."[35] Cf. section 3.5 — Excavated

---

[33] Hackett, *Balaam Text from Deir ʿAllā*, 33–34, 36; idem, "Some Observations on the Balaam Tradition at Deir ʿAllā," 216; Fitzmyer and Kaufman, *Aramaic Bibliography, Part I*, 23–24, section B.1.19. Many scholars accept the ID of the literary figure in Num 22–24 with the literary figure in the Deir ʿAllā inscription, but this inscription of ca. 700 is of questionable *historical* value in identifying the biblical Balaam (ca. 1400).

[34] See preceding note.

[35] Fitzmyer and Kaufman, *Aramaic Bibliography, Part I*, 22–23, section B.1.17. Two matching bronze horse blinders or bridle pieces were discovered at the same temple during different excavations. The engraved blinder in the museum in Athens was originally published in Niki, "Sur une 'Potnia-Gorgone' d'Erétrie au Musée national d'Athènes," 145–53. The other, kept at the Eretria Museum, was published in Charbonnet, "Le dieu au lions d'Erétrie," 140–44, Pl. 33–39. On the decipherment of both, see Ephʿal and Naveh, "Hazael's Booty Inscriptions," 192–200, Pl. 24A, 25A; Bron and Lemaire, "Les inscriptions araméennes de Hazaël," 35–44.

[80] Samos horse frontlet זי נתן הדד למראן חזאל מן עמק Exca-
בשנת עדה מראן נהר, "That which Hadad gave to Lord Ḥaza'el vated
from ʿUmqi in the year (the) Lord crossed the river."[36]

## C.5 In the Remainder, Not the Corpus: Reasonable But Uncertain Identifications: Grade 2

Unless additional evidence surfaces or reliable new information is somehow gleaned to add to the number of identifying marks of these persons, *IDs from this point onward are not reliable.*

**(4) Mikneiah, a Levitical singer and lyrist in the procession of the ark of the covenant into Jerusalem; 1 Chr 15:18, 21:**

[5] seal obv. מקניו עבד יהוה rev. מקניו עבד יהוה, obv. "Mik- Mar-
neyaw, the servant of the LORD" rev. "Belonging to Miqneyaw, the keted
servant of the LORD"[37]

**(24) Hilkiah ( = (27)?), the minister of (23) Hezekiah, king of Judah; 2 Kgs 18:18ff:**

[28 group] bulla ליהוזר / ח בן חלק / יהו · עבד · ח / זקיהו, Mar-
"Belonging to Yehozaraḥ, son of Ḥilqiyahu, the minister of Ḥizqiya- keted
hu" *AHI*, no. 100.321; *WSS*, no. 407; cf. section 4.6

**(25) Shebna ( = (26)?), the overseer of the palace; Isa 22: 15–19:**

[34] Silwan epitaph, line 1: [?שבנ?]יהו אשר על הביתו, "[?Šub- Ob-
na?]yahu, overseer of the palace"[38] served

---

[36] Kyrieleis and Röllig, "Ein altorientalischer Pferdeschmuck aus dem Heraion von Samos," 37–75, Pl. 9–15. On the iconography, see Kantor, "Oriental Institute Museum Notes, No. 13: A Bronze Plaque with Relief Decoration from Tell Tainat," 93–117, Pl. 11–15. Cf. Ephʿal and Naveh, "Hazael's Booty Inscriptions," Pl. 24A and 25A, with Kantor's very similar Figs. 13A and 13B on 108.

[37] Cross, "Seal of Miqneyaw, Servant of Yahweh," 55–63, Pl. IX–X.

[38] Yigael Yadin suggested this potential ID (Avigad, "Epitaph of a Royal Steward from Siloam Village," 150), quite reasonably. The title matches that in Is 22:15, and the rock-cut tomb in a hillside near Jerusalem, dated paleographically to ca. 700, answers to Isa 22:16 (ibid., 137–52). Avigad noted "certain affinities between this passage and the archaeological evidence" (ibid., 151), but he made no ID. Though the biblical Shebna was likely *one of* the successive palace overseers for an interval during Hezekiah's ca. thirty-year reign, still *the absence of all root letters of the PN* makes it possible that the

**(27) Hilkiah, (= (24)?) father of (28) Eliakim the overseer of the palace of (23) Hezekiah, king of Judah; 2 Kgs 18:18ff;**
AND
**(28) Eliakim, son of (27) Hilqiah and the overseer of the palace of (23) Hezekiah; 2 Kgs 18:18ff; Isa 22:20–25:**

[40] bulla [חלקיהו / [ל[א]ליקם], "Belonging to [E]lyaqim, (son of) [Hi]lqiyahu"[39]; cf. section 4.6 — Marketed

**(32) Manasseh, son of (23) Hezekiah, king of Judah (r. 697/6– 642/1); 2 Kgs 20:21ff:**

[45] seal למנשה ב / ן המלך with two-winged scarab beetle, "Belonging to Manašeh, the king's son" *WSS*, no. 16[40] — Marketed

**(33) Meshullam, father of (34) Azaliah, father of (36) Shaphan the scribe, father of (50) Gemariah and (39) Ahikam, father of (60) Gedaliah; 2 Kgs 22: 3ff;**
AND
**(34) Azaliah, son of (33) Meshullam and father of (36) Shaphan the scribe, etc., as immediately above; 2 Kgs 22: 3ff:**

[46] seal לאצליהו / בן משלם, "Belonging to ʾAṣalyahu, the son of Mešullam" *AHI*, no. 100.853; *WSS*, no. 90 — Marketed

**(36) Shaphan the scribe, son of (34) Azaliah, son of (33) Meshullam, and father of (50) Gemariah and of (39) Ahikam, father of (60) Gedaliah; 2 Kgs 22:3ff:**

---

PN is that of another man who held that office. The biblical Shebna's rock-cut tomb may be located elsewhere. Over the millennia, earthquakes could have covered it with debris or caused it to collapse. This ID, based only on title and provenance, is grade 2, a reasonable hypothesis. Cf. Ussishkin, *Village of Silwan*.

If (26) Shebna the scribe of Hezekiah is being considered, this inscription might be referring to the biblical Shebna with a different title at another point in his career in the royal administration. The resulting lack of a match in title, however, reduces the grade of the ID to 1.

[39] Deutsch, *Messages*, 96–97, no. 30.

[40] Paleographic dating at 700 would make this seal owner Hezekiah's successor (Herr, "Paleography and the Identification of Seal Owners," 69), but only if we knew that King Hezekiah were his father. This ID, however, is not certain, because this seal does not name this Manasseh's father. The seal owner could be descended from any earlier king of Judah. Cf. note 47. See Appendix B, note 45, second paragraph.

[47] bulla לְ[א]חִיקָם / [ב]ן שפן, "[Belonging to ʾA]ḥiqam, the [so]n of Šaphan"[41] *WSS*, no. 431; cf. section 3.7 — Marketed

### (37) Hilkiah the high priest, father of (38) Azariah; 2 Kgs 22:4ff:

[51] seal עזריהו / חלקיהו,[42] "ʿAzaryahu, (the son of) Ḥilqiyahu" *AHI*, no. 100.496; *WSS*, no. 307; cf. section 3.9 — Marketed

[52] seal לעזריהו / חלקא, "Belonging to ʿAzaryahu, (the son of) Ḥilqa'" *AHI*, no. 100.728; *WSS*, no. 306; cf. section 3.9 — Marketed

### (38) Azariah, son of (37) Hilkiah the high priest; 1 Chr 5:39; 9:11; Ezra 7:1:

[51] seal עזריהו / חלקיהו,[43] "ʿAzaryahu, (the son of) Ḥilqiyahu" *AHI*, no. 100.496; *WSS*, no. 307; cf. section 3.10 — Marketed

[52] seal לעזריהו / חלקא, "Belonging to ʿAzaryahu, (the son of) Ḥilqa'" *AHI*, no. 100.728; *WSS*, no. 306; cf. section 3.10 — Marketed

### (39) Ahikam, father of (60) Gedaliah and brother of (50) Gemariah and son of (36) Shaphan the scribe, son of (34) Azaliah, son of (33) Meshullam; 2 Kgs 22:12ff:

[47] bulla לְ[א]חִיקָם / [ב]ן שפן, "[Belonging to ʾA]ḥiqam, the [so]n of Šaphan"[44] *WSS*, no. 431 — Marketed

### (40) Asaiah, the minister of (35) Josiah, king of Judah; 2 Kgs 22:12ff:

[53] seal לעשיהו / עבד המלך, "Belonging to ʿAśayahu, the king's minister" section 2.4 — Marketed

### (41) Nathan-melech the eunuch; 2 Kgs 23:11:

[54] bulla לנתנמלך / עבד המלך, "Belonging to Natan-melek, the king's minister"[45] (possibly a grade 1 ID[46]) — Marketed

---

[41] Deutsch, *Messages*, 91–92, no. 25.
[42] Deutsch and Lemaire, *Biblical Period Personal Seals*, 80, no. 74.
[43] Ibid.
[44] Deutsch, *Messages*, 91–92, no. 25.
[45] McCarter, "Bulla of Nathan-melech," 142–53; Deutsch, *Messages*, 73–74, no. 9.

**(42) Elishama, father of Nethaniah, father of (62) Ishmael of royal descent; 2 Kgs 25: 25; Jer 41:1:**

[55] seal לאלשמע ב / ן המלך, "Belonging to ʾElišamaʿ, the king's son" *AHI*, no. 100.072; *WSS*, no. 11 — Marketed

**(43) Jehoahaz, alias Shallum, son of (35) Josiah, king of Judah (r. 609); 2 Kgs 23:30ff:**

[16] seal ליהואחז / בן המלך, Belonging to Yehoʾaḥaz, the king's son" *AHI*, no. 100.252; *WSS*, no. 13; cf. persons (17) and (22) in section C.8 below[47] — Marketed

**(46) Neriah, son of Mahseiah, father of (47) Baruch the scribe and possibly of (49) Seraiah; Jer 32:12ff; 51:59**
**AND**
**(49) Seraiah, son of Neriah ( = (46) Neriah?) and possibly brother of (47) Baruch the scribe; Jer 51:59, 61:**

[58] seal לשריהו / נריהו, "Belonging to Śerayahu, (the son of) Neriyahu" *AHI*, no. 100.780; *WSS*, no. 390; cf. section 4.9 — Marketed

**(51a) Hananiah, father of Zedekiah *śar* of Judah; Jer 36:12**
**AND**
**(51b) Zedekiah, son of Hananiah and a *śar* of Judah; Jer 36:12:**

---

[46] This evaluation as a grade 2 ID follows McCarter in understanding Nathan-melech's biblical designation, הַסָּרִים, "the eunuch," to fall within the scope of the inscription's broader title, עבד המלך which was given to high-ranking royal servants (McCarter, "Bulla of Nathan-melech," 146–47). Significantly, among the 1,217 Northwest Semitic seals and bullae published in *WSS*, only one contains the title סרס, and it is an Aramaic bulla of a eunuch of Sargon which was excavated at Khorsabad (bulla [67] below; *WSS*, 283, no. 755). If later developments should make it clear that these two titles are mutually exclusive in a royal Hebrew governmental context, then this ID should be grade 1. The .1 "decimal" acknowledges the rarity of the seal owner's name in the Bible and in inscriptions, as observed in McCarter, "Bulla of Nathan-melech," 145–46.

[47] Paleographic dating would make this seal owner Josiah's successor (Herr, "Paleography and the Identification of Seal Owners," 69), but only if we knew that King Josiah were his father. This ID, however, is not certain, because this seal does not name this Yehoʾaḥaz's father. The seal owner could be descended from any earlier king of Judah. Cf. note 40. See Appendix B, note 45, second paragraph.

[61] bulla לצדקיהו / בן חנני, "Belonging to Ṣedeqyahu, the son of Ḥanani"[48]  Marketed

**(53) Pedaiah, son of (52) Jehoiachin, king of Judah; 1 Chr 3:16 19:**

[62] seal לפדיהו בן / המלך, "Belonging to Pedayahu, the king's son" WSS, no. 19 (see Appendix B, note 45, second paragraph)  Marketed

**(54) Azzur, father of (55) Jaazaniah; Ezek 11:1;**
AND
**(55) Jaazaniah, son of (54) Azzur; Ezek 11:1:**

[63] accounting ostracon, line 3, II צ III נ עזר בן יאזניהו, "Ya'azanyahu, the son of ʿAzzur, n III ṣ II"[49]  Marketed

**(56) Malchiah, the king's son; Jer 38:6:**

[64] seal למלכיהו / בן המלך, "Belonging to Malkiyahu, the king's son"[50] WSS, no. 15  Marketed

**(57) Azzur of Gibeon, father of (58) Hananiah the false prophet; Jer 28:1ff:**

[65] seal לחנניהו / בן עזריהו, "Belonging to Ḥananyahu, the son of ʿAzaryahu" AHI, no. 100.024; WSS, no. 165  Marketed

[66 group] 7 Gibeon jar handle inscriptions (only 1 complete) גבען גדר / עזריהו, "Gibeʿon. Wall of ʿAzaryahu" AHI, nos. 22.001 through 22.007 (22.012 is doubtful)  Excavated

---

[48] Lemaire, "Nouvelles donées épigraphiques sur l'époque royale israélite," 445–61; idem, "Nouveaux sceaux et bulles paléo-hébraïques," 108* and 111*, no. 10, photograph on 110*, no 22. Numberings (51a) and (51b) are due to an earlier, accidental omission of (51a) Hananiah that was discovered late in the book production process.

[49] Deutsch and Heltzer, *New Epigraphic Evidence from the Biblical Period*, 83–88, no. 77, 84, Fig. 77, and 85, Fig. 77a. They date the ostracon to "the first quarter of the VI cent. B.C.E." (ibid., 83), but without explanation, they allow "no possibility" (ibid., 85) of this ID. Major commentaries date Ezek 8:1 and 11:1 to the same year, which Greenberg affirms is 592 (Greenberg, *Ezekiel 1–20*, 166, 186), and both passages seem to imply that the men who are named (in Ezek 8:11; 11:1, 13) are recognizable public figures.

[50] Deutsch and Lemaire, *Biblical Period Personal Seals*, 29, no. 23. The letter *he* in the upper register is from the late seventh century (Vaughn, "Palaeographic Dating of Judaean Seals," 47, 52–53).

**(58) Hananiah the false prophet, son of (57) Azzur of Gibeon; Jer 28:1ff:**

[65] seal לחנניהו / בן עזריהו, "Belonging to Ḥananyahu, the son of ʿAzaryahu" *AHI*, no. 100.024; *WSS*, no. 165 — Marketed

**(61) Jaazaniah, the son of the Maacathite; 2 Kgs 25: 23; probably called Jezaniah in Jer 40:8:**

[70] Tell en-Naṣbeh seal ליאזניהו / עבד המלך, "Belonging to Yaʾazanyahu, the king's minister" *AHI*, no. 100.069; *WSS*, no. 8 — Excavated

**(62) Ishmael of royal descent, son of Nethaniah, son of (42) Elishama; 2 Kgs 25: 23, 25; Jer 40:8ff:**

[71] bulla לישמעאל / בן המלך, "Belonging to Yišmaʿʾel, the king's son"[51] — Marketed

**(71) Hazael, king of Aram at Damascus (r. 844/842–ca. 800, father of (72) Ben-hadad II or III; 1 Kgs 19:15ff:**

[81] Arslan Tash (ancient Hadattah) ivory piece · זי ק[רב עמא / למראן · חזאל · בשנת] (break) אח[זת · ח]ור[ן?], "That which the people presented to Lord Hazaʾel in the year [(break) sie]zed H[ʔoron?]"[52] cf. section 3.5 — Excavated

**(77) Baalis, king of the Ammonites (r. early sixth century); Jer 40:14:**

[89] Tell el-Umeiri ceramic cone (bottle stopper?) with seal impression למלכמאור / עב / ד בעלישע, "Belonging to Milkomʿur, the minister of Baʿalyašaʿ" (or Baʿalîšaʿ) *WSS*, no. 860 — Excavated

[90] seal [ל[בעל ישע] / מלך / בנ[עמן], "[Belonging to] Baʿalyašaʿ[ʿ], the king of the so[ns of ʿAmmon]"[53] (or Baʿalîša[ʿ]) — Marketed

---

[51] Barkay, "Bulla of Ishmael, the King's Son," 109–14.

[52] Fitzmyer and Kaufman, *Aramaic Bibliography, Part I*, 12–13, section B.1.4; *KAI*, Nr. 232; Gibson, *Aramaic Inscriptions*, 4–5, no. 2, Fig. 6; Puech, "L'ivoire inscrit d'Arslan Tash et les rois de Damas," 544–62, Pl. 12, 13; Mallowan, *Nimrud and Its Remains*, 2:507–8, 598–99, 654 n. 84; Barnett, *Ancient Ivories*, 48.

[53] Deutsch, "Seal of Baʿalis Surfaces," 46–49, 60, color photograph on front cover; Deutsch and Heltzer, *West Semitic Epigraphic News*, 53–57, no. 145 (47).

## C.6 In the Remainder, Not the Corpus: Doubtful Identifications: Grade 1

Because sections C.6, C.7, and C.8, comprising IDs in grades 1, 0, and D, respectively, contain either completely unreliable IDs or else non-IDs, there is little point in repeating the detailed information already listed in Appendix B. Nevertheless, below is a brief list of them in each grade, both to show all categories of results and to illustrate that not all inscriptions that are evaluated in this study name biblical persons.

Of course, a person who is *not* identifiable in *some* inscriptions may well be *reliably* or *certainly* identifiable in *other* inscriptions. Therefore, the lists in sections C.6 through C.8 do *not* amount to an assertion that *no* inscription at all offers a reliable ID of the person.

Appendix B lists at least one grade 1 ID of each of the following persons in an excavated or marketed inscription:

(5) Semachiah, son of Shemaiah, son of Obed-edom and temple gatekeeper; 1 Chr 26:7; in inscription [6]
(8) Jezebel, daughter of (70) Ethbaal, king of the Sidonians, and queen of Israel (r. ca. 873–852); 1 Kgs 16:31ff; in [8]
(13) Zechariah, son of (12) Jeroboam II, king of Israel (r. 750–749); 2 Kgs 15: 8–12; in [11]
(14) Shallum, son of Jabesh and king of Israel (r. 749); 2 Kgs 15:10ff; in [4]
(15) Pekah, king of Israel (r. 750?–732/1); 2 Kgs 15:25ff; in [12], [13], [14]
(19) Zechariah, son of Jehoiada, the priest, under (18) J(eh)oash, son of Ahaziah, king of Judah; 2 Chr 24:20; in [10]
(20) Uzziah/Azariah, son of Amaziah, king of Judah (r. 788/7–736/5); 2 Kgs 14: 21ff; in [19 group], [20 group]
(25) Shebna, the overseer of the palace; Isa 22: 15–19, who might be the same person as (26) Shebna, the scribe, in a different assignment; in [18], [19 group], [20 group], [33], [36], [37 group], [38], [39]
(26) Shebna, the scribe of (23) Hezekiah, king of Judah; 2 Kgs 18:18ff, who might be the same person as (25) Shebna, the overseer of the palace, in a different assignment; in the same inscriptions as (25) Shebna, plus [34]
(28) Eliakim, son of (27) Hilqiah and the overseer of the palace of (23) Hezekiah; 2 Kgs 18:18ff, Isa 22:20–25; in [41 group]
(30) Joah, son of (29) Asaph and the recorder of (23) Hezekiah, king of Judah; 2 Kgs18:18, 26, 37; Isa 36:3, 11, 22; in [27]
(31) Amariah, an overseer of distribution of freewill offerings under (23) Hezekiah, king of Judah, during the chief priesthood of Azariah; 2 Chr 31:15; in [30]
(44) Elnathan, son of Achbor and an official of Jehoiakim, king of Judah; Jer 26:22; 36:12; in [56]

(59) Gedaliah, son of Pashhur; Jer 38:1; in [68], [69]
(60) Gedaliah, governor of Judah under Babylonian rule and son of (39) Ahikam, son of (36) Shaphan the scribe, son of (34) Azaliah, son of (33) Meshullam; 2 Kgs 25: 22ff; in [68], [69]
(74) Sargon II, king of Assyria (r. 721–705); Isa 20:1; in [87]: SI or 1

## C.7 In the Remainder, Not the Corpus: Non-identifications Due to Absence of a Clear Basis: Grade 0 (Zero)

The two opening paragraphs of section C.6 explain the cursory listing below. Appendix B lists only one grade 0 (signifying no clear basis for an ID) non-ID in a provenanced or marketed inscription for each of the following:

(1) "Hophni," son of Eli the priest; 1 Sam 1:3ff; in [1]
(7) Omri, king of Israel, (r. 884–873); 1 Kgs 16:16ff; in [2]
(10) J(eh)oram, son of Ahab, king of Israel (r. 851–842/1); 2 Kgs 3:1ff; in [2]
(17) Ahaziah, son of Jehoram, king of Judah (r. 843/2–842/1); 2 Kgs 8:25ff; in [2]
(68) Ben-hadad I or II, king of Aram at Damascus (r. early ninth century to 844/842); 1 Kgs 15:18ff; in [2]
(74) Sargon II, king of Assyria (r. 721–705); Isa 20:1; in [83]

## C.8 In the Remainder, Not the Corpus: Disqualified Non-identifications Known to be Impossible (or Virtually So): Grade D

The two opening paragraphs of section C.6 explain the cursory listing below. Appendix B lists only one grade D (for disqualified) non-ID in a provenanced or unprovenanced inscription for each of the following persons:[54]

(3) Solomon, son of (2) David, king of Israel (r. ca. 970–931/930); 2 Sam 5:14ff; in [4]
(6) Jeroboam I, son of Nebat and king of Israel (r. 931/30– 909); 1 Kgs 11: 26ff;

---

[54] As this book goes to press, I am aware of only one inscription that both qualifies within the limits of section 3.1 and offers a potential ID but is not in Appendixes B and C. It is a likely sixth-century, unprovenanced, bronze seal ring having a grade D non-ID of Ahab, king of Israel (Uehlinger, "Ahabs königliches Siegel?" 77–116; idem, "The Seal of Ahab, King of Israel?" *Michmanim* 11 [1997]: 39*–52*; Nahman Avigad, Michael Heltzer, and André Lemaire, *West Semitic Seals: Eighth–Sixth Centuries B.C.E.* [in Hebrew and English] [ed. Ronny Reich; The Reuben and Edith Hecht Museum Collection B; Haifa: University of Haifa, 2000], 165, no. 136 [treated by Lemaire]).

in [7]
(9) Obadiah, the overseer of the palace of Ahab, king of Israel (r. 873–852); 1 Kgs 18:3ff; in [9]
(17) Ahaziah, son of Jehoram, king of Judah (r. 843/2–842/1), 2 Kgs 8.25ff, in [16]
(21) Jotham, son of (20) Uzziah, king of Judah (r. 758/7–742/1); 2 Kgs 15:5ff; in [22]
(22) Ahaz, son of (21) Jotham, king of Judah (r. 742/1–726); 2 Kgs 15:38ff; in [16]
(25) Shebna, the overseer of the palace; Isa 22:15–19, who might be the same person as (26) Shebna, the scribe, in a different assignment; in [35]
(26) Shebna, the scribe of (23) Hezekiah, king of Judah; 2 Kgs 18:18ff, who might be the same person as (25) Shebna, the overseer of the palace, in a different assignment; in [35]
(29) Asaph, father of (30) Joah the recorder of (23) Hezekiah, king of Judah; 2 Kgs 18:18, 37; Isa 36:3, 22; in [43]
(32) Manasseh, son of (23) Hezekiah, king of Judah (697/6– 642/1); 2 Kgs 20: 21ff; in [44]
(43) Jehoahaz/Shallum, son of (35) Josiah, king of Judah (r. 609); 2 Kgs 23:30ff; in [4]
(45) Shallum, father of Maaseiah the keeper of the temple threshold; Jer 35:4; in [4]
(48) Jerahmeel, the king's son; Jer 36:26; in [60]
(52) "Jehoiachin"/Jeconiah/Coniah, son of Jehoiakim, king of Judah; 2 Kgs 24: 6ff; in [41 group]
(58) Hananiah the false prophet, son of (57) Azzur of Gibeon; Jer 28:1ff; in [67 group]
(60) Gedaliah, son of (39) Ahikam, son of (36) Shaphan the scribe, and Governor of Judah under Babylonian rule; 2 Kgs 25: 22ff; in [68]
(65) Achish, king of Gath (r. between late eleventh and early to mid-tenth century); 1 Sam 21:11ff; in [73]
(66) Hiram, king of Tyre (r. mid-tenth century); 2 Sam 5:11ff; in [74], [75]
(67) Hadadezer, son of Rehob and king of Zobah (r. early to mid-tenth century); 2 Sam 8: 3ff; in [76]
(68) Ben-hadad I or II, king of Aram at Damascus (r. early ninth century to 844/842); 1 Kgs 15:18ff; in [77]
(70) Ethbaal, king of the Sidonians (r. early to mid-ninth century) and father of (8) Jezebel, queen of Israel; 1 Kgs 16:31; in [74]
(78) Belshazzar (Bel-šarra-uṣur), son and coregent of Nabonidus, king of Babylon (coregency ca. 553–539); Dan 5:1ff; in [91]

# Appendix D

# Index of Biblical Persons in Appendixes B and C

(65) Achish, king of Gath
(22) Ahaz, son of (21) Jotham, king of Judah
(17) Ahaziah, son of J(eh)oram, king of Judah
(39) Ahikam, son of (36) Shaphan the scribe
(31) Amariah, an overseer of distribution of freewill offerings under (23) Hezekiah, king of Judah
(40) Asaiah, the minister of (35) Josiah, king of Judah
(29) Asaph, father of (30) Joah the recorder
(34) Azaliah, son of (33) Meshullam
(38) Azariah, son of (37) Hilkiah the high priest
(54) Azzur, father of (55) Jaazaniah
(57) Azzur of Gibeon, father of (58) Hananiah the false prophet

(77) Baalis, king of the Ammonites
(64) Balaam, son of (63) Beor

(47) Baruch the scribe, son of (46) Neriah
(78) Belshazzar, son and coregent of Nabonidus, king of Babylon
(68) Ben-hadad I or II, king of Aram at Damascus (assassinated by Hazael)
(72) Ben-hadad II or III, son of (71) Hazael, king of Aram at Damascus
(63) Beor, father of (64) Balaam

(2) David, son of Jesse and king of Israel

(28) Eliakim, son of (27) Hilkiah and the overseer of the palace of (23) Hezekiah, king of Judah
(42) Elishama, father of Nethaniah, father of (62) Ishmael
(44) Elnathan son of Achbor and an official of Jehoiakim, king of Judah

## Appendix D

(70) Ethbaal, king of the Sidonians and father of (8) Jezebel, queen of Israel

(59) Gedaliah, son of Pashhur
(60) Gedaliah, son of (39) Ahikam and governor of Judah under Babylonian rule
(50) Gemariah, son of (36) Shaphan the scribe

(67) Hadadezer, son of Rehob and king of Zobah
(51a) Hananiah, father of (51b) Zedekiah who was a *śar* of Judah
(58) Hananiah the false prophet, son of (57) Azzur of Gibeon
(71) Hazael, king of Aram at Damascus, father of (72) Ben-hadad II or III
(23) Hezekiah, son of Ahaz, king of Judah
(37) Hilkiah the high priest, father of (38) Azariah
(24) Hilkiah (= (27)?), the minister of (23) Hezekiah, king of Judah
(27) Hilkiah (= (24)?), father of (28) Eliakim the overseer of (23) King Hezekiah's palace
(66) Hiram, king of Tyre
(1) "Hophni," son of Eli the priest
(16) Hoshea, son of Elah and king of Israel

(62) Ishmael of royal descent, son of Nethaniah, son of (42) Elishama

(55) Jaazaniah, son of (54) Azzur
(61) Jaazaniah, son of the Maacathite
(43) Jehoahaz/Shallum, son of Josiah, king of Judah
(11) J(eh)oash, son of Jehoahaz, king of Israel
(18) J(eh)oash, son of Ahaziah, king of Judah

(52) Jehoiachin/Jeconiah/Coniah, son of Jehoiakim, king of Judah
(10) J(eh)oram, son of Ahab, king of Israel
(48) Jerahmeel, the king's son
(6) Jeroboam I, son of Nebat and king of Israel
(12) Jeroboam II, son of Joash, king of Israel
(8) Jezebel, daughter of (70) Ethbaal, king of the Sidonians, and queen of Israel
(30) Joah, son of (29) Asaph and the recorder of (23) Hezekiah, king of Judah
(35) Josiah, son of Amon, king of Judah
(21) Jotham, son of Uzziah, king of Judah

(56) Malchiah, the king's son
(32) Manasseh, son of (23) Hezekiah, king of Judah
(69) Mesha, king of Moab
(33) Meshullam, father of (34) Azaliah
(4) Mikneiah, a Levitical singer and lyrist in the procession of the ark of the covenant into Jerusalem

(41) Nathan-melech the eunuch
(76) Nebuchadnezzar II, king of Babylon
(46) Neriah, son of Mahseiah and father of (47) Baruch the scribe (see (49) below)

(9) Obadiah, the overseer of the palace of Ahab, king of Israel
(7) Omri, king of Israel

(53) Pedaiah, son of Jehoiachin/Jeconiah/Coniah, king of Judah
(15) Pekah, king of Israel

(74) Sargon II, king of Assyria
(5) Semachiah, son of Shemaiah, son of Obed-edom, and temple gatekeeper
(75) Sennacherib, king of Assyria
(49) Seraiah, the son of Neriah (= (46) Neriah?)
(14) Shallum, son of Jabesh and king of Israel
(45) Shallum, father of Maaseiah the keeper of the Temple threshold
(36) Shaphan the scribe, son of (34) Azaliah
(25) Shebna (= (26)?), the overseer of the palace of (23) Hezekiah, king of Judah
(26) Shebna (= (25)?), the scribe of (23) Hezekiah, king of Judah

(3) Solomon, son of David, king of Israel
(73) Tiglath-pileser III, king of Assyria
(20) Uzziah/Azariah, son of Amaziah, king of Judah
(13) Zechariah, son of Jeroboam II, king of Israel
(19) Zechariah, son of Jehoiada, the priest
(51b) Zedekiah, son of (51a) Hananiah and a *śar* of Judah

# Appendix E

# Is the Biblical King David Named in the Mesha Inscription?

## E.1 Line 31 of the Mesha Inscription (not discussed above)

In 1994, André Lemaire published two articles that show credible grounds for restoring the name of the biblical King David in the phrase ב[ת]דו, "the house of David," in the Mesha Inscription, line 31, based on materials in the Grand Louvre.[1] In the apparent absence of evaluative, let alone corroborative, studies published by other scholars,[2] however, Mykytiuk's 1998 dissertation,

---

[1] Lemaire, "Dynastie Davidique (*byt dwd*) dans deux inscriptions"; idem, "'House of David' Restored in Moabite Inscription." Lemaire had concluded that there is a reference to "the house of David" in the Mesha Inscription "nearly two years before the discovery of the [first] . . . fragment" of the Aramaic stele at Tel Dan (i.e., Tel Qadi) in 1993 (ibid., 32). (Before these articles appeared, the Louvre Museum in Paris had been renamed the Grand Louvre.)

[2] Sometime during 1997, Kitchen published an article expressing approval of Lemaire's restoration of ב[ת]דוד in line 31 (Kitchen, "Possible Mention of David in the Late Tenth Century." Also during 1997, Parker also used Lemaire's restoration, indicating some reserve by a parenthetical question mark: "the House of [Da]vid(?)" (Simon B. Parker, *Stories in Scripture and Inscriptions: Comparative Studies on Narratives in Northwest Semitic Inscriptions and the Hebrew Bible* [New York: Oxford University Press, 1997], 46). He refers to this restoration in three places (ibid., 46 [bis] and 155, n. 13). The beginning of October 1997 was the deadline for publications to be used in the 1998 diss. (see section 3.1 above). Whether Kitchen's article and Parker's book were

266   *Identifying Biblical Persons in Northwest Semitic Inscriptions*

published above (through Appendix D), treated Lemaire's restoration very cautiously. This item appeared in the dissertation version of Appendixes B and C but not as an identification (ID), so it did not receive discussion. Its present evaluation above in Appendixes B and C places it in the grade of an unmistakable match, both on the basis of inscriptional data and, separately, on the basis of biblical data. This is the strongest level of ID. In view of this revised evaluation, this newly added appendix supplies discussion which did not appear in the original dissertation.[3]

**Is the biblical King David named in line 31 of the Mesha Inscription?**

See section 3.3 above on the inscription itself, on the matter of reliability of inscriptional data (i.e., "Question 1"), on the setting of the inscription apart from biblical data, and on how inscriptional information correlates with the historical framework. On how it contributes to that framework, see section 3.3 above and "Remarks" below in this appendix.

**Question 2: whether the setting of the inscription permits a match**

If the biblical David existed, reigned over Judah and Israel, and founded a dynasty that ruled during the tenth and later centuries, then during the ninth century, Mesha, king of Moab, would certainly have known of his dynasty. The Mesha Inscription permits a match in that the setting in which it would place such a personage presents no obstacle to identifying him as the biblical King David.

**Question 3: how strongly the specific data in [3] the Mesha stele from Dhiban count for or against an identification with the biblical (2) King David in line 31 (1 Sam 16:13ff; r. ca. 1010–970)**

A check (√) means that a criterion has been met.
  √ **Name: 5)** The root letters of the name are fragmentary or lacking. In the space occupied by the phrase restored as בת[ד]וד, there is room for only five letters. The first, second, fourth, and fifth letters are, in varying degrees, frag-

---

published and actually available in the United States before or after that deadline, I was unaware of them as of the cutoff point.

[3] This discussion is not located in Chapter 3, because at this point in time, in accordance with the guidelines for this monograph series, the main body of this work (i.e., Chapters 1–5) has been preserved without substantial change. Rather than present current readers with a strong ID but no rationale, discussion appears here at the urging of a series reviewer and with editorial permission.

mentary, but even in the damaged stone enough of each is present to narrow the range of possible letters significantly. The third (middle) letter is destroyed.

With guidance from researchers' published direct observations of the stele or of both it and the squeeze(s) (see below), one can narrow the possibilities for each letter by examining photographs of this phrase in the stele, as follows.[4] The first letter's head and vertical shaft are present, narrowing the possibilities to *beth* and *resh*. A likely, perfectly positioned foot for a *beth* is visible in photographs, making a shallow descent diagonally toward the left but severed from the vertical shaft by a curving crack in the stone. Part of the second letter is discernible in a diagonal stroke from the viewer's upper right to the center of the letter, suggesting a *tav*. This diagonal might also seem to be the right-hand stroke of a *shin* or *kaph* or part of yet other letters, but the other strokes that would form letters besides *tav* do not appear, whereas the photograph at least hints at the other, intersecting diagonal stroke of a *tav*. This cross-stroke is either alongside the curving crack mentioned above or is swallowed up by this crack as it ascends toward the viewer's left. The third letter has been obliterated by a break in the stone. The fourth letter could be either *qoph* or *waw*, depending on the shape of the top of the letter. Photographs of the stele show the top to be open and lacking a vertical line through the middle of the head, making it appear to be a *waw*. The upper portion of the fifth letter could be that of a *daleth*, *beth*, or *resh*, but the vertical shaft of a *beth* or a *resh* is absent, so it seems to be a *daleth*.

For better accuracy and assurance, it is necessary to use the complete paper squeeze that was made before the stele was broken.[5] Although this squeeze has not been published, we have the aid of publications by scholars who have examined it in their attempts to identify the letters.[6] According to these scholars, it makes possible the identification of most of the five letters.

---

[4] Two photographs of the phrase in question as it appears on the stele are published in Lemaire, "'House of David' Restored in Moabite Inscription," 35. The lower photo traces the restored letters in yellow.

[5] Lemaire, "'House of David' Restored in Moabite Inscription," 33–34; a small photograph of the complete squeeze appears in ibid., 36. After the stele was broken, both Charles Warren and Charles Clermont-Ganneau had Arab assistants make squeezes of available fragments; the Louvre Museum became the ultimate repository for all squeezes and recovered fragments (M. Patrick Graham, "The Discovery and Reconstruction of the Mesha Inscription," in Dearman, *Studies*, 69–73, 75).

[6] Charles Clermont-Ganneau, "La stèle de Dhiban," *RAr* (1870): 184–207, 357–386; idem, *La stèle de Mésa roi de Moab 896 av. J.-C.: Lettres à M. le Cte. de Vogüé* (Paris: Librarie Polytechnique de J. Baudry, 1870); idem, "La stèle de Mésa," *Revue Critique* (September 11, 1875): 166–74; idem, "La stèle de Mésa, examen critique du texte" *JA* 9 (8th series, 1887): 107; K. G. Amandus Nordlander, *Die Inschrift des Königs Mesa von Moab* (Leipzig: W. Drugulin, 1896); Mark Lidzbarski, "Eine Nachprüfung der Me-

In their publications, the following read a five-letter phrase:
Clermont-Ganneau (1887): ב[--]וד[7]; 1875: "Serait-ce un nom proper *b..wd*?"[8]
Lidzbarski (1902): בת[-]9וק[10]
Dussaud (1912): ב[-]וד[11]
Lemaire (1994): בת[ד]וד[12]

Others read these letters as part of a longer phrase:
Nordlander (1896): בני[׳] / ח[׳]ור[ן] / א[שר][13]
Sidersky (1920): בת[·]וד .... אש[14]

---

sainschrift," in *Ephemeris für semitische Epigraphik* (Giessen: J. Ricker, Alfred Töpelmann, 1902–1915) 1:1–10; René Dussaud, *Les monuments palestiniens et judaiques: Moab, Judée, Philistie, Samarie, Galilée* (Paris: Ernest Leroux, 1912), 4–20 (at the head of Dussaud's title are the words Musée du Louvre, Département des antiquités orientales, which some read as the beginning of the title); David Sidersky, *Stèle de Mésa: index bibliographique* (Paris: Ernest Leroux, 1920); Henri Michaud, "Le récit de II Rois, III et la Stèle de Mésha," in idem, *Sur la pierre et l'argile: inscriptions hébraïques et l'Ancien Testament* (Cahiers d'archéology biblique 10; Neuchatel: Delachaux et Niestlé, 1958), 29–45. These might not be all the relevant publications of all scholars who have ever used the Mesha Inscription materials in the Louvre firsthand, but these are main publications representing its content.

Among publications which are apparently dependent on the writings of firsthand observers is that of Van Zyl, who reads *bt*[- -]*wd* (A. H. Van Zyl, *The Moabites* [Pretoria Oriental Series 3; Leiden: Brill, 1960], Addendum I). In the same category is Kent P. Jackson and J. Andrew Dearman, "The Text of the Meshaʿ Inscription," pp. 93–95, in Dearman, *Studies*. Apparently following Lidzbarski in reading *qoph*, Jackson and Dearman read *b*[- - -]*wq*[- -] *ʾš*[-] (p. 95, followed in the translation on p. 98). The drawing in Figure 1 of the same book disagrees with their transcription, showing a *beth* followed by a space that might have contained two letters, followed by *waw* and *daleth*. It then omits the last two letters in that line (Figure 1 lacks an attribution of authorship).

[7] Clermont-Ganneau, revising his earlier (1870) reading of the fifth letter as *aleph* ("Stèle de Dhiban," 375), suggests *daleth* in 1887 ("Stèle de Mésa, examen critique du texte," 107).

[8] Clermont-Ganneau, "Stèle de Mésa," 173; cf. idem, "Stèle de Mésa: examen critique du texte," 107.

[9] Lidzbarski, "Nachprüfung der Mesainschrift," 9.

[10] "Das Zeichen nach ב kann man ja für ein נ halten, doch scheint es mir eher ein ת zu sein" (ibid.).

[11] Dussaud, *Monuments palestiniens*, 5.

[12] Lemaire, "Dynastie Davidique" 18; idem, "'House of David' Restored in Moabite Inscription," 36.

[13] Nordlander, *Inschrift des Königs Mesa*, 19, 60.

[14] Sidersky, *Stèle de Mésa: index bibliographique*, 11.

*Appendix E*          269

## Fig. 18

### Portions of the Mesha Inscription Containing the Name of King David

(Excerpted from a drawing by Mark Lidzbarski except for Lemaire's new reading drawn in by the author)

The *daleth* in line 31b is in accordance with Lemaire's new reading:

                                                                                line

                   [Paleo-Hebrew inscription]       31b

Rainey's analysis has shed welcome light on the syntax of the last two words below:

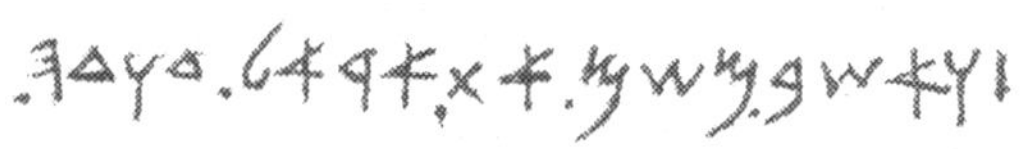

                                                                                line

                   [Paleo-Hebrew inscription]       12b

Lidzbarski's reading of the fifth letter as a *qoph* instead of a *daleth* raises the only serious *epigraphic* question about the reading of David's name in this phrase. He describes part of a letter consisting of a short horizontal line touched at its right tip by the right tip of a short, diagonal line above it. This line above, descending toward the right, forms an acute angle with the horizontal line. He regards this angle as a reliably observable ("sicher") fragment of the right side of a letter.[15] Several other researchers who seem to perceive the same acute angle interpret it as the right corner of a legless, triangular *daleth*. Lidzbarski, however, considers it to be a right corner of the head a *qoph* whose head is flat on the bottom. (Among the variety of *qoph* heads elsewhere in the Mesha Inscription, the lower edges are mostly rounded but in a few instances angular, like this fifth letter.) Lidzbarski compares his interpretation favorably against competing readings which are clearly inferior, i.e., the forced reading of Nordlander, which tries to supply too many letters in the available space, and that of Smend and Socin.[16] But the surprising fact is that Lidzbarski does not treat the possibility that the fifth letter might be *daleth*, as in Clermont-Ganneau's then well-known reading. Instead, he mentions what he sees as pieces of the vertical shaft of a *qoph* which he claims to be visible. With observable consistency, however, other researchers who have examined the broken stele and the complete squeeze firsthand either do not find these alleged shaft fragments or do not interpret such marks as Lidzbarski did.

In sum, the above list of the readings of these firsthand observers shows that they agree with Lidzbarski that the second letter is *tav* and with Clermont-Ganneau that the fifth letter is *daleth*. To these may be added the initial letter *beth* and the fourth letter *waw*, which, as Lidzbarski observes, are secure readings.[17] Combining these four letters, the resulting reading that has attracted the strongest support is בת[-]וד.

Lemaire bases his restoration not only on the epigraphic evidence of the stele and the complete squeeze, but also on the sense of the text, briefly presenting the parallels:

> The term bt[d]wd is the subject of the sentence that begins earlier in line 31 . . . . The sentence begins, "And as for Horonen [a place], dwelt there . . ." Then comes the subject. That what follows identifies who lives in Horonen is clear from parallel passages elsewhere in the inscription involving Israel . . . . For example, in lines 7–8 we read, "Omri [previously identified in lines 4–5 as the king of Israel] had taken possession of the land of Medeba, and he dwelt there . . ." It is clear that bt[d]wd is probably a designation for a king. It appears that the only possible resto-

---

[15] Lidzbarski, "Nachprüfung der Mesainschrift," 9.

[16] Rudolf Smend and Albert Socin, *Die Inschrift des Königs Mesa von Moab für akademische Vorlesungen* (Freiburg im Brisgau: J.C.B. Mohr, 1886).

[17] See note 15.

ration is *bt*[*d*]*wd*, the "House of David," just as the "king of Israel" (*mlk ysr'l*) is mentioned three times earlier. Moreover, referring to the king of Judah by reference to the "House" of David has several parallels in the Bible (2 Samuel 7:26; 1 Kings 2:24, etc.).[18]

To expand on Lemaire's statements, a particular narrative pattern for Mesha's separate campaigns appears no less than three times before line 31 and then once more in lines 31–32: X (an enemy king or a socio-political entity under an enemy king's control) lived in/occupied/settled in Y (a GN) . . . but Kemosh (or: but I, with mention of Kemosh) . . . . After the three earlier occurrences, its fourth occurrence implicitly calls for the five letters in line 31 which are treated above to be once more either an enemy king or a socio-political entity under his control. The excerpts below exhibit this pattern:

*First campaign: the land of Mehadaba*
line
7 . . . . Now Omri had taken possession of the la[n] /
8 d of Mehadaba, and he lived in it during his days and half the days of his son(s), forty years. But
9 Kemosh lived in it during my days. . . .

*Second campaign: ʿAtaroth*
10 . . . . Now the Gadites had always lived in the land of ʿAtaroth, and the king of I /
11 srael had rebuilt ʿAtaroth for himself. But I fought against the city [or: Qir] and took it, and I killed all the people, [so]
12 the city [or: Qir] belonged to Kemosh and to Moab. . . .

*Fourth campaign: Yahaṣ (Jahaz)*
18 . . . . Now the king of Israel had built
19 Yahaṣ, and he occupied it while he was fighting against me. But Kemosh drove him out from before me. . . .

*Fifth campaign: Ḥawronen*
31 . . . . As for Ḥawronen, the house of [Da]vid had settled in it. [ ] ʾš[
32 But] Kemosh said to me, "Go down, fight against Ḥawronen." So I went down[
33 and] Kemosh [retur]ned it in my days. . . .

---

[18] Lemaire, "'House of David' Restored in Moabite Inscription," 36, brackets his, ellipses after the phrase "dwelt there" his, other ellipses mine.

A conquest account that may seem to be an exception to this pattern nevertheless contains each element in this same pattern: the socio-political entity under the control of the enemy king is Israel; it is implicit that Israel must have been occupying Nebo; and Mesha's "I" again accompanies mention of Kemosh:

*Third campaign: Nebo*
14 .... Now Kemosh said to me, "Go seize Nebo from Israel." So I
15 went at night and fought against it from the break of dawn until noon. I sei /zed
16 it and killed all in it—seven thousand native m[e]n, foreign [m]en, native women, [for]eign
17 women, and concubines—for I had devoted it to ʿAshtar-Kemosh. I took from there th[e ves] / sels
18 of Yahweh and dragged them before Kemosh . . . .

As Lemaire observes, all of the conquests except the one in lines 31–33 are defeats of Israel in locations which are north of the Arnon River. This observation leads to the expectation that Mesha's conquests south of the Arnon, of which the surviving text reports only the conquest of Ḥawronen, would be victories over an enemy to the south, either Judah or Edom.[19] Parker's precise grasp of the content of the Mesha Inscription tends to support this view in his arrangement of its content under four headings: A. Introduction (lines 1–4), B. Expulsion of Israel (lines 4–21), C. Building and Other Administrative Activities (lines 21–31), and D. Expulsion of Judah? (Cf. B) (lines 31–34).[20]

It is significant that Mesha does not leave the reader in doubt as to the identity of the founder of the enemy dynasty that ruled the northern kingdom of Israel, naming Omri twice (lines 4 and 7). But interestingly, Mesha names no other Israelite king, only the founder, though he mentions "his son" (line 6) and "his son(s)" (line 8). This way of referring to the Israelite rulers suggests that he would also refer to an enemy whom he fought south of the Arnon by the name of the dynasty's founder, again without naming any of the founder's successors.

---

[19] Lemaire is persuaded that at the time of the events mentioned in lines 31–33 of the Mesha Inscription, "The area southeast of the Dead Sea was apparently controlled by Judah" rather than Edom (Lemaire, "'House of David' Restored in Moabite Inscription," 37; see bibliography in ibid., 37, note marked by asterisk). Margalit provides a different restoration and argues for Edomite control (Baruch Margalit, "Studies in NWSemitic [sic] Inscriptions," *UF* 26 [1994]: 275–76). Parker finds Margalit's position "historically and geographically plausible, though without any textual basis" (Parker, *Stories in Scripture and Inscriptions*, 155, n. 13).

[20] Ibid., 44–46.

For a full year after Lemaire's restoration of the third letter as *daleth*, no scholar suggested any alternative.[21] In lines 31–32, immediately after "*wḥrnn. yšb. bh.,*" the restoration that Margalit proposed in 1995 is "*bt*[*m.*] *qd*[*my.*] *ʾš* [ *ʾdmy.* ]," noting that the letters *taw, qoph,* and *daleth* are uncertain.[22] His translation is, "Now Horoneyn was occupied at the en[d] of [my pre]decessor('s reign) by [Edom]ites." This restoration, in which Margalit states, "the alliterative factor plays a decisive role,"[23] results in forced wording. Too much meaning has to be supplied in and around the word *qd*[*my.*] in order to produce a statement that makes sense. Ultimately, this restoration is not convincing. Kitchen's 1997 comment is still correct:

> No better interpretation has so far been offered by any competent scholar, either for the restoration of [d] or for the rendering 'House of David' dependent on it.[24]

### E.2 Line 12 of the Mesha Inscription

Within the same inscription, a recent analysis discovered a parallel to Lemaire's restoration ד[ד] in line 31, offering support for it.[25] In 1998, Anson F.

---

[21] Lemaire's openness to reasonable alternative suggestions, and indeed his search for any, is clear in his response to a letter to the editor as follows:

... [A] suggestion to study other possible restorations is natural. From the paleographical point of view, the missing letter could be almost any Moabite letter. However there are not many north-west Semitic words in the form "-WD." After trying to find other solutions that would fit contextually, I saw none other than "[D]WD." Since meeting several colleagues during the last few months, none has proposed another letter. I am waiting for any proposition of another reasonable restoration. (André Lemaire, "André Lemaire Replies," *BAR* 20, no. 6 [November/December 1994]: 72)

[22] Margalit, "Studies in NWSemitic [sic] Inscriptions," 275. Notwithstanding the 1994 date given to this publication, it did not appear until after April, 1995. In the same issue, Margalit published a second article whose first sentence begins, "With the recent (April, 1995) publication of two additional fragments (B1 and B2) from the Old-Aramaic stele inscription from t. Dan . . . ." (idem, "The Old-Aramaic Inscription of Hazael from Dan," *UF* 26 [1994]: 317). This dating indicates that for a year after Lemaire published his restoration, other scholars found no alternative to propose.

[23] Ibid., 276.

[24] Kitchen, "Possible Mention of David," 36.

[25] Regarding possible PNs in inscriptions, such as ד[ד] in line 31 of the Mesha Inscription, in which "root letters (and/or letters from another non-theophoric part of the name) . . . are . . . indistinct, . . . fragmentary, or . . . lacking," the identification system set forth in Chapter 1 above states that "In such instances, a sure restoration is usually impossible without a clear parallel in the same inscription or an ancient copy of that inscription" (section 1.29 above, under point 5, italics mine only in this note). Whether a given researcher will see a parallel depends on his or her view of Lemaire's restoration in

Rainey published an article that both adopts Lemaire's restoration of בת[ד]וד in line 31 and proposes Rainey's analysis and interpretation of the Moabite phrase אראל דודה in line 12, translating it as "its Davidic altar-hearth."[26] Although the debate over the meaning of this phrase has extended over 130 years, suggesting that perhaps no proposed solution will ever gather a consensus, Rainey's proposal can be regarded as a genuine solution, and, indeed, it is quite convincing. It certainly deserves serious consideration as a reasonable, well-argued explanation, largely because of the clarity of his syntactic analysis.

A recurring objection to reading -דוד as a PN in אראל דודה has been a supposed rule that a proper noun cannot take a suffix. Such a phenomenon is infrequent but not entirely lacking in Northwest Semitic inscriptions.[27] Rainey's analysis, however, altogether avoids the question of a suffix attached simply to a proper noun by seeing the final ה- as a suffix attached to the end of a construct phrase, אראל דוד-, and modifying the *nomen regens*, אראל, rather than the *nomen rectum*, דוד.[28] Under the heading "Genitive Suffix on Genitive Phrase," Rainey states:

> However, the problem of a personal name with possessive suffix is not directly pertinent to the Meshaʿ passage in question. Actually, the present Meshaʿ passage only places the personal possessive pronoun on the name David (דודה) incidentally. The suffix is really intended for the אראל 'altar hearth' as we will now dem-

---

line 31, his or her analysis of the phrase אראל דודה in line 12, and/or his or her interpretation of דוד in both places.

[26] Anson F. Rainey, "Syntax, Hermeneutics and History," *IEJ* 48 (1998): 244–51. Based on linguistic and philological arguments in this article, and with the later help of digital graphics, Rainey proposed a restoration of the text in Moabite script in idem, "Following Up on the Ekron and Mesha Inscriptions," *IEJ* 50 (2000): 117. The proposed reference to David in line 31 also appears in idem, "Meshaʿ and Syntax," in *The Land that I Will Show You: Essays on the History and Archaeology of the Ancient Near East in Honor of J. Maxwell Miller* (ed. J. Andrew Dearman and M. Patrick Graham; Supplement Series 343; Sheffield, England: Sheffield Academic Press, 2001), 293, 307. Rainey argues for the proposed reference to David in line 12 in ibid., 300–304, 306.

[27] See Chapter 3, note 75, above; Shmuel Aḥituv, *Handbook of Ancient Hebrew Inscriptions: From the Period of the First Commonwealth and the Beginning of the Second Commonwealth (Hebrew, Philistine, Edomite, Moabite, Ammonite, and the Bileam Inscription)* (in Hebrew) (Biblical Encyclopaedia Library 7; Jerusalem: Bialik, 1992), 153–56; Manfried Dietrich and Oswald Loretz, *'Jahwe und seine Aschera': Anthropomorphes Kultbild in Mesopotamien, Ugarit und Israel* (Ugaritisch-biblische Literatur 9; Munster: Ugarit-Verlag, 1992).

[28] For the syntax of such a construction in Hebrew, see Bruce K. Waltke and Michael O'Connor, *An Introduction to Biblical Hebrew Syntax* (Winona Lake, Ind.: Eisenbrauns, 1990), 150, paragraph 9.5.3b, examples 20–23. On the terminology, see ibid., 137, paragraph 9.1b, or GKC 247, paragraph 89a.

demonstrate. It is necessary to explain the entire syntagma. The closest examples presently at hand are from Ugaritic and Hebrew, but they demonstrate the possibilities in the North West Semitic language family.[29]

He then presents four examples in Ugaritic and thirteen in biblical Hebrew.[30]

Before Rainey's proposal was published, Kitchen had discussed the phrase אראל דודה in line 12 as follows:

> The *dwd* here is most unlikely to be either a *David or a *Dod, because of the *-h* suffix, while the *ʾrʾl* can only be interpreted by guesswork, usually as 'altar hearth' or the like. If ritual furnishings are in view, then *dwdh* would also be such—'its vessel'?[31]

On the supposed difficulty with the ה- suffix, see examples to the contrary to which note 27 in this appendix refers. Of course, translating דודה as "its vessel" is a reasonable suggestion in a context of ritual furnishings. But assuming, in the apparent absence of clear syntactical alternatives, that אראל דודה is a construct phrase, this translation seems to create a strange usage. It would be referring to an altar-hearth (or other ritual object) as somehow "of" (belonging to?) "its vessel."

### E.3 The identification of King David paralleled in the Tel Dan stele

A parallel that is external to the Mesha Inscription is, of course, the term ביתדוד in line 9 of the Aramaic stele from Tel Dan, treated in section 3.5 above. It is noteworthy that this stele, written by another neighboring ruler who was hostile to the Hebrews, is dated within a century of the Mesha Inscription. For the sake of thoroughness, it should be mentioned that neither of the two compositions betrays any literary derivation from the other.[32] In the Aramaic

---

[29] Rainey, "Syntax, Hermeneutics and History," 248; the same paragraph appears in idem, "Mesha‛ and Syntax," 301, repeated in this later, fuller discussion "for the sake of completeness" (ibid., 300).
[30] Ibid., 301–303.
[31] Kitchen, "Possible Mention of David," 36.
[32] "The differences among the [Mesha, Tel Dan, and Sefire] inscriptions and their remoteness from one another eliminate any possibility of one inscription having been influenced by another" (Parker, *Stories in Scripture and Inscriptions*, 60). On the other hand, Parker points out the similarities in their narrative patterns and finds like patterns in biblical accounts of military campaigns (ibid., 53, 58, 59–60, 62). He attributes their similar patterns to a common theology of war: "The similarities among them [i.e., the three inscriptions] are best explained on the assumption that these Syro-Palestinian states shared a common ideology . . . and structured their narratives of military campaigns ac-

stele, the preponderance of evidence supports translating this term as "the house of David." It is a reference to the Davidic dynasty and/or the territory it ruled. This translation and interpretation has attracted the dissent of a small minority of scholars but also strong, widespread agreement among many more. The difference of a *yodh* in the spelling of ביתדוד and בת[ד]וד presents no real difficulty; both spellings are used interchangeably, for example, in the Mesha Inscription.[33]

On attestation of the root דוד among PNs in Hebrew, Aramaic, Ugaritic, and Old Akkadian, see Chapter 3, note 87. On the meaning of דוד, see above, section 3.5, under "Question 3," subheading "Name." On the interpretation of בת[ד]וד, see the discussion of the interpretation of the same phrase with the variant spelling ביתדוד above in section 3.5 under the heading "How the inscription contributes to the historical framework," interpretive options 1–7. Interpretive option 4, that בת[ד]וד might be a cultic object, finds a counterpart in Kitchen's proposal regarding the phrase אראל דודה in line 12, briefly discussed above near the end of section E.2.

**Relations**: 2) and 5) Family or other relational information is implicit, and in the inscription, filionymics are absent. See above, section 3.5, under the heading "Question 3," subheading "Relations."

√ **Title(s)**: 2) The title מֶלֶךְ is implied. See section 3.5 above, under the heading "Question 3," subheading "Title(s)."

**Other**: 1) and 3) Some of the inscriptional data agree explicitly and clearly with biblical account and some data are vague or ambiguous. See section 3.3, "Other data," paragraphs 1 through 5.

√ **Singularity**: 1) Available data require an ID on grounds of both inscriptional singularity and biblical singularity. See above, section 3.5, under the heading "Question 3," subheading "Singularity.'

---

cordingly" (ibid., 60; cf. ibid., 75 for a similar view that includes also the biblical accounts).

[33] That the word is spelled בת in lines 7, 23, 27, and 30 (bis), but בית in line 25 indicates that both spellings were then in use in Moabite (Lemaire, "La dynastie Davidique (*byt dwd*) dans deux inscriptions," 19; idem, "'House of David' Restored in Moabite Inscription," 36). The name of David as restored within the five-letter space is in exact agreement with the shorter of the two biblical spellings, i.e., the defective, three-consonant spelling. In general, epigraphers and paleographers usually regard defective spellings as earlier than *plene* spellings. In biblical materials, the three-consonant spelling דוד is more common in materials referring to the First Temple period, and the four-consonant spelling דויד is more common in materials referring to the Second Temple period. See above, section 3.5, under the heading "Name," note 88.

## E.4 Remarks

The evidence and discussion in this appendix, taken together with those in section 3.5 above, lead to the following further development of the statements under the heading "Remarks" at the end of section 3.5 above:

1. Although it is perhaps possible that the phrase בת[ד]וד, considered apart from context, might mean something other than "the house of David," surely in the context of the Mesha Inscription, this phrase is best translated as "the house of David," meaning "the Davidic dynasty" or "the Davidic realm," i.e., Judah. Because of the parallels in the Mesha Inscription which refer to the king of Israel, it is best interpreted there as a reference to the member(s) of the Davidic dynasty who during the decades before the writing of the Mesha Inscription had ruled over the kingdom of Judah. The strength of this interpretation in the Mesha Inscription lends additional plausibility both to the same parallel between "the king of Israel" and "the house of David" in the Tel Dan stele and to the same interpretation of "the house of David" in the Tel Dan stele.

2. Three independent sources attest to the fact that a dynasty called בת[ד]וד, "the house of David" existed. It is mentioned once in the Tel Dan stele, twice in the Mesha Inscription, and many times in the Hebrew Bible.

Further, both stelae document that the rule of the Davidic dynasty extended into the era of their authors. According to biblical chronology, the two stelae were written sometime between a little over a century and a little over two centuries after the dynasty was founded. As to the location of this kingdom, not only the provenance of recovered seals and bullae, but geographic considerations in the Mesha Inscription favor Judah as the location of the realm of the house of David.

3. "The house of David" named in inscriptions and in the Bible was a political entity referred to as such by the use of international terminology appropriate for political entities. Not only the Aramaeans, but also the Moabites applied this terminology to the Davidic dynasty, as did the authors of the books of the Hebrew Bible that pertain to the monarchic period.

4. The house of David was important enough to be recognized internationally and was considered significant enough to be mentioned in both Aramaean and Moabite public monuments, likely as a powerful enemy, so that the rulers who defeated it in battle could justly boast.

5. King David's personal existence and his status as the founder of a dynasty that ruled Judah are now documented in two non-Hebrew monumental inscriptions, as well as in several books of the Hebrew Bible.

# Appendix F

# Numerical Tabulation of Identifications in Appendixes B and C by Grade

*The Key to the Tables and the Definition of an Identification*

The key to the tables below is at the beginning of Appendix B. Appendixes B and C include all identifications (IDs) and non-IDs in this book. In this study, an ID is an instance of a particular inscription referring by name to a biblical person with some degree of likelihood or reasonableness, *regardless of how many times that person's name may occur in that inscription*. This definition attempts to maintain the separateness of each written source of evidence (or related group of written sources) as an attesting "witness." If both a seal and an ostracon clearly refer to the same person, there are two IDs, i.e., two instances of separate sources naming that one person. If the ostracon names the person twice, then it has only one ID but two occurrences of the name.

*Conservative Counting of Identifications*

As in Appendixes B and C, if an ID appears in inscriptions which should, in fairness, be grouped together, e.g., two or more impressions made by the same seal, or a seal and its impression(s), then only one ID is counted for the whole group. In the tables below, suppose that after evaluation, two or more biblical persons remain as competing candidates for one ID in an inscription. Because there is still no specific ID, none is counted. This applies to counting only. For example, [10], the "three shekels" ostracon, has three candidates, so no ID is counted. Also, if there is uncertainty about the grade of an ID, then the lower grade is counted. For example, [87], the Khorsabad bulla, might name (74) Sargon II. This ID that is either grade SI or 1 is counted only as grade 1 (note 1).

*A Range of Options*

Where the tables below include a column representing conditional identifications in marketed inscriptions and totals that include conditional IDs in marketed inscriptions, the intent is not to encourage baseless speculation. Rather, it is to set a limit on the maximum possible number of IDs in these inscriptions. Partly because some IDs are weak and partly because it can be difficult or impossible to establish the authenticity of the inscriptions in which they may be found, the precise number of IDs in authentic inscriptions remains elusive. It is very likely that the maximum possible number is greater than the true number. The amount of difference between the two cannot be calculated, only guessed or estimated. Various researchers will find various levels at which they are comfortable in accepting the numbers of IDs, especially in Table 2 below. Those who, like the author, tend to accept only the conservative figures need to reckon with the two possibilities that: 1) not all of the marketed inscriptions listed are fakes or forgeries and 2) IDs at lower grade levels could still refer to biblical persons. Those who accept a larger number of IDs need to reckon with the opposite possibilities. The tables below are intended to provide readers with data for the exercise of their own judgment.

*Accurate Totals of Numbers of Persons Seem Inaccurate*

The number of persons does not necessarily add up as one would expect, because some persons are named (or conditionally named) in both provenanced and marketed inscriptions. Also, some persons are named in more than one grade of ID. Hazael, for example, is identified in grades SI+SB, 3, and 2. In such instances, simply adding together the numbers of persons listed in each grade, as if multiple IDs of the same person somehow make him more than one person, would produce an inaccurate total; see the notes attached to numbers in the tables. The latter phenomenon can also occur when adding numbers of inscriptions that contain more than one ID.

## Table 1: Identifications and Non-Identifications in the PROVENANCED Inscriptions Listed in Appendixes B and C

The dotted line marks the boundary between reliable and unreliable IDs.

| Grade of ID or non-ID | How many IDs → | Of how many persons → | In how many inscriptions |
|---|---|---|---|
| Certain, both on inscriptional grounds and (separately) on biblical grounds: grade SI + SB | 8 certain SI + SB IDs of | 6 persons in | 5 inscriptions |
| Certain, only on inscriptional grounds: grade SI | 5 certain SI IDs of | 2 persons in | 4[1] inscriptions |
| Certain, only on biblical grounds: grade SB | 1 certain SB ID of | 1 person in | 1 inscription |
| Virtually certain to reliable: grade 3 | 8 grade 3 IDs of | 7 persons in | 5 inscriptions |
| - - - - - - - - - - - | - - - - - - - - | - - - - - - - - | - - - - - - - - |
| Reasonable but uncertain: grade 2 | 5 grade 2 IDs of | 5 persons in | 5 inscriptions |
| Doubtful: grade 1 | 15 grade 1 IDs of | 9[2] persons in | 13 inscriptions |
| No clear basis: grade 0 (zero) | 6 grade 0 non-IDs of | 6 persons in | 3 inscriptions |
| Disqualified: grade D | 14 grade D non-IDs of | 13 persons in | 12 inscriptions |

---

[1] Not six IDs of three persons in five inscriptions, because person (74) in inscription [87] (see Appendix B) could be either a grade SI or a grade 1 ID, and it is counted conservatively as grade 1 only.

[2] Counted as nine rather than ten persons on the supposition that (25) Shebna and (26) Shebna may well be one and the same person.

# Appendix F

## Table 2: Identifications and Non-Identifications in the MARKETED Inscriptions Listed in Appendixes B and C

This table lists the maximum possible number of IDs in marketed inscriptions, arriving at an *upper limit* by counting them as if all were authentic.

| Grade of ID or non-ID | How many IDs → | Of how many persons → | In how many inscriptions |
|---|---|---|---|
| Certain, both on inscriptional grounds and (separately) on biblical grounds: grade SI + SB | **1** certain SI + SB ID of | **1** person in | **1** inscription |
| Certain, only on inscriptional grounds: grade SI | **0** certain SI IDs of | **0** persons in | **0** inscriptions |
| Certain, only on biblical grounds: grade SB | **19** certain SB IDs of | **6** persons in | **15** inscriptions |
| Virtually certain to reliable: grade 3 | **3** grade 3 IDs of | **3** persons in | **2** inscriptions |
| Reasonable but uncertain: grade 2 | **29** grade 2 IDs of | **27** persons in | **20** inscriptions |
| Doubtful: grade 1 | **12** grade 1 IDs of | **9**[3] persons in | **11** inscriptions |
| No clear basis: grade 0 (zero) | **0** grade 0 non-IDs of | **0** persons in | **0** inscriptions |
| Disqualified: grade D | **6** grade D non-IDs of | **6** persons in | **5** inscriptions[4] |

---

[3] See previous note.
[4] This set of three numbers is based on the conservative assumption that the grade D non-ID of person (78) in inscription [91] (see Appendix B) is marketed. Otherwise, they would be five grade D non-IDs of five persons in four inscriptions.

### Table 3: Maximum Total Identifications and Non-Identifications in Both the PROVENANCED and the MARKETED Inscriptions Listed in Appendixes B and C

In each category, this table totals the figures of Tables 1 and 2. As above, the dotted line marks the boundary between reliable and unreliable IDs.

| Grade of ID or non-ID | How many IDs → | Of how many persons → | In how many inscriptions |
|---|---|---|---|
| Certain, both on inscriptional grounds and (separately) on biblical grounds: grade SI + SB | 9 certain SI + SB IDs of | 7 persons in | 6 inscriptions |
| Certain, only on inscriptional grounds: grade SI | 5 certain SI IDs of | 2 persons in | 4 inscriptions |
| Certain, only on biblical grounds: grade SB | 20 certain SB IDs of | 7 persons in | 16 inscriptions |
| Virtually certain to reliable: grade 3 | 11 grade 3 IDs of | 10 persons in | 7 inscriptions |
| ------ | ------ | ------ | ------ |
| Reasonable but uncertain: grade 2 | 34 grade 2 IDs of | 30[5] persons in | 25 inscriptions |
| Doubtful: grade 1 | 27 grade 1 IDs of | 14[6] persons in | 24 inscriptions |

---

[5] Not thirty-two persons, because person (57) has a grade 2 ID both in provenanced inscriptions [66 group] and in marketed inscription [65]; as does person (77) both in provenanced inscription [89] and in marketed inscription [90] (see Appendix B). Adding the same person in two inscriptions still totals only one person.

[6] Not eighteen persons, because person (15) has a grade 1 ID both in provenanced inscription [14] and in marketed inscriptions [12] and [13]; person (28) has a grade 1 ID both in provenanced inscription [41] and in marketed inscription [42]; person (59) has a grade 1 ID both in provenanced inscription [68] and in marketed inscription [69]; and (25) Shebna and (26) Shebna, counted as one person, have grade 1 IDs both in prove-

| | | | |
|---|---|---|---|
| No clear basis: grade 0 (zero) | 6 grade 0 non-IDs of | 6 persons in | 3 inscriptions |
| Disqualified: grade D | 20 grade D non-IDs of | 19 persons in | 17 inscriptions |

**Table 4: Certain. Reliable, and Reasonable Identifications in the PROVENANCED Inscriptions Listed in Appendixes B and C**

This table totals the most valuable portions of Table 1 above. It illustrates increasing inclusiveness at the expense of decreasing security of IDs. Grade 1 IDs and below are not included. Section 5.5 mentions the underlined items.

| Grade of ID or non-ID | How many IDs → | Of how many persons → | In how many inscriptions |
|---|---|---|---|
| IDs that are certain, i.e., grade S only, including SI + SB, SI, and SB | 14 certain IDs of | 9 persons in | 9[7] inscriptions |
| Certain down to reliable IDs: all grade S *and* all grade 3 | 22 certain to reliable IDs of | 15[8] persons in | 14 inscriptions |
| Certain down to reasonable IDs: all grade S, 3, *and* 2 | 27 certain, reliable, or reasonable IDs of | 19[9] persons in | 19 inscriptions |

---

nanced inscriptions [19], [20], [36], [37], and [39] and in marketed inscriptions [18], [33], and [38]. Because of this four-person overlap between provenanced and marketed inscriptions, the total number of persons is four fewer than one might expect.

[7] Not fourteen inscriptions, because inscription [3] contains grade S IDs of persons (2), (7), and (69); inscription [78] contains grade S IDs of persons (71) and (72); inscription [86] contains both a grade SI+SB ID of person (75) and two grade SI IDs: persons (73) and (74). Multiple IDs in a single inscription do not make more than one inscription.

[8] Not sixteen persons, because (71) Hazael has grade SI + SB IDs in provenanced inscriptions [78] and [82] and a grade 3 ID in provenanced inscriptions [79] and [80]. Adding the same person in different grades of ID does not make more than one person.

[9] Not twenty persons, because besides IDs in grades S and 3, (71) Hazael also has a grade 2 ID in inscription [81]. Adding him three times still totals just one person.

## Table 5: Certain, Reliable, and Reasonable Identifications in the MARKETED Inscriptions Listed in Appendixes B and C

This table totals the most valuable portions of Table 2 above, arriving at a maximum limit by treating all the marketed inscriptions as if they were authentic. As the preceding table does, it illustrates the tradeoff between inclusiveness and security of IDs when grade 2 (reasonable but uncertain, below the dotted line) is included. Section 5.5 makes use of the two underlined items.

| Grade of ID or non-ID | How many IDs → | Of how many persons → | In how many inscriptions |
|---|---|---|---|
| IDs that are certain, i.e., grade S only, including SI + SB, SI, and SB | **20** certain IDs of | **7** persons in | **16** inscriptions |
| Certain down to reliable IDs: all grade S *and* all grade 3 | **23** certain to reliable IDs of | <u>**10**[10]</u> persons in | <u>**18** inscriptions</u> |
| Certain down to reasonable IDs: all grade S, 3, *and* 2 | **52** certain, reliable, or reasonable IDs of | **35**[11] persons in | **38** inscriptions |

---

[10] This number is adjusted to nine when used in section 5.5 above, because one person named in provenanced inscriptions is also named in unprovenanced inscriptions: (37) Hilkiah the high priest. See note 12 below.

[11] Not thirty-seven persons, because (37) Hilkiah the high priest has a grade SB ID in marketed inscription [49] and grade 2 IDs in marketed inscriptions [51] and [52]; (46) Neriah has a grade 3 ID in marketed inscriptions [57 group] and a grade 2 ID in marketed inscription [58]. Adding an instances of grade 2 IDs in some inscriptions to instances of higher grades of ID in other inscriptions does not multiply these two individuals.

## Table 6: Certain, Reliable, and Reasonable Identifications in Both the PROVENANCED and the MARKETED Inscriptions Listed in Appendixes B and C

In each category, this table combines Tables 4 and 5 above, summarizing the most valuable portions of Tables 1 and 2 and arriving at a maximum limit by treating all the marketed inscriptions as if they were authentic. As above, grade 2 IDs are below the dotted line. Section 5.5 mentions the underlined item.

| Grade of ID or non-ID | How many IDs → | Of how many persons → | In how many inscriptions |
|---|---|---|---|
| IDs that are certain, i.e., grade S only, including SI + SB, SI, and SB | 34 certain IDs of | 16 persons in | 25 inscriptions |
| Certain down to reliable IDs: all in grade S *and* all in grade 3 | 45 certain to reliable IDs of | 24[12] persons in | 32 inscriptions |
| ------------------------------------------------ | | | |
| Certain down to reasonable IDs: all in grades S, 3, *and* 2 | 79 certain, reliable, or reasonable IDs of | 51[13] persons in | 57 inscriptions |

---

[12] Not twenty-five persons, because (37) Hilkiah the high priest has a grade SB ID in marketed inscription [49] and a grade 3 ID in provenanced inscription [50]. The same person identified in marketed and in provenanced inscriptions is still only one person.

[13] Not fifty-four persons, because (36) Shaphan, (37) Hilkiah the high priest, and the latter man's son (38) Azariah each have both a grade 3 ID in a provenanced inscription and a grade 2 ID in one or two marketed inscriptions. The provenanced inscriptions containing grade 3 IDs are [48], [50], and [50], respectively. The marketed inscriptions that contain grade 2 IDs are [47] for Shaphan, [51] and [52] for Hilkiah, and [51] and [52] for Azariah. As above, various IDs of the same person do not multiply the person.

# Bibliography

# Updated through July 2002

Abramsky, Shmuel, Yohanan Aharoni, Haim M. Y. Gevaryahu, and Ben-Zion Luria, eds. *Shmuel Yeivin Volume: Investigations in the Bible, Archaeology, Language and the History of Israel* (in Hebrew). Jerusalem: Kiryat Sefer, 1970.

Académie des inscriptions et belles-lettres. *Corpus inscriptionum semiticarum ab academia inscriptionum et litterarum humaniorum conditum atque digetum. Pars secunda, inscriptiones aramaicas continens.* Paris: Reipublicae typographeo, 1881– .

———. *Mélanges Syriens offerts à monsieur René Dussaud: secrétaire perpétuel de l'Académie des inscriptions et belles-lettres.* 2 vols. Haut-commissariat de la République francaise en Syrie et au Liban, Service des antiquités, Bibliothéque archéologique et historique 30. Paris: P. Guenther, 1939.

Aharoni, Yohanan. *Arad Inscriptions*. Edited and revised by Anson F. Rainey. Translated by Judith Ben-Or. Jerusalem: Israel Exploration Society, 1981.

———. "Arad: Its Inscriptions and Temple." *Biblical Archaeologist* 31 (1968): 2–32.

———. "Excavations at Tell Arad: Preliminary Report on the Second Season, 1963." *Israel Exploration Journal* 17 (1967): 233–49.

———. "The Israelite Sanctuary at Arad." Pages 25–39 in *New Directions in Biblical Archaeology*. Edited by David Noel Freedman and Jonas C. Greenfield. Garden City, N.Y.: Doubleday, 1969.

———. *Land of the Bible: A Historical Geography*. 2d rev. and emended ed. Edited and translated by Anson F. Rainey. London: Burns & Oates, 1979.

Aharoni, Yohanan, ed. *Excavations and Studies: Essays in Honour of Professor Shemuel Yeivin.* Publications, Tel Aviv University, Institute of Archaeology 1. Tel Aviv: CARTA, 1973.

Aḥituv, Shmuel. *Handbook of Ancient Hebrew Inscriptions: From the Period of the First Commonwealth and the Beginning of the Second Commonwealth (Hebrew, Philistine, Edomite, Moabite, Ammonite, and the Dileum Inscription)* (in Hebrew). Biblical Encyclopaedia Library 7. Jerusalem: Bialik, 1992.

Ahlström, Gösta W. *Psalm 89: Eine Liturgie aus dem Ritual des leidenden Königs.* Lund: Älund, Haakan Ohlssons, 1959.

———. *Royal Administration and National Religion in Ancient Palestine.* Studies in the History of the Ancient Near East 1. Leiden: Brill, 1982.

———. "The Seal of Shema." *Scandinavian Journal of the Old Testament* 7 (1993): 208–15.

Aitken, Martin J. *Thermoluminescence Dating.* Studies in Archaeological Science. Orlando, Fla.: Academic Press, 1985.

Albright, William F. "The Impact of Archaeology on Biblical Research—1966." Pages 2–14 in *New Directions in Biblical Archaeology.* Edited by David Noel Freedman and Jonas C. Greenfield. Garden City, N.Y.: Doubleday, 1969.

———. "King Joiachin in Exile." *Biblical Archaeologist* 4 (1942): 49–55. Repr. Pages 106–12 in *The Biblical Archaeologist Reader, Volume I.* Edited by G. Ernest Wright and David Noel Freedman. Garden City, N.Y.: Anchor Books, 1961. Repr., Missoula, Mont.: Scholars Press, for the American Schools of Oriental Research, 1975.

———. "The Seal of Eliakim and the Latest Pre-Exilic History of Judah, with Some Observations on Ezekiel." *Journal of Biblical Literature* 51 (1932): 77–106.

Alt, Albrecht. *Kleine Schriften zur Geschichte des Volkes Israel.* Munich: C. H. Beck, 1959.

———. "Menschen ohne Namen." *Archiv Orientalni* 18 (1950): 9–24. Repr. pages 198–213 in vol. 3 of *Kleine Schriften zur Geschichte des Volkes Israel.* Munich: C. H. Beck, 1959. ET, *Essays on Old Testament History and Religion.* Translated by R. A. Wilson. Garden City, N.Y.: Doubleday, 1967.

Andersen, Francis I. "Moabite Syntax." *Orientalia* 35 (1966): 81–120.

Ariel, Donald T., ed. *Inscriptions.* Vol. 6 of *Excavations at the City of David 1978–1985. Directed by Yigal Shiloh.* City of David Final Reports 6. Qedem 41. Jerusalem: The Hebrew University of Jerusalem, The Institute of Archaeology, 2000.

Åström, Paul, ed.. *High, Middle, or Low: Acts of an International Colloquium on Absolute Chronology Held at the University of Gothenburg $20^{th}$–$22^{nd}$ August 1987.* 3 parts in 3 vols. Gothenburg, Sweden: Paul Åström Förlag, 1987.

Athas, George. *The Tel Dan Inscription: A Reappraisal and a New Interpretation.* Journal for the Study of the Old Testament Supplement Series 360. Copenhagen International Seminar 12. Sheffield, England: Sheffield Academic Press, 2003.

Aufrecht, Walter E. *A Corpus of Ammonite Inscriptions.* Ancient Near Eastern Texts & Studies 4. Lewiston, N.Y.: Edwin Mellen Press, 1989.

———. "Ammonite Texts and Language." Pages 163–88 in *Ancient Ammon.* Edited by Burton MacDonald and Randall W. Younker. Studies in the History and Culture of the Ancient Near East 17. Boston: Brill, 1999.

Avigad, Nahman. *Ancient Monuments in the Kidron Valley* (in Hebrew). Jerusalem: Mosad Byalik, 1954.

———. "Baruch the Scribe and Jerahmeel the King's Son." *Israel Exploration Journal* 28 (1978): 52–56.

———. *Bullae and Seals from a Post-Exilic Judean Archive*. Translated by Rafi Grafman. Qedem 4. Jerusalem: The Hebrew University of Jerusalem, The Institute of Archaeology, 1976.

———. "The Contribution of Hebrew Seals to an Understanding of Israelite Religion and Society." Pages 195–208 in *Ancient Israelite Religion: Essays in Honor of Frank Moore Cross*. Edited by Patrick D. Miller Jr., Paul D. Hanson, and S. Dean McBride. Philadelphia: Fortress, 1987.

———. *Discovering Jerusalem*. Oxford: Basil Blackwell, 1984.

———. *Hebrew Bullae from the Time of Jeremiah: Remnants of a Burnt Archive*. Translated by Rafi Grafman. Jerusalem: Israel Exploration Society, 1986.

———. "Hebrew Epigraphic Sources." Pages 20–43, 315–17 in *The Age of the Monarchies: Political History*. Edited by Abraham Malamat. Vol. 4, no. 1 of *The World History of the Jewish People*. Edited by Benzion Netanyahu, Benjamin Mazar, Abraham Schalit, Michael Avi-Yonah, and Cecil Roth. New Brunswick, N.J.: Rutgers University Press, 1979.

———. "Jerahmeel & Baruch, King's Son and Scribe." *Biblical Archaeologist* 42 (1979): 114–18.

———. "The Jotham Seal from Elath." *Bulletin of the American Schools of Oriental Research* 163 (1961): 18–22.

———. "A New Class of Yehud Stamps." *Israel Exploration Journal* 7 (1957): 146–53.

———. "New Light on the Naar Seals." Pages 294–300 in *Magnalia Dei, the Mighty Acts of God: Essays in the Bible and Archaeology in Memory of G. Ernest Wright*. Edited by Frank Moore Cross, Werner E. Lemke, and Patrick D. Miller Jr. New York: Doubleday, 1976.

———. "New Names on Hebrew Seals" (in Hebrew). *Eretz-Israel* 12 (Nelson Glueck Volume, 1975): 66–71, Pl. 14, English summary 120*–21*.

———. "A New Seal of a 'Son of the King.'" *Michmanim* 6 (1992): 27*–31*.

———. "On the Identification of Persons Mentioned in Hebrew Epigraphic Sources" (in Hebrew). *Eretz-Israel* 19 (Michael Avi-Yonah Volume, 1987): 235–37, English summary 79*.

———. "The Priest of Dor." *Israel Exploration Journal* 25 (1975): 101–5, Pl. 10: C, D.

———. "The Seal of Jezebel." *Israel Exploration Journal* 14 (1964): 274–76, Pl. 56: C.

———. "A Seal of 'Manasseh, Son of the King.'" *Israel Exploration Journal* 13 (1963): 133–36, Pl. 18: C.

———. "The Seal of Seraiah (Son of) Neriah" (in Hebrew). *Eretz-Israel* 14 (H. L. Ginsberg Volume, 1978): 86–87, Pl. I, no. 3, English summary 125*.

———. "Six Ancient Hebrew Seals" (in Hebrew). Pages 305–8 in *Shmuel Yeivin Volume*. Edited by Shmuel Abramsky, Yohanan Aharoni, Haim M. Y. Gevaryahu, and Ben-Zion Luria. Jerusalem: Kiryat Sefer, 1970.

———. "Titles and Symbols in Hebrew Seals" (in Hebrew). *Eretz-Israel* 15 (Y. Aharoni Memorial Volume, 1981): 303–5, Pl. 57, English summary 85*.

———. "Two Ammonite Seals Depicting the *Dea Nutrix*." *Bulletin of the American Schools of Oriental Research* 225 (1977): 63–64.

Avigad, Nahman, Michael Heltzer, and André Lemaire. *West Semitic Seals: Eighth–Sixth Centuries B.C.E.* (in Hebrew and English). Edited by Ronny Reich. The Reuben and Edith Hecht Museum Collection B. Haifa: University of Haifa, 2000.

Avigad, Nahman, and Benjamin Sass. *Corpus of West Semitic Stamp Seals.* Jerusalem: The Israel Academy of Sciences and Humanities, Israel Exploration Society, and The Hebrew University of Jerusalem, The Institute of Archaeology, 1997.

Avishur, Yitzhak, and Robert Deutsch, eds. *Michael: Historical, Epigraphical and Biblical Studies in Honor of Prof. Michael Heltzer.* Tel Aviv: Archaeological Center Publications, 1999.

Avishur, Yitzhak, and Michael Heltzer. *Studies on the Royal Administration in Ancient Israel in the Light of Epigraphic Sources.* Tel Aviv: Archaeological Center Publications, 2000.

Barkay, Gabriel. "A Bulla of Ishmael, the King's Son." *Bulletin of the American Schools of Oriental Research* 290–291 (1993): 109–14.

———. "The King of Babylonia or a Judaean Official?" *Israel Exploration Journal* 45 (1995): 41–47.

Barkay, Gabriel, and Andrew G. Vaughn. "New Readings of Hezekian Official Seal Impressions." *Bulletin of the American Schools of Oriental Research* 304 (1996): 29–54.

Barnett, Richard D. *Ancient Ivories in the Middle East and Adjacent Countries.* Qedem 14. Jerusalem: The Hebrew University, The Institute of Archaeology, 1982.

———. "Hamath and Nimrud: Shell Fragments from Hamath and the Provenance of the Nimrud Ivories." *Iraq* 25 (1963): 81–85, Pl. XV–XVIII.

Barrick, W. Boyd. "Genealogical Notes on the 'House of David' and the 'House of Zadok.'" *Journal for the Study of the Old Testament* 96 (2001): 29–58.

Barstad, Hans M. "Dod דוד." Pages 259–62 in *Dictionary of Deities and Demons in the Bible DDD.* Edited by Karel van der Toorn, Bob Becking, and Pieter W. van der Horst. 2d extensively rev. ed. Boston: Brill Academic Publishers, 1999.

Beck, Pirhiya. "The Drawings from Ḥorvat Teiman (Kuntillet ʿAjrud)." *Tel Aviv* 9 (1982): 3–86.

Becking, Bob. *The Fall of Samaria: An Historical and Archaeological Study.* Studies in the History of the Ancient Near East 2. New York: Brill, 1992.

———. "Inscribed Seals as Evidence for Biblical Israel? Jeremiah 40.7–41 *par exemple*." Pages 65–83 in *Can a 'History of Israel' Be Written?* Edited by Lester L. Grabbe. Journal for the Study of the Old Testament: Supplement Series 245. European Seminar in Historical Methodology 1. Sheffield, England: Sheffield Academic Press, 1997.

Becking, Bob, and Jan A. Wagenaar. "Het 'Huis van JHWH' en het 'Verzoek van de weduwe': Enkele opmerkingen bij twee recent gepubliceerde oud-Hebreeuwse inscripties." *Nederlands theologisch tijdschrift* 52 (1998): 177–93.

Beech, George. "Prosopography." Pages 185–226 in *Medieval Studies: An Introduction.* Edited by James M. Powell. 2d edition. Syracuse, N.Y.: Syracuse University Press, 1992.

Ben-Zvi, Ehud. "On the Reading '*bytdwd*' in the Aramaic Stele from Tel Dan." *Journal for the Study of the Old Testament* 64 (1994): 25–32.

Benz, Frank L. *Personal Names in the Phoenician and Punic Inscriptions.* Studia Pohl 8. Rome: Biblical Institute Press, 1972.

Biran, Avraham. *Biblical Dan.* Jerusalem: Israel Exploration Society and Hebrew Union College-Jewish Institute of Religion, 1994.

Biran, Avraham, and Joseph Naveh. "An Aramaic Stele from Tel Dan." *Israel Exploration Journal* 43 (1993): 81–98.

———. "The Tel Dan Inscription: A New Fragment." *Israel Exploration Journal* 45 (1995): 1–18.

Blau, Ernst Otto F. H. "Bibliographische Anzeigen." *Zeitschrift der deutschen morgenländischen Gesellschaft* 12 (1858): 715–31.

Bliss, Frederick Jones, and Macalister, Robert A. Stewart. *Excavations in Palestine During the Years 1898–1900.* London: Committee of the Palestine Exploration Fund, 1902.

Boardman, John, I. E. S. Edwards, N. G. L. Hammond, and E. Sollberger, eds. *The Cambridge Ancient History.* 2d ed. New York: Cambridge University Press, 1970.

Bordreuil, Pierre.[1] *Catalogue des sceaux ouest-sémitiques inscrits de la Bibliothèque Nationale, du Musée du Louvre et du Musée biblique de Bible et Terre Sainte.* Paris: Bibliothèque Nationale, 1986.

———. "Inscriptions sigillaires ouest-sémitiques, III: Sceaux de dignitaires et de rois syro-palestiniens du VIIIe et du VIIe siècle avant J.-C." *Syria* 62 (1985): 21–29.

———. "A Note on the Seal of Peqah the Armor-bearer, Future King of Israel." *Biblical Archaeologist* 49 (1986): 54–55.

———. "Les sceaux des grands personnages." *Le monde de la Bible* 46 (1986): 45–46.

———. "Sceaux inscrits des pays du Levant." Cols. 86–212 in vol. 12 of *Dictionnaire de la Bible, Supplément.* Edited by Louis Pirot, André Robert, Jacques Briend, and Édouard Cothenet. Paris: Letouzey & Ané, 1996.

Bordreuil, Pierre, and Felice Israel. "A Propos de la carrière d'Elyaqim: du page au major-dome (?)." *Semitica* 41/42 (1991–1992): 80–87.

Bordreuil, Pierre, Felice Israel, and Dennis Pardee. "Deux ostraca paléo-hébreux de la collection Sh. Moussaïeff: I) Contribution financière obligatoire pour le temple de YHWH, II) Réclamation d'une veuve auprès d'un fonctionnaire." *Semitica* 46 (1997): 49–76, Pl. 7, 8. ET, "King's Command and Widow's Plea: Two New Hebrew Ostraca of the Biblical Period." *Near Eastern Archaeology* 61 (1998): 2–13.

Bordreuil, Pierre, and André Lemaire. "Nouveaux sceaux hébreux, araméens et ammonites." *Semitica* 26 (1976): 45–63.

Botta, Paul E., ed. *Monuments de Ninive découvert et décrit*, 5 vols. Paris: Imprimerie Nationale, 1849.

---

[1] Avishur and Heltzer state, "P. Bordreuil is also preparing his corpus of West-Semitic Seals, including cylinder seals with West-Semitic inscriptions." (Yitzhak Avishur and Michael Heltzer, *Studies on the Royal Administration in Ancient Israel in the Light of Epigraphic Sources* [Tel Aviv: Archaeological Center Publications, 2000], 14).

Botterweck, G. Johannes, Helmer Ringgren, and Heinz-Josef Fabry, eds. *Theological Dictionary of the Old Testament.* 13 vols. to date. Translated by Geoffrey W. Bromiley, David F. Green, Douglas W. Stott, and John T. Willis. Grand Rapids, Mich.: Eerdmans, 1974– .

Branden, Albert van den. *Les inscriptions Dédanites.* Publications de l'Université Libanaise, section des études historiques 8. Beirut: Université Libanaise, 1962.

Bright, John. *A History of Israel.* 4th ed. Louisville, Ky.: Westminster/John Knox, 2000.

Brin, Gershon. "The Title בן (ה)מלך and its Parallels: The Significance and Evaluation of an Official Title." *Annali dell' Istituto Orientale di Napoli* 29 (1969): 433–65.

British Museum, Department of Egyptian and Assyrian Antiquities. *Catalogue of the Cuneiform Tablets in the Kouyunjik Collection of the British Museum.* 6 vols. and Supplement. Edited by Carl Bezold. Supplement edited by Leonard W. King. London: British Museum. 1889–1914.

British Museum, Department of Egyptian and Assyrian Antiquities. *A Selection from the Miscellaneous Inscriptions of Assyria.* Edited by Henry C. Rawlinson and George Smith. Vol. 3 of *The Cuneiform Inscriptions of Western Asia.* Edited by Henry C. Rawlinson. 5 vols. Assyriology Monographs. London: R. E. Bowler, 1870.

British Museum, Department of Egyptian and Assyrian Antiquities. *A Selection from the Miscellaneous Inscriptions of Chaldaea, Assyria, and Babylonia.* Edited by Henry C. Rawlinson and Edwin Norris. Vol. 1 of *The Cuneiform Inscriptions of Western Asia.* Edited by Henry C. Rawlinson. 5 vols. Assyriology Monographs. London: R. E. Bowler, 1861.

Bromiley, Geoffrey W., ed. *The International Standard Bible Encyclopedia.* 4 vols. Fully rev. ed. Grand Rapids, Mich.: Eerdmans, 1979–1988.

Bron, François, and André Lemaire. "Les inscriptions araméennes de Hazaël." *Révue d'Assyriologie et d'Archéologie Orientale* 83 (1989): 35–44.

Broughton, T. Robert S. "Senate and Senators of the Roman Republic: the Prosopographical Approach." Pages 250–65 in vol. 1 of *Von den Anfängen Roms bis zum Ausgang der Republik.* Edited by Hildegard Temporini. Part 1 of *Aufstieg und Niedergang der römischen Welt.* Edited by Hildegard Temporini and Wolfgang Haase. New York: Walter de Gruyter, 1972.

Brown, Francis, Samuel R. Driver, and Charles A. Briggs. *A Hebrew and English Lexicon of the Old Testament with an Appendix Containing the Biblical Aramaic.* Corrected ed. Oxford: Clarendon Press, 1953.

Buccellati, Giorgio. "Review/Essay: Archaeology's Publication Problems." *Near Eastern Archaeology* 61 (1998): 118–20.

Bunimovitz, Shlomo, and Zvi Lederman. "Beth-Shemesh: Culture Conflict on Judah's Frontier." *Biblical Archaeology Review* 23, no. 1 (January/February 1997): 42–49, 75–77.

Buttrick, George A., ed. *The Interpreter's Dictionary of the Bible.* 4 vols. Nashville: Abingdon Press, 1962.

Cahill, Jane M. "Comparing the *LMLK*- and Rosette-Stamped Vessels." Paper presented at the annual meeting of the Society of Biblical Literature and the American Schools of Oriental Research. New Orleans, La., November 26, 1996.

———. "Rosette Stamp Seal Impressions from Ancient Judah." *Israel Exploration Journal* 45 (1995): 230–52.

———. "Rosette-Stamped Handles." Pages 85–108 in *Inscriptions*. Edited by Donald T. Ariel. Vol. 6 of *Excavations at the City of David 1978–1985 Directed by Yigal Shiloh*. City of David Final Report 6. Qedem 41. Jerusalem: The Hebrew University of Jerusalem, The Institute of Archaeology, 2000.
———. "Royal Rosettes Fit for a King." *Biblical Archaeology Review* 23, no. 5 (September/October 1997): 48–57, 68–69.
Carney, Thomas F. "Prosopography: Payoffs and Pitfalls." *Phoenix* 27 (1973): 156–79.
Charbonnet, André. "Le dieu au lions d'Erétrie." *Annali dell' Istituto Orientale di Napoli—Annali del Dipartimento di Studi del Mondo Classico e del Mediterraneo Antico, Sezione di Archeologia e storia antica* 8 (1986): 117–73, Pl. 33–52.
Chase, Debra A. "A Note on an Inscription from Kuntillet ʿAjrūd." *Bulletin of the American Schools of Oriental Research* 246 (1982): 63–67.
Chastagnol, André. "La prosopographie, méthode de recherche sur l'histoire du Bas-Empire." *Annales: Économies, Sociétés, Civilisations* 25 (1970): 1229–35.
Chwolson, Daniel A. *Corpus Inscriptionum Hebraicarum*. St. Petersburg and Leipzig, 1882. Repr. New York: Georg Olms, 1974.
Clermont-Ganneau, Charles. *Les fraudes archéologiques en Palestine*. Paris: Ernest Leroux, 1885.
———. "The Moabite Stone." *Contemporary Review* 52 (1887): 169–83.
———. "Sceaux et cachets israélites, phéniciens et syriens." *Journal asiatique* 8 (1883): 123–59.
———. "La stèle de Dhiban," *Revue archéologique* (1870): 184–207, 357–386.
———. "La stèle de Mésa," *Revue critique* (September 11, 1875): 166–74.
———. "La stèle de Mésa, examen critique du texte" *Journal asiatique* 8/9 (1887): 72–112.
———. *La stèle de Mésa roi de Moab 896 av. J.-C.: Lettres à M. le Cte. de Vogüé*. Paris: Librarie Polytechnique de J. Baudry, 1870.
Clines, David J. A. "X, X ben Y, ben Y: Personal Names in Hebrew Narrative Style." *Vetus Testamentum* 22 (1972): 282–87.
———, ed. *The Dictionary of Classical Hebrew*, 10 vols. projected. Sheffield, England: Sheffield Academic Press, 1993– .
Cody, Aelred. "A New Inscription from Tell āl-Rimaḥ and King Jehoash of Israel." *Catholic Biblical Quarterly* 32 (1970): 325–40.
Cogan, Mordechai, and Hayim Tadmor. *II Kings: A New Translation with Introduction and Commentary*. Anchor Bible 11. N.p.: Doubleday, 1988.
Colless, Brian E. "Recent Discoveries Illuminating the Origin of the Alphabet." *Abr-Nahrain* 26 (1988): 30–67.
Collon, Dominique. *Near Eastern Seals*. Interpreting the Past 2. Berkeley, Calif.: University of California Press, 1991.
Congresso internazionale di studi fenice e punici 1987. *Atti del IIo Congresso Internationale di Studi Fenici e Punici: Roma, 9–14 novembre 1987*. Edited by Enrico Acquaro, Piero Bartoloni, Maria Teresa Francisi, Lorenza-Ilia Manfredi, Federico Mazza, Giovanni Montalto, Gesualdo Petruccioli, Sergio Ribichini, Gabriella Matthiae Scandone, and Paolo Xella. 3 vols. Collezione di Studi Fenici 30. Rome: Consiglio nazionale delle recherche, 1991.

Coogan, Michael D., J. Cheryl Exum, and Lawrence E. Stager, eds. *Scripture and Other Artifacts: Essays on the Bible and Archaeology in Honor of Philip J. King*. Louisville, Ky.: Westminster/John Knox Press, 1994.

Cook, Edward M. "An Aramaic Incantation Bowl from Khafaje." *Bulletin of the American Schools of Oriental Research* 285 (1992): 79–81.

―――. "On the Linguistic Dating of the Phoenician Ahiram Inscription (*KAI* 1)." *Journal of Near Eastern Studies* 53 (January 1994): 33–36.

Cornelius, Izak. "The Lion in the Art of the Ancient Near East: A Study of Selected Motifs." *Journal of Northwest Semitic Languages* 15 (1989): 53–85.

Cowley, Arthur. *Aramaic Papyri of the Fifth Century B.C.* Oxford: Clarendon, 1923. Repr. Osnabrück: Zeller, 1967.

Cross, Frank Moore. "An Ammonite King List." *Biblical Archaeologist* 48 (1985): 171.

―――. "A Bulla of Hezekiah, King of Judah." Pages 62–66 in *Realia Dei: Essays in Archaeology and Biblical Interpretation in Honor of Edward F. Campbell Jr. at His Retirement*. Edited by Prescott H. Williams Jr. and Theodore Hiebert. Atlanta: Scholars Press, 1999.

―――. "King Hezekiah's Seal Bears Phoenician Imagery." *Biblical Archaeology Review* 25, no. 2 (March/April 1999): 42–45, 60.

―――. *Leaves from an Epigrapher's Notebook: Collected Papers in Hebrew and West Semitic Palaeography and Epigraphy*. Harvard Semitic Studies 51. Winona Lake, Ind.: Eisenbrauns, 2003.

―――. "Newly Found Inscriptions in Old Canaanite and Early Phoenician Scripts." *Bulletin of the American Schools of Oriental Research* 238 (1980): 1–20.

―――. "A Philistine Ostracon from Ashkelon." *Biblical Archaeology Review* 22, no. 1 (January/February 1996): 64–65.

―――. "A Phoenician Inscription from Idalion: Some Old and New Texts Relating to Child Sacrifice." Pages 93–107 in *Scripture and Other Artifacts: Essays on the Bible and Archaeology in Honor of Philip J. King*, 93. Edited by Michael D. Coogan, J. Cheryl Exum, and Lawrence E. Stager. Louisville, Ky.: Westminster/John Knox Press, 1994.

―――. "The Seal of Miqnêyaw, Servant of Yahweh." Pages 55–63, Pl. 9–10 in *Ancient Seals and the Bible*. Edited by Leonard Gorelick and Elizabeth Williams-Forte. The International Institute for Mesopotamian Area Studies Monographic Journals of the Near East, Occasional Papers on the Near East, vol. 2/1. Malibu, Calif.: Undena Publications, 1983.

Cross, Frank Moore, Werner E. Lemke, and Patrick D. Miller, eds. *Magnalia Dei, the Mighty Acts of God: Essays in the Bible and Archaeology in Memory of G. Ernest Wright*. New York: Doubleday, 1976.

Cryer, Frederick H. "King Hadad." *Scandinavian Journal of the Old Testament* 9 (1995): 223–35.

―――. "Of Epistemology, Northwest-Semitic Epigraphy and Irony: The '*bytdwd*/House of David' Inscription Revisited." *Journal for the Study of the Old Testament* 69 (1996): 3–17.

―――. "On the Recently-Discovered 'House of David' Inscription." *Scandinavian Journal of the Old Testament* 8 (1994): 3–19.

Culican, William. "Seals in Bronze Mounts." *Rivista di studi fenici* 5 (1977): 1–4, Tables I–III.
Cundall, Arthur E. and Leon Morris. *Judges and Ruth*. Tyndale Old Testament Commentaries. Leicester: Inter-Varsity Press, 1971.
Dalley, Stephanie, C. B. F. Walker, and John D. Hawkins. *The Old Babylonian Tablets from Tell al Rimah*. London: British School of Archaeology in Iraq, 1976.
Davies, Graham I. *Ancient Hebrew Inscriptions: Corpus and Concordance*. New York: Cambridge University Press, 1991.
———. *Megiddo*. Cities of the Biblical World. Grand Rapids, Mich.: Eerdmans, 1986.
Davies, Philip R. "'House of David' Built on Sand: The Sins of the Biblical Maximizers."*Biblical Archaeology Review* 20, no. 4 (July/August 1994): 54–55.
———. *In Search of 'Ancient Israel.'* 2d ed. Journal for the Study of the Old Testament: Supplement Series 148. Sheffield, England: Sheffield Academic Press, 1995.
Davis, Thomas W. "A History of Biblical Archaeology." Ph.D. diss., University of Arizona, 1987.
Dearman, J. Andrew, ed. *Studies in the Mesha Inscription and Moab*. Archaeology and Biblical Studies 2. Atlanta: Scholars Press, 1989.
Dearman, J. Andrew, and M. Patrick Graham, eds. *The Land That I Will Show You: Essays on the History and Archaeology of the Ancient Near East in Honor of J. Maxwell Miller*. Supplement Series 343. Sheffield, England: Sheffield Academic Press, 2001.
Demsky, Aaron. "The ʿIzbet Sartah Ostracon Ten Years Later." Pages 186–97 in Israel Finkelstein, *ʿIzbet Ṣarṭah: An Early Iron Age Site Near Rosh Haʿayin, Israel*. British Archaeological Reports International Series 299. Oxford, England: B.A.R., 1986.
———. "A Proto-Canaanite Abecedary Dating from the Period of the Judges and Its Implications for the History of the Alphabet." *Tel Aviv* 4 (1977): 14–27.
Demsky, Aaron, and Moshe Kochavi. "An Alphabet from the Days of the Judges." *Biblical Archaeology Review* 4, no. 3 (September/October 1978): 22–30.
Deutsch, Robert. "First Impression: What We Learned from King Ahaz's Seal." *Biblical Archaeology Review* 24, no. 3 (May/June 1998): 54–56, 62.
———. *Messages from the Past: Hebrew Bullae from the Time of Isaiah through the Destruction of the First Temple: Shlomo Moussaieff Collection and an Up to Date Corpus* (in Hebrew). Tel Aviv: Archaeological Center Publications, 1997. ET, *Messages from the Past: Hebrew Bullae from the Time of Isaiah through the Destruction of the First Temple*. Translated by Robert Deutsch. Tel Aviv: Archaeological Center Publications, 1999.
———. "New Bullae Reveal Egyptian-Style Emblems on Judah's Royal Seals." *Biblical Archaeology Review* 28, no. 4 (July/August 2002): 42–51, 60–62.
———. "A Royal Ammonite Seal Impression." Pages 121–25 in *Michael: Historical, Epigraphical and Biblical Studies in Honor of Prof. Michael Heltzer*. Edited by Yitzhak Avishur and Robert Deutsch. Tel Aviv: Archaeological Center Publications, 1999.

―――. "Seal of Baʿalis Surfaces: Ammonite King Plotted Murder of Judahite Governor." *Biblical Archaeology Review* 25, no. 2 (March/April 1999): 46–49, 60, front cover color photograph.
Deutsch, Robert, ed. *Shlomo: Studies in Epigraphy, Iconography, History and Archaeology in Honor of Shlomo Moussaieff* [tentative title]. Tel Aviv: Archaeological Center Publications, forthcoming.
Deutsch, Robert, and Michael L. Heltzer. *Forty New Ancient West Semitic Inscriptions*. Tel Aviv: Archaeological Center Publications, 1994.
―――. *New Epigraphic Evidence from the Biblical Period*. Tel Aviv: Archaeological Center Publications, 1995.
―――. *West Semitic Epigraphic News of the 1st Millennium B.C.E.* Tel Aviv: Archaelogical Center Publications, 1999.
Deutsch, Robert, and André Lemaire. *Biblical Period Personal Seals in the Shlomo Moussaieff Collection*. Tel Aviv: Archaeological Center Publications, 2000.
Dever, William G. "Asherah, Consort of Yahweh? New Evidence from Kuntillet ʿAjrûd." *Bulletin of the American Schools of Oriental Research* 255 (1984): 21–37.
―――. "Iron Age Epigraphic Material from the Area of Khirbet el-Kôm." *Hebrew Union College Annual* 40–41 (1969–1970): 139–204.
―――. "Recent Archaeological Confirmation of the Cult of Asherah in Ancient Israel." *Hebrew Studies* 23 (1982): 37–44.
―――. *What Did the Biblical Writers Know and When Did They Know It? What Archaeology Can Tell Us about the Reality of Ancient Israel*. Grand Rapids, Mich.: Eerdmans, 2001.
*Dictionnaire de la Bible, Supplément*. Edited by Louis Pirot, André Robert, Jacques Briend, and Édouard Cothenet. Paris: Letouzey & Ané, 1926– .
Dietrich, Manfred, and Oswald Loretz. *'Jahwe und seine Aschera': Anthropomorphes Kultbild in Mesopotamien, Ugarit und Israel*. Ugaritisch-biblische Literatur 9. Munster: Ugarit-Verlag, 1992.
Diringer, David. *Le iscrizioni antico-ebraiche Palestinesi*. Florence: Felice le Monnier, 1934.
―――. "The Royal Jar-Handle Stamps of Ancient Judah." *Biblical Archaeologist* 12 (1949): 70–86.
DiVito, Robert A. "The Tell el-Kheleifeh Inscriptions." In Gary D. Pratico, *Nelson Glueck's 1938–1940 Excavations at Tell el-Kheleifeh: A Reappraisal*, 51–63, 218, Pl. 79. American Schools of Oriental Research Archaeological Reports 3. Atlanta: Scholars Press, 1993.
Donner, Herbert, and Wolfgang Röllig. *Kanaanäische und aramäische Inschriften*. 3 vols. 3d ed. Wiesbaden: Otto Harrassowitz, 1971–1973.
Dorsey, David A. "The Location of Biblical Makkedah." *Tel Aviv* 7 (1980): 185–93.
Dotan, Aron. "New Light on the ʿIzbet Ṣarṭah Ostracon." *Tel Aviv* 8 (1981): 160–72.
Drews, Robert. "The Babylonian Chronicles and Berossus." *Iraq* 37 (Spring 1975): 39–55.
Dunand, Maurice. "Stèle Araméene Dédiée à Melquart." *Bulletin du Musée de Beyrouth* 3 (1941): 65–76.
Durham. John I., and J. Roy Porter, eds. *Proclamation and Presence: Old Testament Essays in Honour of Gwynne Henton Davies*. Richmond: John Knox Press, 1970.

Dussaud, René. *Les monuments palestiniens et judaiques: Moab, Judée, Philistie, Samarie, Galilée*. Musée du Louvre, Département des antiquités orientales. Paris: Ernest Leroux, 1912.
Ebeling, Erich, and Bruno Meissner, eds. *Ha-a-a–Hystaspes*. Vol. 4 of *Reallexikon der Assyriologie*. Edited by Dietz Otto Edzard. New York: Walter de Gruyter, 1975.
Edelman, Diana V., ed. *The Fabric of History: Text, Artifact and Israel's Past*. Journal for the Study of the Old Testament: Supplement Series 127. Sheffield, England: Sheffield Academic Press, 1991.
Elayi, Josette. "Name of Deuteronomy's Author Found on Seal Ring." *Biblical Archaeology Review* 13, no. 5 (September/October 1987): 54–56.
———. "New Light on the Identification of the Seal of Priest Ḥanan, son of Ḥilqiyahu (2 Kings 22)." *Bibliotheca Orientalis* 49 (1992): cols. 680–85.
———. "Le sceau du prêtre Ḥanan, fils de Ḥilqiyahu." *Semitica* 36 (1986): 43–46.
———. "Les sceaux ouest-sémitiques 'royaux': mythe ou réalité?" *Quaderni ticinesi di numismatica e antichità classiche* 24 (1995): 39–71.
Emerton, John A. "New Light on Israelite Religion: The Implications of the Inscriptions from Kuntillet ʿAjrud." *Zeitschrift für die alttestamentliche Wissenschaft* 94 (1982): 1–20.
Ephʿal, Israel, "On the Identification of the Israelite Exiles in the Assyrian Empire" (in Hebrew). Pages 201–203 in *Excavations and Studies: Essays in Honour of Professor Shemuel Yeivin*. Edited by Yohanan Aharoni. Publications, Tel Aviv University, Institute of Archaeology 1. Tel Aviv: CARTA, 1973.
Ephʿal, Israel, and Joseph Naveh. "Hazael's Booty Inscriptions." *Israel Exploration Journal* 3–4 (1989): 192–200, Pl. 24A, 25A.
Feigin, Samuel I. "The Origin of 'Elôh, 'God,' in Hebrew." *Journal of Near Eastern Studies* 3 (1944): 259.
Finkelstein, Israel. *ʿIzbet Sartah: An Early Iron Age Site Near Rosh Haʿayin, Israel*. British Archaeological Reports International Series 299. Oxford, England: B.A.R., 1986.
Finkelstein, Israel, and David Ussishkin. "Back to Megiddo." *Biblical Archaeology Review* 20, no. 1 (January/February 1994): 26–43.
Fitzmyer, Joseph A., and Stephen A. Kaufman. *An Aramaic Bibliography, Part I: Old, Official, and Biblical Aramaic*. Baltimore: Johns Hopkins University Press, 1992.
Fleming, Stuart J. *Authenticity in Art: The Scientific Detection of Forgery*. New York: Crane, Russack, 1976.
———. *Dating in Archaeology: a Guide to Scientific Techniques*. London: J. M. Dent, 1976.
———. *Thermoluminescence Techniques in Archaeology*. New York: Oxford University Press, 1979.
Flusser, David. "'The House of David' on an Ossuary." *The Israel Museum Journal* 5 (1986): 37–40.
Fowler, Jeaneane D. *Theophoric Personal Names in Ancient Hebrew: A Comparative Study*. Journal for the Study of the Old Testament: Supplement Series 49. Sheffield, England: JSOT Press, 1988.

Fox, Nili Sacher. *In the Service of the King: Officialdom in Ancient Israel and Judah.* Cincinnati: Hebrew Union College Press, 2000.

———. "Royal Functionaries and State-Administration in Israel and Judah During the First Temple Period." Ph.D. diss., University of Pennsylvania, 1997.

Freedman, David Noel. "A Second Mesha Inscription." *Bulletin of the American Schools of Oriental Research* 175 (1964): 50–51.

———. "The Spelling of the Name 'David' in the Hebrew Bible." *Hebrew Annual Review* 7 (1983): 89–104.

———. "Yahweh of Samaria and his Asherah." *Biblical Archaeologist* 50 (1987): 241–49.

Freedman, David Noel, ed. *The Anchor Bible Dictionary.* 6 vols. New York: Doubleday, 1992.

Freedman, David Noel, and Jeffrey C. Geoghegan. "'House of David' Is There!" *Biblical Archaeology Review* 21, no. 2 (March/April 1995): 78–79.

Freedman, David Noel, and Jonas C. Greenfield, eds. *New Directions in Biblical Archaeology.* Garden City, N.Y.: Doubleday, 1969.

Gadd, Cyril J. "Inscribed Prisms of Sargon II from Nimrud." *Iraq* 16 (1954): 173–201, Pl. 45, 46.

Galil, Gershon. *The Chronology of the Kings of Israel and Judah.* Studies in the History and Culture of the Ancient Near East 9. New York: Brill, 1996.

———. "A Re-Arrangement of the Fragments of the Tel Dan Inscription and the Relations between Israel and Aram." *Palestine Exploration Quarterly* 133 (2001): 16–21.

Galling, Kurt. "Beschriftete Bildsiegel des ersten Jahrtausends v. Chr. vornehmlich aus Syrien und Palästina: Ein Beitrag zur Geschichte der phönikischen Kunst." *Zeitschrift des deutschen Palästina-Vereins* 6 (1941): 121–202.

———. "Das Siegel des Jotham von Tell el-Hlefi." *Zeitschrift des deutschen Palästina-Vereins* 83 (1967): 131–34.

Garbini, Giovanni. "L'iscrizione del re Uzzia." *Oriens Antiquus* 24 (1985): 67–75.

Garfinkel, Yosef. "The Eliakim Naʿar Yokan Seal Impressions: Sixty years of Confusion in Biblical Archaeological Research." *Biblical Archaeologist* 53 (1990): 74–79.

Garr, W. Randall. *Dialect Geography of Syria-Palestine, 1000–586 B.C.E.* Philadelphia: University of Pennsylvania Press, 1985.

Geller, Markham J., Jonas C. Greenfield, and Michael P. Weitzman, eds. *Studia Aramaica: New Sources and New Approaches: Papers Delivered at the London Conference of the Institute of Jewish Studies, University College, London, 26$^{th}$–28$^{th}$ June 1991.* Journal of Semitic Studies Supplement 4. New York: Oxford University Press, 1995.

Gesenius, H. F. Wilhelm. *Gesenius' Hebrew Grammar.* Edited and enlarged by Emil F. Kautzsch. Revised and translated by Arthur E. Cowley. 2d English ed. Oxford: Clarendon Press, 1910.

Gibson, John C. L. *Textbook of Syrian Semitic Inscriptions.* Vol. 1: *Hebrew and Moabite Inscriptions.* Corrected ed. New York: Oxford University Press, 1973.

———. *Textbook of Syrian Semitic Inscriptions.* Vol. 2: *Aramaic Inscriptions.* New York: Oxford University Press, 1975.

———. *Textbook of Syrian Semitic Inscriptions*, Vol. 3: *Phoenician Inscriptions*. New York: Oxford University Press, 1982.
Gibson, McGuire. "Summation." In *Seals and Sealing in the Ancient Near East*, 147–53. Edited by McGuire Gibson and Robert D. Biggs. Bibliotheca Mesopotamica 6. Malibu, Calif.: Undena Publications, 1977.
Gibson, McGuire, and Robert D. Biggs, eds. *The Organization of Power: Aspects of Bureaucracy in the Ancient Near East*. Studies in Ancient Oriental Civilization 46. Chicago: The Oriental Institute of the University of Chicago, 1987.
———, eds. *Seals and Sealing in the Ancient Near East*. Bibliotheca Mesopotamica 6. Malibu, Calif.: Undena Publications, 1977.
Gilbert, Felix, and Stephen R. Graubard, eds. *Historical Studies Today*. New York: Norton, 1972.
Ginsberg, Harold L. "Lachish Notes." *Bulletin of the American Schools of Oriental Research* 71 (1938): 24–25.
Gitin, Seymour, Trude Dothan, and Joseph Naveh. "A Royal Dedicatory Inscription from Ekron." *Israel Exploration Journal* 47 (1997): 1–16.
Glueck, Nelson. "Ezion-geber." *Biblical Archaeologist* 28 (1965): 70–87.
———. *The Other Side of the Jordan*. Rev. ed. New Haven, Conn.: American Schools of Oriental Research, 1970.
———. *Rivers in the Desert: A History of the Negev*. New York: Farrar, Strauss & Cudahy, 1959. Repr. as vol. 5 of Evergreen Encyclopedia. New York: Grove Press, Evergreen Books, 1960.
———. "Tell el-Kheleifeh Inscriptions." Pages 225–42, Pl. 1 in *Near Eastern Studies in Honor of William Foxwell Albright*. Edited by Hans Goedicke. Baltimore: Johns Hopkins Press, 1971.
———. "The Third Season of Excavation at Tell el-Kheleifeh." *Bulletin of the American Schools of Oriental Research* 79 (1940): 2–18.
Goedicke, Hans, ed. *Near Eastern Studies in Honor of William Foxwell Albright*. Baltimore: Johns Hopkins Press, 1971.
Gogel, Sandra Landis. *A Grammar of Epigraphic Hebrew*. SBL Resources for Biblical Study 23. Atlanta: Scholars Press, 1998.
Gorelick, Leonard, and A. John Gwinnett. "Ancient Seals and Modern Science: Using the Scanning Electron Microscope as an Aid in The Study of Ancient Seals." *Expedition* 20 (1978): 38–47.
Gorelick, Leonard, and Elizabeth Williams-Forte, eds. *Ancient Seals and the Bible*. International Institute for Mesopotamian Area Studies, Monographic Journals of the Near East, Occasional Papers on the Near East, vol. 2/1. Malibu, Calif.: Undena Publications, 1983.
Grabbe, Lester L., ed. *Can a 'History of Israel' Be Written?* Journal for the Study of the Old Testament: Supplement Series 245. European Seminar in Historical Methodology 1. Sheffield, England: Sheffield Academic Press, 1997.
Graham, M. Patrick. "The Discovery and Reconstruction of the Mesha Inscription." Pages 41–92 in *Studies in the Mesha Inscription and Moab*. Edited by J. Andrew Dearman. Archaeology and Biblical Studies 2. Atlanta: Scholars Press, 1989.

Gray, George Buchanan. *Studies in Hebrew Proper Names*. London: Adam & Charles Black, 1896.
Grayson, Albert Kirk. *Assyrian and Babylonian Chronicles*. Texts from Cuneiform Sources 5. Locust Valley, N.Y.: J. J. Augustin, 1975.
———. *Assyrian Rulers of the Early First Millennium BC, II (858–745 B.C.)*. Royal Inscriptions of Mesopotamia, Assyrian Periods 2. Buffalo, N.Y.: University of Toronto Press, 1996.
Greenberg, Moshe. *Ezekiel 1–20*. Anchor Bible 22. Garden City, N.Y.: Doubleday, 1983.
[Greenfield, Jonas C.] "Professor Nahman Avigad, 1905–1992: In Memoriam." *Israel Exploration Journal* 42 (1992): 1–3.
Gressmann, Hugo, ed. *Altorientalische Texte zum alten Testament*. Vol. 1 of *Altorientalische Texte und Bilder zum alten Testament*. Berlin and Leipzig: Walter de Gruyter, 1926.
Gubel, Eric. "Le sceau de Menahem et l'iconographie royale sigillaire." *Semitica* 38 (1990): 167–71.
———. "Notes sur l'iconographie royale sigillaire." Pages 913–22 in vol. 2 of *Congresso internazionale di studi fenici e punici 1987, Atti del IIo Congresso Internationale di Studi Fenici e Punici: Roma, 9–14 novembre 1987*. Edited by Enrico Acquaro, Piero Bartoloni, Maria Teresa Francisi, Lorenza-Ilia Manfredi, Federico Mazza, Giovanni Montalto, Gesualdo Petruccioli, Sergio Ribichini, Gabriella Matthiae Scandone, and Paolo Xella. Collezione di Studi Fenici 30. Rome: Consiglio nazionale delle richerche, 1991.
Gwinnett, A. John, and Leonard Gorelick. "Seal Manufacture in the Lands of the Bible: Recent Findings." Pages 44–49, Pl. III–VIII in *Ancient Seals and the Bible*. Edited by Leonard Gorelick and Elizabeth Williams-Forte. International Institute for Mesopotamian Area Studies Occasional Papers on the Near East 2/1, Monographic Journals of the Near East. Malibu, Calif.: Undena Publications, 1983.
Hackett, Jo Ann. *The Balaam Text from Deir ʿAllā*. Harvard Semitic Monographs 31. Chico, Calif.: Scholars Press, 1984.
———. "Some Observations on the Balaam Tradition at Deir ʿAllā." *Biblical Archaeologist* 49 (1986): 216–22.
Hallo, William W., ed. *The Context of Scripture*. 3 vols. New York: Brill, 1997–2002.
Halpern, Baruch. "Erasing History: The Minimalist Assault on Ancient Israel." *Bible Review* 11 (December 1995): 26–35, 47.
———. "The Stela from Dan: Epigraphic and Historical Considerations." *Bulletin of the American Schools of Oriental Research* 296 (1994): 64–68.
Haran, Menahem. *Temples and Temple-Service in Ancient Israel: An Inquiry into Biblical Cult Phenomena and the Historical Setting of the Priestly School*. Oxford: Clarendon, 1978. Repr. with corrections, Winona Lake, Ind.: Eisenbrauns, 1985.
Harding, G. Lankester. "The Seals of Adoni Nur, Servant of the Ammonite King: New Finds from a Seventh-Century B.C. Jordanian Tomb." *Illustrated London News* 5759 (September 3, 1949): 351.
———. "Four Tomb Groups from Jordan." *Palestine Exploration Fund Annual* 6 (1953): v–xi, 1–65, Pl. I–VII.
Harris, Rivkah. "Notes on the Nomenclature of Old Babylonian Sippar." *Journal of Cuneiform Studies* 24 (1972): 102–4.

Harris, Zellig S. *Development of the Canaanite Dialects: An Investigation in Linguistic History*. American Oriental Series 16. New Haven, Conn.: American Oriental Society, 1939.
Hayes, John H., and J. Maxwell Miller, eds. *Israelite and Judaean History*. Philadelphia: Trinity Press International, 1977.
Heltzer, Michael. "Eighth Century B.C. Inscriptions from Kalakh (Nimrud)." *Palestine Exploration Quarterly* 110 (1978): 3–9.
———. "Two Ancient West Semitic Seals." *Studi epigrafici e linguistici sul Vicino Oriente antico* 16 (1999): 45–47.
Herr, Larry G. "Paleography and the Identification of Seal Owners." *Bulletin of the American Schools of Oriental Research* 239 (1980): 67–70.
———. "The Palaeography of West Semitic Stamp Seals." *Bulletin of the American Schools of Oriental Research* 312 (1998): 45–77.
———. Review of Robert Deutsch, *Messages from the Past: Hebrew Bullae from the Time of Isaiah through the Destruction of the First Temple*. *Bulletin of the American Schools of Oriental Research* 319 (2000): 77–79.
———. *The Scripts of Ancient Northwest Semitic Seals*. Harvard Semitic Monographs 18. Missoula, Mont.: Scholars Press, 1978.
———. "Seal." Pages 369–75 in vol. 4 of *International Standard Bible Encyclopedia*. Edited by Geoffrey W. Bromiley. 4 vols. Fully rev. ed. Grand Rapids, Mich.: Eerdmans, 1979–1988.
Hestrin, Ruth. "Understanding Asherah: Exploring Semitic Iconography." *Biblical Archaeology Review* 17, no. 5 (September/October 1991): 50–59.
Hestrin, Ruth, and Michal Dayagi. "A Seal Impression of a Servant of King Hezekiah." *Israel Exploration Journal* 24 (1974): 27–29, Pl. 2, B, C.
Hestrin, Ruth, and Michal Dayagi-Mendels. *Inscribed Seals: First Temple Period: Hebrew, Ammonite, Moabite, Phoenician, and Aramaic, from the Collection of the Israel Museum and the Israel Department of Antiquities and Museums*. Jerusalem: Israel Museum, 1979.
Hodder, Ian. *Reading the Past: Current Approaches to Interpretation in Archaeology*. Cambridge, England: Cambridge University Press, 1986.
Hoftijzer, Jacob, and Karel Jongeling. *Dictionary of the North-West Semitic Inscriptions*. 2 vols. Handbuch der Orientalistik, erste Abteilung, Der nahe und mittlere Osten 21. New York: Brill, 1995.
Hoftijzer, Jacob, and Gerrit van der Kooij. *Aramaic Texts from Deir 'Alla*. Documenta et Monumenta Orientis Antiqui 19. Leiden: Brill, 1976.
Hoftijzer, Jacob, and Gerrit van der Kooij, eds. *The Balaam Text from Deir 'Alla Re-Evaluated: Proceedings of the International Symposium held at Leiden, 21–24 August 1989*. New York: Brill, 1991.
Holladay, William L. *Jeremiah 2*. Hermeneia. Minneapolis: Fortress, 1989.
Hopfe, Lewis M., ed. *Uncovering Ancient Stones: Essays in Memory of H. Neil Richardson*. Winona Lake, Ind.: Eisenbrauns, 1994.
Hornblower, Simon, and Anthony J. S. Spawforth. "Prosopography." Pages 1262–63 in *The Oxford Classical Dictionary*. Edited by Simon Hornblower and Anthony J. S. Spawforth. 3d ed. New York: Oxford University Press, 1996.

Hübner, Ulrich. *Die Ammoniter: Untersuchungen zur Geschichte, Kultur und Religion eines transjordanischen Volkes im 1. Jahrtausend v. Chr.* Abhandlungen des deutschen Palästina Vereins 16. Wiesbaden: Harrassowitz, 1992.

———. "Fälschungen ammonitischer Siegel." *Ugarit-Forschungen* 21 (1989): 217–26.

Ingholt, Harald. "Un nouveau thiase à Palmyre." *Syria* 7 (1926): 128–141, Pl. XXXIV.

Israel, Felice. "Inventaire préliminaire des sceaux paléo-hébreux (Études de lexique paléo-hébraïque III)." *Zeitschrift für Althebraistik* 7 (1994): 51–80.

International Organization of Old Testament Scholars. *Congress Volume, Oxford 1959.* Edited by George W. Anderson. Supplements to Vetus Testamentum 7. Leiden: Brill, 1960.

Israel Museum. *Inscriptions Reveal: Documents from the Time of the Bible, the Mishna and the Talmud* (in Hebrew and English). Edited by Efrat Carmon. Translated by Rafi Grafman. Rev. 2d ed. Israel Museum Catalogue 100. Jerusalem: Israel Museum, 1973.

Jackson, Kent P. *The Ammonite Language of the Iron Age.* Harvard Semitic Monographs 27. Chico, Calif.: Scholars Press, 1983.

———. "The Language of the Meshaʿ Inscription." Pages 96–130 in *Studies in the Mesha Inscription and Moab.* Edited by J. Andrew Dearman. Archaeology and Biblical Studies 2. Atlanta: Scholars Press, 1989.

Jackson, Kent P., and J. Andrew Dearman. "The Text of the Meshaʿ Inscription." Pages 93–95 in *Studies in the Mesha Inscription and Moab.* Edited by J. Andrew Dearman. Archaeology and Biblical Studies 2. Atlanta: Scholars Press, 1989.

Janzen, J. Gerald. *Studies in the Text of Jeremiah.* Harvard Semitic Monographs 6. Cambridge, Mass.: Harvard University Press, 1973.

Japhet, Sara. "The Supposed Common Authorship of Chronicles and Ezra-Nehemia Investigated Anew." *Vetus Testamentum* 18 (1968): 338–41.

Jean, Charles-F., and Jacob Hoftijzer. *Dictionnaire des inscriptions sémitiques de l'ouest.* Leiden: Brill, 1965.

Jordan, James R. "Studies in Sumerian Prosopography: Sheshkalla." Ph.D. diss., University of Minnesota, 1971.

Kallai, Zecharia. "The King of Israel and the House of David." *Israel Exploration Journal* 43 (1993): 248.

Kantor, Helene J. "Oriental Institute Museum Notes, No. 13: A Bronze Plaque with Relief Decoration from Tell Tainat." *Journal of Near Eastern Studies* 21 (1962): 93–117, Pl. XI–XV.

Kaufman, Stephen A. "Recent Contributions of Aramaic Studies to Biblical Hebrew Philology and the Exegesis of the Hebrew Bible." Pages 43–54 in *Congress Volume: Basel 2001.* Edited by André Lemaire. Supplements to Vetus Testamentum 92. Boston: Brill, 2002.

Kautzsch, Emil. "Ein althebräisches Siegel vom Tell el-Mutesellim." *Mittheilungen und Nachrichten des Deutschen Palästina-Vereins* 10 (1904): 1–14.

———. "Zur Deutung des Löwensiegels." *Mittheilungen und Nachrichten des Deutschen Palästina-Vereins* 10 (1904): 81–88.

Keel, Othmar. *Corpus der Stempelsiegel-Amulette aus Palästina/Israel: Von den Anfängen bis zur Perserzeit Einleitung.* Orbis Biblicus et Orientalis, Series Archaeologica 10. Göttingen: Vandenhoeck & Ruprecht, 1995.

———. *Die Welt der altorientalischen Bildsymbolik und das Alte Testament: Am Beispiel der Psalmen.* 5th ed. Göttingen: Vandenhoeck & Ruprecht, 1996.
Kempinski, Aharon. "Some Philistine Names from the Kingdom of Gaza." *Israel Exploration Journal* 37 (1987): 20–24.
Kessler, Andreas, Thomas Ricklin, and Gregor Wurst, eds. *Peregrina curiositas: Ein Reise durch den Orbis antiquus: zu Ehren von Dirk Van Damme.* Göttingen: Vandenhoeck & Ruprecht, 1994.
King, Philip J. *Jeremiah: An Archaeological Companion.* Louisville, Ky.: Westminster/John Knox Press, 1993.
Kitchen, Kenneth A. *Ancient Orient and Old Testament.* Downers Grove, Ill.: InterVarsity Press, 1966.
———. "The Basics of Egyptian Chronology in Relation to the Bronze Age." Pages 37–55 in Part I of *High, Middle, or Low: Acts of an International Colloquium on Absolute Chronology Held at the University of Gothenburg $20^{th}$–$22^{nd}$ August 1987.* Edited by Paul Åström. 3 parts in 3 vols.; Gothenburg, Sweden: Paul Åström Förlag, 1987).
———. *On the Reliability of the Old Testament.* Grand Rapids, Mich.: Eerdmans, 2003.
———. "A Possible Mention of David in the Late Tenth Century B.C.E., and Deity *Dod as Dead as the Dodo?" *Journal for the Study of the Old Testament* 76 (1997): 29–44.
———. "Some New Light on the Asiatic Wars of Ramesses II." *Journal of Egyptian Archaeology* 50 (1964): 47–70, Pl. 3–6.
———. "Supplementary Notes on 'The Basics of an Egyptian Chronology.'" Pages 152–59 in Part 3 of *High, Middle, or Low: Acts of an International Colloquium on Absolute Chronology Held at the University of Gothenburg $20^{th}$–$22^{nd}$ August 1987.* Edited by Paul Åström. 3 parts in 3 vols.; Gothenburg, Sweden: Paul Åström Förlag, 1987).
———. *The Third Intermediate Period in Egypt (1100–650 B.C.).* 2d ed. with Supplement. Warminster, England: Aris & Phillips, 1986.
Kloner, Amos. "A Burial Cave of the Second Temple Period at Givʾat Hamivtar, Jerusalem" (in Hebrew). *Qadmoniot* 19–20 (1972): 108–9.
Knauf, Ernst A., Alan de Pury, and Thomas Römer. "*BaytDawid ou *BaytDōd? Une relecture de la nouvelle inscription de Tel Dan." *Biblische Notizen* 72 (1994): 60–69.
Knoppers, Gary N. "The Vanishing Solomon: The Disappearance of the United Monarchy from Recent Histories of Ancient Israel." *Journal of Biblical Literature* 116 (1997): 19–44.
Kochavi, Moshe. "An Ostracon of the Period of the Judges from ʿIzbet Sartah." *Tel Aviv* 4 (1977): 1–13.
———. "The Ostracon." Page 654 of vol. 2 in *New Encyclopedia of Archaeological Excavations in the Holy Land.* Edited by Ephraim Stern. New York: Simon & Schuster, 1993.
Kochavi, Moshe, and Aaron Demsky. "An Israelite Village from the Days of the Judges." *Biblical Archaeology Review* 4, no. 3 (September/October 1978): 18–21.

Kraeling, Emil G.. "Ahiqar, Book of." Pages 68–69 in vol. 1 of *Interpreter's Dictionary of the Bible*. Edited by George A. Buttrick. Nashville: Abingdon Press, 1962.

Kuan, Jeffrey K. *Neo-Assyrian Historical Inscriptions and Syria-Palestine: Israelite/Judean-Tyrian-Damascene Political and Commercial Relations in the Ninth–Eighth Centuries B.C.E.* Jian Dao Dissertation Series 1. Bible and Literature 1. Hong Kong: Alliance Biblical Seminary, 1995.

Kyrieleis, Helmut, and Wolfgang Röllig. "Ein altorientalischer Pferdeschmuck aus dem Heraion von Samos." *Mitteilungen des Deutschen Archäologischen Instituts, Athenische Abteilung* 103 (1988): 37–75, Pl. 9–15.

Lambdin, Thomas O. "Egyptian Loan Words in the Old Testament." *Journal of the American Oriental Society* 73 (1953): 145–55.

Lamon, Robert S., and Geoffrey M. Shipton. *Megiddo I: Seasons of 1925–34, Strata I–V.* Oriental Institute Publications 42. Chicago: University of Chicago Press, 1939.

Lapp, Paul W. *Biblical Archaeology and History*. New York: World Publishing, 1969.

———. "Palestine: Known but Mostly Unknown." *Biblical Archaeologist* 26 (1963): 121–34.

Layton, Scott C. *Archaic Features of Canaanite Personal Names in the Hebrew Bible*. Harvard Semitic Monographs 47. Atlanta: Scholars Press, 1990.

Lemaire, André. "Abécédaires et exercices d'ecolier en épigraphie nord-ouest sémitique." *Journal asiatique* 266 (1978): 221–35.

———. "André Lemaire Replies." *Biblical Archaeology Review* 20, no. 6 (November/December 1994): 72.

———. "Cinq nouveaux sceaux inscrits ouest sémitiques." *Studi epigrafici e linguistici sul Vicino Oriente antico* 7 (1990): 96–109.

———. "Les critères non-iconographiques de la classification des sceaux nord-ouest sémitiques inscrits." Pages 1–26 in *Studies in the Iconography of Northwest Semitic Inscribed Seals: Proceedings of a Symposium Held in Fribourg on April 17–20, 1991*. Edited by Benjamin Sass and Christoph Uehlinger. Orbis Biblicus et Orientalis 125. Göttingen: Vandenhoeck & Ruprecht, 1993.

———. "La dynastie Davidique (*bytdwd*) dans deux inscriptions ouest-sémitiques du IXe s. av. J.-C." *Studi epigrafici e linguistici sul Vicino Oriente antico* 11 (1994): 17–19.

———. "Epigraphie palestinienne: nouveaux documents I. Fragment de stèle araméene de Tell Dan (IXe s. av. J.-C.)." *Henoch* 16 (1994): 87–93.

———. "'House of David' Restored in Moabite Inscription." *Biblical Archaeology Review* 20, no. 3 (May/June 1994): 30–37.

———. "Les inscriptions araméens de Cheikh-Fadl (Égypte)." Pages 77–132 in *Studia Aramaica: New Sources and New Approaches: Papers Delivered at the London Conference of the Institute of Jewish Studies, University College, London, 26$^{th}$–28$^{th}$ June 1991*. Edited by Markham J. Geller, Jonas C. Greenfield, and Michael P. Weitzman. Journal of Semitic Studies Supplement 4. New York: Oxford University Press, 1995.

———. "Les inscriptions de Khirbet el-Qôm et l'Asherah de Yhwh." *Revue biblique* 84 (1977): 597–609.

———. "Joas de Samarie, Barhadad de Damas, Zakkur de Hamat: la Syrie-Palestine vers 800 av. J.C." *Eretz-Israel* 24 (Abraham Malamat Volume, 1993): 148*–57*.

———. "Name of Israel's Last King Surfaces in a Private Collection." *Biblical Archaeology Review* 21, no. 6 (November/December 1995): 48–52.
———. "Note sur le titre *bn hmlk* dans l'ancien Israël." *Semitica* 29 (1979): 59–65.
———. "Nouveaux sceaux et bulles paléo-hébraïques. *Eretz-Israel* 26 (Frank Moore Cross Volume, 1999): 106*–15*.
———. "Nouvelles donées épigraphiques sur l'époque royale israélite." *Revue des etudes juives* 156 (1997): 445–61.
———. "Populations et territoires de la Palestine a l'epoque perse." *Transeuphratene* 3 (1990): 31–74.
———. "Sept nouveaux sceaux nord-ouest sémitiques inscrits." *Semitica* 41–42 (1993): 63–80.
———. "The Tel Dan Stela as a Piece of Royal Historiography." *Journal for the Study of the Old Testament* 81 (1998): 3–41.
———. "Une inscription paléo-hébraïque sur grenade en ivoire." *Revue biblique* 88 (1981): 236–39.
———. "Note sur le titre *bn hmlk* dans l'ancien Israël." *Semitica* 29 (1979): 59–65.
———. "Who or What Was Yahweh's Asherah? Startling New Inscriptions from Two Different Sites Reopen the Debate about the Meaning of Asherah." *Biblical Archaeology Review* 10, no. 6 (November/December 1984): 42–51.
Lemaire, André, ed. *Congress Volume: Basel 2001*. Supplements to Vetus Testamentum 92. Boston: Brill, 2002.
Lemaire, André, and Benedikt Otzen, eds. *History and Traditions of Early Israel: Studies Presented to Eduard Nielsen, May 8th, 1993*. Supplements to Vetus Testamentum 50. New York: Brill, 1993.
Lemche, Niels P. *Ancient Israel: A New History of Israelite Society*. Translated by Frederick H. Cryer. The Biblical Seminar 5. Sheffield, England: Sheffield Academic Press, 1988.
———. "The Old Testament—A Hellenistic Book?" *Scandinavian Journal of the Old Testament* 7 (1993): 163–93.
Lemche, Niels P., and Thomas L. Thompson. "Did Biran Kill David? The Bible in the Light of Archaeology." *Journal for the Study of the Old Testament* 64 (1994): 3–22.
Levine, Louis D. *Two Neo-Assyrian Stelae from Iran*. Art and Archaeology Royal Ontario Museum Occasional Paper 23. Ontario: Royal Ontario Museum, 1972.
Lidzbarski, Mark. *Ephemeris für semitische Epigraphik*. 3 vols. Giessen: J. Ricker, Alfred Töpelmann, 1902–1915.
———. *Handbuch der nordsemitischen Epigraphik nebst ausgewälten Inschriften*. 2 vols. Weimar: Verlag von Emil Felber, 1898. Repr., Hildesheim: Georg Olms, 1962.
———. "Eine Nachprüfung der Mesainschrift." Pages 1–10 in vol. 1 of *Ephemeris für semitische Epigraphik*. Giessen: J. Ricker, 1902.
Lindenberger, James M. *Ancient Aramaic and Hebrew Letters*. Edited by Kent H. Richards. Society of Biblical Literature Writings from the Ancient World 4. Atlanta: Scholars Press, 1994.

Lipiński, Edward. "Etymological and Exegetical Notes on the Meša 'Inscription.'" *Orientalia* 40 (1971): 332–34.

———. *Studies in Aramaic Inscriptions and Onomastics, I.* Orientalia Lovaniensia Analecta 1. Leuven: Leuven University Press, 1974.

———. *Studies in Aramaic Inscriptions and Onomastics, II.* Orientalia Lovaniensia Analecta 57. Leuven: Uitgeverij Peeters en Departement Oriëntalistiek, 1994.

Liverani, Mario. "The Deeds of Ancient Mesopotamian Kings." Pages 2353–66 in vol. 4 of *Civilizations of the Ancient Near East.* Edited by Jack M. Sasson. New York: Charles Scribner's Sons, 1995.

Longman, Tremper III. *Fictional Akkadian Autobiography: A Generic and Comparative Study.* Winona Lake, Ind.: Eisenbrauns, 1991.

Longpérier, Henri Adrien P. de. "Cachet de Sébénias, fils d'Osias." *Comptes Rendus des Séances de l'Académie des Inscriptions et Belles-Lettres* 6 (1863): 288.

Löwy, Albert. *A Critical Examination of the So-Called Moabite Inscription in the Louvre.* 3d ed. London: Printed for private circulation, 1903.

Luckenbill, Daniel D. *Historical Records of Assyria from the Earliest Times to Sargon.* Vol. I of *Ancient Records of Assyria and Babylonia.* Chicago: University of Chicago Press, 1926. Repr. New York: Greenwood Press, 1968.

———. *The Annals of Sennacherib.* University of Chicago Oriental Institute Publications 2. Chicago, University of Chicago Press, 1924.

MacDonald, Burton, and Randall W. Younker, eds. *Ancient Ammon.* Studies in the History and Culture of the Ancient Near East 17. Boston: Brill, 1999.

Maeir, Aren M., and Pierre R. Miroschedji, eds. *I Will Tell Secret Things from Long Ago (Abiah Chidot Menei-Kedem)—Ps. 78:2b): Archaeological and Historical Studies in Honor of Amihai Mazar on the Occasion of his Sixtieth Birthday.* Winona Lake, Ind.: Eisenbrauns, in press.

Malamat, Abraham. "Jeremiah and the Last Two Kings of Judah." *Palestine Exploration Quarterly* (1951): 81–87.

———, ed. *The World History of the Jewish People.* Vol. 4, no. I of *The Age of the Monarchies: Political History.* Edited by Benzion Netanyahu, Benjamin Mazar, Abraham Schalit, Michael Avi-Yonah, and Cecil Roth. Jerusalem: Massada Press, 1979.

Mallowan, Max E. L. *Nimrud and Its Remains.* 2 vols. New York: Dodd, Mead & Co., 1966.

Maraqten, Mohammed. *Die semitischen Personennamen in den alt- und reichsaramäischen Inschriften aus Vorderasien.* Texte und Studien zur Orientalistik 5. New York: Georg Olms Verlag, 1988.

Margalit, Baruch. "Studies in NWSemitic [sic] Inscriptions." *Ugarit-Forschungen* 26 (1994): 271–315.

Martin, William J. "The Jehoiachin Tablets." Pages 84–86 in *Documents from Old Testament Times.* Edited by D. Winton Thomas. London: Thomas Nelson & Sons, 1958. Repr. New York: Harper & Row, Harper Torchbooks, 1961.

Mazar, Amihai. *Archaeology of the Land of the Bible, 10,000–586 B.C.E.* Vol. 1 of *Archaeology of the Land of the Bible.* New York: Doubleday, 1990.

Mazar, Benjamin, and Gaalyahu Cornfeld. *The Mountain of the Lord.* Garden City, N.Y.: Doubleday, 1975.

McCarter, P. Kyle Jr. "'Yaw, Son of 'Omri': A Philological Note on Israelite Chronology." *Bulletin of the American Schools of Oriental Research* 216 (1974): 5–7.

———. "The Bulla of Nathan-melech, the Servant of the King." Pages 142–53 in *Realia Dei Essays in Archaeology and Biblical Interpretation in Honor of Edward F. Campbell, Jr., at His Retirement*. Edited by Prescott H. Williams Jr. and Theodore Hiebert. Atlanta: Scholars Press, 1999.

Meshel, Ze'ev. "Did Yahweh Have a Consort? The New Religious Inscriptions from Sinai." *Biblical Archaeology Review* 5, no. 2 (March/April 1979): 24–35.

———. "Kuntillet 'Ajrud—An Israelite Religious Center in Northern Sinai." *Expedition* 20 (Summer 1978): 50–54.

———. "Kuntillat 'Ajrud—An Israelite Site from the Monarchial Period on the Sinai Border" (in Hebrew). *Qadmoniot* 9 (1976): 118–24.

———. *Kuntillet 'Ajrud: A Religious Centre from the Time of the Judean Monarchy on the Border of Sinai*. Israel Museum Catalogue 175. Jerusalem: Israel Museum, 1978.

Mettinger, Tryggve N. D. *No Graven Image? Israelite Aniconism in Its Ancient Near Eastern Context*. Coniectanea Biblica, Old Testament Series 42. Stockholm: Almqvist & Wiksell International, 1995.

———. *Solomonic State Officials: A Study of the Civil Government Officials of the Israelite Monarchy*. Coniectanea Biblica, Old Testament Series 5. Lund: CWK Gleerup, 1971.

Meyers, Eric M. "The Shelomith Seal and the Judean Restoration: Some Additional Considerations." *Eretz-Israel* 18 (Nahman Avigad Volume, 1985): 35*–37*.

———, ed. *The Oxford Encyclopedia of Archaeology in the Near East*. 5 vols. New York: Oxford University Press, 1997.

Michaud, Henri. "Le récit de II Rois, III et la Stèle de Mésha." Pages 29–45 in *Sur la pierre et l'argile: inscriptions hébraïques et l'Ancien Testament*, by Henri Michaud. Cahiers d'archéology biblique 10. Neuchatel: Delachaux et Niestlé, 1958.

Milano, Lucio. "L'étude prosopographique des textes cunéiformes d'Ebla (IIIe millénaire avant J.-C.): Quelques réflexions à propos du projet et de ses finalités." Pages 91–114 in *Informatique et Prosopographie: Actés de la Table Ronde du CNRS, Paris, 25–26 octobre 1984*. Edited by Hélène Millet. Paris: Éditions du Centre National de la Recherche Scientifique, 1985.

Millard, Alan R. "Alphabetic Inscriptions on Ivories from Nimrud." *Iraq* 24 (1962): 41–51, Pl. XXIII–XXIV.

———. "Assyrian Royal Names in Biblical Hebrew." *Journal of Semitic Studies* 21 (1976): 1–14.

Millard, Alan R., James K. Hoffmeier, and David W. Baker, eds. *Faith, Tradition, and History: Old Testament Historiography in Its Near Eastern Context*. Winona Lake, Ind.: Eisenbrauns, 1994.

Miller, J. Maxwell. "Approaches to the Bible through History and Archaeology: Biblical History as a Discipline." *Biblical Archaeologist* 45 (1982): 211–16.

———. "Is it Possible to Write a History of Israel without Relying on the Hebrew Bible?" Pages 93–102 in *The Fabric of History: Text, Artifact, and Israel's Past*. Edited by Diana V. Edelman. Journal for the Study of the Old Testament: Supplement Series 127. Sheffield, England: Sheffield Academic Press, JSOT Press, 1991.

———. *The Old Testament and the Historian*. Guides to Biblical Scholarship, Old Testament Series. Philadelphia: Fortress, 1976.

Miller, Patrick D. Jr. "Moabite Stone." Pages 396–98 in vol. 3 of *International Standard Bible Encyclopedia*. Edited by Geoffrey W. Bromiley. 4 vols. Fully rev. ed. Grand Rapids, Mich.: Eerdmans, 1979–1988.

Miller, Patrick D. Jr., Paul D. Hanson, and S. Dean McBride, eds. *Ancient Israelite Religion: Essays in Honor of Frank Moore Cross*. Philadelphia: Fortress, 1987.

Millet, Hélène, ed. *Informatique et Prosopographie: Actés de la Table Ronde du CNRS, Paris, 25–26 octobre 1984*. Paris: Éditions du Centre National de la Recherche Scientifique, 1985.

Moorey, P. Roger S. *A Century of Biblical Archaeology*. Louisville, Ky.: Westminster/John Knox Press, 1991.

Morgenstern, Julian. *Amos Studies*. Cincinnati: Hebrew Union College Press, 1941.

Moscati, Sabatino. *L'epigrafia ebraica antica, 1935–1950*. Rome: Pontifical Biblical Institute, 1951.

Muilenburg, James. "Baruch the Scribe." Pages 215–38 in *Proclamation and Presence: Old Testament Essays in Honour of Gwynne Henton Davies*. Edited by John I. Durham and J. Roy Porter. Richmond: John Knox Press, 1970.

Müller, Hans-Peter. "Die aramäische Inschrift von Tel Dan." *Zeitschrift für Althebraistik* 8 (1995): 121–39.

Muraoka, Takamitsu. "Linguistic Notes on the Aramaic Inscription from Tel Dan" *Israel Exploration Journal* 45 (1995): 19–21.

Murphy, Roland E. "Israel and Moab in the Ninth Century." *Catholic Biblical Quarterly* 15 (1953): 409–17.

Mykytiuk, Lawrence J. "Accessing Voices of the Biblical World, Part 2: Tools and Corpora of Northwest Semitic Inscriptions of 1190–333 B.C.E." *Bulletin of Bibliography* 59 (2002): 151–66.

———. "Did Bible Characters Really Exist? Part 1: An Annotated Bibliography on Methods of Evaluating Evidence in Hebrew Inscriptions." *Bulletin of Bibliography* 55 (1998): 243–49.

———. "Did Bible Characters Really Exist? Part 2: An Annotated Bibliography of Northwest Semitic Monumental Inscriptions from before 539 B.C." *Bulletin of Bibliography* 56 (1999): 95–104.

———. "Did Bible Characters Really Exist? Part 3: An Annotated Bibliography of Northwest Semitic Monumental Inscriptions from before 539 B.C., Concluded." *Bulletin of Bibliography* 58 (2001): 135–41.

———. "Is Hophni in the ʿIzbet Ṣarṭah Ostracon?" *Andrews University Seminary Studies* 36 (1998): 69–80.

Naʾaman, Nadav. "Beth-David in the Aramaic Stela from Tel Dan." *Biblische Notizen* 79 (1995): 17–27.

———. "Hazael of ʿAmqi and Hadadezer of Beth-rehob." *Ugarit-Forschungen* 27 (1995): 381–94.

———. "The Historical Background of the Conquest of Samaria (720 BC)." *Biblica* 71 (1990): 206–25.

———, "Sennacherib's 'Letter to God' on His Campaign to Judah." *Bulletin of the American Schools of Oriental Research* 214 (1974): 25–39.

Naveh, Joseph. "Achish-Ikausu in the Light of the Ekron Dedication." *Bulletin of the American Schools of Oriental Research* 310 (1998): 35–37.

———. "Aramaica Dubiosa." *Journal of Near Eastern Studies* 27 (1968): 317–25.

———. "Clumsy Forger Fools the Scholars—But Only for a Time." *Biblical Archaeology Review* 10, no. 3 (May/June 1984): 66–72.

———. *The Development of the Aramaic Script*. The Israel Academy of Sciences and Humanities Proceedings 5, no. 1. Jerusalem: Israel Academy of Sciences and Humanities, 1970.

———. *Early History of the Alphabet: An Introduction to West Semitic Epigraphy and Palaeography*. 2d rev. ed. Jerusalem: The Hebrew University, Magnes Press, 1987.

———. "Graffiti and Dedications." *Bulletin of the American Schools of Oriental Research* 235 (1979): 27–30.

———. "The Greek Alphabet: New Evidence." *Biblical Archaeologist* 43 (1980): 22–25.

———. "Nameless People." *Israel Exploration Journal* 40 (1990): 108–23.

———. "Some Considerations on the Ostracon from 'Izbet Sartah." *Israel Exploration Journal* 28 (1978): 31–35.

———. "Some Recently Forged Inscriptions." *Bulletin of the American Schools of Oriental Research* 247 (1982): 53–58.

———. "Word Division in West Semitic Writing." *Israel Exploration Journal* 23 (1973): 206–8.

———. "Writing and Scripts in Seventh-Century B.C.E. Philistia: The New Evidence from Tell Jemmeh." *Israel Exploration Journal* 35 (1985): 8–21, Pl. 2–4.

Naveh, Joseph, and Hayim Tadmor. "Some Doubtful Aramaic Seals." *Annali dell' Istituto orientale di Napoli* 18 (1968): 448–52, Pl. I–III.

Nicolet, Claude. "Prosopographie et histoire sociale: Rome et l'Italie à l'epoque républicaine." *Annales: Économies, Sociétés, Civilisations* 25 (1970): 1209–28.

Niki, Elly. "Sur une 'Potnia-Gorgone' d'Erétrie au Musée national d'Athènes." *Révue Archéologique*, 6me series, 1 (1933): 145–53.

Ninow, Friedbert, ed. *Wort und Stein: Festschrift Udo Worschech*. Beiträge zur Erforschung der antiken Moabitis (Ard el-Kerak). Frankfurt: Peter Lang Verlag, 2003.

[Nordberg, Heidi L.] "Photoessay: New Photographic Techniques for Documenting Inscribed Objects." *Religious Studies News* 11, no. 3 (September 1996): 12, 23, 29.

Nordlander, K. G. Amandus. *Die Inschrift des Königs Mesa von Moab*. Leipzig: W. Drugulin, 1896.

Noth, Martin. *Geschichte Israels*. 2d ed. Göttingen: Vandenhoeck & Ruprecht, 1954. ET, *The History of Israel*. Translated by Peter R. Ackroyd. New York: Harper & Brothers, 1960.

———. *Die israelitischen Personennamen im Rahmen der gemeinsemitischen Namengebung*. Beiträge zur Wissenschaft vom Alten (und Neuen) Testament 3/10. Stuttgart; W. Kohlhammer, 1928. Repr. New York: Georg Olms, 1980.

Oates, David. "The Excavations at Nimrud (Kalhu), 1961." *Iraq* 24 (1962): 1–25, Pl. I–VII.

Oded, Bustenay. *Mass Deportations and Deportees in the Assyrian Empire*. Wiesbaden: Ludwig Reichert, 1979.

Oppenheim, A. Leo. *Ancient Mesopotamia: Portrait of a Dead Civilization*. Chicago: University of Chicago Press, 1964.

Oppenheim, A. Leo, Erica Reiner, and Robert D. Biggs, eds. *The Assyrian Dictionary: A*. Vol. 1, Part II of *The Assyrian Dictionary of the Oriental Institute of the University of Chicago*. Edited by Miguel Civil, Ignace J. Gelb, Benno Landsberger, A. Leo Oppenheim, and Erica Reiner. Chicago: University of Chicago Press, 1956– .

Overbeck, Bernhard, and Yaakov Meshorer. *Das Heilige Land: Antike Münzen und Siegel aus einem Jahrtausend Jüdischer Geschichte*. Katalog der Sondersusstellung 1993/94. Munich: Staatliche Münzsammlung München in cooperation with the Israel Museum, Jerusalem, 1993.

Owen, David I., and Gordon D. Young. "An Interview with Michael C. Astour on the Occasion of His Being Honored by the Middle West Branch of the American Oriental Society, February 11 and 12, 1996." Pages 1–36 in *Crossing Boundaries and Linking Horizons: Studies in Honor of Michael C. Astour on His 80th Birthday*. Edited by Gordon D. Young, Mark W. Chavalas, and Richard E. Averbeck. Bethesda, Md.: CDL Press, 1997.

Pace, James H. Review of Niels Peter Lemche, *Israelites in History and Tradition*. *Bulletin of the American Schools of Oriental Research* 319 (2000): 71–72.

Page, Stephanie. "A Stela of Adad-Nirari III and Nergal-Eresh from Tell al Rimah." *Iraq* 30 (1968): 139–53, Pl. 38–41.

Paine, John A. "Critical Note: Not Lachish, but Gath." *Bibliotheca Sacra* 47 (1890): 682–91.

Pardee, Dennis. *Handbook of Ancient Hebrew Letters: A Study Edition*. Society of Biblical Literature Sources for Biblical Study 15. Chico, Calif.: Scholars Press, 1982.

Parker, Simon B. *Stories in Scripture and Inscriptions: Comparative Studies on Narratives in Northwest Semitic Inscriptions and the Hebrew Bible*. New York: Oxford University Press, 1997.

Parkes, Penelope A. *Current Scientific Techniques in Archaeology*. New York: St. Martin's Press, 1986.

Parpola, Simo, ed. *The Prosopography of the Neo-Assyrian Empire*. 2 vols. to date. Helsinki: The Neo-Assyrian Text Corpus Project, 1998– .

Paul, Shalom M. *Amos*. Edited by Frank M. Cross. Hermeneia; Minneapolis: Fortress, 1991.

Petrie, William M. Flinders. *Tell el Hesy (Lachish)*. London: Alexander P. Watt, for the Committee of the Palestine Exploration Fund, 1891.

Pinches, Theophilus G.: see Society of Biblical Archaeology (London, England).

Pirot, Louis: see *Dictionnaire de la Bible, Supplément*.

Pitard, Wayne T. *Ancient Damascus: A Historical Study of the Syrian City-State from Earliest Times until its Fall to the Assyrians in 732 B.C.E.* Winona Lake, Ind.: Eisenbrauns, 1987.

———. "The Identity of the Bir-Hadad of the Melqart Stela." *Bulletin of the American Schools of Oriental Research* 272 (1988): 3–21.

Platt, Elizabeth E. "Jewelry, Ancient Israelite." Pages 823–34 in vol. 3 of *The Anchor Bible Dictionary*. Edited by David Noel Freedman. 6 vols. New York: Doubleday, 1992.
Pognon, Henri. *Inscriptions sémitiques de la Syrie, de la Mésopotamie et de la Région de Mossoul*. Paris: Imprimerie Nationale, 1907.
Porten, Bezalel, and Ada Yardeni. *Textbook of Aramaic Documents from Ancient Egypt Newly Copied, Edited and Translated into Hebrew and English*. 4 vols. Texts and Studies for Students. Jerusalem: Hebrew University, Department of History of the Jewish People, 1986–1999.
Powell, James M., ed. *Medieval Studies: An Introduction*. 2d ed. Syracuse, N.Y.: Syracuse University Press, 1992.
Pratico, Gary D. *Nelson Glueck's 1938–1940 Excavations at Tell el-Kheleifeh: A Reappraisal*. American Schools of Oriental Research Archaeological Reports 3. Atlanta: Scholars Press, 1993.
Prignaud, Jean. "Scribes et Graveurs à Jérusalem vers 700 av. J.-C." Pages 136–48 in *Archaeology in the Levant: Essays for Kathleen Kenyon*. Edited by P. Roger S. Moorey and Peter J. Parr. Warminster: Aris & Phillips, 1978.
Pritchard, James B., ed. *Ancient Near Eastern Texts Relating to the Old Testament*. 3d ed. Princeton, N.J.: Princeton University Press, 1969.
Puech, Émile. "Origine de l'alphabet." *Revue biblique* 93 (1986): 161–213.
———. "La stèle araméenne de Dan: Bar Hadad II et la coalition des Omrides et de la maison de David." *Revue biblique* 101–2 (1994): 215–41.
———. "L'ivoire inscrit d'Arslan Tash et les rois de Damas." *Revue biblique* 88 (1981): 544–62, Pl. 12, 13.
Rainey, Anson F. "*Bn hmlk* in Ugarit and among Hittites" (in Hebrew). *Lešonenu* 33 (1969): 304–8.
———. "Following Up on the Ekron and Mesha Inscriptions." *Israel Exploration Journal* 50 (2000): 116–17.
———. "The 'House of David' and the House of the Deconstructionists." *Biblical Archaeology Review* 20, no. 6 (November/December 1994): 47.
———. "Meshaʿ and Syntax." Pages 287–307 in *The Land that I Will Show You: Essays on the History and Archaeology of the Ancient Near East in Honor of J. Maxwell Miller*. Edited by J. Andrew Dearman and M. Patrick Graham. Supplement Series 343. Sheffield, England: Sheffield Academic Press, 2001.
———. "The Prince and the Pauper." *Ugarit-Forschungen* 7 (1975): 427–32.
———. "A Rejoinder to the Eliakim Naʿar Yokan Seal Impressions." *Biblical Archaeologist* 54 (1991): 61.
———. "Syntax, Hermeneutics and History." *Israel Exploration Journal* 48 (1998): 239–51.
———. "The Word *Ywm* in Ugaritic and in Hebrew." *Lešonenu* 36 (1972): 186–89.
Rauh, Nicholas K. "Senators and Business in the Roman Republic, 264–44 B.C." Ph.D. diss., University of North Carolina at Chapel Hill, 1986.
Rawlinson, Henry C.: see British Museum.

Reed, William L., and Fred V. Winnett. "A Fragment of an Early Moabite Inscription from Kerak." *Bulletin of the American Schools of Oriental Research* 172 (1963): 1–9.

Reifenberg, Adolf. *Ancient Hebrew Seals*. London: East & West Library, 1950.

Rendsburg, Gary A. "On the Writing ביתדוד in the Aramaic Inscription from Tel Dan." *Israel Exploration Journal* 45 (1995): 22–25.

Renfrew, Colin, and Paul Bahn. *Archaeology: Theories, Methods and Practice*. London: Thames & Hudson, 1991.

Renz, Johannes. *Schrift und Schreibertradition: eine paläographische Studie zum kulturgeschichtlichen Verhältnis von israelitischem Nordreich und Südreich*. Abhandlungen des Deutschen Palästina-Vereins 23. Wiesbaden: Harrassowitz, 1997.

Renz, Johannes, and Wolfgang Röllig. *Handbuch der althebräischen Epigraphik*. 3 vols. in 4. Darmstadt: Wissenschaftliche Buchgesellschaft, 1995– .

Rogerson, John, and Philip R. Davies. *The Old Testament World*. Englewood Cliffs, N.J.: Prentice-Hall, 1989.

Rollston, Christopher A. "Non-Provenanced Epigraphs I: Pillaged Antiquities, Northwest Semitic Forgeries, and Protocols for Laboratory Tests." *Maarav* 10 (2003): 135–93.

Rosenthal, Franz, ed. *An Aramaic Handbook*, 2 vols. in 4. Porta Linguarum Orientalium 2/10. Wiesbaden: Otto Harrassowitz, 1967.

Sass, Benjamin. *The Genesis of the Alphabet and Its Development in the Second Millenium [sic] B.C.* Ägypten und altes Testament 13. Wiesbaden: Harrassowitz, 1988.

———. "The Pre-Exilic Hebrew Seals: Iconism vs. Aniconism." Pages 194–256 in *Studies in the Iconography of Northwest Semitic Inscribed Seals: Proceedings of a Symposium Held in Fribourg on April 17–20, 1991*. Edited by Benjamin Sass and Christoph Uehlinger. Orbis Biblicus et Orientalis 125. Göttingen: Vandenhoeck & Ruprecht, 1993.

Sass, Benjamin and Christoph Uehlinger, eds. *Studies in the Iconography of Northwest Semitic Inscribed Seals: Proceedings of a Symposium Held in Fribourg on April 17–20, 1991*. Orbis Biblicus et Orientalis 125. Göttingen: Vandenhoeck & Ruprecht, 1993.

Sasson, Jack M., ed. *Civilizations of the Ancient Near East*. 4 vols. New York: Charles Scribner's Sons, 1995.

Sasson, Victor. "The Old Aramaic Inscription from Tel Dan: Philological, Literary, and Historical Aspects." *Journal of Semitic Studies* 40 (1995): 11–30.

———. "Murderers, Usurpers, or What? Hazael, Jehu, and the Tell Dan Old Aramaic Inscription." *Ugarit-Forschungen* 28 (1996): 547–54.

Sayce, Archibald H. *Lectures on the Origin and Growth of Religion as Illustrated by the Religion of the Ancient Babylonians*. London: Williams & Norgate, 1900.

Schneider, Tammi J. "Did King Jehu Kill His Own Family?" *Biblical Archaeology Review* 21, no. 1 (January/February 1995): 26–33, 80, 82.

———. "Rethinking Jehu." *Biblica* 77 (1996): 100–107.

Schneider, Tsvi. "Azariahu Son of Hilkiahu (High Priest?) on a City of David Bulla." *Israel Exploration Journal* 38 (1988): 139–41.

———. "Azaryahu Son of Hilkiyahu (Priest?) on a City of David Bulla" (in Hebrew). *Qadmoniot* 81–82 (1988): 56.

———. "Six Biblical Signatures: Seals and Seal Impressions of Six Biblical Personages Recovered." *Biblical Archaeology Review* 17, no. 4 (July/August 1991): 26–33.
Schniedewind, William M. "Tel Dan Stela: New Light on Aramaic and Jehu's Revolt." *Bulletin of the American Schools of Oriental Research* 302 (1996): 75–90.
Schoville, Keith N. *Biblical Archaeology in Focus.* Grand Rapids: Baker, 1978.
Schroeder, Otto. *Keilschrifttexte aus Assur historischen Inhalts.* 2d issue. Wissenschaftlich Veröffentlichungen der Deutschen Orient-Gesellschaft 37. Leipzig: J. C. Hinrichs, 1922.
———. "Zwei historische Assurtexte nach Abschriften Friedrich Delitzschs." *Archiv für Keilinschriftforschung* 2 (1924): 69–71.
Schumacher, Gottlieb. *Tell el-Mutesellim.* Vol. 1: *Fundbericht,* B. *Tafeln.* Leipzig: Rudolf Haupt, 1908.
Segert, Stanislav. "Die Sprache der moabitischen Königsinschrift." *Archiv Orientální* 29 (1961): 197–267.
Shanks, Hershel. "'David' Found at Dan." *Biblical Archaeology Review* 20, no. 2 (March/April 1994): 26–39.
[———.] "Face to Face: Biblical Minimalists Meet Their Challengers." *Biblical Archaeology Review* 23, no. 4 (July/August 1997): 26–42, 66–67.
———. "Fingerprint of Jeremiah's Scribe." *Biblical Archaeology Review* 22, no. 2 (March/April 1996): 37–38.
———. "Jeremiah's Scribe and Confidant Speaks from a Hoard of Clay Bullae." *Biblical Archaeology Review* 13, no. 5 (September/October 1987): 58–61, 63, 65.
———. "Magnificent Obsession: The Private World of an Antiquities Collector." *Biblical Archaeology Review* 22, no. 3 (May/June 1996): 22–35, 62–64.
[———.] "The Pomegranate Scepter Head—From the Temple of the Lord or from a Temple of Asherah?" *Biblical Archaeology Review* 18, no. 3 (May/June 1992): 42–45.
———. "Should We Have Printed Lemche's Suggestions of Forgeries?" *Biblical Archaeology Review* 23, no. 6 (November/December 1997): 10.
———. "Three Shekels for the Lord: Ancient Inscription Records Gift to Solomon's Temple." *Biblical Archaeology Review* 23, no. 6 (November/December 1997): 28–32.
Shanks, Hershel, ed. *Archaeology's Publication Problem.* Washington, D.C.: Biblical Archaeology Society, 1996.
Shea, William H. "Ancient Ostracon Records Ark's Wanderings." *Ministry* (1991): 14.
———. "Hophni in the Izbet Sartah Ostracon: A Rejoinder." *Andrews University Seminary Studies* 36 (1998): 277–78.
———. "The ʿIzbet Ṣarṭah Ostracon." *Andrews University Seminary Studies* 28 (1990): 59–86.
Shiloh, Yigal. *Excavations at the City of David I, 1978–1982: Interim Report of the First Five Seasons.* Qedem 19. Jerusalem: The Hebrew University, The Institute of Archaeology, 1984.
———. "A Group of Hebrew Bullae from the City of David." *Israel Exploration Journal* 36 (1986): 16–38.

———. "A Hoard of Hebrew Bullae from the City of David" (in Hebrew). *Eretz-Israel* 18 (1985): 73–87, English summary 68*.
———. "A Hoard of Israelite Seal-Impressions on Bullae from the City of David" (in Hebrew). *Qadmoniot* 19 (1986): 2–11.
Shiloh, Yigal, and David Tarler. "Bullae from the City of David: A Hoard of Seal Impressions from the Israelite Period." *Biblical Archaeologist* 49 (1986): 196–209.
Shoham, Yair. "Hebrew Bullae." Pages 29–57 in *Inscriptions*. Edited by Donald T. Ariel. Vol. 6 of *Excavations at the City of David 1978–1985 Directed by Yigal Shiloh*. City of David Final Report 6. Qedem 41. Jerusalem: The Hebrew University of Jerusalem, The Institute of Archaeology, 2000.
Sidersky, David. *Stèle de Mésa: index bibliographique*. Paris: Ernest Leroux, 1920.
Smelik, Klaas A. D. *Converting the Past: Studies in Ancient Israelite and Moabite Historiography*. Oudtestamentische Studiën 28. New York: Brill, 1992.
Smend, Rudolf, and Albert Socin. *Die Inschrift des Königs Mesa von Moab für akademische Vorlesungen*. Freiburg im Brisgau: J.C.B. Mohr, 1886.
Smith, George. *History of Sennacherib, Translated from Cuneiform Inscriptions*. London: Williams & Norgate, 1878.
Smith, W. Robertson. *Kinship and Marriage in Early Arabia*. London: Adam & Charles Black, 1903. Repr. Boston: Beacon Press, n.d.
Society of Biblical Archaeology (London, England). *Proceedings of the Society of Biblical Archaeology* [Succeeded by the title: *Journal of the Royal Asiatic Society of Great Britain & Ireland*]. London: Society of Biblical Archaeology, 1878–1918.
Stamm, Johann J. "Der Name des Königs David." Pages 165–83 in International Organization of Old Testament Scholars, *Congress Volume, Oxford 1959*. Edited by George W. Anderson. Supplements to Vetus Testamentum 7. Leiden: Brill, 1960. Repr. pages 25–43 in Johann J. Stamm, *Beiträge zur hebräischen und altorientalischen Namenkunde: Johann Jakob Stamm zu seinem 70. Geburtstag*. Edited by Ernst Jenni und Martin A. Klopfenstein. Orbis Biblicus et Orientalis 30. Göttingen: Vandenhoeck & Ruprecht, 1980.
Stern, Ephraim. *The Assyrian, Babylonian, and Persian Periods*. Vol. 2 of *Archaeology of the Land of the Bible*. Anchor Bible Reference Library. New York: Doubleday, 2001.
———. *Material Culture of the Land of the Bible in the Persian Period, 538–332 B.C.* Jerusalem: Israel Exploration Society, 1982.
———, ed. *New Encyclopedia of Archaeological Excavations in the Holy Land*. 4 vols. New York: Simon & Schuster, 1993.
Stone, Lawrence. "Prosopography." *Daedalus* 100 (1971): 46–79. Repr. pages 107–40 in *Historical Studies Today*. Edited by Felix Gilbert and Stephen R. Graubard. New York: Norton, 1972.
Streck, Maximilian. *Assurbanipal und die letzten assyrischen Könige bis zum Untergange Niniveh's*. 3 vols. Vorderasiatische Bibliothek 7. Leipzig: J. C. Hinrichs, 1916.
Sublet, Jacqueline. "La prosopographie arabe." *Annales: Économies, Sociétés, Civilisations* 25 (1970): 1236–39.
Suder, Robert W. *Hebrew Inscriptions: A Classified Bibliography*. Selinsgrove, Pa.: Susquehanna University Press, 1984.

Sukenik, Eleazar L. "Funerary Tablet of Uzziah, King of Judah." *Palestine Exploration Quarterly* (1931): 217–21, Pl. I, II.
Tadmor, Hayim. "Azriyau of Yaudi." *Scripta Hierosolymitana* 8 (1961): 232–71.
———. "Historical Implications of the Correct Reading of Akkadian *dakû*." *Journal of Near Eastern Studies* 17 (1958): 129–31.
———. "The Historical Inscriptions of Adad-Nirari III." *Iraq* 35 (1973): 141–50.
———. *The Inscriptions of Tiglath-Pileser III, King of Assyria: Critical Edition, with Introductions, Translations, and Commentary*. Fontes ad Res Judaicas Spectantes. Jerusalem: Israel Academy of Sciences and Humanities, 1994.
Tait, G. A. D. "The Egyptian Relief Chalice." *Journal of Egyptian Archaeology* 49 (1963): 93–138.
Tappy, Ron E. *The Archaeology of Israelite Samaria*. Vol. 2: *The Eighth Century B.C.E.* Harvard Semitic Studies 50. Winona Lake, Ind.: Eisenbrauns, 2001.
Teixidor, Javier. *Bulletin d'épigraphie sémitique (1964–1980)*. Bibliothèque archéologique et historique 127. Paris: Librarie orientaliste Paul Guenther, 1986.
Temporini, Hildegard, and Wolfgang Haase, eds. *Aufstieg und Niedergang der römischen Welt: Geschichte und Kultur Roms im Spiegel der neueren Forschung*. Part 1: *Von den Anfängen Roms bis zum Ausgang der Republik*. Edited by Hildegard Temporini. New York: Walter de Gruyter, 1972.
Thomas, D. Winton, ed. *Documents from Old Testament Times*. London: Thomas Nelson & Sons, 1958. Repr. New York: Harper & Row, Harper Torchbooks, 1961.
Thompson, Henry O., and Fawzi Zayadine. "The Tell Siran Inscription." *Bulletin of the American Schools of Oriental Research* 212 (1973): 5–11.
Thompson, R. Campbell. *The Prisms of Esarhaddon and Ashurbanipal*. London: Trustees of the British Museum, 1931.
Thompson, Thomas L. "Dissonance and Disconnections: Notes on the bytdwd and hmlk.hdd Fragments from Tel Dan." *Scandinavian Journal of the Old Testament* 9 (1995): 236–40.
———. "'House of David': An Eponymic Referent to Yahweh as Godfather." *Scandinavian Journal of the Old Testament* 9 (1995): 59–74.
Tigay, Jeffrey H. *You Shall Have No Other Gods: Israelite Religion in the Light of Hebrew Inscriptions*. Harvard Semitic Studies 31. Atlanta: Scholars Press, for the Harvard Semitic Museum, 1986.
Timm, Stefan. "Die Eroberung Samarias aus assyrisch-babylonischer Sicht." *Die Welt des Orients* 20–21 (1989–90): 64–66.
Toorn, Karel van der, Bob Becking, and Pieter W. van der Horst, eds. *Dictionary of Deities and Demons in the Bible DDD*. 2d extensively revised ed. Boston: Brill, 1999.
Torrey, Charles C. "A Few Ancient Seals." *AASOR* 2–3 (1921–1922): 103–8.
———. "A Hebrew Seal from the reign of Ahaz." *Bulletin of the American Schools of Oriental Research* 79 (1940): 27–29.
Tufnell, Olga. *Lachish III*. New York: Oxford University Press, 1953.

Uehlinger, Christoph. "Ahabs königliches Siegel? Ein antiker Bronzering zwischen Historismus und Reliquienkult, *memoria* und Geschichte." Pages 77–116 in *Peregrina curiositas: Ein Reise durch den orbis antiquus: zu Ehren von Dirk van Damme*. Edited by Andreas Kessler, Thomas Ricklin, and Gregor Wurst. Novum Testamentum et Orbis Antiquus 27. Göttingen: Vandenhoeck & Ruprecht, 1994.

———. "The Seal of Ahab, King of Israel?" *Michmanim* 11 (1997): 39*–52*.

Ussishkin, David. "The Destruction of Lachish by Sennacherib and the Dating of the Royal Storage Jars." *Tel Aviv* 4 (1977): 28–60.

———. "Gate 1567 at Megiddo and the Seal of Shema, Servant of Jeroboam." Pages 410–28 in *Scripture and Other Artifacts: Essays on the Bible and Archaeology in Honor of Philip J. King*. Edited by Michael D. Coogan, J. Cheryl Exum, and Lawrence E. Stager. Louisville, Ky.: Westminster/John Knox Press, 1994.

———. "Royal Judean Storage Jars and Private Seal Impressions." *Bulletin of the American Schools of Oriental Research* 223 (1976): 1–13.

———. *The Village of Silwan: The Necropolis from the Period of the Judean Kingdom*. Translated by Inna Pommerantz. Jerusalem: Izhak Ben-Zvi for the Israel Exploration Society, 1993.

Van Zyl, A. H. *The Moabites*. Pretoria Oriental Series 3. Leiden: Brill, 1960.

Vance, Donald R. "Literary Sources for the History of Palestine and Syria: The Phoenician Inscriptions, Part I." *Biblical Archaeologist* 57 (1994): 6–8.

———. "Literary Sources for the History of Palestine and Syria: The Phoenician Inscriptions, Part II." *Biblical Archaeologist* 57 (1994): 110–20.

Vattioni, Francesco. "I sigilli ebraici [I]." *Biblica* 50 (1969): 370–85.

———. "I sigilli ebraici II." *Augustinianum* 11 (1971): 447–54.

———. "I sigilli ebraici III." *Annali dell' Istituto Orientale di Napoli* 41 (1981): 177–93.

Vaughn, Andrew G. "The Chronicler's Account of Hezekiah: The Relationship of Historical Data to a Theological Interpretation of 2 Chronicles 29–32." Ph.D. diss., Princeton Theological Seminary, 1996.

———. "Methodological Issues in the Palaeographic Dating of Hebrew Seals." Paper presented at the annual meeting of the American Schools of Oriental Research, Philadelphia, Pa., November 19, 1995.

———. "Palaeographic Dating of Judaean Seals and Its Significance for Biblical Research." *Bulletin of the American Schools of Oriental Research* 313 (1999): 43–64.

———. *Theology, History and Archaeology in the Chronicler's Account of Hezekiah*. Archaeology and Biblical Studies 4. Atlanta: Scholars Press, 1999.

Vaughn, Andrew G., and Carolyn Pillers Dobler. "A Provenance Study of Hebrew Seals and Seal Impressions—A Statistical Analysis." In *I Will Tell Secret Things from Long Ago (Abiah Chidot Menei-Kedem)—Ps. 78:2b): Archaeological and Historical Studies in Honor of Amihai Mazar on the Occasion of his Sixtieth Birthday*. Edited by Aren M. Maeir and Pierre M. de Miroschedji. Winona Lake, Ind.: Eisenbrauns, in press.

Vaux, Roland G. de. *Les Institutions de l'Ancien Testament*. Paris: Cerf, 1961. ET, *Ancient Israel*. Vol. 1: *Social Institutions*. Vol. 2: *Religious Institutions*. Translated by John McHugh. London: Darton, Longman & Todd, Ltd., 1961. Repr. *Ancient Israel*. 2 vols. New York: McGraw Hill, 1985.

Veen, Peter G. van der. "Beschriftete Siegel als Beweis für das biblische Israel? Gedalja und seine Mörder *par exemple* (Ein Antwort an Bob Becking)." Pages 238–59 in *Wort und Stein: Studien zur Theologie und Archäologie: Festschrift Udo Worschech*. Edited by Friedbert Ninow. Beiträge zur Erforschung der antiken Moabitis (Ard el-Kerak) 4. Frankfurt am Main: Peter Lang Verlag, 2004.

———. "Two/Too Little Known Bullae: Some Preliminary Notes." Pages 243–54 in *Shlomo: Studies in Epigraphy, Iconography, History and Archaeology in Honor of Shlomo Moussaieff*. Edited by Robert Deutsch. Tel Aviv: Archaeological Center Publications, 2003.

Waltke, Bruce K., and Michael O'Connor. *An Introduction to Biblical Hebrew Syntax*. Winona Lake, Ind.: Eisenbrauns, 1990.

Watzinger, Carl. *Die Funde*. Vol. 2 of *Tell el-Mutesellim*. Leipzig: J. C. Hinrichs, 1929.

Weidner, Ernst F. "Jojachin König von Juda in babylonischen Keilinschrifttexten." Pages 923–35 in vol. 2 of *Mélanges Syriens offerts à monsieur René Dussaud: secrétaire perpétuel de l'Académie des inscriptions et belles-lettres*. Par l'Académie des inscriptions et belles-lettres. Haut-commissariat de la Republique francaise en Syrie et au Liban, Service des antiquites, Bibliothéque archéologique et historique 30. Paris: P. Guenther, 1939.

Williams, Prescott H. Jr. and Theodore Hiebert, eds. *Realia Dei: Essays in Archaeology and Biblical Interpretation in Honor of Edward F. Campbell, Jr., at His Retirement*. Atlanta: Scholars Press: 1999.

Winckler, Hugo. *Altorientalische Forschungen*, 10 vols. in 3. Leipzig: Eduard Pfeiffer, 1893–1905.

———. *Die Keilschrifttexte Sargons*. 2 vols. Leipzig: Eduard Pfeiffer, 1889.

———. *Untersuchungen zur altorientalischen Geschichte*. Leipzig: Eduard Pfeiffer, 1889.

Winter, Irene J. "Legitimation of Authority through Image and Legend: Seals Belonging to Officials in the Administrative Bureaucracy of the Ur III State." Pages 69–106, Pl. 1–10 in *The Organization of Power: Aspects of Bureaucracy in the Ancient Near East*. Edited by McGuire Gibson and Robert D. Biggs. Studies in Ancient Oriental Civilization 46. Chicago: The Oriental Institute of the University of Chicago, 1987.

Wiseman, Donald J. "Babylonia 605–539 B.C." Pages 229–51 in Vol. III, Part II of *Cambridge Ancient History*. 2d ed. Edited by John Boardman, I. E. S. Edwards, N. G. L. Hammond, and E. Sollberger. New York: Cambridge University Press, 1970.

———. "The Bottleneck of Archaeological Publication." *Biblical Archaeology Review* 16, no. 5 (September/October 1990): 60–63.

———. *Chronicles of Chaldean Kings (626–556 B.C.) in the British Museum*. London: Trustees of the British Museum, 1956.

———. "Hazael." Pages 238–39 in vol. 4 of *Reallexikon der Assyriologie*. Edited by Erich Ebeling und Bruno Meissner. Vol. 4 edited by Dietz Otto Edzard. New York: Walter de Gruyter, 1975.

Wright, G. Ernest and David Noel Freedman, eds. *The Biblical Archaeologist Reader, Volume I*. Garden City, N.Y.: Anchor Books, 1961. Repr., Missoula, Mont.: Scholars Press, for the American Schools of Oriental Research, 1975.

Xella, Paolo. "Le dieu et 'sa' déesse: l'utilisation des suffixes pronominaux avec des théonymes d'Ebla à Ugarit et à Kuntillet ʿAjrud." *Ugarit-Forschungen* 27 (1995): 599–610.

Yamauchi, Edwin M. *The Stones and the Scriptures*. New York: J. B. Lippincott, A Holman Book, 1972.

Yeivin, Shmuel. "The Date of the Seal 'Belonging to Shemaʿ (the) Servant (of) Jeroboam.'" *Journal of Near Eastern Studies* 19 (1960): 205–12.

Young, Gordon D., Mark W. Chavalas, and Richard E. Averbeck, eds. *Crossing Boundaries and Linking Horizons: Studies in Honor of Michael C. Astour on His 80th Birthday*. Bethesda, Md.: CDL Press, 1997.

Zadok, Ran. "Notes on Syro-Palestinian History, Toponomy, and Anthroponomy." *Ugarit-Forschungen* 28 (1996): 721–49.

———. *The Pre-Hellenistic Israelite Anthroponomy and Prosopography*. Orientalia Lovaniensia Analecta 28. Leuven: Uitgeverij Peeters, 1988.

Zevit, Ziony. *Matres Lectionis in Ancient Hebrew Epigraphs*. American Schools of Oriental Research Monograph Series 2. Cambridge, Mass.: American Schools of Oriental Research, 1980.

Zorn, Jeffrey R. Review of Niels Peter Lemche, *Israelites in History and Tradition*. *Journal of Biblical Literature* 119 (2000): 544–47.

# Index of Modern Authors and Editors

A letter **n** suffixed to a page number indicates the *footnote* portion of that page. This index gives access by (co)author, (co)editor, or honoree. 1) Pages include references that do not mention authors or editors; e.g., pages that refer to *ANET* are listed under Pritchard, its editor, even though his name does not appear on the page. Unmentioned coauthors and coeditors also have such pages listed by their names. 2) Coverage includes the Bibliography. 3) This index does *not* list pages for idem and ibid. notes, nor does it signal multiple references on a page.

Abramsky, Shmuel   151n, 287, 289
Académie des inscriptions et belles-lettres   287, 306, 317
Acquaro, Enrico   17n, 293. 300
Aharoni, Yohanan   2n, 31n, 64n, 68n, 77n, 104n, 146n, 151n, 182n, 183n, 199n, 224n, 225n, 287, 289, 297; as coeditor with Abramsky: 151n, 287, 289
Ahituv, Shmuel   2n, 3n, 274n, 288
Ahlström, Gösta W.   122n, 123n, 129n, 136, 136n, 215n, 248n, 288
Aitken, Martin J.   44n, 288
Albright, William F.   15, 15n, 18n, 19n, 20–25, 21n, 23n, 25n, 29, 29n, 37, 99n, 158n, 164n, 288, 299
Alexander, Patrick H.   xv
Alt, Albrecht   12n, 288
Ames, Frank R.   xiv
Amiran, Ruth   19n
Andersen, Francis I.   105n, 109n, 123n, 288
Andersen, Leigh   xiv

Anderson, George W.   123n, 302, 314
Ariel, Donald T.   140n, 203n, 288, 293, 314
Astour, Michael C.   310, 318
Åström, Paul   43n, 288, 303
Athas, George   110n, 288
Aufrecht, Walter E.   3n, 288
Averbeck, Richard E.   310, 318
Avigad, Nahman   xii, xiii, xiv, xvi, 2n, 3n, 15, 15n, 20, 21, 21n, 24, 25n, 27–34, 27n, 29n, 30n, 34n–36n, 36–38, 53n, 67, 67n, 68, 68n, 71n–73n, 73, 77, 128n, 142n, 143n, 146, 151n, 183n, 184n, 186n, 191n, 194n–96n, 195, 196, 204n, 213, 214n, 219n, 221n, 224n, 225n, 253n, 260n, 288–290, 300, 307; as coauthor of WSS: xii, xiii, xvi, 2n, 3n, 30n, 42n, 52n, 61, 62n, 68n, 69, 71n, 73, 74n, 77n, 82n, 95, 99n, 100n, 128n, 133n, 137n, 139n, 142n, 145n, 148n, 153n,

319

156n, 159n, 162n, 163n, 166n, 169n, 172n, 173n, 177n, 181n, 182n, 191n, 193n, 208, 208n, 209, 210n, 213, 215–20, 218n, 222–35, 224n, 230n, 237, 241, 242, 248, 250–58, 256n, 290
Avi-Yonah, Michael 15n; as coeditor with Malamat: 29n, 289, 306
Avishur, Yitzhak 242n, 290, 291n, 295

Bahn, Paul 44n, 312
Baker, David W. 307
Barkay, Gabriel xiv, 30, 31n, 173n, 194n, 225n, 235n, 258n, 290
Barnett, Richard D. 239n, 246n, 258n, 290
Barrick, W. Boyd 55n, 290
Barstad, Hans M. 122n, 124n, 125n, 130, 130n, 290
Bartoloni, Piero As coeditor of *Atti*: 17n, 293, 300
Beck, Pirhiya 290
Becking, Bob 157n, 174n, 202n, 205n, 216n; 290; 317; as coeditor of *DDD*: xv, 122n, 290, 315
Beech, George 13n, 290
Ben-Zvi, Ehud 290
Benz, Frank L. 237n, 238n, 291
Bergman, Jan 184n
Bezold, Carl 118n, 292
Biggs, Robert D. 17n, 22n, 299, 310, 317
Biran, Avraham xiii, 77, 77n, 110n, 111, 111n, 112, 112n, 113n, 115n, 121n, 183n, 216, 218, 291, 305
Blakely, Jeffrey A. xiv, 215n
Blau, Ernst Otto F. H. 153n, 291
Bliss, Frederick Jones 224n, 291
Boardman, John As coeditor of *CAH*: xv, 43n, 88n, 213, 291, 317
Bordreuil, Pierre xii, 2n, 3n, 15, 15n, 16, 16n, 17, 27, 42n, 52n, 54n, 210n, 216n, 248n, 291, 291n; as author of *CSOSI*: xv, 2n, 3n,
153n, 154n, 156n, 159n, 208n, 291
Botta, Paul E. 291
Botterweck, G. Johannes As coeditor of *TDOT*: 1n, 103n, 124n, 130n, 159n, 183n, 184n, 186n, 292
Branden, Albert van den 123n, 292
Briend, Jacques As coeditor with Pirot: 42n, 291, 296
Briggs, Charles A. 292
Bright, John 107n, 292
Brin, Gershon 194n, 292
British Museum xv, xvi, 118n, 157n, 158n, 292, 315, 317
Bromiley, Geoffrey W. As editor of *ISBE*: 2n, 99n, 154n, 235n, 292, 301, 308
Bron, François 120n, 239n, 252n, 292
Broughton, T. Robert S. 13n, 292
Brown, Francis 292
Buccellati, Giorgio 199n, 292
Bunimovitz, Shlomo 94n, 292
Buttrick, George A. As editor of *IDB*: 241n, 292, 304

Cahill, Jane M. 140n, 292, 293
Campbell, Edward F. Jr. As honoree of Williams and Hiebert: 221n, 230n, 294, 307, 317
Carmon, Efrat 214n, 302
Carney, Thomas F. 13n, 293
Charbonnet, André 120n, 239n, 252n, 293
Chase, Debra A. 293
Chastagnol, André 13n, 293
Chavalas, Mark W. 310, 318
Chwolson, Daniel A. 214n, 293
Civil, Miguel 310
Clermont-Ganneau, Charles S. 18n, 42n, 95, 95n, 97, 99n, 208n, 210n, 267n, 268, 268n, 270, 293
Clines, David J. A. 2n, 12n, 218n, 293
Cody, Aelred 63n, 293
Cogan, Mordechai 175n, 186n, 293

Colless, Brian E.   293
Collon, Dominique   42n, 293
Congresso internazionale di studi fenice e punici 1987   1/11, 293, 300
Coogan, Michael D.   As coeditor associated with Cross and Ussishkin articles: 45n, 133n, 134n, 136n, 182n, 215n, 248n, 294, 316
Cook, Edward M.   237n, 240n, 294
Cornelius, Izak   139n, 294
Cornfeld, Gaalyahu   171n, 306
Cothenet, Édouard   As coeditor with Pirot: 42n, 291, 296
Cowley, Arthur E.   241n, 294; as reviser of GKC: 274n, 298
Cross, Frank Moore   25n, 29, 29n, 42n, 45n, 79n, 80n, 129n, 143n, 156n, 208n, 215n, 221n, 233n, 253n, 289, 294, 305, 308, 310
Cryer, Frederick H.   117n, 122n, 124n, 126n, 294, 305
Culican, William   182n, 295
Cundall, Arthur E.   295

Dalley, Stephanie   207n, 295
Damme, Dirk van   As honoree of Uehlinger's article: 17n, 260n, 303, 316
Davies, Graham I.   138n, 295; as author of *AHI*: xv, 2n, 68n, 73, 77n, 128n, 133n, 139n, 142n, 145n, 148n, 153n, 156n, 159n, 162n, 163n, 166n, 169n, 172n, 177n, 181n, 183n, 191n, 193n, 208, 213, 215–20, 222–35, 224n, 248, 250–58, 295
Davies, Philip R.   72n, 121n, 122n, 124n, 295, 312
Davies, Gwynne H.   194n, 296, 308
Davis, Thomas W.   19n, 295
Dayagi or Dayagi-Mendels, Michal   2n, 3n, 52n, 128n, 169n, 171n, 301
Dearman, J. Andrew   xiv, 3n, 99n, 101n, 122n, 267n, 268n, 274n, 295, 299, 302, 311
Demsky, Aaron   79n, 295, 303

Deutsch, Robert   2n, 68n, 73n, 74, 74n, 76n, 77n, 208n, 209n, 215n, 217n, 218n, 220n–22n,, 225n–30n, 232n–34n, 242n, 243n, 248n–50n, 254n–58n, 290, 295, 296, 301, 317
Dever, William G.   19n. 296
Dietrich, Manfred   274n, 296
Diringer, David   xv, 2n, 25n, 42n, 133n, 154n, 224n, 296
DiVito, Robert A.   29, 30n, 296
Dobler, Carolyn Pillers   42n, 316
Dommershausen, Werner   186n
Donner, Herbert   As coauthor of *KAI*: xv, xvi, 2n, 62n, 116n, 120n, 123n, 124n, 209n, 236n–40n, 242n, 246n, 247n, 258n, 294, 296
Dorsey, David A.   296
Dotan, Aron   80n, 82n, 296
Dothan, Trude   236n, 299
Drews, Robert   296
Driver, Samuel R.   292
Dunand, Maurice   119n, 296
Durham. John I.   194n, 296, 308
Dussaud, René   158n, 268, 268n, 287, 297, 317

Ebeling, Erich   297, 318
Edelman, Diana V.   297, 308
Edwards, I. E. S.   As coeditor of *CAH*: xv, 43n, 88n, 213, 291, 317
Edzard, Dietz Otto   297, 318
Elayi, Josette   xiii, 16, 16n, 17, 17n, 30, 30n, 150, 177n, 179–81, 179n, 180n, 184n–86n, 190, 297
Emerton, John A.   297
Eph'al, Israel   64n, 120n, 239n, 252n, 253n, 297
Exum, J. Cheryl   As coeditor associated with Cross and Ussishkin articles: 45n, 133n, 134n, 136n, 182n, 215n, 248n, 294, 316

Fabry, Heinz-Josef   As coeditor of *TDOT*: 1n, 103n, 124n, 130n, 159n, 183n, 184n, 186n, 292
Feigin, Samuel I.   123n, 297

Finkelstein, Israel 79n, 295, 297
Fitzmyer, Joseph A. 3n, 236n–41n, 246n, 247n, 252n, 258n, 297
Fleming, Stuart J. 44n, 297
Flusser, David 214n, 297
Fowler, Jeaneane D. xv, 3n, 15n, 61, 69, 100n, 128n, 137n, 138n, 142n, 150n, 156n, 162n, 166n, 172n, 181n, 297
Fox, Michael V. xiii
Fox, Nili S. xiii, 13n, 30, 30n, 31, 31n, 42n–44n, 51n, 52, 52n, 74n, 147n, 231n, 298
Francisi, Maria Teresa As coeditor of *Atti*: 17n, 293, 300
Freedman, David Noel 19n, 105n, 122n, 124n, 129n, 158n, 182n, 287, 288, 298, 311, 318
Friedrich, Johannes 64n

Gadd, Cyril J. 174n, 298
Galil, Gershon xvii, 21n, 43, 43n, 62n, 66n, 87n, 88n, 102n, 111n, 125n, 157n, 167n, 173n, 209n, 213, 298
Galling, Kurt 12n, 298
Garbini, Giovanni 219n, 298
Garfinkel, Yosef 24n, 26n, 29, 29n, 298
Garr, W. Randall 62, 62n, 64n, 107n, 298
Gelb, Ignace 310
Geller, Markham J. 242n, 298, 304
Geoghegan, Jeffrey C. 122n, 298
Gesenius, H. F. Wilhelm As author of GKC: 274n, 298
Gevaryahu, Haim M. Y. As coeditor with Abramsky: 151n, 287, 289
Gibson, John C. L. xv, 2n, 3n, 12n, 19n–21n, 29, 29n, 62n, 133n, 164n, 236n–240n, 246n, 247n, 258n, 298, 299
Gibson, McGuire 17n, 22n, 299, 317
Gilbert, Felix 13n, 299, 314
Ginsberg, Harold L. 143n, 289, 299
Gitin, Seymour 236n, 299

Glueck, Nelson xiii, 19n, 20–23, 20n, 21n, 29, 29n, 30n, 82, 82n, 289, 296, 299, 311
Goedicke, Hans 21n, 299
Gogel, Sandra L. 299
Gorelick, Leonard 29n, 44n, 143n, 156n, 215n, 294, 299, 300
Görg, Manfred 159n
Grabbe, Lester L. 202n, 290, 299
Graham, M. Patrick 267n, 274n, 295, 299, 311
Grant, Elihu 23, 25
Graubard, Stephen R. 13n, 299, 314
Gray, George Buchanan 3n, 15n, 300
Grayson, Albert Kirk xvii, 43, 43n, 87n, 88n, 102n, 118n, 300
Greenberg, Moshe 233n, 257n, 300
Greenfield, Jonas C. 19n, 182n, 219n, 242n, 287, 288, 298, 300, 304
Gressmann, Hugo 300
Gubel, Eric 17, 17n, 300
Gwinnett, A. John 44n, 299, 300

Haase, Wolfgang As coeditor with Temporini: 13n, 292, 315
Hackett, Jo Ann 3n, 9n, 181n, 236n, 252n, 300
Hallo, William W. 300
Halpern, Baruch 115, 115n, 117n, 300
Hammond, N. G. L. As coeditor of *CAH*: xv, 43n, 88n, 213, 291, 317
Hanson, Paul D. 289, 308
Haran, Menahem 183n, 300
Harding, G. Lankester. 208n, 300
Harris, Rivkah 31, 31n, 51n, 300
Harris, Zellig S. 63n, 301
Hawkins, J. David 207n, 295
Hayes, John H. 301
Heltzer, Michael 2n, 68n, 73n, 74, 74n, 76n, 77n, 208n–210n, 217n, 225n, 232n, 233n, 242n, 243n, 257n, 258n, 260n, 290, 291n, 295, 296, 301
Herr, Larry G. 2n, 21, 68n, 191,

191n, 227n, 231n, 235n, 254n, 256n, 301; as author of SANSS: xvi, 2n, 3n, 21, 21n, 29, 29n, 42n, 60n, 84n, 100n, 137n, 156n, 160n, 163n, 166n, 171n, 172n, 181n, 235n, 301
Hérubel, Jean-Pierre V. M.   xiv
Hestrin, Ruth   2n, 3n, 12n, 52n, 128n, 169n, 171n, 301
Hiebert, Theodore   221n, 230n, 294, 307, 317
Hodder, Ian   301
Hoffmeier, James K.   307
Hoffner, Harry A.   130n
Hoftijzer, Jacob   3n, 301; as coauthor of *DISO*: 172n, 302; as coauthor of *DNWSI*: 3n, 100n, 121n–124n, 172n, 181n, 301
Holladay, William L.   71n, 301
Hopfe, Lewis M.   301
Hornblower, Simon   13n, 301
Horst, Pieter W. van der   As coeditor of *DDD*: xv, 122n, 290, 315
Hübner, Ulrich   42n, 302

Ingholt, Harald   121n, 302
International Organization of Old Testament Scholars   123n, 302
Israel, Felice   2n, 216n, 248n, 291, 302
Israel Museum   2n, 3n, 52n, 68, 80, 169n, 214n, 219n, 297, 301, 302, 307, 310

Jackson, Kent P.   xvi, 3n, 100n, 122n–23n, 172n, 181n, 268n, 302
Janzen, J. Gerald   71n, 302
Japhet, Sara   143n, 302
Jean, Charles-F.   As coauthor of *DISO*: 172n, 302
Jenni, Ernst   123n, 314
Jongeling, Karel   As coauthor of *DNWSI*: 3n, 100n, 121n–124n, 172n, 181n, 301
Jordan, James R.   14n, 302
Kallai, Zecharia   302

Kantor, Alon   xiii
Kantor, Helene J.   120n, 239n, 253n, 302
Kaufman, Stephen A.   3n, 113n, 125n, 224n, 236n–241n, 246n, 247n, 252n, 258n, 297, 302
Kautzsch, Emil F.   133n, 139n, 302; as editor of GKC: 274n, 298
Keel, Othmar   12n, 302, 303
Kempinski, Aharon   303
Kenyon, Kathleen M.   19n, 145n, 311
Kessler, Andreas   As one of Uehlinger's editors: 17n, 260n, 303, 316
King, Leonard W.   As supplementer of Bezold: 118n, 292
King, Philip J.   18n, 77n, 199n, 303; as Cross' and Ussishkin's honoree: 45n, 133n, 134n, 136n, 182n, 215n, 248n, 294, 316
Kitchen, Kenneth A.   xvii, 43, 43n, 100n, 214n, 265n, 273, 273n, 275, 275n, 276, 303
Kloner, Amos   214n, 303
Klopfenstein, Martin A.   123n, 314
Knauf, Ernst A.   122n, 129n, 130n, 131, 132n, 303
Knoppers, Gary N.   xiv, 218n, 303
Kochavi, Moshe   79, 79n, 80, 80n, 295, 303
Kooij, Gerrit van der   3n, 301
Kosmala, Hans   103n
Kraeling, Emil G.   241n, 304
Kuan, Jeffrey K.   119n, 304
Kwasman, Theodore   64n
Kyrieleis, Helmut   120n, 239n, 253n, 304

Lambdin, Thomas O.   1n, 304
Lamon, Robert S.   134, 137n, 304
Landsberger, Benno   310
Lapp, Paul W.   199n, 304
Layard, Austen H.   18n
Layton, Scott C.   63n–65n, 64, 304
Lederman, Zvi   94n, 292

Lehman[n?], Manfred R.    215n
Lemaire, André    xiii, 2n, 3n, 28n, 30, 30n, 41n, 47n, 48n, 58, 58n, 93, 93n, 113n, 120n, 182n, 184n, 194n, 209n, 210n, 214n, 215n, 218n, 227n, 229n, 232n–234n, 239n, 242n, 245n, 248n, 252n, 255n, 257n, 260n, 265, 265n, 266, 267n, 268–274, 268n, 271n–73n, 276n, 290–92, 296, 302, 304, 305
Lemche, Niels P.    305, 310, 313, 318
Lemke, Werner E.    25n, 289, 294
Levine, Louis D.    305
Lidzbarski, Mark    xix, 2n, 98, 214n, 267n, 268–270, 268n, 270n, 305
Lindenberger, James M.    2n, 3n, 305
Lipiński, Edward    3n, 117n, 122n, 306
Liverani, Mario    306
Loftus, William K.    102n
Longman, Tremper III    306
Longpérier, Henri Adrien P. de    159n, 306
Loretz, Oswald    274n, 296
Löwy, Albert or Abraham    99n, 306
Luckenbill, Daniel D.    173n–75n, 306
Luria, Ben-Zion    As coeditor with Abramsky: 151n, 287, 289

Macalister, Robert A. Stewart    224n, 291
MacDonald, Burton    288, 306
Maeir, Aren M.    42n, 306, 316
Malamat, Abraham    29n, 158n, 289, 304, 306
Mallowan, Max E. L.    154n, 239n, 246n, 258n, 306
Manfredi, Lorenza-Ilia    As coeditor of *Atti*: 17n, 293, 300
Maraqten, Mohammed    xvi, 3n, 61, 100n, 109n, 128n, 166n, 172n, 193n, 306
Margalit, Baruch    272n, 273, 273n, 306
Martin, William J.    157n, 158n, 306
Matthews, Rex D.    xiv

Mazar, Amihai    19n, 42n, 306, 316
Mazar, Benjamin    19n, 171n, 289, 306; as coeditor with Malamat: 29n, 289, 306
Mazza, Federico    As coeditor of *Atti*: 17n, 293, 300
McBride, S. Dean    289, 308
McCarter, P. Kyle Jr.    62n, 65, 65n, 218n, 230n, 255n, 256n, 307
Meissner, Bruno    297, 318
Meshel, Zeʾev    307
Meshorer, Yaakov    310
Mettinger, Tryggve N. D.    52n, 54n, 307
Meyers, Eric M.    186n, 307
Michaud, Henri    268n, 307
Milano, Lucio    14n, 307
Millard, Alan R.    137n, 307
Miller, Cynthia L.    xiii
Miller, James Ernest    xiii
Miller, J. Maxwell    19, 19n, 85n, 86n, 274n, 295, 301, 307, 308, 311
Miller, Patrick D. Jr.    25n, 99, 99n, 154n, 289, 294, 308
Millet, Hélène    14n, 307, 308
Miroschedji, Pierre R. de    42n, 306, 316
Mobley, Emily R.    xiv
Montalto, Giovanni    As coeditor of *Atti*: 17n, 293, 300
Moorey, P. Roger S.    19n, 145n, 308, 311
Morgenstern, Julian    108n, 308
Morris, Leon    295
Moscati, Sabatino    2n, 308
Muilenberg, James    194n, 308
Müller, Hans-Peter    117n, 308
Muraoka, Takamitsu    117n, 308
Murphy, Roland E.    108n, 308
Mykytiuk, Lawrence J.    3n, 15n, 79n, 80n, 265, 308

Naʿaman, Nadav    64n, 130n, 157n, 308, 309
Naveh, Joseph    2n, 3n, 12n, 29, 29n, 42n, 99n, 110n, 111n, 112, 112n, 113n, 115n, 117n, 118n, 120n,

121n, 123n, 210n, 216, 218, 236n, 239n, 242n, 252n, 253n, 291, 297, 299, 309
Netanyahu, Benzion   As coeditor with Malamat: 29n, 289, 306
Nicolet, Claude   13n, 309
Nielsen, Eduard   305
Niki, Elly   120n, 239n, 252n, 309
Ninow, Friedbert   205n, 309, 317
Nordberg, Heidi L.   60n, 309
Nordlander, K. G. Amandus   267n, 268, 268n, 270, 309
Norris, Edwin   as coeditor of RawlCu 1: xvi, 102n, 292
Noth, Martin   309; as author of IPN: 3n, 15n, 25n, 309

O'Connor, Michael   274n, 317
Oates, David   310
Olyan, Saul M.   xiii
Oppenheim, A. Leo   310
Otzen, Benedikt   1n, 305
Overbeck, Bernhard   310
Owen, David I.   310

Pace, James H.   310
Page, Stephanie   88n, 310
Paine, John A.   215n, 310
Pardee, Dennis   2n, 182n, 216n, 248n, 291, 310
Parker, B.   64n
Parker, Simon B.   265n, 272, 272n, 275n, 310
Parkes, Penelope A.   44n, 310
Parpola, Simo   14n, 64n, 310
Parr, Peter J.   145n, 311
Paul, Shalom M.   129n, 310
Petrie, William M. Flinders   18n, 215n, 310
Petruccioli, Gesualdo   As coeditor of *Atti*: 17n, 293, 300
Pinches, Theophilus G.   198n, 310
Pirot, Louis   42n, 291, 296
Pitard, Wayne T.   119n, 213, 238n, 310
Platt, Elizabeth E.   2n, 311

Pognon, Henri   120, 120n, 311
Porten, Bezalel   3n, 237n, 241n–43n, 311
Porter, J. Roy   194n, 296, 308
Powell, James M.   13n, 290, 311
Pratico, Gary D.   30n, 296, 311
Prignaud, Jean   145n, 311
Pritchard, James B.   As *ANET* editor: 62n, 66n, 87n, 88n, 100n, 101n, 102n, 125n, 157n, 158n, 167n, 173n, 174n, 198n, 208n–210n, 311
Puech, Émile   117n, 216n, 237n, 239n, 258n, 311
Pury, Alan de   122n, 129n, 130n, 131, 132n, 303

Rainey, Anson F.   3n, 23n, 29, 29n, 63n, 122n, 123n, 182n, 194n, 214n, 236n, 245n, 269, 274, 274n, 275, 275n, 311; as editor for Aharoni: 31n, 104n, 182n, 183n, 287
Rauh, Nicholas K.   xiv, 14n, 311
Rawlinson, Henry C.   18n; as coeditor of RawlCu 1: xvi, 102n, 292; as coeditor of RawlCu 3: xvi, 62n, 63n, 88n, 102n, 118n, 125n, 292
Reed, William L.   105n, 312
Reich, Ronny   260n, 290
Reifenberg, Adolf   182n, 312
Reiner, Erica   310
Rendsburg, Gary A.   122n, 125, 125n, 312
Renfrew, Colin   44n, 312
Renz, Johannes   As coauthor of *HAE*: xv, 2n, 3n, 62n, 312
Ribichini, Sergio   As coeditor of *Atti*: 17n, 293, 300
Richards, Kent H.   305
Richardson, H. Neil   301
Ricklin, Thomas   As one of Uehlinger's editors: 17n, 260n, 303, 316
Ringgren, Helmer   183n, 184n; as coeditor of *TDOT*: 1n, 103n, 124n, 130n, 159n, 183n, 184n, 186n, 292
Robert, André   As coeditor with

Pirot: 42n, 291, 296
Robinson, Edward   18n
Rogerson, John   72n, 312
Röllig, Wolfgang   120n, 239n, 253n, 304; as coauthor of *HAE*: xv, 2n, 3n, 62n, 312; as coauthor of *KAI*: xv, xvi, 2n, 62n, 116n, 120n, 123n, 124n, 209n, 236n–240n, 242n, 246n, 247n, 258n, 294, 296
Rollston, Christopher A.   xiv, 42n, 189, 312
Römer, Thomas   122n, 129n, 130n, 131, 132n, 303
Rosenthal, Franz   3n, 241n, 312
Roth, Cecil   As coeditor with Malamat: 29n, 289, 306

Sanmartin-Ascaso, Joaquin   124n
Sass, Benjamin   xii, xiii, 16, 16n, 17n, 30, 30n, 41n, 42n, 80n, 194n, 304, 312; as coauthor of WSS: xii, xiii, xvi, 2n, 3n, 30n, 42n, 52n, 61, 62n, 68n, 69, 71n, 73, 74n, 77n, 82n, 95, 99n, 100n, 128n, 133n, 137n, 139n, 142n, 145n, 148n, 153n, 156n, 159n, 162n, 163n, 166n, 169n, 172n, 173n, 177n, 181n, 182n, 191n, 193n, 208, 208n, 209, 210n, 213, 215–20, 218n, 222–35, 224n, 230n, 237, 241, 242, 248, 250–58, 256n, 290
Sasson, Jack M.   306, 312
Sasson, Victor   131, 131n, 312
Sayce, Archibald H.   122n, 312
Scandone, Gabriella Matthiae   As coeditor of *Atti*: 17n, 293, 300
Schalit, Abraham   As coeditor with Malamat: 29n, 289, 306
Schneider, Tammi J.   88n, 312
Schneider, Tsvi   30, 31n, 148, 148n, 204n, 312, 313
Schniedewind, William M.   111n, 117n, 124n, 313
Schoville, Keith N.   xiii, 44n, 313
Schroeder, Otto   118n, 313
Schumacher, Gottlieb   133n, 134, 136, 313

Seeck, Otto   13n
Segert, Stanislav   123n, 124n, 313
Shanks, Hershel   68n, 74n, 184n, 199n, 215n, 216n, 218n, 248n, 313
Shea, William H.   xix, 79, 79n, 80, 80n, 81, 82n, 313
Shiloh, Yigal   72n, 139n, 140n, 142n, 144, 145, 146, 146n, 148n, 151n, 179n, 181, 190n, 203, 203n, 288, 293, 313, 314
Shipton, Geoffrey M.   134, 137n, 304
Shoham, Yair   203n, 314
Sidersky, David   268, 268n, 314
Smelik, Klaas A. D.   85n, 314
Smend, Rudolf   270, 270n, 314
Smith, George   173n, 314; as coeditor of RawlCu 3: xvi, 62n, 63n, 88n, 102n, 118n, 125n, 292
Smith, W. Robertson   12n, 314
Society of Biblical Archaeology (London, England)   198n, 314
Socin, Albert   270, 270n, 314
Sollberger, E.   As coeditor of *CAH*: xv, 43n, 88n, 213, 291, 317
Spawforth, Anthony J. S.   13n, 301
Stager, Lawrence E.   As coeditor associated with Cross and Ussishkin articles: 45n, 133n, 134n, 136n, 182n, 215n, 248n, 294, 316
Stamm, Johann J.   123n, 129n, 314
Stern, Ephraim   2n, 303, 314
Stone, Lawrence   13n, 314
Streck, Maximilian   101n, 157n, 314
Sublet, Jacqueline   13n, 314
Suder, Robert W.   2n, 3n, 314
Sukenik, Eleazar L.   219n, 315

Tadmor, Hayim   42n, 102n, 122n, 157n, 175n, 186n, 293, 309, 315; as author of *ITP*: 62n, 64n, 66n, 88n, 101n, 125n, 157n, 167n, 168n, 209n, 315
Tait, G. A. D.   153n, 315
Tappy, Ron E.   315
Tarler, David   146, 146n, 151n,

# Index of Modern Authors and Editors

179n, 190n, 203n, 314
Teixidor, Javier   2n, 315
Temporini, Hildegard   13n, 292, 315
Thomas, D. Winton   As editor of *DOTT*: 94n, 119n, 157n, 238n, 246n, 306, 315
Thompson, Henry O.   208n, 315
Thompson, R. Campbell   157n, 315
Thompson, Thomas L.   124n, 305, 315
Tigay, Jeffrey H.   2n, 3n, 15n, 146n, 167n, 315
Timm, Stefan   315
Toorn, Karel van der   As coeditor of *DDD*: xv, 122n, 290, 315
Torrey, Charles C.   164n, 208n, 315
Tucker, J. Mark   xiv
Tufnell, Olga   29n, 224n, 315
Turner, John M.   xiii

Uehlinger, Christoph   16n, 17, 17n, 30n, 42n, 260n, 304, 312, 316
Ussishkin, David   24, 29n, 44n, 45n, 60n, 133n, 134, 134n, 136, 136n, 139, 182n, 215n, 225n, 248n, 254n, 297, 316

Van Zyl, A. H.   268n, 316
Vance, Donald R.   237n, 238n, 316
Vattioni, Francesco   2n, 128n, 316
Vaughn, Amy   xiv
Vaughn, Andrew G.   xiv, 25n, 31n, 42n, 60n, 69n, 73n, 76n, 142n, 148n, 151n, 160n, 171, 171n, 172n, 179n, 191n, 219n, 223n–226n, 234n, 257n, 290, 316
Vaux, Roland G. de   19n, 52n, 186n, 317
Veen, Peter G. van der   205n, 317
Vincent, Louis Hugues   23, 25
Vogüé, E. Melchior, Comte de   95n, 267n, 293

Wagenaar, Jan A.   216n, 290
Walker, Christopher B. F.   207n, 295
Waltke, Bruce K.   274n, 317
Ward, Suzanne M.   xiv
Warren, Charles   267n
Watzinger, Carl   133n, 317
Weidner, Ernst F.   158n, 207, 317
Weitzman, Michael P.   242n, 298, 304
Williams, Prescott H. Jr.   221n, 230n, 294, 307, 317
Williams-Forte, Elizabeth   29n, 44n, 143n, 156n, 215n, 294, 299, 300
Winckler, Hugo   129n, 174n, 198n, 317
Winnett, Fred V.   105n, 312
Winter, Irene J.   17n, 68n, 317
Wiseman, Donald J.   xiv, xvii, 19n, 43, 43n, 158n, 199n, 317, 318
Worschech, Udo   205n, 309, 317
Wright, G. Ernest   19n, 25n, 158n, 288, 289, 294, 318
Wurst, Gregor   As one of Uehlinger's editors: 17n, 260n, 303, 316

Xella, Paolo   124n, 318; as coeditor of *Atti*: 17n, 293, 300

Yadin, Yigael   19n, 225n, 253n
Yamauchi, Edwin M.   199n, 318
Yardeni, Ada   3n, 237n, 241n–243n, 311
Yeivin, Shmuel   64n, 136, 136n, 139n, 151n, 215n, 248n, 287, 289, 297, 318
Young, Gordon D.   xiv, 310, 318
Youngblood, Ronald F.   xiv
Younker, Randall W.   288, 306

Zadok, Ran   2n, 14n, 63, 64n, 318
Zayadine, Fawzi   208n, 315
Zevit, Ziony   29, 30n, 62, 62n, 64n, 65, 143n, 318
Zorn, Jeffrey R.   318

www.ingramcontent.com/pod-product-compliance
Lightning Source LLC
Chambersburg PA
CBHW021818300426
44114CB00009BA/219